*Routledge Revivals*

# Money's Fiscal Dictionary

*Money's Fiscal Dictionary* details information about fiscal terms in encyclopaedic format in relation to British industry in 1910 when originally published. This text originally began as a column in *The Morning Leader* but was expanded upon to present this information in a more accessible and convenient way. This title will be of interest to students of Business and Economics.

# Money's Fiscal Dictionary

L.G. Chiozza Money

Routledge
Taylor & Francis Group
ROUTLEDGE REVIVALS

First published in 1910
by Methuen & Co. Ltd

This edition first published in 2015 by Routledge
2 Park Square, Milton Park, Abingdon, Oxon, OX14 4RN
and by Routledge
711 Third Avenue, New York, NY 10017

*Routledge is an imprint of the Taylor & Francis Group, an informa business*



**Publisher's Note**

The publisher has gone to great lengths to ensure the quality of this reprint but points out that some imperfections in the original copies may be apparent.

**Disclaimer**

The publisher has made every effort to trace copyright holders and welcomes correspondence from those they have been unable to contact.

A Library of Congress record exists under LC control number: 11009187

ISBN 13: 978-1-138-18226-4 (hbk)
ISBN 13: 978-1-315-64654-1 (ebk)

# WORLD'S COAL OUTPUT IN 1907

The Dominating and Determining Factor in Modern Industrial Success

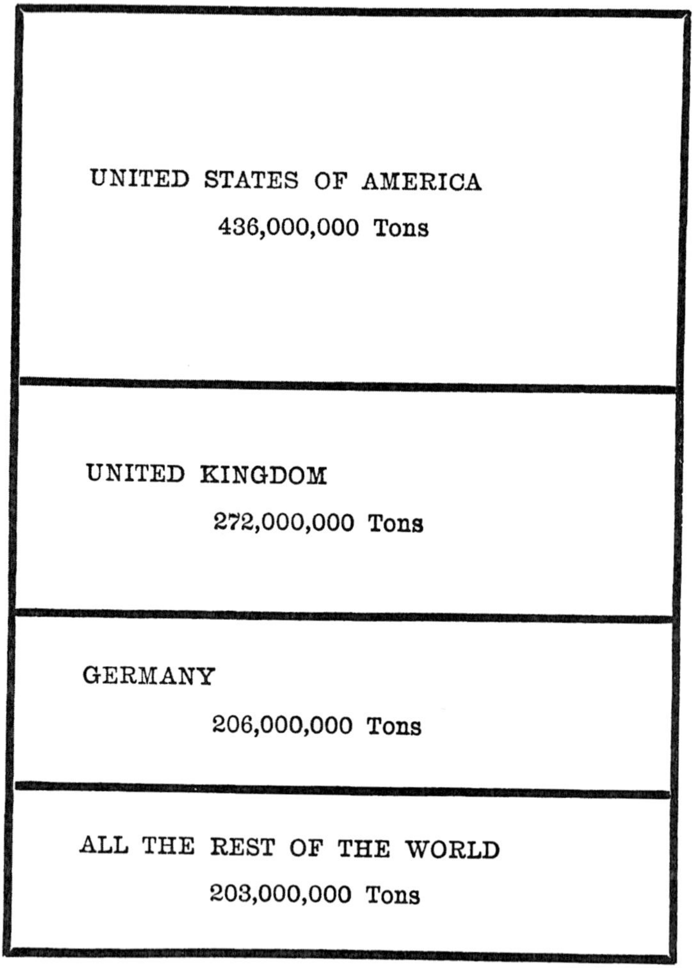


In 1907 the World's Coal Output was 1,117,000,000 metric Tons of 2,204 lbs. America, Britain, and Germany between them produced 914,000,000 Tons, or over 80 per cent. of the whole (see p. 78).

# MONEY'S
# FISCAL DICTIONARY

BY

L. G. CHIOZZA MONEY, M.P.

AUTHOR OF "RICHES AND POVERTY"

METHUEN & CO.
36 ESSEX STREET W.C.
LONDON

*First Published in 1910*

# PREFACE

THIS book is designed to present, in a convenient form, information upon the fiscal question in its relation to British industry and commerce. It was the aim of the author to make it encyclopædic in character, but the protraction of the Parliamentary session of 1909 has compelled him considerably to modify his ambition, and the imminence of a general election seems to render it inadvisable to postpone the publication of a work which, while admittedly incomplete, and far short of what he desired to make it, will, it is believed, prove of some value to the student of affairs. It is the hope of the author that he may be pardoned his sins of omission on account of the very considerable amount of information which his pages, incomplete as they are, afford.

Every care has been exercised in compiling the statistics and statements of fact adduced, but in treating such a large variety of subjects the author cannot hope to have avoided error. He would welcome, and indeed invites, correction from his readers, whatever their fiscal opinions.

This work first took shape in the columns of the *Morning Leader*, in which it was published in an abbreviated form, and the author is indebted to Mr. Ernest Parke, the editor, for permission to publish this expanded version of the widely circulated popular "Fiscal A B C." He has also to thank the editors of the *Daily News*, the *Westminster Gazette*, the *Daily Mail Year Book*, the *Free Trader*, the *Daily Dispatch*, and the *Co-operative Annual* for permission to incorporate in this Dictionary articles which he has contributed during the past few years to those publications.

L. G. C. M.

CHALDON, SURREY
*December 6, 1909*

# MONEY'S FISCAL DICTIONARY

**ACETIC ACID**—In 1908 60,000 cwts. of acetic acid, valued at £67,000 c.i.f., were imported into the United Kingdom. Prior to that year the imports, if any, were not separately recorded. There are no recorded exports, although it is possible that the article may be included in our "Unenumerated" chemical exports. This material of industry is classified in the Board of Trade Returns under Section III., "Articles Wholly or Mainly Manufactured." It is therefore included in the articles upon which Mr. Chamberlain suggested (October 6, 1903) that an import duty should be levied, "not exceeding 10 per cent. on the average."

Acetic acid is used as a solvent, and in the preparation of acetates used as mordants in dyeing, &c. A duty on acetic acid would therefore be a tax on a raw material of industry.

**AERATED WATERS**—The British aerated-water industry is of great dimensions. Owing to our national neglect of industrial statistics, we have no precise computation of the quantity or value of the output, but according to the National Union of Mineral Water Associations, Limited, £30,000,000 is invested in the industry, and the wages bill amounts to £4,000,000 per annum.

In addition to the large home trade, there is a small export trade, which has recently been recorded at the Customs:

BRITISH EXPORTS OF AERATED WATERS

| | Dozen bottles | £ (f.o.b.) |
|---|---|---|
| 1900 (good year) ... ... | 1,105,000 ... ... | 173,000 |
| 1907 (good year) ... ... | 1,415,000 ... ... | 225,000 |
| 1908 (bad year) ... ... | 1,139,000 ... ... | 181,000 |

This trade is chiefly with foreign nations, and the best customers are the United States and France.

There are no recorded imports of aerated waters, and it is impossible, therefore, to offer the trade an import duty. On the other hand, the aerated-water manufacturer would suffer considerably if import duties were levied on articles which he uses as materials, *e.g.*, glass bottles. The cost of laying down an aerated-water plant would, of course, be enhanced by Protective duties, and working costs would be increased all along the line, from the stationery used in the office to the fodder consumed by the horses.

**AEROPLANES**—The manufacture of aeroplanes is a new and rapidly growing industry which owes its sudden emergence to the perfecting of light internal combustion engines of great efficiency by Gottlieb Daimler and his successors in connection with the motor-car industry. As an aeroplane is a manufactured article which "might be made at home," and most certainly ought to be made in the motherland of modern engineering, imports of aeroplanes into the United Kingdom ought to be heavily taxed, according to Protectionist reasoning. The following advertisement appeared in the *Times* of July 28, 1909, after Blériot's flying of the English Channel on July 25, 1909:

"Charles Houry, 23, Rue Royale, Paris, is prepared to furnish without delay the following aeroplanes:

Blériot Monoplane,
Antoinette Monoplane,
Wright Biplane,
Voisin Biplane."

This was the first commercial advertisement of aeroplanes to appear in a British newspaper, and is of historical interest.

The case of aeroplane imports enables us to rate Protection for what it is worth. If we placed a duty upon imported flying machines we should either keep them out altogether or make them dearer. In either case we should injure ourselves by doing so, because, if we are ever to have an aeroplane industry, it is absolutely necessary that we should buy and study the foreign article. Protectionists forget that what is true of aeroplanes is also true of motor-cars and of every other machine and production. Just as free access to foreign aeroplanes is necessary if we are to progress in aeroplane making and using, so free access to the latest varieties of machines, tools, yarns, &c., is necessary in all branches of industry if the greatest efficiency is desired in them.

The rise of the aeroplane reminds us of the final futility of Protection. By improvement of road and rail and tunnel and canal and ship, the engineer in the past has beaten down Customs duties more quickly than Protectionist statesmen could erect them. In the twentieth century the device of Custom houses will be abolished, at least for a very large variety of manufactured articles, by the solution of the problem of aerial transport. The flying man will laugh at Custom houses.

It is amusing to observe that the monthly circular of the British Chamber of Commerce of Paris, for July–August, 1909, announced that the French Customs administration "states that duty will, in future, be imposed on balloons alighting on French territory."

**AGRICULTURAL IMPLEMENTS**—We have both imports and exports of agricultural implements, but only the latter are separately recorded at the Customs, the former being included under the general classification IMPLEMENTS AND TOOLS.

The export record is as follows:

BRITISH EXPORTS OF AGRICULTURAL IMPLEMENTS

| | £ (f.o.b.) |
|---|---|
| 1860 ... ... ... ... ... ... | 254,000 |
| 1870 ... ... ... ... ... ... | 224,000 |
| 1880 ... ... ... ... ... ... | 263,000 |
| 1890 ... ... ... ... ... ... | 391,000 |
| 1900 ... ... ... ... ... ... | 384,000 |
| 1907 ... ... ... ... ... ... | 487,000 |
| 1908 ... ... ... ... ... ... | 431,000 |

The greater part of this trade is with foreign countries, chiefly South America. The trade with British possessions is growing, however, and in 1908 reached £197,000, India, South Africa, Australia, and New Zealand being the chief Colonial buyers. Canada's imports are not large enough to be separately recorded.

By reference to TOOLS it will be seen that our imports of this kind have been falling of recent years. It would be exceedingly unwise to levy an import duty upon them, for to raise the price of agricultural implements would be to inflict serious injury upon the farmer and market gardener.

**AGRICULTURAL MACHINERY**—Britain is one of the largest producers of agricultural machinery. Many of her productions in this industry are unrivalled, but in others the large scale farming of America and consequent great need for machinery has led to the production of excellent, and, in some respects, improved, machinery in the United States and Canada. We export agricultural machinery chiefly to Europe and South America, and import chiefly from the United States, Sweden, and Canada. Our imports for home consumption and exports of British make have been as follows:

BRITISH COMMERCE IN AGRICULTURAL MACHINERY (NOT INCLUDING STEAM ENGINES)

| | Imports for Home Consumption (c.i.f.) £ | Exports of British Make (f.o.b.) £ |
|---|---|---|
| 1860 | Not known | Not known |
| 1870 | ,, | 303,000 |
| 1880 | ,, | 680,000 |
| 1890 | ,, | 688,000 |
| 1900 | ,, | 873,000 |
| 1907 | 269,000 | 1,133,000 |
| 1908 | 322,000 | 1,297,000 |

Our exports in this industry are thus four times as great as our imports, and they have grown considerably in the half century reviewed in the table.

Under Protection the British farmer would be injured by the taxation of agricultural machinery. Messrs. Ransomes, Sims and Jefferies, Limited, of Ipswich, told Mr. Chamberlain's Tariff "Commission" that "the duty should be at least 10 per cent. against countries having a tariff against us," and yet thought that pig-iron should not be taxed. Messrs. Harrison, McGregor & Co., Limited., makers of harvesting machinery, before the same Commission, said, with unconscious humour, that "a 10 per cent. duty on American machines in the case of ordinary harvesting machinery would, in the end, be to the advantage of the farmer." Thus the farmer is threatened with machinery made artificially dearer.

It should be observed that this is an industry in which Colonial competition has already asserted itself. Canada is rapidly increasing her exports of very good agricultural machinery to the Mother Country. She also exports to other countries, and we find her, in Australia and elsewhere, one of our chief competitors. From the Free Trade point of view there is nothing in this to cause us repining, but the point is of great importance in connection with the Protectionist programme. The question which must be faced by British Protectionists is this: Do they include in their scheme the taxation of imports of manufactures from the Colonies?

The use of agricultural machinery has had momentous social and economic effects in all countries. It has been the main cause of rural depopulation in Britain and elsewhere, causing the industry of agriculture to employ an ever decreasing proportion of the population. So potent, indeed, has been its effect in this connection that all other causes of rural depopulation put together are insignificant when compared with it. For a further discussion of this exceedingly important matter *see* AGRICULTURE and RURAL DEPOPULATION.

**AGRICULTURAL WAGES**—High agricultural rents and low agricultural wages were leading characteristics of Britain under Protection. During the first half of the nineteenth century the lot of the men, women, boys, and girls who laboured in our fields was one of abject misery and desperate distress. The authentic records of the days of the Corn Laws tell us of men doing the work of animals, of wages of a few pence a day, of human beings driven by hunger to devour the herbs of the wayside, of the corpses of starved labourers, of outrages upon farmers' property by those driven desperate, of families herding like brutes within mud walls.

Before the Parliamentary Committee which considered agricultural distress in 1821–22 witnesses showed that farmers were too poor to pay wages, and labourers consequently largely unemployed. Mr. T. Barton, a witness, told the Committee that he "could in three or four days bring forward a thousand able-bodied labourers who have no employment." Fifteen years later, at the Parliamentary inquiry of 1836, farmers declared the position "desperate," and spoke of wages extorted by incendiarism. Seven years later, in 1843, the *Times* Commissioner reported of Welsh farmers breakfasting on oatmeal and dining on potatoes, and of labourers who "live entirely on potatoes, and seldom enough of them."

How agricultural wages have risen since the repeal of the Corn Laws is shown by the Board of Trade Report on Agricultural Labourers, by the late Arthur Wilson Fox, published in 1905 (Cd. 2376). Taking cash wages only, apart from payments in kind, of sixty-nine farms in England and Wales, the following great rise is shown:—

RISE OF BRITISH AGRICULTURAL MONEY WAGES

| Year | Per Week s. d. |
|---|---|
| 1850 | 9 3½ |
| 1870 | 11 10½ |
| 1880 | 13 0½ |
| 1900 | 14 5½ |
| 1908 | 14 7½ |

On p. 5 of the same Report the Board of Trade express the facts of the rise in percentages thus:

| Country | 1850 | 1900 |
|---|---|---|
| England and Wales | 64 | 100 |
| Scotland | 50 | 100 |
| Ireland | 56 | 100 |

And not only have money wages risen. It is most important to remember that while wages rose prices fell, so that to-day a shilling buys very much more than in the dark days of Protection. It is within the mark to say that in 1909 the British agricultural labourer receives twice as much return for his labour as his forbear of 1850.

**AGRICULTURE**—Agricultural pursuits still employ more people in the United Kingdom than any other form of occupation. At the Census of 1901 there were 2,262,000 persons returned as farmers, agricultural labourers, nurserymen, &c.

There has been a considerable and continuous decline in the British agricultural population, but not to the extent often supposed, and not through the causes usually represented. The extent of the decline is commonly exaggerated. Thus in his speech at Welbeck, on August 4, 1904, Mr. Chamberlain stated that owing to our system of Free Trade "the number of people cultivating the land has decreased by 600,000 in the last thirty years; and if you go back for fifty years, it has decreased by something like a million." In a speech at Luton he also said that since the repeal of the Corn Laws the number of persons employed in agriculture in England and Wales had fallen by nearly one million. What, he asked, "has become of this million of persons?" And he went on to picture them as having gone to the workhouse, or to foreign countries, or to the slums of our great cities.

### The Decline in Agricultural Employment

This statement as to the loss of 1,000,000 English agricultural labourers has done duty in thousands of speeches, books, pamphlets, and articles, and is generally used by the advocates of Protection and of other political specifics for the cure of rural depopulation. It is based upon Census aggregates quoted by persons who have not taken the trouble to inquire what the aggregates represent. In the Fiscal Blue Book (Cd. 1,761) the Board of Trade give an analysis of the Census reports, 1851–1901, which shows in detail the reduction of agricultural labourers in England and Wales from 1,905,000 in 1851 to 988,000 in 1901:

ENGLAND AND WALES: PERSONS EMPLOYED IN AGRICULTURE, 1851-1901.

| Census of— | Adults (Aged 20 and over) | | | Young Persons (under 20) | | | Total, all Ages | | |
|---|---|---|---|---|---|---|---|---|---|
| | Men | Women | Total | Boys | Girls | Total | Males | Females | Total |
| 1851 | 1,141,000 | 336,000 | 1,477,000 | 328,000 | 100,000 | 428,000 | 1,468,000 | 436,000 | 1,905,000 |
| 1861 | 1,119,000 | 301,000 | 1,420,000 | 323,000 | 60,000 | 383,000 | 1,442,000 | 361,000 | 1,803,000 |
| 1871 | 972,000 | 122,000 | 1,094,000 | 277,000 | 52,000 | 329,000 | 1,249,000 | 175,000 | 1,424,000 |
| 1881 | 884,000 | 50,000 | 934,000 | 254,000 | 11,000 | 265,000 | 1,139,000 | 61,000 | 1,200,000 |
| 1891 | 816,000 | 40,000 | 856,000 | 237,000 | 6,000 | 243,000 | 1,054,000 | 46,000 | 1,099,000 |
| 1901 | 750,000 | 43,000 | 793,000 | 186,000 | 9,000 | 195,000 | 936,000 | 52,000 | 988,000 |

Of the 1,905,000 "agricultural labourers" of 1851, as many as 336,000 were women, and a further 428,000 were boys and girls, leaving only 1,141,000 men aged twenty years and upwards. It is the women and boys and girls who have chiefly disappeared from our fields. Even this statement needs to be modified, for the great decline in adult women is merely apparent, and the result of an alteration in the methods of conducting the Census. The great "reduction" of women and girl workers between 1861 and 1871 resulted from the fact that in 1861 248,500 wives and daughters and other female relatives of farmers were enumerated as employed in agriculture who were not so enumerated in 1871.

To deal with the men only, in 1881 persons no longer working because of old age were for the first time excluded from the Census, and this change accounted for a reduction of 14,000 labourers in that year. As to the 1901 Census, it should be remembered that it was taken when the Army Reserve was called out for the purposes of the South African War.

The reduction of English *men* agricultural workers from 1,141,000 in 1851 to 750,000 in 1901 is also modified by the fact that these figures exclude the large and growing classes of market gardeners and horticultural workers, including florists, seedsmen, and fruit growers. It is, of course, absurd to count as loss the disappearance of an ill-paid ploughman, and not to count as gain the addition of a well-paid market gardener. Nurserymen and gardeners have increased from 76,500 in 1851 to 211,000 in 1901, and the majority of the gardeners included are non-domestic.

Taking these and other points into consideration, Lord Eversley read to the Royal Statistical Society in 1907 a deeply interesting paper in which he arrived at the conclusion that the real extent of the decline in male agricultural employment in England and Wales, counting both men and boys, has been from 1,448,000 in 1861 to 1,079,000 in 1901, or, counting men alone, from 1,121,000 in 1861 to 876,000 in 1901.

In the following table Lord Eversley's figures for Great Britain are summarised:

GREAT BRITAIN: DECLINE IN MALE AGRICULTURAL EMPLOYMENT

(Lord Eversley)

| | | | | |
|---|---|---|---|---|
| 1861 | England and Wales ... | Men ... | 1,121,000 | |
| | | Boys ... | 327,000 | |
| | Scotland ... ... ... | Men ... | 163,000 | |
| | | Boys ... | 46,000 | |
| | | | | 1,657,000 |
| 1881 | England and Wales ... | Men ... | 942,000 | |
| | | Boys ... | 265,000 | |
| | Scotland ... ... ... | Men ... | 136,000 | |
| | | Boys ... | 37,000 | |
| | | | | 1,380,000 |
| 1901 | England and Wales ... | Men ... | 876,000 | |
| | | Boys ... | 203,000 | |
| | Scotland ... ... ... | Men ... | 122,000 | |
| | | Boys ... | 35,000 | |
| | | | | 1,236,000 |

These statistical conclusions successfully ran the gauntlet of a debate at the Royal Statistical Society, and may be accepted as a near approximation to the facts of the case. It will be seen that there has been no such great reduction in agricultural employment as is commonly supposed.

But, of course, the proportion of the population engaged in agricultural pursuits has fallen greatly, and it remains to inquire what has been the cause.

In the first place, as will be seen by a glance at the Census figures at the beginning of this article, the greater part of the decline took place before 1881. That fact at once disposes of the common allegation that it was the fall in prices caused by importations of cheaply grown foreign produce which drove people from the land. The decline was in full swing in the years before so much land passed from arable to pasture; it was marked, indeed, even while the wheat acreage was actually increasing. The decline in arable acreage did not begin until 1875, but there was a great fall in agricultural employment before that date.

### The Main Cause of Rural Depopulation

What, then, is the true cause of the considerable actual and still greater proportionate decline in the number of British agricultural workers? The answer to this question is exceedingly important. It has been given by competent observers again and again, but that it is as yet little realised is shown not only by such utterances as those of Mr. Chamberlain at Welbeck, when he attributed the loss of a "million" English agricultural workers to the shrinkage of arable acreage; it is shown also by the widespread belief that by some magical process or other town dwellers may be turned "back to the land" to the great benefit of themselves and society.

It is the engineer who is the destroyer of agricultural employment in this and in every country. It is the machine which, by economising labour, has made it possible to raise a given quantity of food with an ever decreasing quantity of labour. It follows that, taking the world as a whole, the proportion of the population needed for food production is ever diminishing. The fact is of the most far-reaching importance both from an economic and a sociological point of view. From the economic standpoint it is a great gain to save labour in agriculture, for man does not live by bread alone, and there is for practical purposes an unlimited scope for the application of saved labour in satisfying the other needs of mankind. From a sociological standpoint the destruction of agricultural employment in a society in which towns are permitted to magnify with but scant regard for the health or training of their inhabitants is fraught with grave possibilities of evil for the nation. Full realisation of the dominant fact here insisted upon, that agricultural employment is declining and must decline, cannot but concentrate the attention of statesmen upon the all-important problem of town life and the means of improving it. "Back to the land" is idle talk, but there is, of course, no reason why a practical working town may not be made a sanatorium combining all the amenities of the city with the healthfulness of rural life.

The conclusion as to the effect of machinery upon agri cultural employment here stated is confirmed in the Board of Agriculture Report on the Decline in Agricultural Population published in 1906, from the pen of Mr. R. H. Rew, the Secretary of the Board. This document was based upon the collection of reports from well-qualified correspondents in every county of Great Britain. After giving due weight to the cancellation of agricultural labour through the laying down of land to grass, the Report says:

> "There is little doubt that the saving of labour on the 15½ million acres which in 1901 still remained under the plough was in the aggregate greater during the twenty years than on the two million acres laid down to grass. Many expedients, other than actually stopping the plough, were adopted to reduce the labour bill. But while manual labour has no doubt been economised to some extent by curtailing some of the operations which require it, the main cause of its reduction is undoubtedly the expended use of labour-saving machinery. This is referred to by the large majority of correspondents in all parts of the country. With the exception of the self-binding harvester, which was introduced into this country in the early eighties, few machines for the performance of a specific manual operation have perhaps been invented since 1881 (unless milking machines, shearing machines, and, perhaps, potato diggers come within that category), but whereas twenty years ago labour-saving machinery was fully employed by comparatively few, it has now become almost universal on all holdings of sufficient size to make its use practicable. The substitution of mechanical or horse or hand power for fixed machinery,—*e.g.*, thrashing machines, chaff-cutters, pumps, &c.—has taken place largely, although it has made, comparatively speaking, little progress for tractive purposes. It may, indeed, be questioned if steam is so largely employed in the cultivation of the land as it was twenty years ago. But the displacement of manual labour arising from the greatly extended use of drills, horse-shoes, mowers, binders, manure distributors, and the like must have been in the aggregate very great, and probably to this more than to any other single cause the reduced demand for farm labourers may be attributed."

Mr. Rew's report deals only with the period 1881–1906, but agricultural machinery was in use at a much earlier period. Steam was employed in agricultural operations from the beginning of the nineteenth century, and mechanical reapers were exhibited at the Paris Exhibition of 1855.

As to the universality of the relative decrease of agricultural employment, see the discussion under RURAL DEPOPULATION.

### THE CULTIVATED AREA: ARABLE AND PASTURE

I now pass to the statistics illustrating the progress of British agriculture. Unfortunately, acreage statistics were not officially collected until 1867, and it was not until 1884 that official estimates of the produce of crops were made. The following table shows the variation in the cultivated area of the United Kingdom from 1867 to 1908:

UNITED KINGDOM: THE CULTIVATED AREA

(In Millions of Acres)

| | Cultivated Area | Arable Land | Permanent Pasture. |
|---|---|---|---|
| 1867 | 44·1 | 22·0 | 22·1 |
| 1870 | 44·5 | 22·4 | 22·1 |
| 1875 | 47·3 | 23·5 | 23·8 |
| 1880 | 47·6 | 22·9 | 24·7 |
| 1885 | 47·9 | 22·3 | 25·6 |
| 1890 | 48·0 | 20·9 | 27·1 |
| 1895 | 47·9 | 20·1 | 27·8 |
| 1900 | 47·8 | 19·5 | 28·3 |
| 1905 | 47·7 | 18·8 | 28·9 |
| 1908 | 47·0 | 19·5 | 27·5 |

The total cultivated area of the United Kingdom increased until 1891, in which year it was returned at 48,179,000 acres. Since then the cultivated area has slightly declined.

The chief feature of the table, however, is the gain of permanent pasture, chiefly at the expense of arable land. The area under tillage not only held its own, but considerably increased between the repeal of the Corn Laws and the early seventies. The year 1877 was the last in which the average price of British wheat exceeded 50s. per quarter. Then began the great fall in prices due to the rapid extension of wheat areas in the United States, Argentina, and other countries, and the fall in freight charges, and the British corn area rapidly contracted. The contraction was continuous until 1905, when the arable area was 18,807,000 acres. Since then it has risen and is now rising.

### The Decline in Corn Crops

The table on page 15 examines the acreage under corn and the production of corn so far as the particulars are known in 1867–1908:

It will be seen that the considerable shrinkage in the British corn area has been chiefly caused by the decline in the cultivation of wheat. The shrinkage in area has been partly balanced by an increased yield of wheat per acre, the result chiefly of the abandonment of the poorest wheat fields. Barley has shown a smaller decline, while the oat crop has remained almost constant. It is of interest to contrast the British wheat production with the imports and the fall of prices. This is done in the following table:

UNITED KINGDOM: WHEAT ACREAGE AND PRODUCTION, PRICE OF BRITISH WHEAT, AND WHEAT IMPORTS, 1867–1908

| Year | Wheat Area | Wheat Production | Price of British Wheat per Quarter | Wheat Imports |
|---|---|---|---|---|
| | Acres | Bushels | s. d. | Bushels |
| 1867 ... ... | 3,640,000 | Not known | 64 5 | 72,800,000 |
| 1870 ... ... | 3,770,000 | ,, | 46 11 | 69,000,000 |
| 1875 ... ... | 3,510,000 | ,, | 45 2 | 110,000,000 |
| 1880 ... ... | 3,060,000 | ,, | 44 4 | 126,900,000 |
| 1885 ... ... | 2,550,000 | 79,630,000 | 32 10 | 151,200,000 |
| 1890 ... ... | 2,480,000 | 75,990,000 | 31 11 | 153,000,000 |
| 1895 ... ... | 1,450,000 | 38,280,000 | 23 1 | 199,700,000 |
| 1900 ... ... | 1,900,000 | 54,320,000 | 26 11 | 182,900,000 |
| 1905 ... ... | 1,830,000 | 60,330,000 | 29 8 | 212,800,000 |
| 1908 ... ... | 1,660,000 | 53,920,000 | 32 0 | 203,400,000 |

These interesting comparisons show how the British wheat area contracted with increasing imports. The lowest price of

UNITED KINGDOM; CORN CROPS, AREA AND PRODUCTION, 1867–1908.

(Area in Millions of Acres. Production in Millions of Bushels.)

| Year | Wheat | | Barley | | Oats | | Beans | | Peas | | Total | |
|---|---|---|---|---|---|---|---|---|---|---|---|---|
| | Area | Product | Area | Product | Area | Product | Area | Product | Area | Product | Area | Product |
| 1867 | 3·64 | — | 2·44 | — | 4·42 | — | 0·54 | — | 0·32 | — | 11·43 | — |
| 1870 | 3·77 | — | 2·62 | — | 4·42 | — | 0·53 | — | 0·31 | — | 11·75 | — |
| 1875 | 3·51 | — | 2·75 | — | 4·17 | — | 0·57 | — | 0·31 | — | 11·39 | — |
| 1880 | 3·06 | — | 2·69 | — | 4·19 | — | 0·43 | — | 0·23 | — | 10·67 | — |
| 1885 | 2·55 | 79·63 | 2·44 | 85·72 | 4·28 | 160·44 | 0·44 | 9·12 | 0·23 | 4·33 | 10·01 | 339·24 |
| 1890 | 2·48 | 75·99 | 2·30 | 80·79 | 4·13 | 171·29 | 0·36 | 11·85 | 0·22 | 6·31 | 9·57 | 346·23 |
| 1895 | 1·45 | 33·28 | 2·34 | 75·02 | 4·52 | 174·47 | 0·24 | 5·62 | 0·20 | 4·73 | 8·86 | 298·12 |
| 1900 | 1·90 | 54·32 | 2·17 | 68·54 | 4·14 | 165·13 | 0·26 | 7·46 | 0·15 | 4·07 | 8·70 | 299·52 |
| 1905 | 1·83 | 60·33 | 1·87 | 65·00 | 4·13 | 166·28 | 0·25 | 8·26 | 0·17 | 4·44 | 8·35 | 304·31 |
| 1908 | 1·66 | 53·92 | 1·82 | 61·56 | 4·18 | 176·00 | 0·29 | 8·91 | 0·16 | 4·36 | 8·20 | 304·75 |

British wheat ever reported was reached in 1894, when the average for the year was 22s. 10d. per quarter; in 1895, as the table shows, the price was a trifle above this. The British wheat crop of 1895 yielded only 38,280,000 bushels, but in spite of this the price for the year was only 23s. 1d. per quarter, the great oversea supply ruling the price.

Since 1895 the price of wheat has risen in consequence of the world demand for wheat rising more rapidly than the world's supply. This factor, which is discussed elsewhere under WHEAT, is in 1909 bringing a larger British area into wheat cultivation.

### THE INCREASE IN ROOTS AND HAY

I now give the United Kingdom production of potatoes, roots, and hay since 1885, the second year in which the statistics were collected:

UNITED KINGDOM: PRODUCTION OF POTATOES, ROOTS, AND HAY

(In Millions of Tons)

| Year | Potatoes | Turnips and Swedes | Mangolds | Hay | |
|---|---|---|---|---|---|
| | | | | Clover and Rotation Grasses | From Permanent Pasture |
| 1885 ... | 6·4 | 24·1 | 6·0 | 12·9 | |
| 1890 ... | 4·6 | 32·0 | 6·7 | 4·8 | 9·6 |
| 1895 ... | 7·1 | 29·2 | 6·4 | 4·3 | 8·0 |
| 1900 ... | 4·6 | 28·4 | 9·6 | 4·6 | 9·2 |
| 1905 ... | 7·2 | 26·6 | 9·5 | 4·5 | 9·0 |
| 1908 ... | 7·1 | 29·2 | 10·6 | 5·1 | 9·5 |

This table brings out the fact that British root crops have increased as corn crops have decreased. Doubtless the figures for earlier years, if available for the purposes of comparison, would accentuate this point.

### The Gain in Horses and Cattle

To complete the record of the chief features of British agricultural production, the following table shows the numbers of horses, cattle, sheep, and pigs in the United Kingdom for the period 1867–1908:

UNITED KINGDOM: NUMBERS OF HORSES, CATTLE, SHEEP, AND PIGS

| Year | Horses | Cattle | Sheep | Pigs |
|---|---|---|---|---|
| 1867 ... ... | Not known | 8,731,000 | 33,817,000 | 4,221,000 |
| 1870 ... ... | 1,267,000 | 9,235,000 | 32,787,000 | 3,651,000 |
| 1875 ... ... | 1,820,000 | 10,163,000 | 33,492,000 | 3,495,000 |
| 1880 ... ... | 1,930,000 | 9,871,000 | 30,240,000 | 2,863,000 |
| 1885 ... ... | 1,909,000 | 10,869,000 | 30,086,000 | 3,687,000 |
| 1890 ... ... | 1,965,000 | 10,790,000 | 31,667,000 | 4,362,000 |
| 1895 ... ... | 2,112,000 | 10,753,000 | 29,775,000 | 4,239,000 |
| 1900 ... ... | 2,000,000 | 11,455,000 | 31,055,000 | 3,664,000 |
| 1905 ... ... | 2,117,000 | 11,674,000 | 29,077,000 | 3,602,000 |
| 1908 ... ... | 2,089,000 | 11,739,000 | 31,332,000 | 4,056,000 |

The figures for horses relate to animals used solely for agriculture, mares kept for breeding, and unbroken horses.

It will be seen that the number of horses and cattle has increased very considerably in the period reviewed, while that of sheep has slightly declined and that of pigs has been almost stationary. The decline in the number of sheep is not peculiar to this country. There has been a similar decline in France, and a very much greater decline in Germany, where at the present time there are less than 8,000,000 sheep.

The reader has now before him a broad survey of the main features of British agriculture under Free Trade. The chief change which has occurred owing to untaxed imports is that the cultivation of wheat, and to a smaller extent that of barley, has been increasingly abandoned, while the production of meat and milk and, as a concomitant, the growth of fodder, has very greatly increased. The present position is broadly that the cultivation of corn employs only some 8,000,000 acres, while the raising of meat and dairy produce employs nearly

40,000,000 acres. Our farmers and graziers have been much better employed in increasing the number of our horses and cattle by about 50 per cent. in forty years than they would have been in attempting, through artificial prices created by Protective import duties, to grow wheat in competition with the virgin soils of the United States, Canada, and South America. It is not commonly realised how greatly the demand for meat in the United Kingdom has increased by virtue of the fact that cheap bread has left the workman in town and country with the means to eat meat every day. A tax on wheat must necessarily cause a decline in the demand for meat, as it did in Britain under the Corn Laws, and as it does in Germany to-day.

### The Small Holder and Protection

And it is not only the stock farmer and grazier who would be hit by the higher prices of corn, feeding stuffs, manures, machinery, and other materials under Protection. Many people believe that the future of British agriculture is largely bound up with the prosperity of the small holder. A small farmer is a buyer rather than a seller of corn, and his land, when it is not employed in the production of meat and dairy produce, is given to the cultivation of fruit, vegetables, or root and green crops. Import duties offer the small holder little or no assistance directly, while indirectly they must greatly increase his costs of production. Free Trade combined with the practice of co-operation and science in agriculture have made the Danish small farmer flourish. The British small holder needs to hold fast the advantages which he derives from Free Trade, and to add to them the other factors of Danish success.

### Protection a Lever to Raise Rent

Nor should the corn farmer believe that Protection would be an unmixed blessing in his case. Protection is the friend not so much of the corn grower as of the corn-grower's landlord. If the British people consented to pay an enhanced price for bread, in order to stimulate British wheat production, they would be engineering not greater profits for the farmer, or higher wages for the agricultural labourer, but higher rents for the landlord. The landed interest is with good reason strongly Protectionist in policy. The owner of land plays a comparatively small part in the sharing of the profits of manufacturing, for land is an exceedingly small item in the capital of a manufacturing business. In agriculture, however, the landlord *qua* landlord is a sleeping partner who is in a position to secure through rent any artificial profits which the State is foolish enough to attach to the growing of corn. The history of British agriculture under Protection offers the gravest warning to those who would revert to the system under which British farmers groaned for a generation. The Protective enactments of 1815–46, which will be found described under CORN LAWS, were a curse to British agriculture. They were passed in order to sustain the high prices and high rents caused by the French wars. The Corn Law of 1815, which enacted that wheat could only be taken out of bond for home consumption when the price of British wheat was not less than 80s. per quarter, was passed because it was shown to the House of Commons Committee of 1814 that the rent of land had doubled in twenty years, and that the farmer needed a very high price in order to make any profit at all after satisfying his landlord and meeting the enormous poor rates. As soon as the Corn Law passed, rents rose, and the greatest distress soon befell the agricultural interest.

### AGRICULTURAL DISTRESS UNDER PROTECTION

In 1821 farmers poured their woes into the ears of a House of Commons Committee. Mr. John Ellman, farmer, showed the Committee that his rent had risen between 1790 and 1815 from £680 to £1,000 a year. Mr. S. Capper, farmer, said that his rent had increased between 1796 and 1815 from £300 to £500 a year. Mr. E. Wakefield, an Essex land valuer, gave it as his opinion that rents had trebled between 1797 and 1813. All the evidence went to show that while rents rose under

Protection, farmers were insolvent and labourers considerably worse off. One witness told the Committee that he could "in three or four days bring forward a thousand able-bodied labourers who had no employment." (Those who are unable to consult the original Parliamentary reports can obtain a most informing account of this and other evidence put before the Committee of 1821 in Mr. I. S. Leedham's "What Protection does for the Farmer and Labourer," published by the Cobden Club and Messrs. Cassell and Co.)

The Committee of 1821 could not fail to be impressed with the evidence of ruin and insolvency placed before them. They found themselves unable to make any specific recommendation or to advise that Protection could be carried further. Their report contained the following passage, showing how much their faith in Protection had been shaken:

"Your Committee may entertain a doubt (a doubt, however, which they wish to state with that diffidence which a subject so extensive naturally imposes upon their judgment) whether the only solid foundation of the flourishing state of agriculture is not laid in abstaining, as much as possible, from interference, either by Protection or prohibition, with the application of capital in any branch of industry."

In 1829 the Corn Laws were tinkered and a sliding scale enacted (*see* CORN LAWS). Agricultural distress, which was severe down to 1828, and somewhat mitigated in 1829–31, deepened in 1832–3, and in 1833 another Committee of the House of Commons made a report in which they said:

"The Committee of 1821 arrived at the conclusion 'that the returns of farming capital were at that time considerably below the ordinary rate of profit'; and no evidence produced before your Committee of diminished outgoing, contrasted with the change of prices in the interval, would warrant at this moment (1833) a different conclusion."

The Committee of 1833 were as powerless as their predecessors to help the farmers to pay the excessive rents which had been fastened on farmers by the Corn Laws. Distress continued and deepened, and in 1836 there was another Parliamentary inquiry, at which the most distressing evidence was submitted by farmers. Witnesses spoke of the desperate condition to which agricultural labourers were reduced, and how wages were wrung from insolvent farmers by incendiarism. The following is a typical extract from the evidence given before this inquiry, a Lords' Committee, the witness being Mr. R. Hope, a farmer of Haddingtonshire:

*Q.* "Have the farmers who hold their farms at money rent suffered?"

*A.* "Yes; they suffer much at present and they complain much."

*Q.* "These money rents were fixed under the operation of the old Corn Law of 1815?"

*A.* "Yes; under the expectation that the prices upon wheat would be maintained at something like what the Corn Law proposed."

The experience of the British farmer in 1815–1846 may be summed up by saying that in none of these years was agriculture prosperous, and that in most of them it was in distress.

### The Town Argument and the Country Argument

In the fiscal agitation of 1902–1909 those who advocate Protection have found themselves involved in some strange contradictions. In the towns they have been anxious to assure the working men that there is no possibility of food prices rising under a Protective system. The artisan is told that the foreigner pays the import duty, and that, therefore, a tax on corn could not possibly affect the price of bread. When the farmer is approached, however, a picture is drawn of Protection as an infallible cure for low prices.

In connection with the Colonial Preference, again, we meet with a similar example of what it is charitable to call confusion of thought. The urban elector is told that the conception of the Preference proposals is to substitute Colonial food supplies for foreign food supplies in order to promote Imperial solidarity. The farmer, on the other hand, is told that the

Preference proposals will raise price, and in order to secure that object a duty on Colonial food as well as on foreign food has been already suggested by the leaders of the tariff agitation, a differential duty being suggested in lieu of a Preference based on untaxed Colonial food.

### The Tariff "Commission's" Report on Agriculture

This brings me to the report of the Agricultural Committee of the Tariff "Commission." As explained elsewhere, the Tariff "Commission" is a body of Protectionist gentlemen who generally favour Mr. Chamberlain's Protectionist proposals of 1903, and which constituted itself in 1904 in order to examine those proposals in detail, and to suggest in what particular they could be improved or amended. The Commission appointed various Committees to examine the different branches of industry, and the Agricultural Committee was set up, we are told, "to report to the Commission as to: (1) the effect of Mr. Chamberlain's proposals on present agricultural conditions; (2) whether any modifications in detail are desirable, and, if so, what shall be the nature of such modifications, having due regard to the general interests of the community; and (3) the best way in which the interests of the manufacturing and the agricultural industries, where they conflict, can be harmonised."

It is not surprising that the Committee frankly shirked the last term of reference, leaving "harmonising" to the "final report" of the Commission itself, which has not yet (1909) been published. The Chairman of the Agricultural Committee was Mr. Henry Chaplin.

It is amusing to note that the Committee begins its report with what purports to be a historical sketch "of agricultural policy before 1846." It consists of a bald, incomplete, and uniforming catalogue of dates and duties, and nothing is said of the terrible distress of British agriculture under the Corn Laws. As a fair sample of the Committee's historical method, all it says about the Commons Committee of 1821 is as follows:—

"Another Committee on the Corn Trade sat in 1821,

and in the following year a further Act was passed to amend the laws relating to the importation of corn."

It is difficult to believe that these Tariff "Commissioners" were not aware that the Committee of 1821 was not a Committee on the "Corn Trade," but a Committee to inquire into the causes of agricultural distress consequent upon the Corn Law of 1815.

The Committee does not even refer to the Commons Committee of 1833 on the same subject, and there is not a single word, in a report of many hundreds of pages, which would even hint or suggest to a foreign reader unacquainted with British history that farmers and labourers were involved in common ruin under our abandoned Protective system. Yet the Commissioners, guilty in this extreme degree of *suppressio veri*, have the assurance to conclude their misleading account of the Corn Laws with these words: "It is clear from this historical review that popular ideas as to the operation of the Corn Laws require revision."

To come to the concrete recommendations of the Committee, the "Commissioners" set out what they call a "provisional scale of duties," which they are careful to tell us is merely an "indication of the nature of the scheme which may hereafter be recommended when the inquiry in other trades and interests has been completed." I give the Committee's scale *verbatim* on page 24.

If this scale is contrasted with that suggested by Mr. Chamberlain on October 6, 1903 (*see* CHAMBERLAIN PROGRAMME), it will be seen that some important modifications have been introduced. These are: (1) the abandonment of free imports of Colonial food; (2) the suggested taxation of maize; (3) the suggested taxation of bacon; (4) the suggested taxation of market-garden produce, potatoes, and hops; and (5) the suggested taxation of hay.

Very little has been said in public speeches or writings of the Tariff "Commission's" abandonment of the cardinal point of Mr. Chamberlain's proposals, which was the substitution of the Colonies for foreign countries as food suppliers of the British market, and the consequent building up and

FROM THE REPORT (1906) OF THE AGRICULTURAL COMMITTEE OF THE TARIFF "COMMISSION" (VOL. III. PARAGRAPH 394).

PROVISIONAL SCALE OF DUTIES

| | General Tariff | Preferential Tariff |
|---|---|---|
| Wheat ... ... | 6d. per cwt. (or about 2s. per quarter) | 3d. per cwt. (or about 1s. per quarter) |
| Barley, Oats, Rye, Maize, &c. | Duties equivalent to those on wheat | Duties equivalent to those on wheat |
| Wheaten and other Flour and Meal | 1s. 3d. per cwt | Subject to negotiation with Colonies |
| Animals and Meat, including Bacon | General level to be 5 per cent | Ditto |
| Dairy Produce, including Poultry and Eggs | Specific duties equivalent in general to from 5 per cent. to 10 per cent. *ad valorem;* though in particular cases some duties when calculated may be proved to be lower and in others rather higher than these limits | Ditto |
| Market garden produce, including Potatoes and Hops | Ditto | Ditto |
| Hay and Straw ... | Ditto | Ditto |

NOTE.—The subject of agricultural machinery will be dealt with in the report on the Engineering Industry and in the Final Report. In regard to feeding-stuffs and fertilisers the general rule would be that they should be imported free; but the subject belongs in the main to the Chemical Industry and will be dealt with in the report on that industry and in the final report.

cementation of the Empire. I am not aware that this change of front has been made plain in Canada, or that it is commonly known here.

The footnote appended to the scale by the Commissioners is worth special attention. It deals with the delicate subject of the position of feeding-stuffs and fertilisers and machinery under Protection. The Agricultural Committee shirk the issue by reference to other reports to come, but the little they say betrays an extraordinary ignoring of the economic position of many British farmers. They indicate that "feeding-stuffs" should be imported free; yet their own scale of duties suggests the taxation of maize, of which Mr. Chamberlain in making his original proposals on October 6, 1903, said: "I propose to put no tax whatever on maize, partly because maize is a food of some of the very poorest of the population, and partly also because it is a raw material for the farmers, who feed their stock with it." What Mr. Chamberlain said is true, of course, of much more than maize in the Committee's scale of duties. It is clear that the Committee, in drafting their report, have not paid sufficient attention to the adverse evidence submitted to them, which, to do them justice, they have the fairness to print. I take the following typical statements from the evidence of farmers published in this report of a Protectionist body:—

By Mr. A. Amos, Wye, Kent, Farmer. "Anything that makes corn, cake, or any feeding-stuff dearer would handicap me in producing meat."

By Mr. A. Macintyer, Isle of Bute, Farmer. "A decided disadvantage in every way, as I pay over £200 yearly for feeding stuffs, mostly grinding beans (Egyptian or Smyrna)."

By Mr. A. F. Davies, Broughton, Chester, Farmer. "As nearly all the wheat, oats, and beans, besides hay and roots grown on this farm are consumed by the live stock on it, and in addition between £300 and £400 of other feeding-stuffs are bought, any duty on foreign stuffs would be a disadvantage."

By Mr. W. Barber, Moniaive, Dumfries-shire, Farmer. "To sheep farmers like myself a duty on corn, which would tend to raise the price, would be a distinct disadvantage."

The Committee print many statements from farmers who are in favour of Protection, but their provisos are so many and so far-reaching that the Committee's scale of duties quoted above would utterly fail to satisfy them. The Committee, indeed, is constrained to say, par. 210:

"Witnesses do not, as a rule, state precisely under what conditions they think that wheat-growing would be remunerative. Their statements generally take the form of expressing a general opinion as to the efficacy of Mr. Chamberlain's proposals, but they are unanimous that in order to obtain a substantially increased acreage under wheat, *prices would have to be considerably higher than they are at present.*"

It is also significant that the "Commissioners" are compelled to admit that many classes of farmers are doing well under Free Trade. Paragraph 276 says: "Those breeding special classes of sheep would seem to be doing fairly well." Paragraph 256 says: "The successful dovelopment of market gardening in the Evesham district is described in the evidence." Paragraph 252 is constrained to quote a Herefordshire fruit grower, who says: "The fruit-growing industry is flourishing, and likely to reach considerable dimensions." Paragraph 215 states "the most detailed evidence with regard to potato growing given by farmers is from Lincolnshire, where they state that potato growing has, on the whole, increased of late years in the districts with which they are concerned." Paragraph 271 admits "the continuous increase in the number of cattle in each country in the United Kingdom in recent years." Paragraph 272 says: "An increase in milk production is generally spoken of by farmers living near large towns. It is often the only branch of their farming which is regarded as remunerative." It is difficult to say which is more remarkable, the wide significance of these admissions in a document drawn up by avowed Protectionists, or the fact that the "Commissioners'" scale of duties, quoted above, is calculated most obviously to inflict severe injury upon the main and progressive branches of British agriculture.

This report by Mr. Chamberlain's political supporters as to the designs of Protectionists upon agriculture should serve to remind the farmer, the grazier, the small holder, and the agricultural labourer that it is proposed to re-introduce a *system which would tax and raise the price of foods and materials which are more largely purchased by, than sold by, the majority of those engaged in British agriculture;* a system which would raise the cost of corn, cake, and other feeding-stuffs, of chemical manures and other fertilisers, of agricultural machinery and implements, and other plant, of clothes and furniture and boots and every common necessity with which manufacturing industry offers exchange for farming produce. (*See also* WHEAT, MEAT, MILK, BUTTER, CHEESE, RURAL DEPOPULATION, CHAMBERLAIN PROGRAMME, &c.)

**ALCOHOL, METHYLIC**—The value of the British production of wood spirit is unknown, but our external commerce in this article is as follows:

BRITISH COMMERCE IN METHYLIC ALCOHOL

| Year | Imports for Home Consumption | | Exports of British Make | |
|---|---|---|---|---|
| | Gallons | Value (c.i.f.) | Gallons | Value (f.o.b.) |
| | | £ | | £ |
| 1900 | 271,000 | 43,000 | 17,000 | 2,000 |
| 1907 | 450,000 | 37,000 | 130,000 | 18,000 |
| 1908 | 473,000 | 37,000 | 221,000 | 26,000 |

The growth in exports and imports has been considerable. It will be seen that the import price has fallen greatly in the last ten years. In the Board of Trade Returns this article is classified as a "manufacture," and the imports of this raw material of industry are therefore included in the aggregate of imports which Protectionists propose to tax in order to increase employment. Our imports are chiefly derived from the United States.

**ALIZARINE**—The manufacture of alizarine is almost a German monopoly, and it must be confessed that the Germans deserve it. Alizarine is the essential colouring matter of the madder root, and until the last generation this valuable dye was entirely produced from madder. In 1868 two German chemists, Graebe and Liebermann, succeeded in producing alizarine synthetically. This was a triumph of industrial chemistry, for it was the first instance of the artificial production of a vegetable colouring matter. The German artificial alizarine has its base in anthracene, a liquid derived from the distillation of coal-tar. Briefly, oxydised anthracene is treated with fuming sulphuric acid and the product fused with caustic soda. The red crystals of alizarine obtained form the base of a wide range of colours, which, unlike many of the coal-tar colours, are permanent.

The Custom House (1909) record our imports of alizarine dyes as follows:

BRITISH IMPORTS FOR HOME CONSUMPTION OF ALIZARINE AND OTHER ANTHRACENE DYES

| | Quantity. Cwts. | Value (c.i.f.) £ |
|---|---|---|
| 1900 ... ... | Not known ... ... | 184,000 |
| 1907 ... ... | 63,000 ... ... | 268,000 |
| 1908 ... ... | 47,000 ... ... | 206,000 |

It is hardly necessary to add that these imports are from Germany.

It is noteworthy that Germany imposes no customs duties on alizarine or other dyes; her "protection" in this matter takes the only form which is not futile—that of efficiency. (*See also* ANILINE.)

**ALKALI**—The manufacture of the group of industrial chemicals generally described as alkalis, including caustic soda, soda ash, bicarbonate of soda, bleaching powder, &c., is an exceedingly important branch of British industry, and on the whole it has been worthily sustained. The United Kingdom, possessing plentiful supplies of coal and salt, early availed itself of the invention of Leblanc, the Frenchman, for the utilisation of common salt in alkali manufacture, and so gained a lead in a trade which she could not expect for ever to monopolise. The Leblanc process has now been largely superseded by the ammonia-soda process of Solvay and the electrolytic process of Le Sueur and Rieckmann. The last named has been largely developed in Germany, and German manufacturers of bleach made by this process have been able to market their production here with some success.

The following figures relate to British imports and exports of the soda compounds and of bleach:

BRITISH COMMERCE IN ALKALI

| | Imports for Home Consumption | | Exports of British Make | |
|---|---|---|---|---|
| | Cwts. | Value (c.i.f.) | Cwts. | Value (f.o.b.) |
| | | £ | | £ |
| 1860 ... ... | 12,000 | 11,000 | 2,050,000 | 965,000 |
| 1870 ... ... | 86,000 | 142,000 | 3,853,000 | 1,485,000 |
| 1880 ... ... | 58,000 | 69,000 | 6,888,000 | 2,398,000 |
| 1890 ... ... | 27,000 | 21,000 | 6,332,000 | 2,089,000 |
| 1900 ... ... | 291,000 | 161,000 | 4,923,000 | 1,488,000 |
| 1907 ... ... | 517,000 | 169,000 | 6,783,000 | 2,120,000 |
| 1908 ... ... | 408,000 | 162,000 | 5,423,000 | 1,735,000 |

The import figures of the earlier years are probably not strictly comparative, as varying compounds seem from time to time to have been included under the heading "alkali."

The export trade suffered a great check through the development of the American alkali manufacture and the Dingley Tariff of 1897. It was not, of course, to be expected that the United States, more favoured than ourselves in raw material, would be dependent upon us indefinitely for the products of processes which were not even of British invention. The loss of a great part of the American trade, which accounts for the check in exports in the decade 1890–1900, has been atoned for, however, by great expansion in other markets.

Imports are comparatively small, and largely consist of bleach produced by electrolysis in Germany.

Large as is the external trade, it forms but a small part of our production. The output of alkali in the United Kingdom is now probably as much as 20,000,000 cwts. a year. This is the most important feature, for the alkalies are exceedingly valuable raw materials of industry in the soap, glass, textiles, paper, and other trades. To these industries the cheapening of alkali, clearly shown in the above figures, has been a great stimulus.

The relation of the imports and exports of alkali to foreign competition is worth consideration. We cannot, of course, export alkali without assisting foreign industry, any more than foreign nations can export chemicals to this country without assisting British industry. This is an obvious observation, but it is quite necessary to make it, and its application goes far. It is a curious fact that it rarely occurs to Protectionists that it is our exports of manufactures, and not our imports, which form the chief assistance we render to foreign manufacturers. Still more curious, while some Protectionists, unaware of the real nature of our coal exports (*see* Coal Exports), deplore them as of special assistance to foreign industry, which they are not, they do not appear to deplore our exports of such products as chemicals, the essence of cheap coal, which are essential raw materials of important trades in which foreigners compete with us in the home and export markets. The early British Protectionists were more logical. Both Henry III. and Edward III. saw so clearly that exports of British material aided foreign manufacturers that they prohibited the exportation of wool from England.

**ALUM**—No record of commerce in alum appeared in the Custom House returns until 1901, when exports were first noted:

BRITISH EXPORTS OF ALUM AND ALLIED COMPOUNDS

| | Cwts. | £ (f.o.b.) |
|---|---|---|
| 1901 ... ... | 160,000 ... ... | 36,000 |
| 1907 ... ... | 192,000 .. ... | 46,000 |
| 1908 ... ... | 196,000 ... ... | 47,000 |

There are no recorded imports. The exports represent the supply to foreign and Colonial manfacturers of a valuable raw material used in the leather, paper, and dyeing trades, chiefly as a mordant in the last named. If there were any imports it would be obviously unwise to tax them, although alum is a "manufacture."

**AMERICA**—*See* United States.

**AMMONIA**—The manufacture of ammonical salts is carried on in connection with the alkali industry, and the value of the production, although not precisely known, is considerable. The Custom House returns of recent years give records of commerce in (1) sulphate of ammonia; (2) carbonate of ammonia (*sal-volatile*); and (3) muriate of ammonia (ammonium chloride or sal-ammoniac).

### 1. Sulphate of Ammonia

There are no recorded imports of this salt, and the exports were at one time included under the heading "Chemical Manures." Since 1899 the exports have been separately recorded:

BRITISH EXPORTS OF AMMONIUM SULPHATE

| | Tons | Value (f.o.b.) £ |
|---|---|---|
| 1900 | 145,000 | 1,637,000 |
| 1907 | 231,000 | 2,753,000 |
| 1908 | 234,000 | 2,764,000 |

The export trade is seen to be a large and growing one. As I have said, there are no imports, but if there were, to tax them would be to tax agriculture. It may be added that there are some imports of sulphuric acid, and ammonium sulphate is prepared commercially by the addition of sulphuric acid to gas-water.

### 2. Carbonate of Ammonia

British commerce in carbonate of ammonia was for the first time recorded in 1908:

BRITISH EXPORTS OF AMMONIUM CARBONATE

| | Cwts. | Value (f.o.b.) £ |
|---|---|---|
| 1908 | 62,000 | 96,000 |

The uses of ammonium carbonate are varied. Commercial ammonia is employed in dyeing, in wool scouring, &c. It is thus a raw material of industry, and if imports arise they ought not to be taxed.

### 3. Muriate of Ammonia.

Both imports and exports of sal-ammoniac have been recorded in recent years, the first figures being published in 1904:

BRITISH COMMERCE IN AMMONIUM CHLORIDE.

| Imports for Home Consumption | | | Exports of British Make | |
|---|---|---|---|---|
| Year | Cwts. | Value (c.i.f.) | Cwts. | Value (f.o.b.) |
| | | £ | | £ |
| 1904 | 4,200 | 6,200 | 81,000 | 108,000 |
| 1907 | 4,800 | 6,600 | 154,000 | 194,000 |
| 1908 | 4,700 | 6,500 | 83,000 | 110,000 |

In this case there are some recorded imports, to tax which would be to tax industry, since sal-ammoniac has many industrial uses. It is employed in galvanising iron, in soldering, &c.

**AMMUNITION**—The following table shows the extent of British commerce in ammunition since 1860. The early figures stand chiefly for shot and shell, gunpowder, and percussion caps; in later years the growing complexity of ammunition and explosives brings a large variety of articles into the composition of the totals:

BRITISH COMMERCE IN AMMUNITION

| | Imports for Home Consumption (c.i.f.) | Exports of British Make (f.o.b.). |
|---|---|---|
| | £ | £ |
| 1860 | 4,000 | 384,000 |
| 1870 | 8,000 | 490,000 |
| 1880 | 19,000 | 486,000 |
| 1890 | 146,000 | 957,000 |
| 1900 | 266,000 | 1,365,000 |
| 1907 | 129,000 | 2,262,000 |
| 1908 | 125,000 | 1,703,000 |

The export trade is thus very extensive, while imports on the whole now tend to fall. Since 1901 the official records have been given in greater analysis, and the following table is added to show the composition of the totals in recent years :

BRITISH COMMERCE IN AMMUNITION ANALYSED

| Description | Imports for Home Consumption (c.i.f.) | | | Exports of British Make (f.o.b) | | |
|---|---|---|---|---|---|---|
| | 1901 £ | 1907 £ | 1908 £ | 1901 £ | 1907 £ | 1908 £ |
| Shot and shell... ... | 3,000 | — | 200 | 205,000 | 81,000 | 16,000 |
| Gunpowder ... ... | 3,000 | 8,000 | 5,000 | 172,000 | 184,000 | 158,000 |
| Cordite and other smokeless powders | 5,000 | 6,400 | 2,000 | 240,000 | 376,000 | 161,000 |
| Dynamite, &c. ... | 57,000 | 9,000 | 14,000 | 443,000 | 807,000 | 720,000 |
| Cartridges for small arms ... ... ... | 29,000 | 44,000 | 51,000 | 255,000 | 328,000 | 248,000 |
| Cartridges, other ... | 1,000 | — | — | 77,000 | 91,000 | 34,000 |
| Cartridges, empty ... | 2,000 | — | 700 | 11,000 | 400 | 3,000 |
| Fuses, &c. ... ... | 10,000 | 5,000 | 7,000 | 40,000 | 30,000 | 55,000 |
| Percussion caps ... | — | 400 | 400 | 25,000 | 27,000 | 19,000 |
| Rockets and miscellaneous ... ... | 43,000 | 56,000 | 45,000 | 182,000 | 338,000 | 289,000 |
| Total ... ... | £153,000 | £128,800 | £125,300 | £1,650,000 | £2,262,400 | £1,703,000 |

The imports, it will be seen, are comparatively small, and foreign competition in the home market does not appear to have made any progress save in respect of small arms ammunition.

**ANILINE**—This important substance is a hydro-carbon produced from benzine, which, in its turn, is derived from the destructive distillation of coal. Itself a colourless liquid, it is the base of a marvellous series of beautiful dyes, although some of the colours commonly called "aniline dyes" are derived not from aniline, but from allied substances. The progress of the aniline dye industry is worth particular attention, for it serves to remind us of the chief factors of modern industrial progress.

The fact that aniline produced a beautiful blue when treated with alkali was first noticed as long ago as 1836 by a German chemist, Runge, but an Englishman, Perkin, was the first to produce a practical aniline dye (1856), and a British dyer, Pullar, was the first to employ it. What might have been a magnificent British industry was thus founded, but it was left for German chemists to build upon the work of Perkin, and to produce from benzine, anthracene, naphthalene, and other hydro-carbons derived from coal-tar, the wonderful range of artificial dyes which have become almost exclusively the dyers' colouring materials. After allowance has been made for the fact that the industrial use of alcohol, so necessary in this industry, was unwisely limited by British law, it is impossible not to deplore the lack of scientific application in the United Kingdom which resigned to the Germans this peculiarly creditable branch of industrial production.

Some have deplored the fact that in connection with this industry we did not have, long ago, such a patent law as that enacted by Mr. Lloyd George in 1907, which compels those who patent processes here to work them here if they desire to retain their patents. By this means we might indeed have compelled German chemical manufacturers to establish on British soil works for the exploitation of German scientific research, but surely that is a poor substitute for that application of science to industry which is the secret of German success all along the line. Here we are reminded that science is the only reliable basis of industrial progress apart from the possession of natural resources, and while the aniline dye industry is an outstanding example of the true explanation of the rise of modern industrial Germany, we shall do well to remember that in greater or less degree every German industry has been affected by the same cause.

Our imports of aniline dyes are shown in the following table:

BRITISH IMPORTS OF ANILINE AND NAPHTHALENE DYES FOR HOME CONSUMPTION

| | Quantity Cwts. | Value (c.i.f.) £ |
|---|---|---|
| 1890 ... ... | Not known ... ... | 245,000 |
| 1900 ... ... | Not known ... ... | 505,000 |
| 1907 ... ... | 217,000 ... ... | 1,263,000 |
| 1908 ... ... | 196,000 ... ... | 1,106,000 |

Down to 1900 the figures represent imports of "aniline" dyes. The Custom House now use the not very scientific heading, "Aniline and Naphthalene Dyestuffs" (the aniline and naphthalene dyes are distinct series of colours), so that the earlier and later figures are probably not strictly comparative. Nevertheless they show sufficiently the great growth of the imports of these indispensable colours, which, I need hardly add, are almost entirely from Germany.

These imports, of course, are the raw materials of the dyer, and to tax them would be an obvious folly.

We have no exports classified as strictly "aniline," but under "dyestuffs: products of coal-tar," we exported in 1908 43,596 cwts., valued at £152,000 f.o.b. Our exports under this general heading are thus much less in value than our imports from Germany under the classification above given.

**APPAREL**—The British production of apparel is of an enormous value, but its precise dimensions are unknown. The industry is chiefly concerned with home trade, but the external trade, while relatively small, is not unimportant. The following table shows our imports for home consumption and exports of British make:

BRITISH COMMERCE IN APPAREL

| | Imports for Home Consumption (c.i.f.) £ | Exports of British Make (f.o.b.) £ |
|---|---|---|
| 1860 | Not known | 2,156,009 |
| 1870 | ,, | 2,205,000 |
| 1880 | ,, | 3,212,000 |
| 1890 | ,, | 5,036,000 |
| 1900 | ,, | 5,287,000 |
| 1907 | 2,726,000 | 5,634,000 |
| 1908 | 2,424,000 | 5,018,000 |

It will be seen that our exports of apparel are nearly twice as great as our imports. Our imports are an insignificant fraction of our total consumption.

The above figures do not include BOOTS, HATS, &c., *which see.*

**ARMS**—The value of our total production of arms is not known, but it is considerable. There are certain small imports, but these have only recently been recorded separately at the Customs House. The following table gives an analysis of both our imports and exports since 1901, the year in which a detailed classification was adopted by the officials:

BRITISH COMMERCE IN ARMS

| Description | Imports for Home Consumption (c.i.f.) | | | Exports of British Make (f.o.b.) | | |
|---|---|---|---|---|---|---|
| | 1901. | 1907. | 1908. | 1901. | 1907. | 1908. |
| | £ | £ | £ | £ | £ | £ |
| CANNON: | | | | | | |
| Guns, howitzers, &c. ... | — | — | 13,000 | 106,000 | 157,000 | 264,000 |
| Machine and quick-firing guns ... ... ... | 5,000 | 6,000 | 8,000 | 103,000 | 85,000 | 73,000 |
| Gun mountings ... ... | — | — | 1,000 | 115,000 | 31,000 | 378,000 |
| SMALL ARMS (FIREARMS): | | | | | | |
| Sporting guns and rifles | } 46,000 | 33,000 | 25,000 | } 309,000 | } 302,000 | 176,000 |
| Military rifles ... ... | | | 1,000 | | | 114,000 |
| Miniature rifles ... ... | | | — | | | 2,000 |
| Air guns ... ... ... | not known | not known | 9,000 | not known | not known | 3,000 |
| Revolvers and pistols ... | 8.000 | 10,000 | 11,000 | 7,000 | 12,000 | 11,000 |
| Tubes for barrels ... | — | — | — | — | — | 3,000 |
| Other parts... ... ... | not known | not known | 49,000 | not known | not known | 23,000 |
| SWORDS, CUTLASSES, &C.: | 3,000 | 2,000 | 1,000 | 17,000 | 5,000 | 9,000 |
| TORPEDOES, MINES, &C.... | — | 6,000 | — | — | 2,000 | 58,000 |

It will be seen that there is considerable competition in the home market in small arms. An extended view of our commerce in small arms (firearms) only is given in the following table:

BRITISH COMMERCE IN SMALL FIREARMS

| | Imports for Home Consumption (c.i.f.) | Exports of British Make (f.o.b.) |
|---|---|---|
| | £ | £ |
| 1880 ... ... ... | 13,000 ... ... | 345,000 |
| 1900 ... ... ... | 86,000 ... ... | 208,000 |
| 1907 ... ... ... | 42,000 ... ... | 314,000 |
| 1908 ... ... ... | 97,000 ... ... | 332,000 |

These figures appear to point to a considerable decline in our small-arms industry followed by revival. The export trade has recovered to such purpose that the figures of 1907–8 are half as great again as those of 1900.

**AUSTRALIA**—The Commonwealth of Australia was formed in 1901 by the Federation of the six colonies—New South Wales, Victoria, Queensland, South Australia, West Australia, and Tasmania. The area of the Commonwealth is 2,974,581 square miles, or about twenty-five times the size of the United Kingdom. A great part of this vast territory, however, is desert, and the remainder subject to extremes of heat and recurrent drought. The entire population at the present time is only about 4,500,000, of whom about 150,000 are aborigines. The greater part of the population, or, say, 2,750,000, live in New South Wales and Victoria, which between them have an area of about only 400,000 square miles, forming the south-east corner of the island.

Australia's wealth lies chiefly in her pastures and her mines, and, except in years of drought, she is a large producer and exporter of mutton and wool. She supplies us with considerable quantities of butter, wheat, fruit, leather, mutton, rabbits, copper, lead, silver, tin, skins, furs, tallow, timber, wool, and, of course, gold. In years of drought, such as 1903, Australia is forced to import food. Unfortunately, she has comparatively little coal, the foundation of modern economic industry.

The external commerce of Australia in 1903–1907 was as follows:

COMMERCE OF AUSTRALIAN COMMONWEALTH
(In Millions of £)

| | Imports from | | Exports to | |
|---|---|---|---|---|
| | 1903 | 1907 | 1903 | 1907 |
| United Kingdom ... ... ... | 19·8 | 31·9 | 20·0 | 34·0 |
| Remainder of British Empire ... | 5·0 | 6·7 | 15·6 | 13·1 |
| Foreign Countries ... ... | 13·0 | 13·2 | 12·7 | 25·7 |
| Total ... ... | 37·8 | 51·8 | 48·3 | 72·8 |

The exports of Australia exceed her imports because she has raised public loans abroad, and has to export to pay interest due. The above figures include both merchandise and precious metals. Australia, of course, is a large gold producer. The above export figures include, in 1903, £19,000,000 worth, and in 1907 £12,000,000 worth, of gold and silver.

It is important to note that as far as the imports of Australia consist of manufactured articles they are chiefly drawn from the United Kingdom. The facts are:

AUSTRALIAN IMPORTS ANALYSED

(In Millions of £)

| From | Manufactured Articles | | Total Imports | |
|---|---|---|---|---|
| | 1903 | 1907 | 1903 | 1907 |
| United Kingdom ... ... | 17·7 | 28·3 | 19·8 | 31·9 |
| Remainder British Empire ... | 1·0 | 2·0 | 5·0 | 6·7 |
| Foreign countries ... ... | 6·0 | 8·9 | 13·0 | 13·2 |
| Total ... ... ... | 24·7 | 39·2 | 37·8 | 51·8 |

We have thus much more than held our own in the Australian market in recent years.

**AUSTRALIAN PREFERENCE**—The Australian Preferential tariff, embodied in the Australian Customs Tariff of 1908, can only be described, in plain English, as a sham. The chief idea of the new Australian tariff was to give increased protection to Australian manufacturers, and to give that protection against the chief exporter to Australia, viz., the United Kingdom. With this object a large number of the old duties, which applied equally to British and foreign goods, were raised. A double tariff was constructed, giving a maximum and minimum scale, the maximum applying to foreign goods, and the minimum or "preferential" rates to British goods.

What has been really done is to make a considerable increase in the Australian tariff against British manufacturers. Where before, say, 20 per cent. was levied on our goods, 25 per cent. is to be levied in future, and we are to find what consolation we can in the fact that 30 per cent. is to be levied on foreign goods. Well may the British trader say, "If Australia be not fair to me, what care I how unfair she be to others?" If 25 per cent. is enough fully to protect the Australian producer, 30 per cent. protects him no more.

This is no fancy illustration, unfortunately. Examination of the details shows that the tariff is raised against us all round by the alleged "Preference."

Take wearing apparel as an example. Before we received the advantage of the Australian "Preference" a duty of 25 per

THE AUSTRALIAN "PREFERENTIAL" TARIFF

| | Old Duties | New Preferential Duties on British Goods | New Duties on Foreign Goods |
|---|---|---|---|
| | Per cent. | Per cent. | Per cent. |
| Machine tools... ... | Free | 15 | 15 |
| Furniture ... ... | 20 | 30 | 35 |
| Traction engines ... | Free | 25 | 30 |
| Locomotives ... ... | 12½ | 20 | 25 |
| Perfumery ... ... | 20 | 25 | 30 |
| Cycles ... ... ... | 20 | 25 (Minimum £5) | 30 (Minimum £5 5s.) |
| Agricultural Machinery | Free | Free | Free |

cent. *ad valorem* was imposed upon British wearing apparel. Under the advantage of the "Preference" a duty of 40 per cent. *ad valorem* is levied. Where, then, does the "Preference" come in? Let the reader control his enthusiasm. The "Preference" lies in the fact that while the British wearing apparel is in future to be taxed 40 per cent., foreign wearing apparel is to be taxed 45 per cent.!

Here is an even brighter example of the virtues of the new Preference which I commend to Coventry. If a British cycle maker exported a £5 bicycle to Australia under the old tariff the duty levied was £1, or 20 per cent. Under the

Preference a "preferential" duty of £5, or 100 per cent., is levied. If the £5 machine is foreign, however, a duty of £5 5s. is levied, which constitutes the "Preference." As a matter of fact, however, the £5 is quite enough to exclude British cycles altogether, and the odd 5s. is a fancy piece of tariff trimming.

On page 39 I give a short list of other examples which will help to show how the thing is done.

It will be seen that the new "preferential" duties are higher —sometimes much higher—than the old rates. The foreign duty is a little higher still, but it is the minimum that counts. Sometimes, again, there is no preference at all, as with agricultural machinery, where we most need it. Only in cases where there is no Australian home manufacture of an article, and no desire immediately to foster such manufacture, is a real Preference given to British goods. An example may be found in the surgical instruments. These, if of British make, go in as heretofore, duty free; while, if foreign-made, they are charged to duty at 10 per cent. *ad valorem*. This case only serves to accentuate the guiding principle of Preference. (*See* CANADIAN MANUFACTURERS' ASSOCIATION.)

**AUSTRIA-HUNGARY**—The dual monarchy, which has an area about twice as great as that of Britain, and a population rather larger than ours, is one of the minor manufacturing nations. She has little coal. Her customs tariff is highly Protectionist, her duties averaging about 35 per cent *ad valorem* on manufactured articles. The figures given opposite show the degree and nature of her commerce in recent years.

Unfortunately there were some changes in the classifications in 1906 which somewhat vitiate the comparison with 1900.

The Protectionist should carefully note that in 1906 Austria-Hungary imported £43,700,000 worth of manufactures, and that although iron and steel, copper, &c., are classified in the "raw materials" category.

Germany is by far the largest exporter to Austria. This is due to (1) proximity, (2) language, and (3) energy.

COMMERCE OF AUSTRIA-HUNGARY

(In Millions of £)

| Category | Imports for Home Consumption | | Exports of Austrian Produce | |
|---|---|---|---|---|
| | 1900 | 1906 | 1900 | 1906 |
| Food ... ... ... | 11·5 | 9·4 | 13·1 | 10·6 |
| Raw materials ... | 29·9 | 44·4 | 21.1 | 25·6 |
| Manufactures ... | 29·2 | 43·7 | 46·7 | 62·9 |
| Totals ... ... | 70·6 | 97·5 | 80·8 | 99·1 |

**BACON**—The United Kingdom imports large quantities of bacon, chiefly from foreign countries. During the last three years the imports have been about 5,500,000 cwts., worth about £14,500,000 per annum. In 1908 the imports were:

BRITISH IMPORTS OF BACON, 1908

| From— | Cwts. | | £ |
|---|---|---|---|
| Denmark ... ... ... ... | 2,051,000 | ... | 5,686,000 |
| United States ... ... ... | 2,542,000 | ... | 6,035,000 |
| Total above and other Foreign | 4,682,000 | ... | 11,962,000 |
| Canada ... ... ... ... | 1,004,000 | ... | 2,518,000 |
| Grand total ... ... | 5,686,000 | ... | 14,480,000 |

Under Protection these valuable supplies would undoubtedly be taxed. When Mr. Chamberlain outlined his programme on October 6, 1903, he proposed to leave bacon untaxed. His words were:

"*I propose to exclude bacon, because bacon is a popular food with some of the poorest of the population.*"

Thus Mr. Chamberlain confessed that food duties raised prices.

But Mr. Chamberlain's programme has since been thrown over by his own "Tariff Commission." Paragraph 394 of vol. iii., Report of the "Tariff Commission's" Agricultural Committee, proposes *a 5 per cent. tax on bacon, and does not even propose that Canadian bacon should come in free.*

**BAGS AND SACKS** (empty, for packing merchandise)—There are no recorded imports of these articles, but we have a considerable export trade in them, almost entirely to foreign countries. In 1900 our exports were worth £538,000, in 1907 £926,000, and in 1908 £778,000. Protection cannot offer an import duty to this industry, for the imports are negligible.

**BAKERS**—The baker, master and man, would be heavily hit by import duties, for while cost of production and cost of living would be enhanced, Protection cannot offer the baker any compensation, because there are no imports of bread. In this connection it should be noted that the trade of bread-making is a branch of manufacturing industry which is "*protected" by nature*, as we cannot eat imported bread. Here lies a complete proof that Protection is not a remedy for unemployment, for unemployment exists amongst bakers as much as in the trades which are exposed to foreign competition.

**BALANCE OF TRADE**—The term "balance of trade" is hundreds of years old—as old as the MERCANTILE SYSTEM (*which see*), from which Protection is lineally descended. It was the name given to the difference between the respective values of the imports and exports of a country. The conception of the mercantile system was, in brief, that wealth and the precious metals were one and the same thing, and that the whole object of a nation was to export more merchandise than it imported in order to obtain payment of "the balance" in gold. It was this ridiculous notion which Adam Smith overthrew in Book IV. of his celebrated "Wealth of Nations." Yet to-day many people are Protectionists because British imports are greater than British exports, and because they believe that the "balance" is paid out by us in money.

Our *visible* imports, like those of Germany, always largely exceed our *visible* exports. That is because we have such large exports of *services*. The following statement shows broadly how our exports were paid for in 1907 :

BRITISH IMPORTS AND EXPORTS, 1907

(In Millions of £)

| Imports | | Exports | |
|---|---|---|---|
| Of Goods ... ... | ... 646 | Of British Goods ... | ... 426 |
| ,, Gold and Silver ... | ... 73 | ,, Imported Goods ... | ... 92 |
| | | ,, Gold and Silver ... | ... 68 |
| | 719+ | ,, Shipping Services | ... 90 |
| | | ,, Capital ,, (*i.e.*, Interest receivable) | ... 100 |
| | | | 776 + |

The above statement gives the chief details, but banking services, remittances of pay, imports of diamonds (not recorded), &c., of uncertain but comparatively small dimensions, are not included. Nevertheless, it gives the essential items, and shows that we do not import all that we have the power to import. (*See also* Mercantile System, Gold, Imports, Exports, &c.)

The fallacy that gold is exported to pay foreign workmen is frequently at the root of Protectionist thought, and I read without surprise in a leading article in the *Daily Mail* of January 15, 1909, that:

> "So long as our sales to the foreigner are less than his sales to us he can always take our gold when it suits him to do so. The golden sovereigns do in actual fact go abroad to pay for foreign imports."

If the *Daily Mail*, before writing this "leader," had consulted the official record of gold and silver imports and exports for recent years it would have found that taking one year with another we are always adding to the stock of the precious metals in the country. In 1908 our exports of bullion and specie were rather larger than our imports, and that occasionally happens within the limits of a single year, month, or week, but taking any few years together our imports of gold always exceed our exports. (*See* Gold.)

What is particularly misleading about the *Mail* article is its implied assumption that it is only Britain which has an excess of imports. "So long," it says, "as our sales to the foreigner are less than his sales to us." It is apparently unaware that that sentence might with equal truth be written of both France and Germany. As to the former the facts for 1907 are:

MERCHANDISE IMPORTS AND EXPORTS OF FRANCE IN 1907

| | £ |
|---|---|
| Imports ... ... ... ... ... | 241,906,000 |
| Exports ... ... ... ... ... | 221,681,000 |
| Excess of Imports ... ... | 20,225,000 |

The case of Germany is as follows:

MERCHANDISE IMPORTS AND EXPORTS OF GERMANY IN 1907

| | £ |
|---|---|
| Imports ... ... ... ... ... | 422,707,000 |
| Exports ... ... ... ... ... | 337,722,000 |
| Excess of Imports ... ... | 84,985,000 |

According to the wisdom of the *Daily Mail*, Germany has to export nearly £85,000,000 of gold every year to pay for her excess of imports. According to common sense, she does nothing of the kind. She pays for her excess of imports as we do, chiefly by shipping earnings and interest receivable from abroad. The £85,000,000 excess of imports is smaller than ours. In 1907 the British excess of imports amounted to £128,000,000. The explanation is that we have more ships than the Germans, a larger international banking business than the Germans, and have more interest owing to us than the Germans. But the difference is one of degree, not of kind.

The United States, unlike Germany and Britain, has an excess of exports which varies in size from year to year. For 1907 the facts were:

MERCHANDISE IMPORTS AND EXPORTS OF THE UNITED STATES, 1907

| | £ |
|---|---|
| Imports ... ... ... ... ... | 296,519,000 |
| Exports ... ... ... ... ... | 394,859,000 |
| Excess of Exports ... ... | 98,340,000 |

While Britain and Germany have great mercantile marines, America has very little ocean shipping. Therefore she has to pay out exports to the nations, chiefly Britain, which carry her goods for her. A great part of the ocean traffic of America is done by Britain, and we are paid in corn and cotton for doing the work, a fact which at one and the same time explains part of the American excess of visible exports, and part of the British excess of visible imports. Then America has to export interest on the American bonds and securities held abroad. Again, her rich citizens are constantly travelling abroad and calling out exports to cover their letters of credit.

Taking the world as a whole, adding the imports of all countries together and the exports of all countries together, imports exceed the exports. At first sight this seems strange, but reflection shows that it ought to be so. In the Fiscal Bluebook the Board of Trade give the facts for the years 1891, 1896, and 1901. They say:

"The following table shows for the three years 1891, 1896, and 1901 the aggregate imports into and exports from all the principal countries of the world:

| | Imports Million £ | Exports Million £ | Excess of Imports Million £ |
|---|---|---|---|
| 1891 ... ... | 2,000 ... | 1,850 ... | 249 |
| 1896 ... ... | 2,147 ... | 1,898 ... | 249 |
| 1901 ... ... | 2,516 ... | 2,292 ... | 224 |

"It will be seen that the average excess of imports over exports, taking the whole external trade of the world into account, bears a fairly definite relationship to the aggregate of trade. The amount of the excess in 1901 was, however, somewhat less than in either of the other years, viz., about 224 million pounds."

The Board of Trade then go on to give the explanation, viz., "the imports and exports of the whole world are, for the most part, the same goods valued at the point of arrival and departure respectively." That is to say, if we export a locomotive to Brazil, the value of the locomotive is entered in our trade returns at what is called the f.o.b. (free on board) value. But when the locomotive arrives at Brazil it is worth more. Brazil has to take into account the freight to Brazil and the cost of insurance, and the Brazilian authorities enter the locomotive at the "c.i.f." (cost, insurance, and freight) value. So that the same item figures for more in the Brazilian import returns than it does in the British export returns. And so it is generally.

Now as this fortunate country owns more than one-half of the ocean shipping of all the world, *it follows that the difference between the value of the world's imports and the value of the world's exports is as to more than one-half accounted for by the earnings of British ships.* When a man once understands this interesting and all-important fact it is difficult for him to be a "Tariff Reformer."

**BALFOUR, THE RIGHT HON. A. J., M.P.**—That the result of Protection is to enable would-be monopolists to make profit by raising their prices against the public is sometimes denied by Protectionists. On this point Mr. Balfour, speaking at Edinburgh, on October 3, 1904, gave a definition of Protection "in a nutshell," which could hardly be improved. Mr. Balfour said:

> "*The object of Protection is to encourage home industry. The means by which it attains that object is by the manipulation of a fiscal system to raise home prices. If the home prices are not raised, the industry is not encouraged. If the industry is encouraged, it is by the raising of prices. That is, in a nutshell, Protection properly understood.*"

This limpid utterance demands no comment from me, but for proofs that in practice Protection raises price, and that the consumer pays the import duty, *see* WHEAT, IMPORT DUTY, DRAWBACKS, &c.

**BANK RATE**—The Bank rate is the Bank of England minimum rate of discount, or the lowest rate at which the Bank of England will discount first-class bills of exchange or lend money on good security for short periods. The rate is settled every Thursday morning at the Bank of England, and it varies with the proportion which the gold reserve bears to the aggregate deposits. The Bank of England is the custodian of the national reserve of gold, and if at any time there is a run upon that reserve the Bank raises its official rate of discount in order to preserve it. Gold moves to the point where it can be most profitably employed, and when the Bank of England raises the Bank rate it raises the price of money (*i.e.*, the rate of interest paid for the loan of money) and so checks the call upon its gold, or causes gold to flow back to London. This check is brought into operation whenever there is any danger of the depletion of the gold reserve. Those Protectionists who fear that we pay for our imports in gold confess themselves unacquainted with the essential facts to which I have briefly referred. (*See* also GOLD.)

**BANKERS' CLEARING HOUSE RETURNS**—In order to facilitate the clearance of cheques and bills of exchange the London bankers long ago—in 1775—established a central Clearing House at which all the various promises to pay in the shape of cheques and bills drawn upon or payable at the different banks are set off against each other by simple book-keeping. This saves each bank the trouble of settling up with each other bank, and thus economising time and labour. The Clearing House and the banks each have accounts with the Bank of England, and so whatever differences are shown by the Clearing House to be due from one bank to another are easily settled.

It will be seen that the total value of the cheques cleared at the London Bankers' Clearing House is an excellent clue to the growth of business transactions. The following table shows the amounts cleared since 1885 :

| Year | | £ | Year | | £ |
|---|---|---|---|---|---|
| 1885 | ... | 5,511,000,000 | 1897 | ... | 7,491,000,000 |
| 1887 | ... | 6,077,000,000 | 1899 | ... | 9,150,000,000 |
| 1889 | ... | 7,619,000,000 | 1901 | ... | 9,561,000,000 |
| 1891 | ... | 6,848,000,000 | 1903 | ... | 10,120,000,000 |
| 1893 | ... | 6,478,000,000 | 1905 | ... | 12,288,000,000 |
| 1895 | ... | 7,593,000,000 | 1907 | .. | 12,730,000,000 |

These stupendous figures exhibit both the fluctuation of trade (*see* TRADE CYCLES) and the enormous growth of business transacted in twenty-two years. They are, of course, quite inconsistent with the Protectionist allegation that British home trade is declining. As to whether business is more or less profitable than of old, *see* INCOME TAX.

**BARLEY**—Barley, perhaps the most ancient cereal used by mankind, is now chiefly used in Britain as the primary raw material of beer and whisky. Its taxation under Mr. Chamberlain's programme would affect the industries of the maltster, the brewer, and the distiller, and through them the consumers of alcoholic liquors.

We import a varying quantity of barley, sometimes less and sometimes more than 20,000,000 cwts. a year. Our chief suppliers are foreign countries—the United States, Russia, Turkey, and Roumania. Mr. Chamberlain proposed to tax foreign barley only, but Mr. Chamberlain's Tariff "Commission" proposes to tax both foreign and Colonial barley.

**BARTER**—Barter, strictly speaking, is the direct exchange of commodities without the intervention of a medium of exchange, but, in essence, all trade is barter, for the use of money merely disguises what is, in effect, an exchange of goods or services for goods or services. The man who works for a weekly wage barters his services, not for money, but for what the money will buy—for house-room, food, clothes, &c. Trade is barter facilitated by the use of money, which is at once a measure of value and a medium of exchange.

The commerce of the United Kingdom with other nations is simply an expression of barter. Possessing great manufacturing power, we, in effect, barter exports, chiefly consisting of manufactured articles, for imports, consisting chiefly of food and raw materials (for details *see* IMPORTS and EXPORTS). The bartering of exports for imports is carried out in practice by a form of paper money known as Bills of Exchange, *which see*.

Imports thus pay for exports, and exports pay for imports.

The Protectionist who fears imports fears the only form by which we can take payment for our exports. We export not to get rid of valuable commodities, and not to get "money" in exchange for them, but to acquire imports, and it is only because the nation is full of valuable imports, earned by our exports, that Britain, which is poor in a large variety of natural resources, is counted amongst the richest nations of the world.

**BASKETS AND BASKETWARE**—This is a humble branch of manufacturing industry in which we have no recorded exports. We import baskets and basketware from the Continent of Europe and from Japan to the value of about £200,000 a year. Broadly speaking, our relation to these imports is that we do better work and barter some of it for baskets. An import duty on baskets would be a great folly, because it would increase the expenses of those trades which buy baskets, and because it would be of no advantage whatever to this country to stimulate the production of baskets here by Protection.

**BEACONSFIELD, BENJAMIN DISRAELI, EARL OF**—The political career of the Earl of Beaconsfield strikingly illustrates the consensus of opinion which was arrived at in this country, after the adoption of Free Trade, that Free Trade was right. Benjamin Disraeli achieved his position as leader and educator of the Tory Party when, in 1846, Sir Robert Peel was converted from Protection to Free Trade and repealed the Corn Laws. Disraeli thereupon became the champion of Protection, but when he achieved power he did not undo Free Trade. So great was the triumph of Free Trade in practice that, when Disraeli himself rose to power, there was no reversal of fiscal policy. Upon this hangs a famous anecdote, which I may recount in the following extract from the "Letters of John Richard Green," pp. 237, 238:

"Long after Free Trade had come in, Neate remained unconvinced, and at last wrote a pamphlet advocating a restoration of Protection, and got a friend to submit it to Disraeli. 'Tell him,' replied D., 'that Protection is dead.' 'But Mr. Neate,' replied the friend, 'believes in its resurrection.' 'Then tell him,' Dizzy whispered, 'tell him Protection is not only dead, but d——d.'"

**BEEF**—The greater part of the beef we consume is raised in the United Kingdom. Nevertheless our imports are very large, and an import duty would have the effect of raising the price of the entire supply. The following is a careful estimate of British beef supplies, by Mr. R. H. Hooker, of the Board of Agriculture:

BEEF SUPPLY OF THE UNITED KINGDOM

| Year. | Home Supply | Imported | Total Supply | Per Cent. of Home to Total |
|---|---|---|---|---|
| | Million Cwts. | Million Cwts. | Million Cwts. | |
| 1900–1 | 13·4 | 8·3 | 21·7 | 61·7 |
| 1902–3 | 13·3 | 7·2 | 20·5 | 64·8 |
| 1904–5 | 13·4 | 8·8 | 22·2 | 60·3 |
| 1906–7 | 14·3 | 9·3 | 23·6 | 60·5 |
| 1907–8 | 13·9 | 8·9 | 22·8 | 60·8 |

So common is the erroneous idea that nearly all our food comes from abroad that few people are aware that we produce far more beef than we import.

Our beef imports are drawn chiefly from the United States and Argentina. The third largest supplier is Canada, and we get smaller quantities from New Zealand, Australia, and Uruguay.

Mr. Chamberlain, in his "practical" programme of October 6, 1903, proposed to put a tax of 5 per cent. on foreign beef only, but Mr. Chamberlain's Tariff "Commission" indicates that the agricultural Protectionists would not be satisfied with free meat imports from the Colonies.

**BELGIUM**—Belgium is a little country of only 11,000 square miles with a population of about 7,000,000 people—nearly 600 to the square mile—the most dense in Europe except Saxony. She occupies a favourable position for commerce, and has cleverly developed the fine port of Antwerp. Her territory is rich in coal, iron, and zinc.

The tariff of Belgium is liberal. Wheat and some other foods are on the free list. Her duties on manufactures are low, averaging about 12 per cent. *ad valorem.* Her duty on pig-iron, for example, is only 5 per cent., which means that she is less protected against German iron competition than the United Kingdom, although we have no iron duty, because the extra freight from Germany to the United Kingdom must be more than equal to a 5 per cent. duty.

COMMERCE OF BELGIUM

| Year. | Imports for Home Consumption £ | Exports of Belgian Produce £ |
|---|---|---|
| 1900 | 88,630,000 | 76,915,000 |
| 1907 | 146,625,000 | 113,036,000 |
| 1908 | 129,497,000 | 99,131,000 |

The large transit trade of Belgium is not included in these figures.

Belgium is a good customer of the United Kingdom, her 7,000,000 people buying from us about £18,000,000 worth of our produce per annum.

**BELTING**—*See* MACHINE BELTING.

**BILL OF EXCHANGE**—A Bill of Exchange is simply an order in writing from A to B requiring that B shall pay a certain sum, either on demand or at some future date, to A or to some third person. A is said to "draw" the Bill upon B. B. "accepts" the bill by signing his name across it.

The instrument of exchange created in this simple manner is beautifully effective, and is the foundation of the machinery of foreign trade. It renders the sending of gold between nations in payment for goods only exceptionally necessary. Practically all transactions are carried out by the machinery of the Bill of Exchange. Bills are drawn against the actual shipment of goods, and the slip of paper bearing the requisition to pay by the exporter in one country to the importer in another country becomes a symbol for the produce to which it relates. The bill is a piece of negotiable "money" if the names upon it are reputable, and the sending of these slips of paper between nations is the only form of payment which usually passes. They stand for goods, and symbolise the bartering of goods.

**BOARD OF TRADE RETURNS**—What are commonly called the "Board of Trade Returns" are compiled monthly at the Custom House, London, E., and the full title of the Return is "Accounts Relating to Trade and Navigation of the United Kingdom." They are published monthly at three o'clock on the seventh day of each month for the month previous. They can be bought through any bookseller, and the December issue, which costs 1s. 4d., gives complete figures for the current and two previous years.

The present form of the Board of Trade Returns was introduced in the year 1903, upon representations made by myself and largely accepted by a joint committee of the Board of Trade and Customs. They have since been further improved, and are now the clearest and best arranged national trade returns in the world.

The Returns show imports, exports, and re-exports of merchandise and the precious metals, and figures relating to shipping. All important articles are shown separately in the categories.

**BOOM AND SLUMP**—*See* Trade Cycles

**BOOTS AND SHOES**—The relation of the fiscal question to this trade is exceedingly important. All the raw materials of the bootmaker are manufactured articles. The bootmaker buys, from other manufacturers, leather for uppers and leather for soles, linings, thread, eyelets, nails, buttons, machinery, &c., not to mention the manufactured articles which have to be bought when his factory is built and equipped, and in the upkeep of his establishment. The avowed policy of the Protectionists is to tax manufactured articles in order to raise home prices (*see* BALFOUR). The immediate result of the adoption of Mr. Chamberlain's programme, or of the programme of Mr. Chamberlain's Tariff "Commission," would be to raise the price of leather and of the other materials of the boot manufacturer.

That would mean a severe blow to masters and men in the boot trade, for which they could not be compensated by being granted a duty on the imports of boots. Under Protection British leather makers would always be fighting for higher duties, and no tax on boots could atone to the bootmaker for dear leather.

Our imports and exports of boots since 1860 have been:

BRITISH COMMERCE IN LEATHER BOOTS

| Year | Imports for Home Consumption | | Exports of British Make | |
|---|---|---|---|---|
| | Quantity Doz. pairs | Value (c.i.f.) £ | Quantity Doz. pairs | Value (f.o.b.) £ |
| 1860 ... ... | 62,000 | 128,000 | Not known | Not known |
| 1870 ... ... | 52,000 | 143,000 | 372,000 | 1,148,000 |
| 1880 ... ... | 64,000 | 272,000 | 420,000 | 1,282,000 |
| 1890 ... ... | 89,000 | 297,000 | 696,000 | 1,898,000 |
| 1900 ... ... | 215,000 | 645,000 | 630,000 | 1,479,000 |
| 1907 ... ... | 170,000 | 728,000 | 787,000 | 2,041,000 |
| 1908 ... ... | 161,000 | 673,000 | 764,000 | 2,084,000 |

There was a considerable growth in foreign competition, which had long existed, between 1890 and 1900, in both the home and foreign markets. Since then the British boot trade has well maintained its position, as will be seen.

But an endeavour should always be made to get our external trade into perspective with our home trade, and in this case we are able to do it. The home production, imports, and exports of boots compare thus:

NUMBER OF PAIRS OF BOOTS (1) PRODUCED; (2) IMPORTED FOR HOME CONSUMPTION; AND (3) EXPORTED. 1908

| | No. of Pairs |
|---|---|
| Estimate of production ... ... ... | 100,000,000 |
| Imported for home consumption ... ... | 1,927,000 |
| Exports of British make ... ... ... | 9,146,000 |

The reader will see from these facts that in the boot trade foreign competition is a small factor in the home market.

Nothing is more remarkable in this industry than the manner in which British bootmakers, with the aid of Free Trade in leather, have beaten American competition. The Americans endeavoured to enter the British wholesale boot trade, and utterly failed. Yet, strange to say, British bootmakers work largely with American leather, and entirely with the clever boot machinery which the Americans invented.

**BOTTLES**—Glass bottles figure in both our import trade and our export trade. The facts are as follows:

BRITISH COMMERCE IN GLASS BOTTLES

| | Imports for Home Consumption (c.i.f.) | Exports of British Make (f.o.b.) |
|---|---|---|
| | £ | £ |
| 1900 ... ... | 665,000 ... ... | 421,000 |
| 1907 ... ... | 586,000 ... ... | 554,000 |
| 1908 ... ... | 565,000 ... ... | 501,000 |

The bottles we export are of a class different from the bottles we import.

The glass trade is one in which in some departments we have great need to reconsider our methods. On this head *see* GLASS.

An import duty on bottles would be most injurious to the general trade of the country. Glass bottles of every kind are raw materials of industry, used by many trades, and especially by food manufacturers. The cost of bottles is a considerable item in the expenses of these trades, and to add to it by taxation would diminish business and throw many workers out of employment.

**BOUNTIES**—The bounty system "encourages" an industry by making it a grant out of public funds. It is a form of Protection more direct, and often less objectionable, than the imposition of import duties to enable producers to levy private taxes on the public through raising prices. The bounty system is not very widely practised, but examples are to be found in the bounties until recently paid by Germany to her sugar producers, and the bounties paid by Canada to her iron manufacturers.

**BREAD**—All flesh is grass, but the nature of the grass used by different nations varies considerably. The best of the grasses is wheat, and the wealthiest nations of the world use wheaten bread almost exclusively. At the time of Cobden, while the American workman had wheaten bread, the British workman had often to use inferior foods, and Cobden, in one of his speeches, looked forward to every British workman having wheaten bread on his table like an American workman as something to hope for and work for.

During the last two years the price of wheat has risen through shortage of supplies, and this fact has been most unfairly used by Protectionists in their attack on Free Trade. What Free Trade does is to give us the best and cheapest supplies the world has to offer at any given time. If the world's harvests are good, then the loaf is cheap, and there is no tax to make it artificially dear. If the world's harvests are poor, and bread is dear from natural causes, then there is no tax to make it dearer still. That is the Free Trade position.

As I write (late in 1909) the Protectionists are retaliating upon the Free Trade Big and Little Loaf cartoons of the General Election of 1906 by placarding the walls of the United Kingdom with a poster which reads:

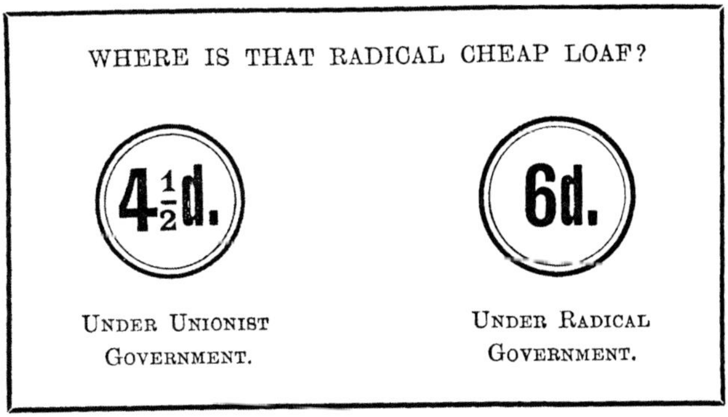

It is said that the public has a short memory, but it may be doubted if that memory is short enough to make it advisable to issue such a poster. So far as London is concerned, the average price of bread has not been below 5d. under any Administration during the last twenty-five years—I speak of the ordinary household loaf. So far as Great Britain as a whole is concerned, I have extracted the following figures from the Board of Trade *Labour Gazette*:

AVERAGE PRICE OF BREAD IN GREAT BRITAIN

(Ordinary Household Bread of Average Quality)

| Year | June 1 Pence | December 1 Pence |
|---|---|---|
| 1900 | 4·87 | 5·12 |
| 1901 | 5·12 | 5·00 |
| 1902 | 5·12 | 5·08 |
| 1903 | 5·10 | 5·27 |
| 1904 | 5·31 | 5·54 |
| 1905 | 5·43 | 5·39 |
| 1906 | 5·34 | 5·18 |
| 1907 | 5·31 | 5·98 |
| 1908 | 5·85 | 5·83 |
| 1909 | 6·30 | — |

It will be seen that between 1900 and June, 1907, the average price of bread in Great Britain was about fivepence, with a tendency to rise—a tendency which has since increased. As the table covers six "Unionist" years and four "Radical" years it is ludicrously at variance with the Protectionist poster referred to.

The actual rise of the price of bread is a phenomenon of great interest and importance, and it furnishes a striking example of the obscuration of really important matters at the hands of politicians. For years past I have pointed out in many places (*e.g.*, "Riches and Poverty," pp. 228–232) that wheat would appreciate in price. It is simply a matter of the world's wheat production failing to respond to the great increase in the number of eaters of the aristocrat of the grass family, which in its turn is a symbol of the increase of the standard of living in the world as a whole.

Faced with this natural increase in the price of wheat, free imports of grain become more and not less necessary to our working population. It is somewhat puzzling that there can be found public men willing to obscure that plain fact. At the present moment British wheat producers are enjoying high prices such as a considerable degree of Protection would have been needed to effect some years ago. With the loaf at sixpence and Essex wheat lands in great demand our industrial Protectionists may be excused for wishing in their hearts for the suppression of the Chamberlain food-tax programme, but they are as helpless before the landed interest as their prototypes in Germany.

Sooner or later wheat will fall again, although it may be after an interval of some years. If, when the fall comes, we are under the bondage of Protection, the power of Protection will be used to deprive our people of the benefit of the fall, and to sustain the prices and the rents based in the interim upon natural dearness plus Protection.

If I stopped here the average Protectionist, while admitting that his party poster is a discreditable document, might be inclined to use the *tu quoque* with reference to the Free Trade Big and Little Loaf cartoons of 1905–6. I hardly think the average Protectionist is aware that the little Protectionist loaf is a very real danger in the United Kingdom, in spite of the fall in freights and the consequent cheapening of bread which has occurred since the Hungry Forties. The table on page 58, which is taken from the Blue Book on "British and Foreign Trade and Industry" (Cd. 4954), is worth careful examination.

The conditions as to food production of the four nations dealt with in this table vary enormously. The United States, of course, still produces more wheat than she requires. As to the three European countries, France has 190 inhabitants per square mile, Germany 290, and the United Kingdom 342 (last census figures in each case). France, with her stationary population, is in many years independent or almost independent of imported wheat. Germany finds herself growing an ever-decreasing proportion of the food she requires, in spite of

Protection. Britain, more crowded even than Germany, is less able than Germany to feed herself, and, Protection or no Protection, will be found importing an increasing proportion of

AVERAGE RETAIL PRICES OF BREAD PER 4 LB. IN LONDON, PARIS, BERLIN, AND NEW YORK

| Year | London (Wheaten) | Paris (Wheaten) | Berlin (Rye) | New York (Wheaten) |
|---|---|---|---|---|
| | Pence | Pence | Pence | Pence |
| 1886 ... ... ... | 6·25 | 6·3 | 4·5 | — |
| 1887 ... ... ... | 5·6 | 6·7 | 4·4 | — |
| 1888 ... ... ... | 5·7 | 6·7 | 4·5 | — |
| 1889 ... ... ... | 6·0 | 6·9 | 5·3 | — |
| 1890 ... ... ... | 6·0 | 7·0 | 5·8 | 10·0 |
| 1891 ... ... ... | 6·2 | 7·4 | 6·8 | 10·0 |
| 1892 ... ... ... | 6·2 | 7·0 | 6·3 | 10·0 |
| 1893 ... ... ... | 5·75 | 6·6 | 4·7 | 10·0 |
| 1894 ... ... ... | 5·5 | 6·2 | 4·4 | 10·0 |
| 1895 ... ... ... | 5·1 | 6·1 | 4·4 | 10·0 |
| 1896 ... ... ... | 5·1 | 6·1 | 4·5 | 10·0 |
| 1897 ... ... ... | 5·5 | 6·8 | 4·8 | 10·0 |
| 1898 ... ... ... | 6·0 | 7·2 | 5·4 | 10·0 |
| 1899 ... ... ... | 5·1 | 6·5 | 5·2 | 10·0 |
| 1900 ... ... ... | 5·2 | 6·5 | 5·1 | 10·0 |
| 1901 ... ... ... | 5·0 | 6·1 | 5·2 | 10·0 |
| 1902 ... ... ... | 5·3 | 6·1 | 5·2 | 10·0 |
| 1903 ... ... ... | 5·6 | 6·5 | 5·1 | 9·4 |
| 1904 ... ... ... | 5·5 | 6·4 | 5·0 | 9·8 |
| 1905 ... ... ... | 5·5 | 6·3 | 5·2 | 10·7 |
| 1906 ... ... ... | 5·5 | 6·4 | 5·8 | 10·7 |
| 1907 ... ... ... | 5·4 | 6·5 | 6·6 | 10·7 |
| 1908 ... ... ... | 5·75 | 6·5 | 6·8 | 10·7 |

her food. Thus Germany presents the nearest comparison to our own conditions, but even in Germany food taxes are not felt as much as they would be felt here.

This said, a glance at the price of 4 lb. of rye bread in Germany should convince the most hardened Protectionist that a cartoon picturing the Free Trade loaf as big and the Protectionist loaf as little does not trifle with fact.

It will be seen that 4 lb. of German black bread are now (November, 1909), selling at a higher price than 4 lb.

of British wheat bread. It will be seen that whereas *circa* 1900 the Berlin black loaf was at parity with the British white loaf, and while both have since risen, the German black loaf has risen to a much higher point than the British white loaf. The British rise is the natural one, the German rise adds Protectionist folly to natural scarcity.

Perhaps it may be well to add that the white wheaten loaf is now nearly twice as dear in Berlin as it is in London.

**BRICKMAKING**—The making of bricks is a trade protected by nature. A few fancy bricks are from time to time imported, but their quantity is quite negligible, and for practical purposes the whole of the bricks used in the United Kingdom are, and must be, made at home. That is to say, the trade of brickmaking is as much "protected" from foreign competition as though we gravely drew up a Protectionist tariff and levied a duty of sixpence a brick on imported bricks.

This trade is therefore a test of whether or not foreign competition is the cause of unemployment, and of whether Protection is a cure for unemployment. As everybody knows, brickmakers are unfortunately just as much subject to unemployment as workers in trades which have imports.

**BRICKLAYING**—The bricklayers' trade is another industry which enjoys natural and complete "Protection" from foreign competition. Houses cannot be imported, and bricklaying, like bread-making, must be done at home. No German or Frenchman can be alleged to deprive the British bricklayer of work. Here, then, is another proof as to the efficacy of Protection from foreign competition as a remedy for unemployment. Bricklayers suffer terribly from unemployment in every country in the world, under every sort and kind of fiscal policy, clearly showing that in legislating for unemployment we must have regard to matters other than fiscal policy.

We may go further with justice, and point out that, if we

adopt Protection, many of the raw materials, such as cement, used by the bricklaying and other branches of the building industry will be taxed and made dearer, so that, while import duties can do nothing for the bricklayers' own trade, they will increase the cost of building, reduce the number of houses built, and so decrease bricklaying.

The British bricklayer is the best paid in Europe. From the report above referred to, and from the corresponding report on France, Cd. 4512, the following facts are taken :

BRICKLAYERS' WAGES

| | | | |
|---|---|---|---|
| In Britain | ... | ... | 37s. 6d. to 40s. 6d. per week. |
| In France | ... | ... | 21s. 7d. to 28s. 10d. ,, |
| In Germany | ... | ... | 26s. 11d. to 31s. 3d. ,, |

As to what these wages will buy in the three countries, *see* Cost of Living.

The rise of bricklayers' wages in the United Kingdom has been as follows since 1875 :

GROWTH OF BRICKLAYERS' WAGES

(Per Hour)

| Year | Birmingham | Cardiff | Leicester | Liverpool | London | Manchester |
|---|---|---|---|---|---|---|
| | Pence | Pence | Pence | Pence | Pence | Pence |
| 1875 | 7½ | 7½ | 7 | 7¾ | 9 | 8½ |
| 1885 | 8 | 7½ | 7½ | 8 | 9 | 8½ |
| 1895 | 9 | 8½ | 8 | 9 | 9½ | 9½ |
| 1905 | 9½ | 9 | 9 | 9½ | 10½ | 10 |
| 1909 | 9½ | 9 | 9 | 9¾ | 10½ | 10 |

**BRITISH EMPIRE**—The British Empire has an area of about 11,300,000 square miles, or nearly one hundred times that of the United Kingdom. Its population is now over 400,000,000, or about one-third of the world's population.

Covering every range of latitude, and embracing many peoples, its productions are exceedingly varied and its trade enormous. Its manufacturing power, however, is chiefly concentrated in the United Kingdom, and the explanation of this is that what coal it possesses is chiefly situate in the Mother Country. Thus, in 1906, the British Empire produced 284,000,000 tons of coal, and 251,000,000 of these tons were raised in the United Kingdom. To understand fully the importance of this, see the discussion under COAL.

The white population of the British Empire, neglecting the few white men in India and the Crown Colonies, is approximately as follows:

WHITE POPULATION OF THE BRITISH EMPIRE, 1909

| | |
|---|---|
| United Kingdom ... ... ... ... | 45,000,000 |
| Australia ... ... ... ... ... | 4,250,000 |
| New Zealand ... ... ... ... ... | 950,000 |
| Canada and Newfoundland... ... ... | 7,000,000 |
| South Africa ... ... ... ... ... | 900,000 |
| Total ... ... ... ... | 58,100,000 |

There are thus only about 13,000,000 white people in the Empire outside the British Isles. It is of great importance to the nation, the Empire, and the world that this number should be increased, and the Colonial emigration offices are doing much to redistribute the Empire's white population. The result of these efforts is curiously attributed by Protectionists to the operations of Free Trade. (*See* EMIGRATION.)

The present prosperity and solidarity of the British Empire is a result of the triumph of the Liberal policy of Colonial freedom and self-government. In South Africa, as in Canada, the loyalty and co-operation of white men of other than British race has been secured neither by political nor fiscal restrictions or regulations, but by the wise grant of free institutions. It is not true that the United Kingdom needs to give a food preference to the Colonies, and so to make the bread of her people dearer, in order to "cement the Empire." On this head, *see* CANADIAN FARMERS AND PREFERENCE.

The Board of Trade give us a calculation of the trade of the British Empire, considered as a whole, with foreign countries. In the following table I give an interesting comparison of the trade of the Mother Country and the Empire:

TOTAL EXTERNAL COMMERCE OF (1) UNITED KINGDOM AND (2) BRITISH EMPIRE

(In Millions of £)

| | Total Imports | Total Exports |
|---|---|---|
| United Kingdom ... ... | 608 ... ... | 461 |
| British Empire ... ... | 610 ... ... | 520 |

These figures remind us how enormously the United Kingdom bulks in the Empire's trade. Of course, in the United Kingdom figures, British commerce with the British Empire is included, whereas in the British Empire figures inter-Imperial trade is excluded because it is internal.

**BRITISH TRADE**—*See* United Kingdom, the various trade headings, &c.

**BROADENING THE BASIS OF TAXATION**—This is a euphemism for increasing the taxation of the middle and working classes. It expresses the desire of the Protectionists to substitute indirect for direct taxation. To broaden the basis of taxation is to levy taxes on a large variety of commodities in common consumption. By that means a larger part of the national revenue can be shifted on to the less wealthy members of the community, since the consumption of common articles is almost as great by the poor individually as by the rich individually. For example, if a tax is levied on bacon, as desired by Mr. Chamberlain's Tariff "Commission," the chief part of the tax would be paid by the working classes, who consume the greater part of the bacon used by the whole nation. However rich a man is he can only eat a little bacon, so that a bacon tax spares the rich and hits the poor.

**BROOMS AND BRUSHES**—The United Kingdom both imports and exports brooms and brushes, as will be seen by the following figures:

BRITISH COMMERCE IN BROOMS AND BRUSHES

| | Imports for Home Consumption (c.i.f.) | Exports of British Make (f.o.b.) |
|---|---|---|
| | £ | £ |
| 1900 (good year) ... | ... 269,000 ... | ... 147,000 |
| 1907 (good year) ... | ... 351,000 ... | ... 199,000 |
| 1908 (bad year) ... | ... 339,000 ... | ... 186,000 |

The quantity manufactured for the home trade is not precisely known, but it is very much greater than these figures.

A tax on brushes would be a tax on industry, since the brush is a tool of industry.

**BUILDING TRADES**—The building trades have made enormous progress in the United Kingdom in the last fifty years. The following figures are taken from the Census Returns:

PERSONS EMPLOYED IN BUILDING TRADES (UNITED KINGDOM)

| | |
|---|---|
| Census of 1851... ... ... ... ... | 508,634 |
| „ 1861... ... ... ... ... | 596,173 |
| „ 1871... ... ... ... ... | 714,987 |
| „ 1881... ... ... ... ... | 833,386 |
| „ 1891... ... ... ... ... | 836,413 |
| „ 1901... ... ... ... ... | 1,124,387 |

The most rapid progress was made, it will be seen, between 1891 and 1901.

The building trades in every branch would be severely hit by Protection. A house is made of a large variety of materials, many of them manufactured, and under Protection the following would be taxed: Glass, cement and lime, iron pipes, joists and girders, stoves and ranges, nails, screws, baths, &c., glue, colours, varnish, oils and turpentine, paper, electrical fittings, brushes, tools, machinery, felt, slate, tiles and earthenware.

That would mean dearer houses, therefore fewer houses, therefore less building. The value of the annual output of houses in the United Kingdom is fully £100,000,000 a year, and this gigantic trade could only be harmed by Protection.

All the building trades, it should be observed, are "protected" by nature, for houses must be made at home.

The building trades are peculiarly subject to unemployment in all countries: (1) because they are organised under competitive masters who surround themselves with a labour reserve out of which to draw workers when they win contracts; (2) for seasonal reasons, building being inconvenient in winter; and (3) through the cycles of trade. (*See also* JOINERY, BRICKLAYING, TRADE CYCLES, &c.)

**BUTTER**—Our imports of butter are considerable. In 1900, 1907, and 1908, they were as follows:

BRITISH IMPORTS OF BUTTER FOR HOME CONSUMPTION

(In Millions of £)

| Year | Foreign | Colonial | Total Imports | Re-Exports | Retained for Home Consumption |
|---|---|---|---|---|---|
| 1900 | 14·3 | 3·2 | 17·5 | 0·3 | 17·2 |
| 1907 | 17·7 | 4·7 | 22·4 | 0·4 | 22·0 |
| 1908 | 20·3 | 3·8 | 24·1 | 0·3 | 23·8 |

We import about 450,000,000 lb. of butter a year, or, say, a lb. a week for each family in the country.

Mr. Chamberlain proposed (October 6, 1903) to tax foreign butter 5 per cent., which would raise the price of the whole supply. Mr. Chamberlain's Tariff "Commission" propose to tax all butter, foreign or Colonial.

Our largest foreign supplier of butter is Denmark, which flourishes under Free Trade for agriculture.

**C.I.F.**—The meaning of these letters, which will be found at the head of many of the tables in this work, is "cost *plus* insurance *plus* freight." That is to say, when the price of goods is quoted C.I.F. at any place it means that the price includes freight and insurance to that place. Our imports are declared at the Customs at C.I.F. value.

**CANADA**—Canada has an area of 3,745,000 square miles, or rather more than that of the United States, but she is not gifted with the wonderful natural resources of her southern neighbour. The United States is the greatest coal nation; Canada has comparatively little coal. Hence we get the following striking contrast:

UNITED STATES AND CANADA: COAL AND POPULATION

| | Coal Production Metric tons | Population |
|---|---|---|
| United States ... ... | ... 436,000,000 ... | ... 87,000,000 |
| Canada ... ... ... | 9,500,000 ... | ... 7,500,000 |

Canada naturally trades with the great nation over her border, but it is to be doubted whether we put enough energy into our Canadian trade relations. According to the British Official Trade Commissioner, we do not.

The facts as to Canada's commerce are:

COMMERCE OF CANADA

(In Millions of £)

| | Imports from | | Exports to | |
|---|---|---|---|---|
| | 1903 | 1907 | 1903 | 1907 |
| United Kingdom ... ... | 12·1 | 19·5 | 27·0 | 27·7 |
| Remainder of Empire ... | 1·3 | 3·3 | 2·2 | 2·7 |
| Foreign countries (U.S.A. chiefly) ... ... ... | 34·7 | 50·8 | 17·2 | 27·2 |
| Totals ... ... | 48·1 | 73·6 | 46·4 | 57·6 |

We are the second largest supplier of, and the largest buyer from, Canada.

CANADIAN IMPORTS ANALYSED

(In Millions of £)

| From | Manufactured Articles | | Total Imports | |
|---|---|---|---|---|
| | 1900 | 1907 | 1900 | 1907 |
| United Kingdom ... | 10·0 | 16·7 | 12·1 | 19·5 |
| Remainder of British Empire... | — | 0·3 | 1·3 | 3·3 |
| Foreign countries (chiefly U.S.A.)... | 18·0 | 26·7 | 34·7 | 50·8 |
| Total ... ... | 28·0 | 43·7 | 48·1 | 73·6 |

From this table it will be seen that we supplied £16,700,000 worth of the manufactures imported by Canada in 1907. The Canadian Preference leaves the United States Canada's chief supplier.

**CANADIAN FARMERS AND PREFERENCE**—The conception of the policy of "Preference" is that we should tax foreign food in order to enable Colonial food-raisers to get a higher price in the British market. Are the Canadian farmers so unthinking as to desire that we should burden our people with food taxes for their benefit?

The answer is to be found in the fact that when the news of the great Free Trade victory of 1906 reached Canada, Mr. Fisher, the Canadian Minister of Agriculture, and himself a farmer, speaking for the farmers of Canada, said:

"We farmers of Canada want no Preference in the English market. . . . England has not adopted the Preference, and I think she did right. . . . England to-day, being a Free Trade country, could not give a Preference without changing her fiscal policy. It would mean a tax on imported goods for the express purpose of giving a preference to Canada and the other Colonies. That would mean the obstruction of her own trade, increased taxation, and the entering into the complicated problem of a protective policy. It would, in England's case, be a radical change for the worse."

And he added:

"It is a calumny to say that unless Canadian products are granted a preference in the English market, Canada would be liable to break away from the Empire."

And the editor of the great Canadian journal, the *Toronto Globe*, writing in the *Westminster Gazette* of July 24, 1909, said:

"Quite as unthinkable and even more offensive, is the notion that the farmers of Canada, the most favoured farmers under the sun, either need a Preference or ask for it."

**CANADIAN MANUFACTURERS' ASSOCIATION**—This is an Association of Canadian manufacturers, whose policy it is so to pull the strings of the Canadian tariff that the lowest or British so-called "preferential" duties shall be high enough to protect them. Their policy is expressed in the famous resolution which they passed in 1902:

"That while such tariff should be primarily framed for Canadian interests, it should nevertheless give substantial preference to the Mother Country. . . . RECOGNISING ALWAYS THAT THE MINIMUM TARIFF MUST AFFORD ADEQUATE PROTECTION TO ALL CANADIAN PRODUCERS."

**CANADIAN PREFERENCE**—The Canadian Preferential Tariff has passed through many changes since it was first introduced in 1898. The chief details are:

1898, Aug. 1.—The then existing Canadian duties were reduced by one-fourth in their application to British goods.

1900, July 1.—The preferential reduction was increased to one-third.

1904, June 8.—The "preference" on British woollens was reduced at the demand of the Canadian Manufacturers' Association. British woollens were denounced in the Canadian Parliament as "shoddy."

1906, Nov. 29.—The percentage preference was abolished, and a triple tariff arranged, the highest for foreign goods, the intermediate for negotiation with foreign countries, and the lowest for British goods.

It has been difficult to distinguish any great benefit to British trade through the Preference. The only item strikingly affected was woollens, but the Canadian manufacturers soon altered that, demanding and getting a reduction of the Preference.

The facts as to the growth of dutiable imports into Canada from the United States and Britain respectively are as follows (from Canadian Trade Returns, 1909). Dutiable imports alone are shown, because they alone could be affected by the Preference:

IMPORTS OF DUTIABLE GOODS INTO CANADA

(In Millions of Dollars)

| | From U.S.A. | From United Kingdom |
|---|---|---|
| 1892 | 29 | 31 |
| 1893 | 28 | 32 |
| 1894 | 26 | 27 |
| 1895 | 26 | 23 |
| 1896 | 29 | 24 |
| 1897 | 30 | 20 |
| (Preference First Established 1898) | | |
| 1898 | 38 | 22 |
| 1900 | 54 | 31 |
| 1902 | 60 | 35 |
| 1904 | 77 | 45 |
| 1906 | 89 | 53 |
| 1908 | 110 | 71 |

Protectionists sometimes claim that the growth of British imports into Canada since 1898 has been due to the Preference. It should be difficult to argue *post hoc ergo propter hoc* in this matter in view of the great increase in American trade with Canada since 1898.

**CANDLES**—There are no recorded imports of candles, but we have an export trade in them. For 1900, 1907, and 1908 the figures are:

BRITISH EXPORTS OF CANDLES (f.o.b.)

| | £ |
|---|---|
| 1900 (good year) ... ... ... | 398,000 |
| 1907 (good year) ... ... ... | 551,000 |
| 1908 (bad year) ... ... ... | 504,000 |

The Protectionist cannot promise to tax imports of candles, because there are none to tax.

**CARPENTERS**—There is very little foreign competition with the British carpenter and joiner. What little there is will be found recorded under JOINERY. The greater part of all carpentery must necessarily be done at home, and no import duty can even pretend to help.

Under Protection, however, the carpenter, while himself unaided, would find himself compelled to buy taxed tools, taxed clothes, and taxed food, reducing his real wages. (*See also* BUILDING TRADES).

I give the comparison of carpenters' wages in Britain, France, and Germany given in the Board of Trade Yellow Books (Cd. 4512 and Cd. 4032 recently issued):

CARPENTERS' WAGES PER WEEK

| | s. d. | | s. d. | |
|---|---|---|---|---|
| In Britain ... ... ... | 36 2 | to | 39 4 | per week |
| In France ... ... ... | 24 0 | to | 30 3 | ,, |
| In Germany ... ... ... | 26 11 | to | 31 3 | ,, |

For real value of these wages *see* COST OF LIVING and WAGES.

The rise of carpenters' wages in the British Kingdom since 1875 has been as follows:

GROWTH OF BRITISH CARPENTERS' WAGES

(Per Hour)

| Years | Birmingham | Cardiff | Leicester | Liverpool | London | Manchester |
|---|---|---|---|---|---|---|
| | Pence | Pence | Pence | Pence | Pence | Pence |
| 1875 | 7½ | 7½ | 7 | 7½ | 9 | 8 |
| 1885 | 8 | 7½ | 7½ | 7½ | 9 | 8 |
| 1895 | 9 | 8½ | 8 | 8½ | 9½ | 8½ |
| 1905 | 9½ | 9 | 9 | 9½ | 10½ | 9½ |
| 1909 | 9½ | 9 | 9 | 10 | 10½ | 9½ |

These facts are taken from the Board of Trade record (Cd. 4954).

**CARPETS**—The British carpet trade is large and important and chiefly concerned with the home market. The exports are considerable :

BRITISH COMMERCE IN CARPETS

| | Imports for Home Consumption (c.i.f.) | Exports of British Make (f.o.b.) |
|---|---|---|
| | £ | £ |
| 1900 (good year) | 398,000 | 920,000 |
| 1907 (good year) | 390,000 | 1,232,000 |
| 1908 (bad year) | 233,000 | 776,000 |

The imports are chiefly Oriental carpets, which are non-competitive. London is the chief market for Oriental carpets. When I was last in one of our largest carpet warehouses I found a German wholesale buyer buying Turkey carpets in London.

According to the Census of Production Preliminary Tables, our output of carpets in 1907 (without rugs) was worth £3,337,000.

**CARRIAGES**—Our external trade in carriages and carts is not very great:

BRITISH COMMERCE IN CARRIAGES AND CARTS

| | Imports for Home Consumption (c.i.f.) £ | Exports of British Make (f.o.b.) £ |
|---|---|---|
| 1900 (good year) | ... Not recorded ... | ... 331,000 |
| 1907 (good year) | ... 100,000 ... | ... 763,000 |
| 1908 (bad year) | ... 104,000 ... | ... 470,000 |

There are very few imports in this trade. The home industry is of considerable but unmeasured dimensions; it is undergoing great changes owing to the rise of the motor-car.

**CEMENT**—The importance of this article has considerably increased of late years, owing to the introduction of the ferro-concrete process into the building trade. The facts as to our imports and exports are as follows:—

BRITISH COMMERCE IN CEMENT

| | Imports for Home Consumption (c.i.f.) £ | Exports of British Make (f.o.b.) £ |
|---|---|---|
| 1900 (good year) ... | ... 208,000 ... | ... 673,000 |
| 1907 (good year) ... | ... 151,000 ... | ... 1,267,000 |
| 1908 (bad year) ... | ... 115,000 ... | ... 957,000 |

This is a trade as to which Protectionists are constantly alleging that we are ruined by increasing imports. The facts of the case, it will be seen, are very different. Imports are falling; exports are rising.

**CHAMBERLAIN, ARTHUR**—Mr. Arthur Chamberlain, brother of Mr. Joseph Chamberlain, made a pregnant utterance at Bolton in September, 1903, expressing a warning which may serve to remind the reader of one of the greatest dangers inherent in Protection. He said:

"Give us Protection, and we manufacturers will show you something in the way of trusts, rings, and syndicates that you little dream of. The Free Trade policy has alone protected the people of England from the proceedings of trusts and rings. Relieve us of foreign competition, and you will have an experience you will not enjoy. Protection would change the entire course of business. With the possibility of getting a duty put upon things which are necessary to your competitors, and the possibility of keeping duty off the things that are necessary to you, lobbying would become more important to the manufacturer than the slow process of the factory. I can make more money in an evening in the House of Commons by arranging for the taxation of my opponents' necessities, and for the maintenance of a free market for myself, than I can make by honest industry in a month." (On this *see also* CORRUPTION AND PROTECTION and TRUSTS.)

**CHAMBERLAIN, JOSEPH**—The history of Mr. Chamberlain's conversion to Protection deserves to be noted, for it gives not merely a record of one man's opinion, but reminds us of many things which it is well to remember.

Mr. Chamberlain was one of the leading opponents of the Fair Trade League, which was founded in July, 1881. "Fair Trade," of course, like the "Tariff Reform" of 1909, was an alias for Protection. In 1885 "Fair Trade" was much to the fore at the elections, and Mr. Chamberlain delivered many effective utterances. He pointed out at Birmingham that while there was depression here "it is nothing to the depression and privation in Germany." At Ipswich he reminded the agricultural interest that "the condition of the farmer was never so hopeless and the state of the labourer never so abject as when corn was kept up at high value by a prohibitive or protective duty."

It was in 1881 Mr. Chamberlain put into a terse sentence in the House of Commons an economic fact of great importance: "A tax on food would mean a decline in wages."

"Fair Trade" faded. The League broke up and disappeared, and no more was heard of Protection until 1896, when the suggestion was made that we should revive the old-time "Preference" for the Colonies. On this Mr. Chamberlain, become Colonial Secretary in a Unionist Government, said at the Congress of Chambers of Commerce of the Empire on June 9, 1896:

"This proposal (for Imperial Reciprocity) requires that we should abandon our system in favour of theirs, and it is in effect that while the Colonies should be left absolutely free to impose what Protective duties they please both on foreign imports and upon British commerce, they should be required to make a small discrimination in favour of British trade, in return for which we are expected to change our whole system, and impose duties on food and raw material. Well, I express again my own opinion when I say that *there is not the slightest chance that in any reasonable time this country or the Parliament of this country would adopt so one-sided an agreement.* The foreign trade of this country is so large, and the foreign trade of the Colonies is comparatively so small, that a small preference given to us upon that foreign trade by the Colonies would make so trifling a difference—would be so small a benefit to the total volume of our trade—that I do not believe the working classes of this country would consent to make a revolutionary change for what they would think to be an infinitesimal gain."

The next year, 1897, the Colonial Conference was held, when Mr. Chamberlain again pointed out that a British Zollverein was impracticable.

Five years elapsed, and another Colonial Conference was held. In the interim, in 1898 (*see* CANADIAN PREFERENCE), the Canadian Government had granted a Preference to British manufactures.

At the Colonial Conference Mr. Chamberlain clearly pointed out how disappointing the Canadian Preference had proved to be. He said:

"While I cannot but gratefully acknowledge the intention of this proposal, and its sentimental value as a proof of goodwill and affection, yet that its substantial results have been altogether disappointing to us, and I think they must have been equally disappointing to its promoters."

Then comes a curious change. A year later, on May 15, 1903, he reversed his opinion (Mr. Ritchie had just abolished the shilling corn duty with Mr. Balfour's approval). Breaking out into vigorous speech, he asked: "Now what has Canada done for us?" and answered his own question by declaring that the Preference "had had an important result."

How little ground there was for this change of opinion will be seen by reference to Canadian Preference.

On May 28, 1903, in the House of Commons, he acknowledged that "if you are to give a Preference to the Colonies you must put a tax on food." On June 26, 1903, he declared that the preference was "the only system by which the Empire can be kept together."

Finally, came the tacking on to the unpopular and discredited preference of a policy of taxing imports of manufactures to save British trade from destruction, and Mr. Chamberlain completed his conversion to Protection.

**CHAMBERLAIN PROGRAMME**—On October 6, 1903, at Glasgow, Mr. Chamberlain, after much consideration of the details with many advisers, made the following concrete proposals:

New Taxes on Food

(To be levied on foreign imports only, to give a "Preference" for Colonial supplies)

1. Corn, except maize, a duty of 2s. per quarter.
2. Flour, a duty at a somewhat higher rate than on corn to "protect" the miller.
3. Meat, except bacon, a duty of 5 per cent.
4. Dairy produce, a duty of 5 per cent.

Reductions on Present Taxes on Food

1. Tea duty, three-fourths to be remitted.
2. Sugar duty, one-half to be remitted.
3. Cocoa and coffee duties to be reduced.

Colonial wine growers to be assisted by preferential duties.

A duty not exceeding an average of 10 per cent. *ad valorem* to be levied on foreign manufactures.

In the year 1909 this programme is obsolete, as will be seen by reference to Agriculture, and Revenue from Protection.

The Free Trade Government of 1906 has abolished one-half

of the sugar duty and reduced the tea duty by one penny per pound.

In any case, it should be borne in mind that the consumer is not compensated when a Protectionist import duty, such as a wheat duty, is substituted for a revenue import duty, such as a tea duty. The former takes much more from the public than it gives to the Treasury, while the latter gives to the Treasury all that it takes from the public, less only the cost of collection. On this head *see* TEA, WHEAT, IMPORT DUTY, &c.

Mr. Chamberlain's trumpery scale of duties, if enacted, would be but the beginning of worse things. Before Mr. Chamberlain's Tariff "Commission" witness after witness has declared that small duties are useless. The Protectionists who supported Mr. Chamberlain's programme did so because they hoped to be excused the introduction of Protective taxes by pleading that they are "so small." Here is the evidence of two of the Protectionist manufacturers who appeared before Mr. Chamberlain's Tariff "Commission."

Mr. Hugo Hirst, of the General Electric Co.: "A protective tariff of at least 50 per cent. would be required for a number of years." (On carbons.)

Mr. A. Ransome: "A 10 per cent. duty would not be of any use." (*See also* REVENUE FROM PROTECTION.)

**CHEAPNESS**—Cheapness means plentifulness, and those who sneer at cheapness sneer at plenty. Free Trade cannot of itself confer plenty upon a nation, but it can and does open our ports to the world's plenty when plenty there is. The Protectionist, by imposing an artificial barrier between the British people and the world's produce, would deny them the right to exchange their work for the best value which the entire world has to offer.

**CHEESE**—The United Kingdom imports large quantities of this valuable food. There are some very small exports of our own production, but they are not worth recording here. The record of imports is as follows:

BRITISH IMPORTS OF CHEESE FOR HOME CONSUMPTION

(In Millions of £)

| | Foreign | Colonial | Total Imports | Re-Exports | Retained for Home Consumption |
|---|---|---|---|---|---|
| | £ | £ | £ | £ | £ |
| 1900 | 2,820,000 | 4,018,000 | 6,838,000 | 168,000 | 6,670,000 |
| 1907 | 1,318,000 | 5,587,000 | 6,905,000 | 173,000 | 6,732,000 |
| 1908 | 1,325,000 | 5,359,000 | 6,684,000 | 183,000 | 6,501,000 |

The Colonies—chiefly Canada—thus supply us with the greater part of our cheese imports. Mr. Chamberlain proposed to leave Colonial cheese untaxed, but the Chamberlain Tariff "Commission" propose to tax all food imports, and undoubtedly a British Protectionist Government would be no more able than the German Government has been to resist the pressure of the landed interest to tax food increasingly.

**CHEMICALS**—The British production, importation, and exportation of chemicals is very large. The value of our production is unfortunately unknown, but our imports and exports are as follows:

BRITISH COMMERCE IN CHEMICALS, DRUGS, DYES, AND COLOURS

| | Imports for Home Consumption (c.i.f.) | Exports of British Make (f.o.b.) |
|---|---|---|
| | £ | £ |
| 1900 (good year) ... | ... 6,625,000 ... | ... 11,343,000 |
| 1907 (good year) ... | ... 9,915,000 ... | ... 17,053,000 |
| 1908 (bad year) ... | ... 8,414,000 ... | ... 16,289,000 |

A very large number of widely varying substances are included in these figures—bleach, alkali, coal products, such as aniline dyes, benzol, naphtha, tar, carbolic acid, and pitch, sulphate of copper, dyes, glycerine, manures, sulphate of ammonia, basic slag, drugs, painters' colours, sulphuric acid, and tartaric acid.

Some of these substances are crude manufactures, and

others are highly refined, but all alike are indispensable raw materials of industry. Here, as in other directions, we see how our imports strengthen our industries, and how our exports strengthen foreign and Colonial industries, the commerce expressing mutual service.

A tax on imported chemicals would be a tax on industry. To tax bleach, for example, would be to tax the textile industries. It is this all-important fact which Protectionists overlook when they imagine that by taxing imports they can make more work. (*See* ALKALI, &c.).

**CHINA AND EARTHENWARE**—*See* EARTHENWARE.

**CLAY**—*See* POTTER'S CLAY.

**CLERKS AND FISCAL POLICY**—At the Census of 1901 there were 439,972 commercial or business clerks in the United Kingdom. Clerks, in common with the middle classes to which they belong, stand to lose heavily by Protection. Receiving fixed salaries, which could not be increased by Protective duties, the value of their earnings would be decreased in a marked manner by the incidence of import duties. Not long since the German Government had to raise the salaries of their clerks in order to compensate them for the increased cost of living, but what of the clerks who have not the fortune to serve under Government? The clerk should bear in mind that under Protection he would have to pay more for every necessary of life—for every article of food, for every detail of clothing, for utensils and furniture—while there could be no Customs duty to enable him to sell his product of labour at a higher figure. The London *Daily Mail* of July 22, 1909, recorded that the German Imperial Statistical Office has just reported on the systematic book-keeping of 800 families which they cause to be kept. The report shows, in the words of the *Daily Mail*, "how people of small means have to struggle for existence in modern Germany." Amongst the cases mentioned is that of a married clerk with two children, aged four and five, who earned £86, and ended the year with a deficit of £11 10s." The clerk who votes for Protection votes his own undoing.

**CLOCKS**—In clocks of a good class British makers hold their own, but in the production of the cheap modern household clock American and Continental makers are easily supreme. The record of our imports and exports of clocks is as follows:

BRITISH COMMERCE IN CLOCKS AND PARTS OF CLOCKS

| | Imports for Home Consumption (c.i.f.) | Exports of British Make (f.o.b.) |
|---|---|---|
| | £ | £ |
| 1900 (good year) ... | ... 533,000 ... | ... 84,000 |
| 1907 (good year) ... | ... 471,000 ... | ... 68,000 |
| 1908 (bad year) ... | ... 396,000 ... | ... 27,000 |

The exports, it will be seen, are insignificant. The imports have declined considerably, which appears to indicate that British makers of popular clocks are making an impression on the home market.

**CLOTHING**—*See* APPAREL.

**COAL**—Coal is the most important but least discussed factor in modern industrial prosperity.

In the first place, coal is the only great source of power which man yet possesses. Some parts of the world, as, for example, Italy and Canada, have water-power; but, taking the world as a whole, we are dependent on coal for the steam or electricity with which to drive our machinery.

In the second place, the importance of the possession of native coal must be clearly understood if the distribution of modern industry is to be understood. Coal is so bulky that it is costly to move about the world. As a consequence economic industry can only be carried on near coal. If a country has to import coal it is out of the running in industrial competition. Nay, even in a coal-producing country industries will be found chiefly situated not far from the coal mines. *Coal has the remarkable property of drawing to it industry and population.*

It follows that if one has a map of the world, with the great coal areas clearly marked on it, one has also a map of the world's chief industrial areas. Fiscal policy cannot erase this fact; *it can only modify it.* Not to understand this fact is, therefore, not to understand modern industry. In my "Elements of the Fiscal Problem" (1903), page 46, I wrote:

"The industry must go to the coal, not the coal to the industry. This was first demonstrated by Jevons, and a moment's reflection will show that it is true. For instance, Cornish potters' clay is taken to Staffordshire to be near coal. Coal is not taken to the clay in Cornwall.

"That is why, to put it bluntly and frankly, the United Kingdom, the United States, and Germany are the three greatest industrial nations. They have the coal. Not any fiscal policy whatsoever—good, bad, or indifferent—can make a country industrially great if it lacks coal in the Age of Coal. And the length of the Coal Age? Who shall say?"

But how often is this made clear to the fiscal student? I turn to the index of one of the latest works on the subject. It has two slight references to coal, but no reference at all to the real meaning and importance of coal.

In the following table I give the world's coal output for 1907 in metric tons of 2,204 lb.:

THE WORLD'S COAL, 1907

| | Metric Tons | Per Cent. of Total |
|---|---|---|
| United States ... ... ... | 436,000,000 | 39 |
| United Kingdom ... ... | 272,000,000 | 24 |
| Germany ... ... ... | 206,000,000 | 19 |
| America, Britain, and Germany | 914,000,000 | 82 |
| All the rest of the world ... | 203,000,000 | 18 |
| All the world ... ... ... | 1,117,000,000 | 100 |

This is the most remarkable and the least realised set of statistics that the world has to show. It will be seen that three countries—America, Britain, and Germany—have a practical monopoly of the world's coal, between them producing eight out of every ten tons of coal.

Fiscal policy, I repeat, can only *modify* the results of this coal distribution.

How often the Free Trader is asked to explain, "If Protection means ruin, how is it that America and Germany have great and successful industries?" The answer is, of course, that Protection cannot rob a nation of coal—all it can do is to modify the effect of its possession. If Protectionists want to know what Protection can do for a nation which lacks coal, let them turn to the effect of Tariff "Reform" in Spain, or Portugal, or Italy. If they want to know what Protection does to injure a coal nation, let them ponder the fact that America's natural resources are monopolised by the few to a degree which is happily unknown here, unequal as is our own distribution of wealth. Free Trade has enabled Britain to make the best use of her coal and seaboard, two of her greatest gifts. While Britain, possessing coal and seaboard, has more than half the world's ocean shipping, America, possessing more coal and more seaboard, has very few seagoing ships.

**COAL EXPORTS**—From what has been said under COAL, the reader will understand how untenable is the Protectionist argument that Britain exports coal to feed foreign industries. Competitive industry cannot be carried on with imported coal. Why, then, does Britain export coal? The explanation is that our coal exports are chiefly sent to foreign ports for the use of steamships. As will be seen by reference to SHIPPING, we own more than one-half of the effective steam tonnage of all the world. It follows that *our coal exports are chiefly made for our own use abroad*, and they are a symbol of the magnificent growth of British ships.

This extraordinary record at once shows the triumph of British shipping and the chief explanation of the growth of British coal exports.

COMPARATIVE GROWTH OF BRITISH STEAM TONNAGE AND BRITISH COAL EXPORTS

| | Growth of British Steamships Million Net Tons | Growth of British Coal Exports Million Tons |
|---|---|---|
| 1860 ... ... ... | 0·4 ... ... ... | 7·3 |
| 1870 ... ... ... | 1·1 ... ... ... | 11·7 |
| 1880 ... ... ... | 2·7 ... ... ... | 18·7 |
| 1890 ... ... ... | 5·0 ... ... ... | 30·1 |
| 1900 ... ... ... | 7·2 ... ... ... | 46·0 |
| 1906 ... ... ... | 9·6 ... ... ... | 57·8 |

In 1903, when the fiscal controversy began, Mr. J. L. Garvin wrote a series of articles in the *Daily Telegraph* entitled "Imperial Reciprocity," and their contents briefed Mr. Chamberlain and others. The sixth of the articles was entitled "Coal and Commerce." It made great play with our coal exports, and said, "Do not let us think that we are maintaining our manufacturing position because we are merely selling more coal."

The reader will see how entirely Mr. Garvin misunderstood the significance of British coal exports. As for the facts, the following table will speak for itself:

BRITISH EXPORTS OF BRITISH PRODUCE, SHOWING (1) MANUFACTURES, (2) COAL, AND (3) TOTAL EXPORTS

| | Manufactures £ | Coal £ | Total Exports £ |
|---|---|---|---|
| 1900 (good year) ... | 228,800,000 | 38,600,000 | 291,200,000 |
| 1907 (good year) ... | 342,000,000 | 42,100,000 | 426,000,000 |
| 1908 (bad year) ... | 297,100,000 | 41,600,000 | 377,200,000 |

It will be understood from these facts why the leading "argument" of 1903, invented by Mr. J. L. Garvin, that our exports are merely sustained by coal, is no longer heard in 1909.

Protectionists threaten to reimpose an export duty on coal. The folly of this will be understood from consideration of the great part which coal cargoes play in British shipping. We chiefly import food and raw material, which are bulky. We chiefly export manufactures, which take up little space in a ship. Consequently, if we had no other export but manufactures, many of our ships would have to go out nearly empty, which would mean unprofitable shipping. Fortunately, coal exports redress the balance, because, being bulky, they furnish outward cargoes. The British ship thus earns freights both inwards and outwards. Yet Protectionists talk of levying a coal export duty, which would be a grave blow at our valuable shipping trade.

**COBDEN CLUB**—The Cobden Club (Caxton House, Westminster, London, S.W.) was founded in 1866 to further Free Trade in all parts of the world. In pursuance of this proper object it elects to honorary membership the distinguished Free Traders of foreign countries and British Colonies, such as Sir Wilfrid Laurier, of Canada, and Professor John Graham Brooks, of Massachusetts.

It is unfortunately to be recorded that Mr. Chamberlain, who in 1883 presided at the annual Cobden Club dinner, permitted himself to say in 1904:

"The Cobden Club appears to be an institution mainly supported by foreigners whose interest it is that we should maintain our present system of free imports."

Mr. Chamberlain was informed that this was false, and that the club received not a single penny from the honourable and well-known foreigners and colonists who are its "foreign members."

Yet Mr. Chamberlain has not retracted his accusation.

**COBDEN, RICHARD**—It is not true that Mr. Cobden based his argument for Free Trade upon the belief or promise that other nations would follow our example. On this point Mr. Chamberlain has said at Birmingham on November 9, 1903:

"Mr. Cobden based the whole of his argument upon the assumption, made in good faith, that if we adopted Free Trade five or ten years would not pass without all other nations adopting a similar system. That was his belief, and upon the promise—the prediction which he offered—the country adopted Free Trade."

There is not a single word or passage in the speeches and writings of Cobden during the great fight in which any such prediction or promise was made. It was not until 1846, when the battle was won, that Cobden, in the hour of triumph, expressed the belief that other nations would follow our example. That is a very different thing from Mr. Chamberlain's statement that Cobden induced the country to become Free Trade by promising that others would do the same. Indeed, Mr. Chamberlain's statement was the very reverse of the truth. At Dundee, on January 16, 1844, Mr. Cobden said what Free Traders repeat now, that:

"If foreign countries exclude us it is only a stronger reason why we should throw open our ports more widely to them."

It was also in 1844 that he said at Aberdeen:

"The greater the restrictions in other countries the more necessity there is for Free Trade in this."

Again, in 1849, Mr. Cobden said:

"I remember at the last stage of the Corn Law agitation our opponents were driven to this position: 'Free Trade is a very good thing for us, but you cannot have it until other countries adopt it too'; and I used to say, 'If Free Trade be a good thing for us we will have it. Let others take it if it be a good thing for them; if not, let them do without it.'"

**COCOA**—Our imports of cocoa, raw and manufactured, are of the following value:

COCOA: IMPORTS FOR HOME CONSUMPTION

| | Raw | Manufactured |
|---|---|---|
| | £ | £ |
| 1900 ... ... | 1,368,000 ... ... | 643,000 |
| 1907 ... ... | 1,674,000 ... ... | 888,000 |
| 1908 ... ... | 1,723,000 ... ... | 850,000 |

I also give the figures relating to cocoa imports and exports in 1908:

IMPORTS (FOR HOME CONSUMPTION)

| | £ |
|---|---|
| Raw cocoa ... ... ... ... ... | 1,723,257 |
| Husks and shells... ... ... ... ... | 2,113 |
| Cocoa butter ... ... ... ... ... | 42,369 |
| Manufactured cocoa ... ... ... ... | 849,664 |
| Confectionery containing chocolate ... ... | 57,532 |

EXPORTS OF BRITISH MAKE

| | £ |
|---|---|
| Manufactured cocoa ... ... ... ... | 154,935 |
| Confectionery containing chocolate ... ... | 314,126 |

Our imports of manufactured cocoa was thus nearly twice as great as our exports; this is a result of the fact that our cocoa duty protects foreign cocoa manufacturers in the export trade from British competition. To explain this, I must explain the cocoa duties, which are as follows:

COCOA IMPORT DUTIES

| | Per lb. Pence |
|---|---|
| Raw cocoa ... ... ... ... ... ... ... | 1 |
| Cocoa and chocolate, ground, prepared or manufactured | 2 |
| Confectionery containing upwards of 50 per cent. of chocolate ... ... ... ... ... ... ... | $1\frac{3}{4}$ |
| Confectionery where chocolate does not exceed 50 per cent. ... ... ... ... ... ... ... | $1\frac{1}{4}$ |

The differential duty as between raw and manufactured cocoa was not designed for Protection, but in order to allow for the loss of weight in manufacturing. The idea is the same as in the cases of tobacco and coffee, which see. The cocoa and coffee duties compare thus:

COCOA AND COFFEE DUTIES

| | On Raw | On Prepared |
|---|---|---|
| Cocoa, per lb. ... ... | 1d. ... ... ... | 2d. |
| Coffee, per cwt. ... ... | 14s. ... ... ... | 18s. 8d. |

In each case the higher rate on the prepared article is levied theoretically to *equalise* the duties. In practice, however, two unforeseen and unintended effects arise.

1. The British cocoa manufacturer is slightly protected in the home market, because the 2d. per lb. on the manufactured article is fractionally too great.

2. The British cocoa manufacturer is injured in his export trade (as the above statistics show) because no rebate of the duty which he has paid on his raw material is allowed him under the law.

It may fairly be said that the unintended benefit and the unintended injury balance each other.

Those Protectionists, and they are many, who allege that the British cocoa trade thrives on Protection unconsciously condemn Protection. For Holland has no cocoa duties, and her export trade in manufactured cocoa is as follows:

HOLLAND'S EXPORTS OF MANUFACTURED COCOA (NOT INCLUDING COCOA PREPARED WITH SUGAR)

| | Kilogs. |
|---|---|
| 1904 ... ... ... ... ... ... | 4,351,000 |
| 1905 ... ... ... ... ... ... | 4,046,000 |
| 1906 ... ... ... ... ... ... | 4,484,000 |
| 1907 ... ... ... ... ... ... | 5,715,000 |
| 1908 ... ... ... ... ... ... | 5,358,000 |

A kilogram is 2·2 lb., so that in 1908 Holland exported 11,787,000 lb. of manufactured cocoa. I now compare British and Dutch manufactured cocoa exports:

BRITISH AND DUTCH COMMERCE IN COCOA

| In 1908 | "Protected" Great Britain Lb. | Free Trade Holland Lb. |
|---|---|---|
| Imports of manufactured cocoa for home consumption ... ... ... ... | 10,294,000 | 112,000 |
| Exports of manufactured cocoa ... | 2,643,000 | 11,787,000 |

If, therefore, it is true that British cocoa makers are "protected," Protection does not gain much by the above comparison. On the contrary, it will be seen how much British cocoa manufacturers stand to gain by the entire removal of the duties which on a thousand platforms are alleged to be to the great advantage of the British industry.

British cocoa manufacturers are in need of Free Trade in cocoa, and it is to be hoped that this stupid duty, which has been retained by both parties through *vis inertiæ*, may soon be removed.

**COFFEE**—Our consumption of coffee is very small; the imports for home consumption are worth only about £1,000,000 per annum. This is another stupid impost which British Chancellors of the Exchequer ought long ago to have cleared from the Statute Book.

As in the case of cocoa, a higher duty is levied on manufactured than on raw coffee, in order to compensate for the loss of weight in preparation. The duties are—raw coffee, 14s. per cwt.; prepared coffee, 18s. 8d. per cwt.

**COLONIAL PREFERENCE**—*See* PREFERENCE.

**COMPOSITORS**—*See* PRINTING.

**COPPER**—British native supplies of this valuable metal are exceedingly poor. The United States, on the other hand, is the greatest copper country in the world, producing more than one-half of the entire world's product.

COPPER OUTPUT FROM ORE ACTUALLY RAISED IN THE DIFFERENT COUNTRIES, 1907

| | Metric Tons |
|---|---|
| United States ... ... ... ... ... | 394,174 |
| Mexico ... ... ... ... ... ... | 80,330 |
| Spain ... ... ... ... ... ... | 64,731 |
| Germany ... ... ... ... ... ... | 22,858 |
| United Kingdom ... ... ... ... ... | 677 |
| Total above and other countries ... ... | 781,955 |

In spite of these remarkable facts we are the largest consumers of copper—the fact illustrating how British wealth depends on imports. Our imports of copper are as follows :

BRITISH IMPORTS OF COPPER FOR HOME CONSUMPTION

| Years | Ore | Regulus and Precipitate | Unwrought and Wrought (chiefly Unwrought) |
|---|---|---|---|
| | £ | £ | £ |
| 1900 (good year)... | 1,152,000 | 3,515,000 | 5,166,000 |
| 1907 (good year)... | 1,272,000 | 3,568,000 | 5,348,000 |
| 1908 (bad year) ... | 1,086,000 | 2,501,000 | 6,064,000 |

Nearly the whole of this table relates to raw material. Yet the second and third columns figure as imports of "manufactures" in the Board of Trade Returns. Strictly speaking, a bar of copper is a manufactured article, but to suggest that its importation is an evil, as the Protectionists do when they denounce our imports, illustrates the absurdity of the promises that import duties would "make work."

In addition to an enormous home trade in goods made from copper imports, we have the following export trade:

BRITISH EXPORTS OF COPPER MANUFACTURES

| Years | Brass and Brass Goods | Unwrought Copper | Wrought Mixed Metal | Wrought Copper |
|---|---|---|---|---|
| | £ | £ | £ | £ |
| 1900 (good year) ... | 631,000 | 1,397,000 | 585,000 | 942,000 |
| 1907 (good year) ... | 1,390,000 | 2,520,000 | 631,000 | 1,891,000 |
| 1908 (bad year) ... | 1,059,000 | 932,000 | 931,000 | 1,583,000 |

The greater part of the copper we import is used at home.

**CORN**—*See* Wheat, &c.

**CORN LAWS**—The history of the British Corn Laws dates from the fifteenth century. There have been import duties and export duties, and under William and Mary, Anne, and George III., bounties were paid to encourage exportation.

Import duties on a sliding scale existed from the time of Charles II. until 1774, when a scale was arranged which made the duty only 6d. per quarter when wheat was at or above 48s., high duties being levied when the price was less than that figure.

During the Napoleonic Wars prices were naturally high (119s. in 1801), and the landlords did well. With peace came a fall in prices, and Parliament, which may be truthfully described as then consisting of two Houses of Landlords, the lower largely in the pocket of the upper, enacted in 1815 a Corn Law altogether prohibiting importation when wheat fetched less than 80s. per quarter, at which figure or at any higher figure it was duty free. Subsequently this Corn Law was mitigated by the introduction of a sliding scale. By the Act of 1828 the duty varied from 1s. per quarter with wheat at 73s. to 20s. 8d. with wheat at 66s., thereafter rising by a shilling for every shilling by which the price of wheat was less than 66s. In 1842 this scale was varied. In 1846 came Sir Robert Peel's conversion to Free Trade, and the repeal of the Corn Law, to take effect in 1849. In 1847–48, however, the duties were suspended in consequence of scarcity. From 1849 there remained only a registration duty of a shilling per quarter, and this was entirely repealed in 1869.

In 1902 Sir Michael Hicks-Beach reimposed the shilling duty on corn, but it was repealed the following year by Mr. Ritchie.

**CORRUPTION AND PROTECTION** — Under Protection every manufacturer must keep in close touch with the Legislature which can make him or mar him. As Mr. Arthur Chamberlain has put it: "I can make more money in an evening in the House of Commons by arranging for the taxation of my opponents' necessities and for the maintenance of a free market for myself than I can make by honest industry in a month." When it comes to arranging a tax on a commodity which A sells and which B buys, both A and B must be in the Parliamentary lobby to protect their individual interests and to hunt for votes. A Parliament arranging a Protective tariff is a welter of private interests scrambling for profits. What between monetary corruption and the more reputable but no less injurious purchase of political support by voting for a particular interest, protective tariffs, when enacted, simply represent a triumph of certain interests at the expense of other interests. Party funds are zealously fed by men desiring duties, and Parliament becomes dominated by trade interests vested in the tariff. Protection offers a premium to business men to corrupt the legislature, and as the experience of the United States and Canada has bitterly shown, it is almost impossible to bring reason to bear when once trade interests have established themselves in politics. *Protection is a Socialism in which the State creates monopolies without controlling them.*

**COST OF LIVING**—In 1908 and 1909 the Board of Trade issued two detailed Reports on the Cost of Living in France and Germany which throw light on the value of wages under a Protective tariff. As is shown elsewhere, British wages are considerably higher than French and German wages. The Reports in question show that the purchasing power of money in Britain is considerably higher than in either France or Germany. It is impossible to give all the details, but I quote the official conclusions:

(1) As to Germany (Cd. 4032, page liii):

"It appears, therefore, that an English workman in Germany, living so far as possible as he had been accustomed to live in England, would find his expenditure on rent (exclusive of local taxation), food and fuel increased by some 19 per cent. (or, roughly by one-fifth)."

(2) As to France (Cd. 4512, page xlvi):

"It appears, therefore, that an English workman living in France and maintaining as far as possible his English mode of life and his English dietary, would have found his expenditure on rent (not including local taxation), food and fuel increased by some 14 per cent. (or nearly one-seventh)."

Under the Dingley Tariff the cost of living has increased very greatly in America since 1897. According to the New York State Department of Labour's calculation, the cost of living in New York City was 22 per cent. higher in 1907 than 1897. The British Consul at Boston quotes the highest authorities to the effect that the cost of living at that place has increased 42 per cent. in the last seven years. Since 1903 earthenware has advanced 25 per cent., kitchen utensils 10 per cent., furniture 20 per cent., linen 30 per cent., cotton goods 15 per cent., underwear 15 per cent.

The British workman may therefore confidently expect dearer living under Protection.

**COTTON**—The British cotton trade has prospered so marvellously that it may well be termed an industrial miracle. It is a case in which we challenge comparison, as we do in shipping and shipbuilding, not with any other nation, not even with any other group of nations, but with all the world. Here is the record of the world's spindles on March 31, 1909, as officially estimated by the International Federation of Master Cotton Spinners' and Manufacturers' Associations:

THE WORLD'S COTTON SPINDLES AT WORK ON MARCH 31, 1909

| | |
|---|---|
| United Kingdom ... ... ... ... | 53,472,000 |
| U.S.A. ... ... ... ... ... | 27,846,000 |
| Germany ... ... ... ... ... | 9,881,000 |
| Russia ... ... ... ... ... | 7,829,000 |
| France... ... ... ... ... ... | 6,750,000 |
| India ... ... ... ... ... ... | 5,756,000 |
| Total above and other ... ... | 130,796,000 |

Or, if we take the Board of Trade's estimate of spindleage, based on Messrs. Ellison & Co's. figures, we get the following comparison between the four leading industrial nations:

COTTON SPINDLES OF BRITAIN, FRANCE, GERMANY, AND AMERICA

(Compiled by the Board of Trade from Reports by Messrs. Ellison & Co.)

| Years | United Kingdom | France | Germany | United States |
|---|---|---|---|---|
| | Millions | Millions | Millions | Millions |
| Aver. 1875–9 ... | 39·0 | 3·8 | 4·8 | 10·4 |
| ,, 1880–4 ... | 41·2 | 3·9 | 4·9 | 12·1 |
| ,, 1885–9 ... | 42·9 | 4·2 | 5·1 | 13·6 |
| ,, 1890–4 ... | 44·9 | 4·4 | 5·9 | 15·2 |
| ,, 1895–9 ... | 45·1 | 5·1 | 7·4 | 17·2 |
| ,, 1900–4 ... | 46·6 | 5·9 | 8·4 | 21·4 |
| ,, 1905 ... | 48·5 | 6·2 | 8·8 | 24·1 |
| ,, 1906 ... | 50·0 | 6·5 | 9·5 | 24·8 |
| ,, 1907 ... | 52·0 | 6·6 | 9·7 | 25·9 |
| ,, 1908 ... | 54·6 | 6·7 | 9·8 | 26·7 |
| ,, 1909 ... | 55·6 | 6·9 | 10·2 | 27·8 |

This record, which is more complete than the other for the countries dealt with, shows that 120 years after Arkwright made his fortune, Britain possesses far more spindles than France, Germany, and America put together.

But the spindle record, good as it is, does less than justice to Lancashire. We do far more fine spinning than foreign nations, which means that our output per spindle is worth more than the output per spindle of foreign nations. Again, our spindles are, as to a larger proportion, faster running than foreign spindles.

As to growth, in 1875–9 we possessed only 39,000,000 spindles; in 1909 we possess about 56,000,000 spindles; and the spindles of 1909 are vastly more efficient than those of 1874.

To sum up the position, it is Lancashire against the world, and Lancashire easily first.

And this has been accomplished under the fiscal system which Protectionists are trying to undermine. Æsop's fable of the dog who snatched at the shadow and lost the substance of his meal might specially have been written to illustrate the folly of Protection in its relation to Lancashire.

The world's cotton is, as to the greater part, produced in that Protectionist nation, the United States of America. We have to buy American cotton in order to carry on our industry. A comparison of British and American imports and exports of cotton goods is, therefore, of the deepest interest, as showing what is achieved by (1) the Protectionist nation which can grow cotton, and (2) the Free Trade nation which cannot grow cotton.

First, as to imports. The record for 1905–8 is as follows:

BRITISH AND AMERICAN IMPORTS OF COTTON GOODS FOR HOME CONSUMPTION

| | Imported into Britain £ | Imported into U.S.A. £ |
|---|---|---|
| 1905 ... ... ... | 6,500,000 ... ... ... | 10,900,000 |
| 1906 ... ... ... | 6,700,000 ... ... ... | 13,800,000 |
| 1907 ... ... ... | 7,000,000 ... ... ... | 15,900,000 |
| 1908 ... ... ... | 7,600,000 ... ... ... | 11,300,000 |

So that the United States imports twice the value of cotton goods that we do. Yet America has high duties to keep out cotton goods, while we have no duties.

Second, as to exports. The record for 1905–1908 is:

BRITISH AND AMERICAN EXPORTS OF COTTON GOODS

| | British Exports | American Exports |
|---|---|---|
| | £ | £ |
| 1905 | 92,000,000 | 11,300,000 |
| 1906 | 99,600,000 | 8,600,000 |
| 1907 | 110,400,000 | 5,300,000 |
| 1908 | 95,100,000 | 5,300,000 |

So that Lancashire takes American cotton and beats America with it to such an extent that Britain's cotton trade exports are about twenty times as great as those of America.

Here is a fact even more striking. America cannot sell us cotton goods. Taking the latest year for which I have the official analysis of the Board of Trade, the following table shows our imports from America of cotton and cotton goods respectively in 1906:

IMPORTS INTO U.K. OF (1) RAW COTTON AND (2) COTTON GOODS FROM U.S.A.

| | £ |
|---|---|
| Raw cotton | 38,700,596 |
| Cotton yarn and goods | 253,448 |
| | £38,954,044 |

America, the great cotton land, can sell us only £253,448 worth of cotton goods in a year, although we have no duties to keep her out.

On the other hand, we sold to America £2,071,066 worth of cotton yarn and goods in 1906, although she has "Protection."

What is the explanation? The answer is the key to the whole position. America, through Protection, denies herself cheap production—denies herself, that is, the power to export. *Her duties protect us.* Britain, on the other hand, through

Free Trade has cheap and efficient production, and is able to sell abroad in a fortnight as many cotton goods as America is able to sell in a year.

Eighty per cent. of the work of Lancashire's great industry is done for oversea markets. To retain export business worth £2,000,000 a week it is absolutely necessary to retain cheap production. The increase of cost by even a small percentage would be ruinous. And what the Tariff Reformers propose to do is to increase cost.

In his brilliant reply to the Tariff "Commission's" "report" on the cotton industry Professor S. J. Chapman shows what even such a small import duty as 5 per cent. would mean to the trade. A weaving shed of 800 looms is estimated to cost £27,625, of which about £20,000 would be affected by the 5 per cent. duties. That means an extra capital cost of £1,000 in setting up the shed, entailing an extra annual cost of £125 for interest and depreciation. But that is only part of the increased cost of running. Flour, sago, faring, leather, oil, tallow, &c., would all be high in price, costing an extra £180 a year. Thus the working costs of the shed under a 5 per cent. duty would increase by £305 a year.

Or take a cotton mill of 80,000 spindles costing £100,000; £75,000 of this would be affected by a 5 per cent. tariff, making an extra capital cost £3,750. This means an extra £468 a year for interest and depreciation. Adding £145 extra for the tax on materials (cotton not included), brings the extra annual cost up to £613.

But if we get Tariff Reform it will not stop at 5 per cent. or 10 per cent., and *Lancashire, without any possibility of gaining by Protection, for there is nothing to protect, as we have seen, would be charged extra costs by every trade which could get a duty out of Legislature.*

It is because the United States spinners and weavers cannot establish mills or work them so cheaply as we can that they cannot compete with us. If Lancashire gives up Free Trade it will emulate American impotence in the world's markets.

The Colonial Preference side of the Tariff Reform agitation, sufficiently unsatisfactory in regard to any British industry, is particularly so in regard to the cotton trade.

Our magnificent cotton exports go chiefly to foreign nations and to India, not to the British Colonies. Here are the facts for 1907 :

BRITISH EXPORTS OF COTTON YARN AND MANUFACTURES, 1907

| | £ |
|---|---|
| To foreign countries... ... ... ... | 67,000,000 |
| To India ... ... ... ... ... | 27,000,000 |
| To other British possessions ... ... | 16,000,000 |
| | 110,000,000 |

It comes to this : we are asked to risk the £67,000,000 of foreign trade, and the £27,000,000 of Indian trade, to make a problematic increase in the £16,000,000, only part of which is strictly "Colonial" trade.

In the words of a Lancashire friend of mine, Mr. William Edge, of Bolton, the Lancashire cotton trade works thus, if we imagine the days of the week divided up amongst Lancashire's customers. On Monday the British cotton trade works for the home market. On the first *four hours* of Tuesday it works for the Colonies. For the remainder of Tuesday and until, say, 3 o'clock on Wednesday it works for India. For the remainder of the week until Saturday closing time it works for the foreign markets.

The case of India is most important, and Tariff "Reformers" continue to refuse to meet it. We ourselves make India a Free Trade country, but if we adopt Protection we must allow India to have cotton duties. If we did not, it would be grossly unfair; it would justify an Indian revolt against us. Only while we are Free Traders can we honestly retain the Indian cotton market, so that to adopt Protection is to cut off one-fifth of our export trade in cottons on this account alone.

And for what should we be risking our foreign and Indian cotton trade? Our exports of cottons to British Colonies are small, but they form nine-tenths of the cottons which the Colonies buy, so that we stand to gain nothing and to lose everything. Australia, New Zealand, Canada, South Africa—all alike are necessarily small buyers of cotton goods, but what cotton goods they buy are procured almost entirely from Lancashire.

As for the alleged "Preference" in Colonial markets, Colonial manufacturers have shown us only too plainly that they have not the slightest intention of admitting British manufacturers to their markets on equal terms with their own. The Canadian Preference simply consists in charging manufactures with high duties, and then, for the sake of form, charging an even higher duty on foreign goods. What matters is not the maximum foreign duty, but the minimum British duty.

The Canadian manufacturers are determined to have thorough protection against the home country. The competition of Britain is, of course, the chief competition which they have to meet, and so long as there is a stiff duty against us, the Canadian manufacturer does not mind in the least if, by way of a little pleasantry, another column is added to the tariff showing even stiffer duties against goods coming from foreign countries.

In view of these considerations we need not be surprised that at a thoroughly representative cotton conference held in Lancashire in July, 1903, the following resolution was carried unanimously:

> "This Conference of the Cotton Employers' Parliamentary Association and the United Textile Factory Workers' Association (*representing the whole cotton trade as employers and operatives*), firmly convinced that the great cotton industry of the United Kingdom owes its pre-eminence to, and can only be maintained by, the policy of *Free Trade*, pledges itself to oppose to the utmost of its power any proposals which, by imposing taxes on food or raw materials, and so raising the cost of production and living, will cripple it in its already severe struggle to uphold its position in foreign markets, by which 80 per cent. of its productions are absorbed."

Such is the considered opinion of the British cotton trade.

The Census of Production (1907) Preliminary Report, issued

late in 1909, shows the value of the gross output in the British cotton industry to be :

BRITISH COTTON OUTPUT, 1907

| | Quantity | Value |
|---|---|---|
| | | £ |
| Yarn, lbs. ... ... ... ... | 1,529,601,000 | 79,621,000 |
| Piece goods, yds. ... ... ... | 7,091,485,000 | 82,167,000 |
| Belting, cwts. ... ... ... | 40,000 | 317,000 |
| Other manufactures ... ... | — | 9,097,000 |
| Cotton waste, lbs. ... ... | 461,942,000 | 4,450,000 |
| All other products ... ... | — | 1,288,000 |
| Total gross output... ... | — | 176,940,000 |

The cost of materials used was £129,095,000. Adding £904,000 for payments for work "given out," this figure is increased to £129,999,000. The net output, or fund providing profit, wages, &c., is thus about £47,000,000. It will be clear that a slight increase in the cost, £129,999,000, would make a serious diminution in this fund.

As to wages in the cotton trade, the recent Board of Trade inquiry into textile wages (Cd. 4,545), shows that rates have grown considerably in recent years:

RISE IN BRITISH COTTON WAGES

| | Men | | Women | |
|---|---|---|---|---|
| | s. | d. | s. | d. |
| 1886 ... ... ... | 23 | 7 | 15 | 0 |
| 1906 ... ... ... | 28 | 10 | 18 | 8 |
| Increase per cent.... | 22 | | 24 | |

A note must be added on the question of raw cotton supplies.

There is a growing feeling of solidarity amongst the leading agents of the world's great industries, a feeling which finds practical expression in such gatherings as the Fifth International Congress of Cotton Masters, held at Paris in 1908.

The official report of this Conference is of deep interest to us, especially in its references to the question of raw material. One-fourth of our exports in 1907 (£110,438,000 out of £426,204,000) consisted of cotton yarn and manufactures. More extraordinary still, according to Mr. C. W. Macara, we actually manufacture about one-fourth, measured by value, of all the cotton goods produced by all the world. In producing this enormous output, we call for a great share of the world's cotton—about one-third of the whole crop. The world's cotton is almost entirely produced in the Southern States of North America. That was the chief point which concerned the Cotton Congress. It was of serious import to all the nations represented, but to ourselves, the chief cotton manufacturers of the world, it was supremely important.

The American cotton monopoly will be understood from the following eloquent figures submitted to the Congress:

THE WORLD'S COTTON CROP IN 1906

| | Bales of 500 lb. each |
|---|---|
| United States ... ... ... ... ... | 13,016,000 |
| East Indies ... ... ... ... ... | 3,708,000 |
| Egypt ... ... ... ... ... ... | 1,400,000 |
| Russia ... ... ... ... ... ... | 675,000 |
| China ... ... ... ... ... ... | 418,000 |
| Brazil ... ... ... ... ... ... | 275,000 |
| Mexico ... ... ... ... ... ... | 130,000 |
| Other sources ... ... ... ... ... | 320,000 |
| Total bales ... ... ... ... | 19,942,000 |

The demand for cotton grows rapidly. An additional 500,000 bales are called for every year. The United States now consumes about 5,000,000 bales out of the 13,000,000 bales which she grows. She would consume more if she had Free Trade, or low duties, instead of her absurd tariffs, which protect *us*. Tho facts on this head now stand thus:

UNITED STATES EXPORTS OF (1) RAW COTTON, AND (2) COTTON GOODS, 1907

| Exports of | £ |
|---|---|
| Raw Cotton ... ... ... ... ... | 94,000,000 |
| Cotton Manufactures ... ... ... ... | 5,300,000 |

That is a typical Protectionist triumph. America cannot sell her cotton goods abroad. She can only find a market for raw cotton. We take her cotton (in our own ships) and do the export cotton trade for her.

The consideration by the Congress of the question of raw cotton supplies was made more serious by the new combination movement amongst the Southern cotton planters.

No one can blame the cotton growers for combining. For long years they have seen the fruit of their labour taken from them and juggled with. Bales of cotton became counters in a game of speculation by the parasitic agents who stand between the planters and the cotton users. Prices fluctuated wildly, doubling, or, perchance, halving in a single year. As Mr. Moritz Schanz, of Chemnitz, pointed out in his paper read to the Congress, cotton prices have varied between 5 cents. in 1898 and 18 cents. in 1904. In consequence of a mad fever of speculation in New York a fall took place from 17 cents in May, 1904, to under 7 cents in January, 1905, causing severe and undeserved losses to honest farmers.

Who can wonder if the planters have sought by combination to fight the speculators? Working alone, the planter is a helpless tool of the cotton middleman. Working in association with his fellows, the cotton planter is learning that he can control price.

But, being of the same earth as the middlemen, the cotton planters in combination are beginning, in their turn, to play the middlemen's game. The growers see the strength of the position so eloquently set out in the above table of cotton supplies. They see the cotton world dependent on American cotton. They want higher prices, and do their best to fix a high minimum.

The average price of a pound of American cotton in 1897–1906 was 8⅔ cents. The cotton growers think the minimum should be 15 cents. On a crop of 12,000,000 bales that would mean an additional levy on the cotton world of £60,000,000 for raw materials.

Europe, which draws 75 per cent. of her cotton supplies from America, must clearly find fresh sources of supply.

Britain, France, and Germany are all doing their best to promote Colonial cotton growing, but so far with little success. The British Cotton Growing Association is doing admirable work, but in 1907 the bales of cotton produced under its auspices only amounted to 26,000, a negligible quantity.

The experts of the Association are exceedingly hopeful, however. Much is looked for from the development of Nigeria. Mr. Howarth believes that 10,000,000 bales or so a year will be produced there in twenty years' time. The British Government has granted some thousands to help on the experimental work, and it might well do much more. It is by such straightforward means, and not by the indirect, clumsy, and wasteful method of preferential duties that the Empire's resources should be developed.

**CUSTOMS DUTIES**—The word Customs is exceedingly old, and in ancient times applied to any "customary" dues or payments. Its use came to be restricted to duties payable upon the exportation or importation of goods. The first customs duty of which we can trace the legislative origin was an export duty on wool and leather for war purposes, levied in the reign of Edward I. in 1297. Then came Tonnage and Poundage—the former levied at so much a ton on wine and the second at so much a pound of value on goods—and these came to be granted to each successive Sovereign at the beginning of his reign. The Tonnage and Poundage Act of 1660 (Charles II.), afterwards called the Old Subsidy, remained law until 1787, and between those dates so many duties and imposts were added that the complexity became bewildering. By 1785, when Pitt determined to reform the Customs, there were 68 different branches of the law. A single imported article paid not one but a dozen or more different duties, beginning with the old Poundage of 5 per cent. of 1660.

After Pitt's codification of 1787 the tariff contained 1,414 articles. Thereafter the war with France led to many additions and complications. In 1801 each article imported paid four different rates of duty—three, that is, in addition to the duty set out in the Act of 1787. In 1826 the Customs law was codified by Hume, and the musty laws of five hundred years swept away and serious Tariff Reform commenced. In 1842 Gladstone, under Peel, after the Report of the Committee of 1840, made many reductions. In 1845–6 came the repeal of the Corn Laws and an exceedingly large measure of reform. In 1853 Gladstone, then Chancellor of the Exchequer, continued the reforms, and 1860 saw the completion of the work and the removal of all duties save twenty-four, ten of which merely remained to countervail Excise duties.

Looking at Customs duties as revenue producers, it is remarkable that the complicated tariff upon many articles before 1846 yielded no more revenue than the simplified tariff on a few articles after 1860.

**CUSTOMS UNION**—A Customs Union is a union of States for Customs purposes, each party to the union enjoying Free Trade with the others, while the group of States as a whole has a general Customs tariff applied to all the world outside it. Instances are (1) the German Zollverein, which includes Luxemburg, (2) the Australian Commonwealth, and (3) the Union of South Africa. A Customs Union is a practical recognition of the virtue of Free Trade.

**CUTLERY**—There is a considerable and growing exportation and importation of cutlery, in addition to a very large manufacture for the home market. The figures for external commerce are:

BRITISH COMMERCE IN CUTLERY

| | Imports for Home Consumption (c.i.f.) £ | Exports of British Make (f.o.b.) £ |
|---|---|---|
| 1900 (good year) ... ... | 15,000 ... ... | 639,000 |
| 1907 (good year) ... ... | 117,000 ... ... | 770,000 |
| 1908 (bad year) ... ... | 118,000 ... ... | 614,000 |

It will be seen that, in spite of a considerable growth of the imports, we export more than five times as much cutlery as is imported. Sheffield cutlery is still the best known in the world.

**CYCLES**—The growth of this trade in recent years, both for home and export, has been very great, through the introduction of popular prices. We shall not know the value of the home production until the results of the Census of Production are got out, but the external trade is as follows:

BRITISH COMMERCE IN CYCLES, INCLUDING PARTS

| | Imports for Home Consumption (c.i.f.) | Exports of British Make (f.o.b.) |
|---|---|---|
| | £ | £ |
| 1900 (good year) | Not recorded | 531,000 |
| 1907 (good year) | 161,000 | 1,288,000 |
| 1908 (bad year) | 143,000 | 1,419,000 |

The above table does not include motor cycles, which will be dealt with under MOTOR CARS. In 1900 the imports of cycles were not recorded separately. The British exports of cycles are very large and growing, and are ten times as great as our imports. American cycles were freely imported for a little while some years ago, but quite failed in the British market.

**CYCLES OF TRADE**—*See* TRADE CYCLES.

**DINGLEY TARIFF**—The Dingley Tariff of the United States was passed into law in 1897. It was highly Protectionist in character, and levied import duties upon food and raw materials, and on partly and wholly manufactured articles. The import duties on food were practically inoperative, as America has little need to import food; the food duties were shams put into the schedule to placate the agricultural States. The tariff had high duties on many raw materials, put in at the bidding of those interested in their production. Amongst the materials taxed were timber, iron ore, hides, skins, leather, paper, hemp, tallow, basic slag, &c. Indeed, duties were levied on 100,000,000 dollars' worth of raw materials every year. It is also interesting to observe that, in spite of the tariff, America imports more manufactured articles than are imported into the United Kingdom.

On August 5, 1909, a new American Tariff, almost as stupid as the Dingley Tariff, became law. It only passed the American Senate by 47 votes to 31.

**DRAWBACK**—This is the name given to a return, upon exportation of an imported article, of the duty paid when that article was imported. It is a system practised by most countries. For example, Section 25 of the new American Payne Tariff reads as follows:

"Section 25: That where imported materials on which duties have been paid are used in the manufacture of articles manufactured or produced in the United States, there shall be allowed on the exportation of such articles a drawback equal in amount to the duties paid on the materials used, less one per centum of such duties."

Thus, if an article which has been taxed on import into the United States becomes part of the American manufacture which is exported out of the country, the American Government returns to the American exporter 99 per cent., or nearly the whole, of the import duty on the imported material. To take a case in point, British tinplate, imported into America, is taxed. If an American tinned food exporter exports tin cans made out of imported tinplate, the American Government hands him back the duty which was paid on the imported British tinplate. This would be absurd if the American citizen did not pay the import duty in the first place. If the British tinplate maker paid it, the American Government would be committing the egregious folly of returning to the American tin can exporter a duty which he had not paid.

This drawback system, which is practised all over the world, is a complete and conclusive proof that the Governments of all countries know and recognise in practice that the importer pays the import duty.

**DUMPING**—Dumping is a term applied to the exportation of articles at a price either below the cost of production or much below the home selling price. In the first Fiscal Blue

Book the Board of Trade made a careful examination of the export policy of the Trusts of Germany and America. In each case they showed that the dumping policy is occasionally practised, but there is no evidence whatever of any deliberate attempt to injure British industry by continuous under-selling. Thus as to Germany, the Blue Book says, page 297:

"It is, of course, easy to suppose a state of things in which a kartell (syndicate) or a combination of kartells, might deliberately export at a low price with the principal or the exclusive aim of injuring and ultimately of entirely ruining and bringing to a close a particular industry in a foreign country. But it cannot be said that there is any clear evidence of such action on the part of the German combinations, whose export policy up to the present time appears to be mainly the result of supply exceeding demand in the German domestic markets."

The trade depression of 1901–2 was marked by German dumping, but that it was occasioned by depression is clearly shown by the fact that Germany actually dumped coal. Thus the Rhenish-Westphalian Coal Syndicate in 1902 sold coal abroad at 9·84 marks per metric ton, while they were selling it at home at 10·45 marks per metric ton.

Germany was thus dumping coal in Europe even as she was dumping steel at the same time in Europe and America.

From its very nature, dumping of this character cannot be a continuous process, for it would ruin the country which practised it. There was little dumping noticeable in the trade depression of 1908. Both German and American exports fell off heavily.

If dumping were practised with the deliberate object of ruining an industry, the imposition of small or even moderate duties would be quite ineffective. As has been said, there is no evidence whatever of dumping with a view to deliberate injury; if such evidence existed it would be a case not for trumpery import duties, but for representations of quite a different character.

**EARTHENWARE**—Like most of our industries, this manufacture is chiefly concerned with the home market. The home production has been estimated to be worth over £15,000,000 a year, but we shall not have a reliable figure before the Census of Production Act of the present Government has done its work. The external trade is as follows:

BRITISH COMMERCE IN EARTHENWARE

| | Imports for Home Consumption (c.i.f.) | Exports of British (Make (f.o.b). |
|---|---|---|
| | £ | £ |
| 1900 (good year) ... ... | 777,000 ... | 2,038,000 |
| 1907 (good year) ... ... | 880,000 ... | 2,649,000 |
| 1908 (bad year) ... ... | 792,000 ... | 2,344,000 |

These figures relate to many widely varying articles, from china to sanitary ware, from tiles to porcelain electrical fittings. In some lines there is considerable foreign competition, as, for example, in cheap artistic earthenware, in which there is great room for improvement in British design. On the whole, as our exports are three times as great in value as our imports, it cannot be said that we are doing badly, but Staffordshire might do much better if (1) she gave greater attention to design and colouring in the cheaper productions, and (2) if she could get her clay more cheaply from Cornwall and her goods more cheaply transported whether for home or export. On this *see* Potters' Clay and Railways.

**EGGS**—As many as 2,185,000,000 eggs were imported in 1908, their value being £7,183,000, or about three-farthings each. Eggs were included in the Chamberlain food taxation programme of October 6, 1903, the suggested impost on dairy produce being 5 per cent. Not only would such a tax raise the price of eggs to the consumer, but it would probably raise it by more than the amount of the tax. In all probability the retail price of eggs would rise by about 10 per cent., which would be a serious addition to the food bill of the poor.

**ELECTRICAL TRADES**—It is only in the last few years that any official records have been made of our commerce in electrical machinery. This was one of the reforms which I urged in 1902, and which were made in 1903. The available records are as follows:

BRITISH COMMERCE IN ELECTRICAL GOODS AND ELECTRICAL MACHINERY

| Year | Electrical Goods and Apparatus | | Electrical Machinery | |
|---|---|---|---|---|
| | Imports Home Consumption (c.i.f.) | Exports British Make (f.o.b.) | Imports Home Consumption (c.i.f.) | Exports British Make (f.o.b.) |
| | £ | £ | £ | £ |
| 1900 (good year) | 1,229,000 | 546,000 | Not known | Not known |
| 1907 (good year) | 1,081,000 | 2,470,000 | 669,000 | 996,000 |
| 1908 (bad year) | 1,131,000 | 1,942,000 | 547,000 | 1,354,000 |

Owing to the changes in the classifications, there is some doubt as to whether the figures are strictly comparative. So far as they go, however, they show that we are building up a valuable export trade in electrical goods and machinery.

**EMIGRATION**—Emigration statistics are difficult, because the mere figures do not show why persons are voyaging from one country to another; they may relate to emigrants and again they may not. With regard to the United Kingdom, the following figures show the total numbers of inward and outward passengers of all classes and nationalities, and the excess of outward-bound over inward-bound passengers, to and from non-European countries only:

BRITISH OUTWARD AND INWARD PASSENGERS: TO AND FROM NON-EUROPEAN COUNTRIES

| Year | Outward Bound | Inward Bound | Excess of Outward Bound |
|---|---|---|---|
| 1900 | 298,561 | 175,747 | 122,814 |
| 1903 | 449,006 | 199,685 | 249,321 |
| 1906 | 557,737 | 230,165 | 327,572 |
| 1907 | 634,949 | 293,633 | 341,316 |
| 1908 | 386,411 | 342,922 | 43,489 |

All we can assume is, and it is a common-sense deduction, that inward and outward travellers for pleasure and business balance each other, and that the excess of outward passengers roughly represents emigrants.

It will be seen that up to 1907 there was considerable increase in recent years. This has been attributed by Protectionists to the evil effect of Free Trade. It is due, of course, to the great activity of the emigration offices established by our Colonies in recent years. In 1908, it will be seen, owing to bad trade all over the world, emigrants wisely held back. Indeed, in 1908, the third-class outward passengers were fewer than the third-class inward passengers.

No other country, of course, has oversea possessions like ours, inviting its people to go abroad. When we remember that there is also our great daughter nation, the United States, we should expect British emigration to be the largest in Europe, but as a matter of fact it is not.

Nearly the whole of our emigrants go to English-speaking places. The foreign emigrant, on the other hand, has actually to go to a foreign place. This makes the following emigration statistics the more interesting:

EMIGRATION STATISTICS (ROUGHLY COMPARABLE), 1907

| Emigrants from | Number |
|---|---|
| Austria-Hungary ... ... ... ... ... | 386,528 |
| Italy ... ... ... ... ... ... ... | 428,255 |
| Spain (1906) ... ... ... ... ... | 118,042 |
| Germany ... ... ... ... ... ... | 31,543 |

It will be seen that, in spite of the facts referred to, Protectionist countries head the emigration list. The figures are not strictly comparable, however, as the Board of Trade point out. They are compiled in different ways; for instance, the German figures refer only to emigration by sea.

German emigration is comparatively small, but, of course, there are practically no German Colonies, and there is no German-speaking "new" country to invite a German to emigrate.

**ENGINEERING**—Britain is the motherland of modern engineering, and the various branches of this noble industry occupy much of her activities. The following Census figures will show how enormous has been the growth of British engineering:

ENGLAND AND WALES: PERSONS EMPLOYED IN MACHINE MAKING AND SHIPBUILDING

| | | |
|---|---|---|
| Census of | 1851 ... ... ... ... ... | 80,528 |
| ,, | 1871 ... ... ... ... ... | 172,948 |
| ,, | 1891 ... ... ... ... ... | 292,239 |

Unfortunately, the classifications of the 1901 Census do not permit of a comparative statement for that year, but there is no doubt that a further great increase was made. This is evident from the following figures, which combine the classifications of the various metal, engineering, and shipbuilding trades of the United Kingdom:

UNITED KINGDOM: PERSONS EMPLOYED IN METAL, ENGINEERING, AND SHIPBUILDING

| | | |
|---|---|---|
| Census of | 1851 ... ... ... ... ... ... | 504,968 |
| ,, | 1871 ... ... ... ... ... ... | 789,230 |
| ,, | 1891 ... ... ... ... ... ... | 1,056,724 |
| ,, | 1901 ... ... ... ... ... ... | 1,435,835 |

The total value of British production in the industry is unknown, but the following figures exhibit the external trade:

BRITISH COMMERCE IN MACHINERY

(Exclusive of Machinery in Ships Exported)

| | | Imports for Home Consumption (c.i.f.) | | Exports of British Make (f.o.b.) |
|---|---|---|---|---|
| | | £ | | £ |
| 1900 (good year) | ... | 2,869,000 | ... | 19,620,000 |
| 1907 (good year) | ... | 3,879,000 | ... | 31,743,000 |
| 1908 (bad year) | ... | 3,456,000 | ... | 31,019,000 |

The exports exhibit a magnificent growth, having nearly

| Year | Steam Engines, Agricultr'l | Locomotives | Steam Engines, other kinds | Sewing Machines | Agricultural Machinery | Mining Machinery | Textile Machinery |
|---|---|---|---|---|---|---|---|
| | £ | £ | £ | £ | £ | £ | £ |
| 1846 | | 316,000 | | | | 802,000 | |
| 1847 | | 441,000 | | | | 822,000 | |
| 1848 | | 234,000 | | | | 583,000 | |
| 1849 | | 152,000 | | | | 548,000 | |
| 1850 | | 424,000 | | | | 618,000 | |
| 1851 | | 404,000 | | | | 765,000 | |
| 1852 | | 338,000 | | | | 913,000 | |
| 1853 | | 458,000 | | | | 1,527,000 | |
| 1854 | | 567,000 | | | | 1,364,000 | |
| 1855 | | 883,000 | | | | 1,360,000 | |
| 1856 | | 819,000 | | | | 1,897,000 | |
| 1857 | | 1,069,000 | | | | 2,814,000 | |
| 1858 | | 1,097,000 | | | | 2,502,000 | |
| 1859 | | 973,000 | | | | 2,758,000 | |
| 1860 | | 1,238,000 | | | | 2,599,000 | |
| 1861 | | 1,258,000 | | | | 2,955,000 | |
| 1862 | | 1,625,000 | | | | 2,468,000 | |
| 1863 | | 1,595,000 | | | | 2,773,000 | |
| 1864 | | 1,617,000 | | | | 3,231,000 | |
| 1865 | | 1,958,000 | | | | 3,264,000 | |
| 1866 | | 1,761,000 | | | | 2,998,000 | |
| 1867 | | 2,026,000 | | | | 2,942,000 | |
| 1868 | | 1,725,000 | | | | 3,005,000 | |
| 1869 | | 1,852,000 | | | | 3,267,000 | |
| 1870 | | 1,997,000 | | | | 3,296,000 | |
| 1871 | | 2,055,000 | | | | 3,887,000 | |
| 1872 | | 2,595,000 | | | | 5,606,000 | |
| 1873 | | 2,929,000 | | | | 7,092,000 | |
| 1874 | | 3,256,000 | | | | 6,535,000 | |
| 1875 | | 2,631,000 | | | | 6,427,000 | |
| 1876 | | 1,939,000 | | | | 5,271,000 | |
| 1877 | | 2,019,000 | | | | 4,704,000 | |
| 1878 | | 2,408,000 | | | | 5.090,000 | |
| 1879 | | 2,198,000 | | | | 5,080,000 | |
| 1880 | | 2,786,000 | | | | 6,477,000 | |
| 1881 | | 3,167,000 | | | | 6,793,000 | |
| 1882 | | 3,556,000 | | | | 8,376,000 | |
| 1883 | | 4,297,000 | | | | 9,136,000 | |
| 1884 | | 4,179,000 | | | | 8,895,000 | |
| 1885 | | 3,725,000 | | | | 7,362,000 | |
| 1886 | | 3,013,000 | | | | 7,124,000 | |
| 1887 | 479,000 | 827,000 | 1,489,000 | 503,000 | 506,000 | | 7,322,000 |
| 1888 | 569,000 | 1.024,000 | 1,856,000 | 445,000 | 545,000 | | 8,499,000 |
| 1889 | 625,000 | 1,444,000 | 1,758,000 | 602,000 | 554,000 | | 10,291,000 |
| 1890 | 717,000 | 1,848,000 | 1,877,000 | 697,000 | 688,000 | | 10,583,000 |
| 1891 | 684,000 | 1,617,000 | 1,622,000 | 748,000 | 731,000 | | 10,415,000 |
| 1892 | 789,000 | 984,000 | 1,445,000 | 818,000 | 817,000 | | 9,035,000 |
| 1893 | 934,000 | 843,000 | 1,498,000 | 717,000 | 935,000 | 410,000 | 5,256,000 |
| 1894 | 880,000 | 750,000 | 1,435,000 | 770,000 | 1,018,000 | 387,000 | 5,479,000 |
| 1895 | 647,000 | 798,000 | 1,338,000 | 914,000 | 797,000 | 716,000 | 6,151,000 |
| 1896 | 541,000 | 1,078,000 | 1,667,000 | 955,000 | 664,000 | 1,048,000 | 6,746,000 |
| 1897 | 523,000 | 1,006,000 | 1,495,000 | 1,074,000 | 662,000 | 869,000 | 5,702,000 |
| 1898 | 688,000 | 1,484,000 | 1,455,000 | 1,088,000 | 850,000 | 716,000 | 6,628.000 |
| 1899 | 762,000 | 1,467,000 | 1,647,000 | 1,281,000 | 945,000 | 731,000 | 6,804,000 |
| 1900 | 755,000 | 1,497,000 | 1,843,000 | 1,452,000 | 873,000 | 562,000 | 6,214,000 |
| 1901 | 621,000 | 1,911,000 | 1,726,000 | 1,552,000 | 733,000 | 509,000 | 4,726,000 |
| 1902 | 632,000 | 2,299,000 | 1,849,000 | 1,840,000 | 812,000 | 548,000 | 4,511,000 |
| 1903 | 876,000 | 2,359,000 | 2,014,000 | 2,035,000 | 979,000 | 782,000 | 4,730,000 |
| 1904 | 931,000 | 1,929,000 | 2,168,000 | 2,269,000 | 1,082,000 | 874,000 | 5,001,000 |
| 1905 | 1,099,000 | 2,384,000 | 2,311,000 | 1,968,000 | 1,047,000 | 832,000 | 5,606,000 |
| 1906 | 1,136,000 | 2,895,000 | 2,831,000 | 1,577,000 | 1,171,000 | 733,000 | 6,710,000 |
| 1907 | 1,022,000 | 3,433,000 | 3,445,000 | 1,831,000 | 1,133,000 | 875,000 | 8,039,000 |

FROM THE UNITED KINGDOM, 1846 TO 1907

| Electrical Machinery | Machinery other kinds | Machinery forming part of new Ships exported | Cycles. | Motor Cycles and Parts | Motor Cars and Parts | Total | Year |
|---|---|---|---|---|---|---|---|
| £ | £ | £ | £ | £ | £ | £ | |
| | | Not recorded before 1899 | Not separately distinguished before 1892 | Not separately distinguished before 1902 | | | |
| | | | | | | 1.118,000 | 1846 |
| | | | | | | 1,263,000 | 1847 |
| | | | | | | 817 000 | 1848 |
| | | | | | | 700,000 | 1849 |
| | | | | | | 1,042,000 | 1850 |
| | | | | | | 1,169,000 | 1851 |
| | | | | | | 1.251,000 | 1852 |
| | | | | | | 1,985.000 | 1853 |
| | | | | | | 1.931,000 | 1854 |
| | | | | | | 2,243 000 | 1855 |
| | | | | | | 2,716,000 | 1856 |
| | | | | | | 3.883,000 | 1857 |
| | | | | | | 3,599,000 | 1858 |
| | | | | | | 3,731,000 | 1859 |
| | | | | | | 3 837,000 | 1860 |
| | | | | | | 4,213,000 | 1861 |
| | | | | | | 4,093,000 | 1862 |
| | | | | | | 4,368,000 | 1863 |
| | | | | | | 4,848,000 | 1864 |
| | | | | | | 5.222,000 | 1865 |
| | | | | | | 4,759,000 | 1866 |
| | | | | | | 4'968,000 | 1867 |
| | | | | | | 4,730 000 | 1868 |
| | | | | | | 5,119,000 | 1869 |
| | | | | | | 5,293,000 | 1870 |
| | | | | | | 5,942 000 | 1871 |
| | | | | | | 8,201,000 | 1872 |
| | | | | | | 10,021,000 | 1873 |
| | | | | | | 9,791,000 | 1874 |
| | | | | | | 9,058,000 | 1875 |
| | | | | | | 7,210,000 | 1876 |
| | | | | | | 6,723,000 | 1877 |
| | | | | | | 7,498,000 | 1878 |
| | | | | | | 7,278,000 | 1879 |
| | | | | | | 9,263,000 | 1880 |
| | | | | | | 9,960,000 | 1881 |
| | | | | | | 11,932,000 | 1882 |
| | | | | | | 13,433,000 | 1883 |
| | | | | | | 13,074,000 | 1884 |
| | | | | | | 11,087,000 | 1885 |
| | | | | | | 10,137,000 | 1886 |
| | | | | | | 11,126,000 | 1887 |
| | | | | | | 12,938.000 | 1888 |
| | | | | | | 15,274,000 | 1889 |
| | | | | | | 16,410,000 | 1890 |
| | | | | | | 15,817,000 | 1891 |
| | | | 916,000 | | | 14,804,000 | 1892 |
| 3,325,000 | | | 1,033,000 | | | 14,951,000 | 1893 |
| 3,486,000 | | | 1'201,000 | | | 15,406,000 | 1894 |
| 3,788,000 | | | 1,386,000 | | | 16,535,000 | 1895 |
| 4,314,000 | | | 1.856,000 | | | 18,869,000 | 1896 |
| 4,924,000 | | | 1,430,000 | | | 17,685,000 | 1897 |
| 5,485,000 | | | 961,000 | | | 19,450,000 | 1898 |
| 6,017'000 | | 2,452,000 | 662,000 | | | 22,768,000 | 1899 |
| 6,424,000 | | 2,256,000 | 530,000 | | | 22,406 000 | 1900 |
| 6,034,000 | | 1,893,000 | 577,000 | | | 20,282,000 | 1901 |
| 6,264,000 | | 1,466,000 | 718,000 | 172,000 | | 21,111,000 | 1902 |
| 437,000 | 5,846,000 | 1,222,000 | 849,000 | 344,000 | | 22,473,000 | 1903 |
| 523,000 | 6,288.000 | 1,165,000 | 740,000 | 38,000 | 321.000 | 23,329,000 | 1904 |
| 644,000 | 7,368,000 | 1,516,000 | 1,037,000 | 41,000 | 502,000 | 26.355,000 | 1905 |
| 842,000 | 8,876,000 | 1,669,000 | 1,140,000 | 51.000 | 819,000 | 30,450,000 | 1906 |
| 996,000 | 10,970,000 | 2,551,000 | 1,288,000 | 53,000 | 1,325,000 | 36,961,000 | 1907 |

doubled in eight years. The imports are small, yet they ought on no account to be taxed. Such machinery as we bring in is of special character, and it is bought by British manufacturers to equip their works.

It should be explained that the figures given in this table do not include cycles or motor-cars, *which see.* On pages 108 and 109 a complete record of British exports of engines and machinery, including the machinery in new ships, &c., is presented. The total, it will be seen, reached nearly £37,000,000 in 1907.

British engineers' wages have grown thus since 1875:

GROWTH OF BRITISH ENGINEERS' WAGES

(Per Week)

| Year | Fitters and Turners | | Pattern-makers | |
|---|---|---|---|---|
| | London | Glasgow | Birmingham | Manchester |
| | s. d. | s. d. | s. d. | s. d. |
| 1875 | 36 0 | 27 0 | 34 0 | 36 0 |
| 1885 | 38 0 | 28 0 | 34 0 | 36 0 |
| 1895 | 38 0 | 30 4 | 36 0 | 38 0 |
| 1905 | 39 0 | 35 0 | 38 0 | 40 0 |
| 1909 | 40 0 | 36 0 | 39 0 | 42 0 |

Protectionists frequently allege that unemployment is constantly increasing in this country. If it were, it would be quite impossible for the above figures to obtain.

**ENTREPÔT TRADE**—Our entrepôt or storehouse trade is a minor but important branch of our commerce. The fact that Britain is a great free port makes her a world-market for many things she does not herself produce, such as gold, cotton, skins, indiarubber, ivory, palm oil, hemp, jute, Oriental wares, and many other raw and manufactured articles. The following figures will show the extent and, broadly, the nature of our entrepôt trade in 1908:

BRITISH IMPORTS AND ENTREPÔT TRADE IN 1908

| Classification | Total Imports | Entrepôt Trade (Re-exports of Imported Goods) | Imports for Home Consumption |
|---|---|---|---|
| | £ | £ | £ |
| Food, drink, and tobacco | 244,248,000 | 10,879,000 | 233,369,000 |
| Raw materials ... ... | 203,489,000 | 45,317,000 | 158,172,000 |
| Manufactures ... ... | 143,124,000 | 23,291,000 | 119,833,000 |
| Miscellaneous ... ... | 2,280,000 | 179,000 | 2,101,000 |
| Total ... ... | 593,141,000 | 79,666,000 | 513,475,000 |

The third column of figures shows the imports for home consumption, *i.e.*, our total imports less the entrepôt trade.

**EXCISE DUTIES**—The word Excise simply means tax, but the term is used exclusively to designate taxes on home productions or on licenses connected with home trade.

**EXPORTS**—Exports are goods or products passing outwards over a political boundary line. They may represent various things. They may stand (1) for an ordinary sale of goods by a person in country A to a person in country B; (2) for a payment of interest due by a person in country A to a person in country B; (3) for an investment of capital by a person in country A with a person in country B; or (4) for payment by a person in country A for use of a ship belonging to a person in country B.

In the case of (1) the export will presently produce a corresponding import, since the person in country A will take payment either from some one in country B direct, or from a fellow countryman who will draw an import from country B.

In the case of (2) there will be no corresponding import, and the export will represent an economic drain on the country.

In the case of (3) there will be a corresponding import either if the investment pays interest, or if A sells out his investment and withdraws the proceeds.

In the case of (4) the export has gone out in satisfaction of the use of a ship, and the service of the ship forms the corresponding import.

The services, such as the loan of a ship or of money, rendered by persons of one country to persons of another country are not recorded at Custom houses. They have been sometimes called "invisible exports" or "invisible imports," according to whether given or taken. It follows that the visible recorded exports and imports of goods by any nation never balance each other, for a certain amount of these invisible exports and imports enter into the oversea transactions of every nation.

**EXPORTS, COMPARATIVE**—The following is a comparative statement of the exports (home productions only) of ten leading nations, giving both the total values and the values of the exports of manufactured goods only:

EXPORTS OF TEN NATIONS

(In Millions of £)

| Nation | Year | Exports of Manufactures only | Total Exports | Percentage of Manufactured to Total Exports |
|---|---|---|---|---|
| United Kingdom | 1907 | 342 | 426 | 80 |
| Germany ... | 1907 | 236 | 337 | 70 |
| United States ... | 1907 | 154 | 386 | 40 |
| France ... ... | 1907 | 134 | 224 | 60 |
| Austria-Hungary | 1906 | 63 | 99 | 64 |
| Switzerland ... | 1906 | 32 | 43 | 74 |
| Holland... ... | 1906 | 32 | 173 | 19 |
| Italy ... ... | 1906 | 18 | 77 | 23 |
| Russia ... ... | 1906 | 10 | 116 | 8 |
| Spain ... ... | 1906 | 10 | 36 | 7 |

This table brings out the great supremacy of this country as an exporter of manufactured articles. In this respect she is easily first, exporting almost as many manufactures as Germany and America put together. America is a large exporter, but she chiefly exports food and raw materials, her exports of manufactures being scarcely larger than those of France.

## EXPORTS OF UNITED KINGDOM, FRANCE, GERMANY, AND UNITED STATES COMPARED

(In each case Exports of Home Production are given)

| Years. | United Kingdom | | | | France | | | | Germany | | | | United States | | | |
|---|---|---|---|---|---|---|---|---|---|---|---|---|---|---|---|---|
| | Total Exports | | Manufactures Only | | Total Exports | | Manufactures Only | | Total Exports | | Manufactures Only | | Total Exports | | Manufactures Only | |
| | Amount | Per Head | Amount | Per Head | Amount | Per Head | Amount | Per Head | Amount | Per Head | Amount | Per Head | Amount | Per Head | Amount | Per Head |
| | Mill. £ | £ s. d. | Mill. £ | £ s. d. | Mill. £ | £ s. d. | Mill. £ | £ s. d. | Mill. £ | £ s. d. | Mill. £ | £ s. d. | Mill. £ | £ s. d. | Mill. £ | £ s. d. |
| 1854 ... ... | 97 | 3 10 3 | 88 | 3 3 6 | 56 | 1 11 2 | not | known | not a | vailable | not a | vailable | 45 | 1 13 10 | 7 | 0 5 3 |
| Aver. 1855-9 ... | 116 | 4 2 4 | 104 | 3 13 8 | 76 | 2 1 9 | ,, | ,, | ,, | ,, | ,, | ,, | 53 | 1 16 5 | 8 | 0 5 5 |
| ,, 1860-4 ... | 138 | 4 14 8 | 125 | 4 5 7 | 96 | 2 11 5 | ,, | ,, | ,, | ,, | ,, | ,, | 43 | 1 6 1 | 9 | 0 5 6 |
| ,, 1865-9 ... | 181 | 5 19 0 | 165 | 5 8 8 | 120 | 3 2 8 | ,, | ,, | ,, | ,, | ,, | ,, | 45 | 1 5 0 | 13 | 0 7 2 |
| ,, 1870-4 ... | 235 | 7 7 4 | 210 | 6 11 9 | 135 | 3 13 9 | ,, | ,, | 114 | 2 15 0 | ,, | ,, | 96 | 2 7 6 | 19 | 0 9 4 |
| ,, 1875-9 ... | 201 | 6 0 0 | 178 | 5 6 0 | 138 | 3 14 10 | 69 | 1 17 5 | 132 | 3 1 5 | ,, | ,, | 125 | 2 13 9 | 26 | 0 11 3 |
| ,, 1880-4 ... | 234 | 6 13 2 | 206 | 5 17 3 | 138 | 3 13 4 | 73 | 1 18 9 | 153 | 3 7 8 | 91 | 2 0 4 | 165 | 3 3 0 | 31 | 0 11 8 |
| ,, 1885-9 ... | 226 | 6 3 8 | 197 | 5 7 7 | 132 | 3 9 2 | 70 | 1 16 7 | 151 | 3 3 10 | 98 | 2 1 5 | 146 | 2 9 10 | 32 | 0 10 10 |
| ,, 1890-4 ... | 234 | 6 2 10 | 199 | 5 4 5 | 137 | 3 11 4 | 74 | 1 18 4 | 152 | 3 0 5 | 99 | 1 19 1 | 185 | 2 16 9 | 39 | 0 11 11 |
| ,, 1895-9 ... | 238 | 5 18 11 | 200 | 4 19 10 | 144 | 3 14 8 | 79 | 2 1 2 | 181 | 3 7 5 | 117 | 2 3 5 | 213 | 2 19 5 | 62 | 0 17 2 |
| ,, 1900-4 ... | 283 | 6 14 9 | 225 | 5 7 1 | 169 | 4 6 4 | 95 | 2 8 5 | 236 | 4 1 3 | 154 | 2 13 2 | 292 | 3 14 0 | 100 | 1 5 3 |
| 1905 ... ... | 324 | — | 264 | — | 195 | — | 110 | — | 282 | — | 188 | — | 311 | — | 127 | — |
| 1906 ... ... | 367 | — | 297 | — | 211 | — | 123 | — | 313 | — | 216 | — | 358 | — | 143 | — |
| 1907 ... ... | 416 | — | 332 | — | 224 | — | 134 | — | 337 | — | 236 | — | 386 | — | 154 | — |
| 1908 ... ... | 366 | — | 286 | — | 202 | — | 118 | — | 315 | — | 213 | — | 382 | — | 156 | — |
| Aver. 1905-8 ... | 368 | 8 7 11 | 295 | 6 14 4 | 208 | 5 5 11 | 121 | 3 1 10 | 311 | 5 0 8 | 213 | 3 9 0 | 359 | 4 4 5 | 145 | 1 14 2 |

A fuller comparison, covering half a century so far as the figures are available, is given in the deeply interesting table on page 113, which is based upon the Board of Trade's tables in Cd. 4954.

Germany is seen to have made the greatest comparative progress since she had the chance to make progress in 1872. In the period 1880–4 her commerce was almost at a parity with that of France. Now she has left France far in the rear. In the same period she has greatly bridged the gulf between the size of her commerce and that of the United Kingdom, a fact which will not surprise those who appreciate the causes of her progress (*see* GERMANY). Those who attribute the growth of German commerce to her Protection should compare her figures with those of France, who in the same period has pursued the same fiscal policy.

The progress of the United States has also been great, but in view of her superior natural resources it is not nearly as remarkable as that of Germany or Britain.

In our own case, the increase of our exports of manufactures from £3 3s. 6d. per head in 1854 to £6 14s. 4d. in 1905–8 is eminently satisfactory.

**F.O.B.**—These letters are shorthand for "free-on-board." This expression is used in quoting prices, and signifies the price of goods, including the cost of placing them on board ship at the point of exportation. The values of British exports are declared at the Customs f.o.b.

**FAIR TRADE**—This is an alias for Protection. The experience of Protection in Britain was so bitter that the word Protection came to be shunned. Consequently every time that an attempt has been made to revive Protection in this country it has been called by another name. In the seventies the word used was "Reciprocity." In the eighties the name "Fair Trade" was adopted. At the end of the nineteenth century the term "Tariff Reform" was thought of. All over the world, however, the thing denoted by these names is called Protection, and the fact that British Protectionists are afraid to use the name is very significant.

The Fair Trade League was a Protectionist organisation formed in 1881. It published a weekly paper called *Fair Trade*, which collapsed, I believe, in 1891. The Fair Trade agitation was a complete failure. Lord Salisbury snubbed it and Mr. Joseph Chamberlain pulverised it with Free Trade argument.

**FISCAL**—The word "fiscal" is derived from the Latin *fiscus*, which designated the State Treasury. Hence all matters relating to the raising of revenue are "fiscal." Protection, of course, is not really a "fiscal" policy, as its avowed aim is to levy Customs duties not for revenue purposes (since that implies the admission of imports), but to restrict or keep out imports. In so far, therefore, as a Customs duty is Protectionist it cannot be "fiscal."

**FLOUR**—*See* MILLING.

**FOOD CONSUMPTION**—The following broad view of the growth of the consumption of certain articles of food, prepared by the Board of Trade, is eloquent of the increased welfare and purchasing power of the British people:

UNITED KINGDOM, CONSUMPTION PER HEAD

| Imported Articles— | | 1871 | 1907 |
|---|---|---|---|
| Bacon and ham | lbs. | 3·38 | 16·12 |
| Beef ... ... | ,, | Not known | 22·53 |
| Butter and margarine | ,, | 4·69 | 12·71 |
| Cheese ... | ,, | 4·25 | 5·89 |
| Eggs ... ... | number | 12·75 | 50·11 |
| Rice ... ... | lbs. | 7·47 | 15·53 |
| Cocoa ... ... | ,, | 0·23 | 1·00 |
| Coffee ... ... | ,, | 0·97 | 0·66 |
| Tea ... ... | ,, | 3·92 | 6·21 |
| Wheat... ... | ,, | 150·63 | 279·14 |
| Sugar ... ... | ,, | 46·80 | 87·74 |
| Tobacco ... | ,, | 1·36 | 2·03 |
| Mutton, fresh ... | ,, | Not known | 11·61 |
| Pork ... ... | ,, | Not known | 2·06 |

In the case of some of the items there are home supplies, which cannot be included, but the improvement shown in items like rice, tobacco, tea, where the supplies are entirely imported, is conclusive as to the growth of purchasing power or real wages.

**FOOD IMPORTS**—As is generally known, our food imports are enormous and indispensable. In 1908 they were valued at about £239,000,000.

BRITISH IMPORTS OF FOOD AND DRINK, 1908

| | £ |
|---|---|
| From foreign countries ... ... ... ... | 185,700,000 |
| From British possessions ... ... ... | 53,300,000 |
| Total imports ... ... ... ... | £239,000,000 |
| Re-exported (entrepôt trade) ... ... ... | 10,600,000 |
| **Net imports for home consumption** ... ... | **£228,400,000** |

It will be seen that more than three-fourths of our imported food, bought in the cheapest and best markets in the world, are derived from foreign countries. There are about 9,000,000 families in Britain, so that our imported food is worth about 10s. per week per family of the population. This helps one to realise what a tax of 10 per cent., or even 5 per cent., on imported food would mean to large numbers of our people.

**FOREIGN INVESTMENTS**—*See* Oversea Investments

**FRANCE**—France has an area about twice as great as ours, and a population rather smaller—about 40,000,000. Having more area and a much better climate, she is more easily able to grow her own food, and only in years of bad harvest has need to import much wheat. She has an excellent geographical position and seaboard, but is comparatively poor in coal. Her Customs tariff is Protectionist, and her commerce and shipping have been somewhat stationary. The following figures show the degree and nature of her commerce in recent years:

COMMERCE OF FRANCE

(In Millions of £)

| | Imports for Home Consumption | | Exports of French Produce | |
|---|---|---|---|---|
| | 1900 | 1907 | 1900 | 1907 |
| Food ... ... | 32·8 | 41·5 | 30·8 | 29·9 |
| Raw materials ... | 121·4 | 160·5 | 43·4 | 60·3 |
| Manufactures ... | 33·7 | 46·9 | 90·2 | 133·7 |
| Total ... ... | 187·9 | 248·9 | 164·3 | 223·8 |

It is remarkable that as long ago as 1875—thirty-four years ago—French imports amounted to £141,000,000 and French exports to £155,000,000. There has been a little progress in the last ten years, but there was plenty of room for it.

In spite of her tariff France imports, it will be seen, nearly £47,000,000 of manufactures per annum. (*See also* IMPORTS, COMPARATIVE, and EXPORTS, COMPARATIVE, POPULATIONS, &c.)

**FREE TRADE**—In its political sense Free Trade simply means the *absence of import or export duties of a Protective character.* These words should be carefully considered. Free Trade does not mean the absence of Customs duties, but the absence of *Protective* Customs duties. That is to say, it is opposed to Customs duties designed to favour private or sectional interests, or designed to create entire or partial monopolies in the home market. It is not that Free Trade means opposition to Government interference in trade, or opposition to the idea that Governments ought to help trade. Thus we find modern Free Traders, who have happily sloughed off the idea that opposition to Protective duties necessarily involves opposition to every sort of Government interference, actively engaged in promoting British trade interests by such measures as the Lloyd George Patent law and the Development and Road Improvements Fund Act of 1909. These measures directly assist trade, but they do not, by the stupid and roundabout process of taxing imported competitive articles, deliver the nation over, bound hand and foot, to the mercy of private monopolists.

To illustrate in the concrete, the Free Trader believes that it is the duty of the Government to foster agriculture. He regards as legitimate means to that end public expenditure upon agricultural education, agricultural research, the establishment of agricultural experimental stations or farms for the improvement of strains of plants or animals, the afforestation of suitable districts to improve climate and to foster local industries which, in their turn, react upon agriculture, the construction of improved roads, or the making of light railways. He knows that all these things can be wisely done, and that all of them will not raise but lower the price of food. Public money is spent in the process, but no private individual is set up to tax his fellow-countrymen.

Contrast the process of Protection. The Protectionist would assist agriculture by the dubious process of making imported food dearer in order to enable the home producer to get more for his food in the market. What does that mean? It means that the Government would only get the taxes collected at the ports on the imported food. The agricultural interest, by raising its prices behind the tariff wall, would be in a position to tax, as a private tax-collector, every eater of food. Thus, agriculture would be assisted, but assisted most improperly, not by creating agricultural efficiency, but by giving British agriculture monopoly.

In a wider sense, Free Trade is the work not of the statesman but of the engineer. That is to say, the contribution of the statesman towards Free Trade can only be *the decision not to impose protective duties.* The contribution of the engineer, on the other hand, is not negative but positive. The engineer, by levelling a road, cutting a canal, tunnelling a mountain, making a railway, or constructing a ship, creates the possibility of trade, and by every improvement in these devices which he invents establishes Free Trade on a surer foundation.

Surveying the activities of mankind as a whole from the earliest times, progress is seen largely to be the triumph of the engineer over Natural Protection. While man possessed only man-power, horse-power, and inefficient ships, his statesmen could at best give him freedom to enjoy such imports as he could gain through the agency of these poor means of transport. The invention of the railway and the steamship made Free Trade a reality, and for ever reduced the idea of Protection to an absurdity. *Protection now represents an attempt to make ineffective the work of the engineer.*

Free Trade negatives one particular form of Government interference. It is opposed to the idea that a Customs officer should, by levying at the ports duties on products which are also produced in the country, give to the private producers concerned the power to tax their fellow-countrymen. It considers that such a system amounts to the resignation of the powers of taxation and monopoly (which should be wielded by the State alone) from the State to the individual.

Economically, Free Trade leads to the devotion of the powers of a nation to those tasks which it is best fitted to perform, since, in view of the absence of Protective duties, no private interest can establish an unsuitable or uneconomic industry at the expense of the nation. The economic reason why a nation has imports is the economic reason why the reader of these lines did not make his own hat or boots. Just as the reader buys or imports a hat in exchange for some other work which he does, and which he can perform better than he can make a hat himself, so the individuals forming our nation import from other nations, by virtue of individual transactions, products which, for divers economic reasons, are secured in greater abundance or in more suitable form *through not producing them at home*, but through buying them *by means of other work done at home which we are better fitted to do.* (*See also* PROTECTION.)

**FRUIT**—At present all fruit except dried currants and raisins (which are taxed for revenue purposes only) are imported free of duty, unless it is preserved with sugar, when it is taxable under the Tory sugar duty, half of which was remitted by the present Free Trade Government. In 1908,

£10,372,000 worth of fruit was imported free of duty. Mr. Chamberlain did not propose to tax any of this, but it should be carefully noted that Mr. Chamberlain's Tariff "Commission" (par. 387 of their report) propose a duty of 5 to 10 per cent. on fruit, and apparently they do not even suggest that Colonial fruit, such as Canadian apples, should come in untaxed. The Free Trader has thus even to fight for untaxed fruit.

**FURNITURE**—Owing to differences of taste, &c., the larger part by far of the furniture used in all countries is made at home. Our commerce in furniture is therefore small:

BRITISH COMMERCE IN FURNITURE AND CABINET WARE

| | Imports for Home Consumption (c.i.f.). £ | Exports of British Make (f.o.b.). £ |
|---|---|---|
| 1900 (good year) ... | ... Not known ... | ... 637,000 |
| 1907 (good year) ... | ... 543,000 ... | ... 802,000 |
| 1908 (bad year) ... | ... 423,000 ... | ... 662,000 |

The great growth of the home trade in furniture, while it cannot be measured by value, can be traced in part through the importations of furniture woods. In 1887 95,000 tons of furniture woods were imported; in 1907 the quantity imported was 260,000 tons—an increase of 200 per cent. in 20 years.

**GERMANY**—Germany is an Empire consisting of four kingdoms, eleven duchies, seven principalities, the territory of Alsace-Lorraine, and the three free ports of Hamburg, Bremen, and Lübeck. The kingdom of Prussia covers more than one-half the German area of 208,800 square miles, and the Prussian population includes about 38,000,000 out of its total population of 63,000,000. Germany is not favoured in seaboard like the United Kingdom, but, on the other hand, her central position in Europe and her fine national railway system, with freights and advantages much more favourable than those which obtain on our private railways, enable her pushful traders to beat us in some of the Continental trade.

Germany is one of the three great coal countries, and she is also rich in iron, zinc, and copper. She has magnificent forests, which she has carefully conserved. As the railways are national, canals have not been neglected, but developed into a fine auxiliary system of transport.

So far as internal trade is concerned, the German now enjoys more Free Trade than the Briton; but this has only been the case in recent years.

The progress of Germany in the last generation represents an emergence out of absolute Protection of the most absurd character into a condition of comparative Free Trade. A century ago Germany was divided into about 200 States with high protective duties against each other, and with different systems of coinage and weights and measures. In 1833 a Customs Union was formed, but coinage and weights and measures remained unreformed, and not until 1868 did internal Free Trade become really effective. The three great ports of Hamburg, Bremen, and Lübeck did not join the Customs Union respectively until 1866, 1888, and 1889.

Germany, the honest Tariff Reformer feels, has undoubtedly been making rapid strides where of old she did little or nothing. She has had a protective tariff since the eighties. *Ergo*, the charmingly simple argument runs, the tariff has done it. It would, of course, be just as logical to attribute the stationariness of Spain or Russia or the backwardness of Portugal entirely to the fact that these countries practise Protection.

The German nation has made, in an incredibly short space of time, almost unparalleled advance, but the better the circumstances of the case are understood, the less this will be found surprising. The bound forward which Germany has made simply represents the long-delayed development in peace of a great people whose soil has been for about 270 years, or, say, nine generations, the cockpit of war. A cultured German gentleman remarked to me not long ago that Germany is only just recovering from the effects of the Thirty Years' War. This may be regarded as somewhat of an exaggeration in view of the dates of that war—1618–1648—

but the more closely German history is studied the less exaggerated it will appear. Germany's position in the heart of Europe made her a constant battle-ground, and until recent times she was "a geographical expression." The awful Thirty Years' War left her prostrate, halved her population, razed many of her towns, made deserts of great districts, paralysed her trade, and, worst of all, took the spirit out of her people. At the end of the seventeenth century very little recovery had been made, and in the eighteenth century, while Prussia had developed, Germany as a whole grew weaker, and, if possible, more disunited. Then came Napoleon and the disastrous years ending in the Treaty of Tilsit. After the fall of Napoleon Germany remained torn by internal dissensions, and by the jealousies of Prussia and Austria. Germany was not a nation, but a collection of scores of weak and petty States, each practising High Protection against the other. Thus during many generations, while Britain enjoyed internal peace and unity, Germany's strength was exhausted in ways that utterly prevented the display of the great gifts which she possessed. Not until 1833 was Free Trade set up between the States of Prussia and Bavaria. During the first half of the nineteenth century it is the fact that Germany had declined in trade and industry from the point to which she had attained before the outbreak of the Thirty Years' War in 1618, when the celebrated Hanse cities were world-centres of trade.

In the sixties rose Bismarck. In 1866 he gave Prussia a decisive victory over Austria, and decided the leadership of the German people. Then came the final cementing in "blood and iron" through the Franco-German War in 1870, when Napoleon III. found to his astonishment South Germany one with Prussia in the fight. The Prussian King was proclaimed German Emperor in January, 1871, and at last Germany was united, and with the frontier secured by her mighty army, at peace to develop. A people great in the arts, in music, in literature, in philosophy, in science, and in war, were, so to speak, slipped from the leash. If they had not progressed it would indeed have been astonishing. There was blundering at first. The 5,000,000,000 francs paid over by France within the few years after 1871, and paid sooner than was expected, swept over Germany, as Bismarck himself puts it, "like a waterspout." There was wild extension of industry and mad speculation, something like that of our South Sea Bubble days, ending in inevitable disaster and collapse. Wages fell heavily, and there was a large amount of unemployment. Recovery began in 1879, and has since continued, and Germany has cause to be proud of what she has done since then in every department of industry and research, or, as perhaps I ought to say, research and industry.

Tariff "Reformers" have been known to attribute the whole of the progress made to the fact that Germany enacted a moderate Protective tariff in 1879, which came into operation in January 1, 1880, but the real causes of German progress are to be found in far more important factors, which may be thus summed up:—

1. The gifts of the people themselves, at last set free;
2. Continuous peace, untroubled even by such external wars as we have constantly waged;
3. The development of her wonderful supplies of coal and iron.
4. The scientific education and technical training of her people.
5. The development of the nationalised railways, which actually give Germany more internal Free Trade than is possessed by Britain;
6. The State compulsory insurance system, which has had an enormous influence upon German work by giving security to German workers, and which has prevented some of the worse evils of poverty;
7. The discovery by Thomas, the Englishman, of the method of utilising phosphoric iron ore, which gave value to Germany's great ore deposits of this character, beforetime useless;
8. The German quality of "thorough," which is really part of number 1;
9. Last, but perhaps not least, the fact that German cities have possessed municipal Home Rule, *i.e.*, have

> been free to do what they pleased for the good of their cities without going cap in hand to Parliament for leave to run a tramway, or to buy land, or to build houses, or to do any other good and useful thing.

It is not a little curious that the year 1879, which was the date of the Protectionist tariff, was also the date of Sydney Thomas's invention of the basic steel process, and the date of the beginning of active German railway nationalisation. Only two years later William I. sent his famous message to the Reichstag on the subject of organising State insurance. We, in 1909, are only just about to do for the workman what the Germans began twenty-eight years ago, and as for railway nationalisation, which I regard as one of the chief things which has made German industry, we seem no nearer to getting rid of the private railway shareholder than when Gladstone passed his Railway Act in the forties.

No intelligent man who considers all these facts, and especially no man who assists his intelligence by visiting and studying modern Germany, can again be so foolish as to compare Britain and Germany with regard to fiscal policy only. The wise man will find in Germany, not an examplar of tariffs, but a gifted exponent of what can be achieved by science, education, and thoroughness.

And something must be attributed to German "pushfulness." It is a point which may be strikingly illustrated in the concrete. In 1908 as many as 7,097 foreign commercial travellers visited Switzerland. How many of these came from the United Kingdom? The Swiss records show that just 61 British commercial travellers attempted to sell goods in Switzerland in 1908.

Let us see where the others came from. I find that 4,711 came from Germany; 1,531 from France; 1,405 from Italy; 248 from Austria-Hungary; 85 from Belgium. Britain is thus a bad sixth in the record.

What is the explanation? Switzerland is a delightful place which possesses national railways. Cheap circular tickets can be bought (at the well-appointed office in Pall Mall) at prices which astonish the British traveller, accustomed to a higher scale of charges. The Swiss peoples are exceedingly well disposed towards us. It is perfectly true that the German, the Frenchman, or the Austrian has not to take a sea passage to reach Switzerland; but can this be considered a satisfactory explanation of the extraordinary disparity between 4,711 German travellers and 61 British ones?

The reader will not be surprised to learn, after the figures just given, that Germany is the chief exporter to the Swiss market. The details under this head are of considerable interest:

SWITZERLAND: IMPORTS AND TRAVELLERS' VISITS

| | Imports into Switzerland 1906 Million Francs | Commercial Travellers visiting Switzerland 1908 |
|---|---|---|
| Germany | 482 | 4,711 |
| France | 360 | 1,531 |
| Italy | 204 | 1,405 |
| Austria-Hungary | 93 | 248 |
| Belgium | 29 | 85 |
| United Kingdom | 84 | 61 |
| Holland | 7 | 32 |
| Spain | 6 | 9 |
| U.S.A. | 58 | 4 |
| Total above and all other countries | 1,554 | 7,097 |

It will be seen that Britain is sixth in the travellers' record and fifth in the import record. Of course, trade is not directly proportionate to travellers' visits, but, on the whole, there is an unmistakable correspondence between the figures in the respective columns. Germany stands out as the most pushful country. She sends more commercial travellers to Switzerland in a year than France, Italy, and Austria put together, and she does nearly as much trade in Switzerland as France and Italy put together. America stands out as the least pushful, and her exports to Switzerland are only as large as they are because she is a seller of cotton and other things which do not need pushing.

(The imports in the table are the latest for which I have details, but I have followed the Swiss commercial traveller returns for some years and know that in 1906 the proportions of travellers from various countries were much the same as in 1908.)

The reader will see from the above table that Germany's progress in European markets is not undeserved. She has to meet precisely the same duties that we have to meet. Switzerland applies the same tariff to Germany that she applies to ourselves. True it is that to the German a visit to Switzerland is as commonplace as a journey within the confines of the Fatherland. True it is also that the German national railway system makes exportation to Switzerland a much simpler matter than it is to us. When this is said, however, this Swiss record remains an indictment of British enterprise which calls seriously for the attention of the traders concerned.

Fortunately, I am able to add a practical note which may be of use to many British traders. I am indebted to Mr. George Gifford, United States Consul at Basle, for an analysis of the dealings of the commercial travellers who visited Switzerland in 1908. Here it is:

COMMERCIAL TRAVELLERS VISITING SWITZERLAND

| Merchandise | Total Number of Travellers | Number of German Travellers |
|---|---|---|
| Textiles | 1,948 | 1,305 |
| Machinery | 187 | 149 |
| Metals | 771 | 644 |
| Jewellery, clocks, watches | 305 | 188 |
| Hardware | 378 | 281 |
| Food products | 833 | 245 |
| Leather, boots, shoes | 314 | 226 |
| Glass | 118 | 81 |
| Paper, literature, art | 762 | 566 |
| Pottery, cement | 128 | 76 |
| Chemicals, drugs, perfumery, colours, wood | 376 | 261 |
| Grease | 272 | 230 |
| Fertilisers | 93 | 36 |
| Rubber | 11 | 5 |
| Total above and other | 7,097 | 4,711 |

I particularly invite those who believe German progress to be due to tariffs to ponder these hard facts. I further invite the British trader to reflect, if sixty-one British commercial travellers can do some £3,000,000 worth of trade with Switzerland in a year, how much more might be done if we profited in this particular by German example.

The nature of German commerce is analysed in the following table:

COMMERCE OF GERMANY

(In Millions of £)

| | Imports for Home Consumption | | Exports of German Produce | |
|---|---|---|---|---|
| | 1900 | 1907 | 1900 | 1907 |
| Food ... ... ... | 86·7 | 119·5 | 25·5 | 26·6 |
| Raw Materials ... ... | 137·8 | 218·0 | 54·6 | 73·8 |
| Manufactures ... ... | 59·0 | 92·5 | 146·6 | 236·4 |
| Total ... ... | 283·5 | 430·0 | 226·7 | 336·8 |

Germany, it will be seen, is a large and growing importer of food. She is also a considerable exporter of raw materials, exporting £73,800,000 worth in 1907 against our £52,578,000. Her exports of manufactures have grown considerably. (*See also* EXPORTS, COMPARATIVE.)

Germany, in spite of her great progress, is still a much poorer country than the United Kingdom. Thus, in Prussia, the official Income Tax returns show that out of her 38,000,000 people as many as 21,000,000 belong to families which are excused from paying Income Tax, because they are below the Income Tax line of £45 a year or 17s. 3d. per week. As to German wages, *see* WAGES, COMPARATIVE.

With such a low scale of incomes it will be understood how bitterly the Germans feel their oppressive food duties (*see* WHEAT and MEAT for details of these). The Social Democrats of Germany, by far the largest German political party, wage constant war on the taxes on necessaries of life. Their opinions may be gathered from the following extract from the Election Manifesto of the Social Democratic Party, issued in connection with the elections to the Reichstag in 1907. It was published in *Vorwaerts* on December 16, 1906, and signed by 78 Socialist Members of the Reichstag:

"The Government policy of taxing and excluding foreign imports, supported hitherto by an Agrarian majority in the Reichstag, has introduced an unprecedented rise in the cost of necessaries, especially of meat. This policy throws over 50 millions a year into the laps of our Agrarians at the expense of the non-Agrarian population. This policy means not only continually dearer food, but increasingly dearer food, because the population of Germany increases about a million annually, and the production of food within the Empire cannot keep pace with it. While the Agrarian chiefs reap gigantic profits, and are in the seventh heaven of delight, want and misery come into millions of the German families. The pieces of meat on the tables of our workmen, of our lower middle classes, and of the lower official classes grow smaller and smaller, and hundreds of thousands cease to eat meat at all. The result is chronic underfeeding of millions of human beings, with all that it implies in the diminution of physical strength and incapacity for effort, the multiplication of illnesses, and the shortening of lives. At the same time, the Budgets of the State and Local Authorities are rapidly swollen by increased expenditure on poor relief, on hospitals, on infirmaries, on prisons of all kinds, and on maintaining soldiers and sailors; and that in turn means a further rise in the duties. Not only meat, but bread, butter, eggs, and, above all, milk—the principal food of our children—have risen greatly in price already, and the leaders of the Agrarian organisations are already considering how they can further take advantage of the situation in order to make life still harder for the poor and the very poor in town and country. If another great crisis comes the misery of the masses that proceeds from the maintenance of our Agrarian Protectionist policy will be beyond all computation. If you do not wish the hunger whip of the Agrarian chiefs swung yet further over your heads and the heads of your families, elect representatives who will make an end of this starvation policy."

It only remains to add that each successive election in Germany shows a great gain in the votes of the party opposing food duties. The latest news (1909) is of more Socialist victories at German by-elections. This fact should be pondered by the British Protectionists who represent their "Tariff Reform" as an *alternative to Socialism.* (*See also* IMPORTS, COMPARATIVE, EXPORTS, COMPARATIVE, POPULATION, RURAL DEPOPULATION, WAGES, BREAD, MEAT, IRON AND STEEL, etc.)

**GLADSTONE, THE RIGHT HON. W. E.**—Elsewhere, under TARIFF REFORM, I remind the reader that true Tariff Reform may be said to have commenced in 1842. The revision of the Customs Tariff in that year, under Peel, was really the sole work of Mr. Gladstone. Out of some 1,200 duties as many as 750 were either abolished or reduced. The harassing taxes upon raw materials were made low or nominal; the duties on partly manufactured articles were reduced to a point not exceeding 12 per cent. *ad valorem;* the duties on manufactured goods were reduced to a point not exceeding 20 per cent. Mr. Gladstone showed extraordinary ability in putting such an enormous mass of detail through the House of Commons in Committee, and when the Bill was passed in June, 1842, he had shown that a master of finance had arisen in the State. Mr. Gladstone did not take an active part in the debates on the Repeal of the Corn Laws, but 1853 found him in office as Chancellor of the Exchequer, abolishing unproductive duties, and generally continuing the movement towards absolute Free Trade. Mr. Gladstone's first Budget was introduced on May 18, 1853, when he passed, amidst the execrations of the Tory party, the Succession Duties which were the foundation of our existing Death Duties. This Budget reduced the duties on 250 articles, including tea, butter, cheese, cocoa, fruit, and soap.

But it was the great Budget of 1860 which was Mr. Gladstone's financial masterpiece. In the words of Mr. Pittars' official history of the "Customs Tariffs of the United Kingdom," this Act "carried the process of the simplification of the tariff almost to the extremest limit of which it was susceptible." It reduced our Customs tariff to twenty-six generic denominations, of which ten, viz., those on beer, cards, chicory, dice, essence of spruce, hops, malt, paper, vinegar, and plate, were solely for the purpose of countervailing duties of Excise on the like articles produced in the United Kingdom, while two others, those on corks and hats, were to disappear at fixed dates. The remaining fourteen articles were retained in the tariff for revenue purposes only, and whilst in 1859–60 the Customs revenue was £24,460,000, in the following year, notwithstanding the reductions, it only fell by about £1,200,000.

It was the Budget of 1860 which carried out the Cobden Commercial Treaty with France. There were not wanting, of course, those who said that this treaty indicated subserviency to France, but we may note that Mr. Gladstone held that the alterations in the British tariff consequent upon the treaty would be beneficial to the United Kingdom even if nothing were to be received in exchange.

It should also be pointed out that in this same year, 1860, Mr. Gladstone's attempt to repeal the paper Excise duty, with its complement the paper Customs duty, was foiled by the House of Lords, and that Mr. Gladstone defeated the Lords by including the repeal of the paper duty in his Budget of 1861, challenging them to accept the entire Finance Bill or to reject the entire Finance Bill, paper duty repeal and all. This was the origin of the combination of all the financial measures of one year in a single Bill. The Lords in 1861 dared not continue their opposition to the repeal of the taxes on knowledge, and Mr. Gladstone won his case. Since then, until the Budget of 1909, the House of Lords has made no attempt to interfere with the financial provisions of the House of Commons.

The whirligig of time brings about its revenges, and when in 1909 I have so frequently heard Mr. Gladstone's finance held up as a sort of white background upon which to limn the fiscal depredations and heresies of Mr. Lloyd George, I have recalled to mind the virulence of the language which assailed Mr. Gladstone while he accomplished his great work.

**GLASS**—Glass is one of the few branches of manufacture in which our imports exceed our exports, signifying that it is an industry in which, on the whole (not by any means in all branches) we are inferior.

BRITISH COMMERCE IN GLASS

| | | Imports for Home Consumption (c.i.f.) | | Exports of British Make (f.o.b.) |
|---|---|---|---|---|
| | | £ | | £ |
| 1900 (good year) | ... | 2,488,000 | ... | 1,033,000 |
| 1907 (good year) | ... | 3,967,000 | ... | 1,400,000 |
| 1908 (bad year) | ... | 3,615,000 | ... | 1,355,000 |

An inquirer who desires to know why Britain is behind in some branches of the glass trade should read the report made by Mr. Frederick Carder at the request of the Staffordshire County Council Technical Instruction Committee. In 1902 Mr. Carder toured the glass-making districts of Germany and Austria. He shows that the Continental makers deserve their success because their machinery and their methods are so much better than ours. To name two points. At Ehrenfeld, near Cologne, he found machinery melting the tops of wine glasses at 3,000 an hour. Again, the Austrian and German makers work with regenerative gas furnaces, instead of by direct firing with coal as in England, so that they have greater control of temperature.

These hard facts, and many more that might be named, will show how futile it is to trust to duties and not to skill and enterprise.

**GOLD**—Although this country produces only a few ounces of gold a year, many Protectionists still believe that we pay for our imports in gold, and speeches are often made in which by implication money is pictured to be pouring out of the country. As a matter of fact, it is very rarely that a year passes in which our exports of the precious metals exceed our imports. Thus, in the sixteen years 1893–1908, our exports of gold and silver exceeded our imports of gold and silver in only four years, and in that period imports have exceeded exports enormously. In the ten years 1898–1907 we imported on balance £47,000,000 worth of gold and silver.

The following table exhibits the British imports and exports of gold and silver for the last fifty years:

GOLD AND SILVER; BRITISH IMPORTS AND EXPORTS.

| Years | GOLD | | | | SILVER | | | |
|---|---|---|---|---|---|---|---|---|
| | Imports | Exports | Excess of Imports | Excess of Exports | Imports | Exports | Excess of Imports | Excess of Exports |
| Average. | Mill. £ | Mill. £ | Mill. £ | Mill. £ | Mill. £ | Mill. £ | Mill. £ | Mill. £ |
| 1860–4 | 16·1 | 14·3 | 1·8 | — | 10·1 | 10·8 | — | 0·7 |
| 1865–9 | 16·9 | 10·0 | 6·9 | — | 8·0 | 7·4 | 0·6 | — |
| 1870–4 | 19·5 | 16·0 | 3·5 | — | 12·7 | 10·9 | 1·8 | — |
| 1875–9 | 19·2 | 17·6 | 1·6 | — | 13·5 | 12·8 | 0·7 | — |
| 1880–4 | 10·4 | 11·7 | — | 1·3 | 8·4 | 8·4 | — | — |
| 1885–9 | 13·8 | 12·9 | 0·9 | — | 8·0 | 8·6 | — | 0·6 |
| 1890–4 | 25·6 | 17·7 | 7·9 | — | 10·7 | 12·7 | — | 2·0 |
| 1895–9 | 33·5 | 28·1 | 5·4 | — | 14·1 | 14·7 | — | 0·6 |
| 1900–4 | 26·2 | 21·7 | 4·5 | — | 11·3 | 12·2 | — | 0·9 |
| 1905 | 38·5 | 30·8 | 7·7 | — | 13·0 | 14·5 | — | 1·5 |
| 1906 | 46·0 | 42·6 | 3·4 | — | 17·2 | 18·8 | — | 1·6 |
| 1907 | 57·1 | 50·9 | 6·2 | — | 15·9 | 16·9 | — | 1·0 |
| 1908 | 46·1 | 49·9 | — | 3·8 | 10·3 | 13·3 | — | 3·0 |
| Average. 1905–8 | 46·9 | 43·6 | 3·3 | — | 14·1 | 15·9 | — | 1·8 |

It will be seen that it is quite an exceptional thing for exports of the precious metals to exceed imports.

Gold is only used in settlement of transactions in international trade on the rare occasions when it is cheaper to remit gold than to send a Bill of Exchange. (*See* Bill of Exchange.)

**HAMILTON, LORD GEORGE**—Lord George Hamilton, Unionist and Free Trader, was Chairman of the recent Royal Commission on the Poor Laws, whose arduous labours have produced reports of so much interest and value. The majority report of the Chairman, and the minority report drawn up by Mr. and Mrs. Sidney Webb, differed in many things, but agreed in this, that they ignored the fiscal question in proposing remedies for unemployment. That there was good reason for this will be understood from the discussion of the subject under UNEMPLOYMENT, *which see.* Speaking at Acton on November 12, 1908, Lord George Hamilton said: "I have seen a number of vans set out from Westminster bearing the words 'Tariff Reform means work for all unemployed, and a reduction of the income tax.' The Poor Law Commission over which I presided have made the most exhaustive inquiries into the causes of unemployment. It is an *absolute delusion* to suppose that we could ever remove them by any fiscal alterations."

**HARDWARE**—The various departments of the hardware trade chiefly supply the home market, but there is a considerable oversea trade:

BRITISH COMMERCE IN HARDWARE

| | Imports for Home Consumption (c.i.f.) £ | Exports of British Make (f.o.b.) £ |
|---|---|---|
| 1900 (good year) ... | ... 640,000 ... | ... 1,500,000 |
| 1907 (good year) ... | ... 895,000 ... | ... 2,540,000 |
| 1908 (bad year) ... | ... 890,000 ... | ... 2,159,000 |

Under Protection the British hardware trade would suffer from dear materials and increased standing charges. The price of metals and the price of machinery would rise, which would more than set off higher prices if charged by hardware makers, to say nothing of the fact that dearer hardware would mean diminished consumption and decreased exporting power.

**HARNESS TRADE**—*See* SADDLERY AND HARNESS.

**HATS**—The consumption of hats in the United Kingdom is of very great value, and only an exceedingly small part of it is of foreign make. There is a considerable export trade, about six times as large as the import:

BRITISH COMMERCE IN HATS

| | Imports for Home Consumption (c.i.f.) | Exports of British Make (f.o.b.) |
|---|---|---|
| | £ | £ |
| 1900 (good year) ... | ... 171,000 ... | ... 1,212,000 |
| 1907 (good year) ... | ... 370,000 ... | ... 1,543,000 |
| 1908 (bad year) ... | ... 273,000 ... | ... 1,503,000 |

The British hat trade, whether the felt hat trade of Stockport or the straw hat trade of Luton, would be severely hit by Protection. All the materials it uses, including felt, velvet, plush, shellac, cloth, straw-plait, silk, satin, ribbons, chenille, crinoline, linings, bindings, thread, &c., are manufactured. As they would be taxed under Protection, and consequently raised in price, the hat-maker would be injured both in his home and export trade; in the home trade because the necessarily raised price of hats would diminish consumption, and in the export trade because the increased cost of production would lose us our markets.

British cotton yarn is exported to Germany and bought by the German silk weaver as a warp upon which to weave his silk ribbons or galloons. The British hat-maker in turn imports from Germany the silk galloons, woven on British cotton warp, to trim his British hats. Such are the complications of modern industry, expressing the interdependence of nations and the "territorial division of labour," as Free Trade has been aptly termed. It is with such division of labour that Protection would blindly interfere.

**HOPS**—The agitation for a duty on hops varies in strength with the fluctuations of the crop from year to year. Before the Hop Committee of 1908 the growers demanded a duty of not less than 40s. per cwt. Mr. Chamberlain's Tariff "Commission" recommend a small duty as of 5 to 10 per cent. Mr. Chamberlain, however, proposed no duty on hops, and he distinctly promised not to tax raw materials. Hops form a brewers' raw material, and we see that under Protection no material would be safe from taxation. As a matter of fact, foreign competition in the hop market has not increased, and on the average the home growers already possess the greater part of the market. What the hop-growers want to do, of course, is to raise prices; as the Hop Committee reported to the House of Commons:

"The object of the proposed duty, they explained frankly, was to raise the price of the home produce."

So that the hop-growers very sensibly believe that the foreigner does *not* pay the import duty.

**HOSIERY**—There is considerable foreign competition in the hosiery trade:

BRITISH COMMERCE IN HOSIERY

| Year. | Cotton Hosiery | | Woollen Hosiery | |
|---|---|---|---|---|
| | Imports for Home Consumption (c.i.f.) | Exports of British Make (f.o.b.) | Imports for Home Consumption (c.i.f.) | Exports of British Make (f.o.b.) |
| | £ | £ | £ | £ |
| 1900 (good year) | 576,000 | 394,000 | Not known | 899,000 |
| 1907 (good year) | 1,206,000 | 522,000 | 262,000 | 1,486,000 |
| 1908 (bad year) | 1,334,000 | 424,000 | 300,000 | 1,276,000 |

In cotton hosiery, imports exceed exports: in woollen hosiery, exports exceed imports.

Before Mr. Chamberlain's Tariff "Commission" a number of hosiery manufacturers suggested duties varying from 10 per cent. to 33 per cent. and upwards. One firm spoke of 60 per cent. on gloves, and another of 35 per cent. on stockings, another firm quoted with approval the *Nottingham Guardian*, "If our trade is to be conserved we must have not merely a protective duty but a prohibitive one." The Tariff "Commission" made no recommendation, but it is quite clear that Mr. Chamberlain's "10 per cent." would not satisfy those who desire to bestow upon us the gift of dear hosiery. Given effective methods, it should not be more difficult to hold our own in cotton hosiery than to hold it in cotton spinning and manufacturing, and we cannot afford to give duties to hosiery manufacturers to help their trade while ruining the cotton trade generally.

**HOURS OF LABOUR**—In the Fiscal Blue Book for 1903 the Board of Trade pointed out that not only are Continental wages lower than British wages, but that the lower wages are earned in longer hours. The Board of Trade say: "Generally speaking, the countries compared stand in the following order as regards the length of the current hours of labour: Germany, France, United States, United Kingdom." Thus of the four leading industrial nations Britain has the shortest hours of labour. The Saturday half-holiday, a commonplace here, is unknown on the Continent.

**IMPLEMENTS**—*See* Tools.

**IMPORT DUTIES, INCIDENCE OF**—In the general case, and in the long run, import duties are paid by the consumers of the importing country. They are an element in price, just as much as cost of material, or cost of freight, or cost of labour. This is universally recognised in the practice of all business men and in the practice of all Protectionist Governments. It ought not to be necessary to support such a common-sense proposition as that here laid down by the weight of authority, but it may be useful to quote the opinion of our most distinguished economist, Professor Alfred Marshall, as stated in his memorandum, "Fiscal Policy of International Trade," published as a House of Commons paper in 1908. Professor Marshall says:

"It is my opinion that, in nearly all important cases, import duties are borne almost exclusively by the consumer. But there is no absolute rule in the matter. Cases can be conceived on a large scale, and have actually existed on a small scale, in which a perceptible part of the burden of an import duty is borne by foreigners. And, of course, a part of the pressure of every new tax of whatever kind is apt to rest temporarily on producers, merchants, shippers, and others, until they are able to shift it to its permanent resting-place on the shoulders of consumers."

*De minimis non curat lex*, and a Government, in making laws, must have regard to the general case, and not to the exceptional instance which proves the general case. As I have said, all foreign Governments recognise the general case as stated at the beginning of this article.

For example, the American Government, under Section 25 of the new Payne Tariff, continuing the provisions of the Dingley Tariff, repays to American exporters 99 per cent. of any import duty which has been paid upon any raw or manufactured dutiable material incorporated in exported articles. That is to say, they recognise that the American import duties are paid by American citizens, and not by foreigners. Under the Dingley Tariff millions of dollars have been returned every year to American citizens in this way.

Most other countries adopt the same practice. France, for example, returns to a French file maker the steel duty if he shows on export that he has made his files out of imported steel.

The Protectionist who understands Protection, indeed, is a Protectionist because he has the assurance that in the general case the consumer and not the foreigner pays the duty. Thus, when the German Government introduced the last German tariff, in 1902, they published with it, as is their custom, a printed *explanation of the reasons for its introduction.* In this they said:

"A means whereby the agricultural interests are enabled to cover their cost of production is to be found, under the given circumstances, by *creating a factor which will determine the inland selling price through relative Protective duties. . . . Inland prices are raised*, so far as a consideration of the circumstances of the last ten years will allow us to judge, *in proportion to the duties.* This is seen from the following tables . . ."

The tables showed, amongst other things, that the Berlin price of wheat in the years 1889–1900 was higher than the

London price of wheat by about the amount of the wheat duty. The German Government memorandum went on to say :

> " These tables show that the difference between the inland price and the price of foreign wheat (exclusive of duty) *varies according to the amount of duty.* It is therefore to be expected that a raising of duties will favourably affect our internal agricultural interests."

So that the policy which is said by Protectionists here not to raise price, *in Germany is introduced deliberately with the purpose of raising price.*

A moment's consideration will show that *if the foreigner pays the import duty, there is no such thing as Protection.* For, if the foreigner pays the duty, and the price of a taxed competitive article is not raised by the duty, the foreign competition remains where it was before the duty was imposed, and the home producer stands precisely where he did before the duty was imposed. This ought to be so obvious that it is surprising that Protectionists can at one and the same time (1) complain of foreign under-selling, (2) claim Protective duties as a relief from that under-selling, and (3) gravely tell the public that the foreigner will pay the duty.

**IMPORTS**—Imports are goods or products passing inwards over a political boundary line. The receipt of imports by a country is proof that that country has either exported goods to pay for them, or that it has rendered services (" invisible exports ") to pay for them, or that foreign capital has been invested in the country. (*See* EXPORTS.)

**IMPORTS AND UNEMPLOYMENT**—*See* UNEMPLOYMENT, COMPARATIVE.

**IMPORTS, COMPARATIVE**—The following table gives comparative imports for home consumption of ten nations :

IMPORTS FOR HOME CONSUMPTION

(In Millions of £)

| Nation | Year | Imports of Manufactures only | Total Imports | Percentage of Manufactures to Total Imports |
|---|---|---|---|---|
| United States ... ... | 1907 | 131 | 298 | 44 |
| United Kingdom ... ... | 1907 | 128 | 554 | 23 |
| Germany ... ... ... | 1907 | 88* | 430 | 21 |
| Italy ... ... ... ... | 1906 | 47 | 103 | 46 |
| France ... ... ... | 1907 | 47 | 249 | 19 |
| Austria-Hungary ... ... | 1906 | 44 | 98 | 45 |
| Holland ... ... ... | 1906 | 41 | 210 | 19 |
| Russia ... ... ... ... | 1906 | 35 | 85 | 41 |
| Switzerland ... ... ... | 1906 | 20 | 59 | 33 |
| Spain ... ... ... ... | 1906 | 11 | 40 | 28 |

* If classed as ours this figure would be higher.

These figures dispose of the common Protectionist belief that Britain is the only country which permits manufactures to be imported. The chief importer is America, we are second, and Germany is a close third.

On page 140 will be found an extended comparison of the four chief commercial nations in point of comparative imports. It should be borne in mind that the figures relating to comparative imports of manufactures are not strictly comparative, owing to differences of classification. It will be seen that both Britain and Germany have doubled their imports of manufactures since 1880–4, while America has also made a very great increase. France, although exhibiting increase in this respect, still imports but £45,000,000 or so of manufactures per annum. Thus the country of the four which is least progressive in commerce and industry has by far the smallest importation of manufactured articles. According to Protectionist reasoning she should be the most prosperous of the four nations.

In point of imports Britain is easily first, and as the sole object of exportation is to secure imports the success of British commerce could not be subjected to a truer criterion.

IMPORTS OF UNITED KINGDOM, FRANCE, GERMANY, AND UNITED STATES COMPARED

(In each case Imports for Home Consumption are stated)

| Years | United Kingdom | | | | France | | | | Germany | | | | United States | | | |
|---|---|---|---|---|---|---|---|---|---|---|---|---|---|---|---|---|
| | Total Imports | | Manufactures Only | | Total Imports | | Manufactures Only | | Total Imports | | Manufactures Only | | Total Imports | | Manufactures Only | |
| | Amount | Per Head | Amount | Per Head | Amount | Per Head | Amount | Per Head | Amount | Per Head | Amount | Per Head | Amount | Per Head | Amount | Per Head |
| | Mill. £ | £ s. d. | Mill. £ | £ s. d. | Mill. £ | £ s. d. | Mill. £ | £ s. d. | Mill. £ | £ s. d. | Mill. £ | £ s. d. | Mill. £ | £ s. d. | Mill. £ | £ s. d. |
| 1854 ... ... | 134 | 4 16 8 | 18 | 0 13 2 | 52 | 1 8 6 | Not | known | Not a | vailable | Not a | vailable | 57 | 2 3 5 | Not | known |
| Aver. 1855-9 ... | 146 | 5 3 8 | 18 | 0 12 6 | 69 | 1 18 2 | " | " | " | " | " | " | 59 | 2 0 10 | " | " |
| " 1860-4 ... | 194 | 6 12 9 | 26 | 0 18 0 | 92 | 2 9 2 | " | " | " | " | " | " | 55 | 1 13 4 | " | " |
| " 1865-9 ... | 238 | 7 16 3 | 38 | 1 4 9 | 119 | 3 2 5 | " | " | " | " | " | " | 73 | 2 0 0 | " | " |
| " 1870-4 ... | 291 | 9 2 4 | 48 | 1 9 10 | 136 | 3 14 4 | " | " | " | " | " | " | 113 | 2 15 9 | 59 | 1 9 2 |
| " 1875-9 ... | 319 | 9 10 4 | 59 | 1 15 4 | 160 | 4 6 4 | 22 | 0 12 2 | " | " | " | " | 96 | 2 1 6 | 40 | 0 17 4 |
| " 1880-4 ... | 344 | 9 15 3 | 65 | 1 16 9 | 191 | 5 1 2 | 28 | 0 14 11 | 152 | 3 7 2 | 43 | 0 18 11 | 140 | 2 13 4 | 66 | 1 5 1 |
| " 1885-9 ... | 319 | 8 14 2 | 67 | 1 16 6 | 166 | 4 6 10 | 24 | 0 12 5 | 160 | 3 7 7 | 43 | 0 18 3 | 139 | 2 7 6 | 64 | 1 1 9 |
| " 1890-4 ... | 357 | 9 7 1 | 76 | 1 19 8 | 169 | 4 8 0 | 25 | 0 12 10 | 199 | 3 18 10 | 44 | 0 17 5 | 163 | 2 10 0 | 66 | 1 0 5 |
| " 1895-9 ... | 393 | 9 16 5 | 94 | 2 7 2 | 164 | 4 4 8 | 25 | 0 13 0 | 233 | 4 6 6 | 49 | 0 18 3 | 145 | 2 0 8 | 58 | 0 16 3 |
| " 1900-4 ... | 466 | 11 2 2 | 113 | 2 14 1 | 182 | 4 13 3 | 32 | 0 16 7 | 287 | 4 19 0 | 57 | 0 19 8 | 186 | 2 7 1 | 79 | 0 19 11 |
| 1905 ... ... | 487 | — | 121 | — | 191 | — | 35 | — | 350 | — | 65 | — | 227 | — | 88 | — |
| 1906 ... ... | 523 | — | 130 | — | 225 | — | 40 | — | 394 | — | 82 | — | 250 | — | 108 | — |
| 1907 ... ... | 554 | — | 128 | — | 249 | — | 47 | — | 430 | — | 88 | — | 293 | — | 131 | — |
| 1908 ... ... | 513 | — | 120 | — | 226 | — | 45 | — | 377 | — | 76 | — | 243 | — | 108 | — |
| Aver. 1905-8 ... | 519 | 11 16 8 | 125 | 2 16 11 | 223 | 5 13 6 | 42 | 1 1 2 | 388 | 6 5 5 | 78 | 1 5 2 | 253 | 2 19 7 | 109 | 1 5 8 |

**INCOME TAX RETURNS**—The growth of British incomes and of British trading profits is shown by the official Income Tax returns of the Inland Revenue Commissioners to be as follows:

OFFICIAL ASSESSMENTS TO INCOME TAX

| Financial Years Ended March 31 | Profits of Trades and Professions Only Schedule D Millions of £ | Total Profits All Schedules Millions of £ |
|---|---|---|
| 1855 | 91 | 308 |
| Aver. 1856–60 | 91 | 322 |
| ,, 1861–5 | 107 | 363 |
| ,, 1866–70 | 166 | 429 |
| ,, 1871–5 | 227 | 515 |
| ,, 1876–80 | 259 | 576 |
| ,, 1881–5 | 277 | 612 |
| ,, 1886–90 | 298 | 642 |
| ,, 1891–5 | 357 | 707 |
| ,, 1896–1900 | 397 | 770 |
| ,, 1901–5 | 491 | 914 |
| 1906 | 509 | 960 |
| 1907 | 519 | 979 |
| 1908 | 519 | 982 |
| 1909 | 575 | 1,040 |

These remarkable figures call for little comment. They show how thoughtless is the common Protectionist statement that British trade is not as profitable as it used to be.

The figures *understate* growth, because in recent years the extension of the exemption limit has cut out incomes which of old were included in the statistics.

**INDIA**—Although India contains about three-fourths of the population of the British Empire, she found no place in Mr. Chamberlain's programme of preference and protection. India bulks very largely in British commerce, and it is important to observe that of her total imports in 1908, 178,783,000 tens of rupees, as much as Rx 116,660,000 worth was imported from the United Kingdom, chiefly in the form of manufactured articles. Protectionists have never yet told us what is their programme for India. It is clear that if we need Protection against foreign competition, India must need Protection against British competition. We are trustees for India's welfare, and if we adopt Protection without giving India import duties against ourselves, we shall be convicted of the rankest injustice. At present India has a Free Trade revenue tariff, but that can only remain while we are ourselves a Free Trade country. Protection means giving up a large share of the Indian market.

**INVISIBLE EXPORTS**—*See* EXPORTS.

**IRON AND STEEL**—In considering this important industry it should first of all be remembered that three countries are specially favoured by nature in respect of iron ore and coal:

WORLD'S IRON ORE PRODUCTION, 1906

| Nation | Tons | Per Cent. |
|---|---|---|
| United States ... ... | 47,750,000 | 37·97 |
| Germany ... ... ... | 26,735,000 | 21·26 |
| United Kingdom ... ... | 15,500,000 | 12·33 |
| America, Germany, and Britain together... ... | 89,985,000 | 71·56 |
| All the rest of the world | 35,775,000 | 28·44 |
| Total ... | 125,760,000 | 100·00 |

Thus America, Germany, and Britain together produce 7 out of every 10 tons of iron ore produced by all the world. By reference to coal it will be seen the same three nations produce 8 out of every 10 tons of the world's coal.

It naturally follows that the same three countries produce 7 to 8 tons out of every 10 tons of iron and steel produced by all the world. Fiscal policy can only modify these facts; it cannot materially alter them, for Protection cannot rob a country of its native coal and iron, or Free Trade confer native coal and iron upon a nation.

The broad progress of the British iron trade is exhibited in the accompanying table (page 143) headed "British Pig Iron Production," which gives the basic statistics for every year since 1873.

## BRITISH PIG IRON PRODUCTION

Table showing (1) Number of Furnaces in Blast, (2) Quantity of Pig Iron Produced, (3) Quantities of Ore and Coal used in its Production, and of Iron Ore Imported, and Price of Exported Pig Iron, 1873 to 1908

| Year | Furnaces in Blast | Pig Iron Produced | Total Iron Ore Used. British and Imported | Iron Ore Imported | Coal Used | Average Price of Exported Pig, f.o.b. |
|---|---|---|---|---|---|---|
| | Number | Tons | Tons | Tons | Tons | s. d. |
| 1873 | 683 | 6,566,000 | 16,820,000 | 968,000 | 16,718,000 | 124 3 |
| 1874 | 649 | 5,991,000 | 15,854,000 | 754,000 | 15,292,000 | 94 0 |
| 1875 | 629 | 6,365,000 | 16,560,000 | 459,000 | 15,646,000 | 72 6 |
| 1876 | 585 | 6,556,000 | 17,814,000 | 672,000 | 15,598,000 | 62 4 |
| 1877 | 541 | 6,609,000 | 18,250,000 | 1,142,000 | 15,342,000 | 57 3 |
| 1878 | 498 | 6,381,000 | 17,300,000 | 1,173,000 | 14,112,000 | 53 4 |
| 1879 | 497 | 5,995,000 | 15,797,000 | 1,085,000 | 13,117,000 | 51 6 |
| 1880 | 567 | 7,749,000 | 21,087 000 | 2,633,000 | 16,983,000 | 63 10 |
| 1881 | 565 | 8,144,000 | 20,249,000 | 2,451,000 | 17,485,000 | 55 3 |
| 1882 | 570 | 8,587,000 | 21,249,000 | 3,285,000 | 17,796,000 | 56 1 |
| 1883 | 552 | 8,529,000 | 21,013,000 | 3,191,000 | 17,775,000 | 51 10 |
| 1884 | 476 | 7,812,000 | 18,887,000 | 2,731,000 | 16,078,000 | 46 0 |
| 1885 | 424 | 7,415,000 | 17,938,000 | 2,823,000 | 15,287,000 | 43 1 |
| 1886 | 399 | 7,010,000 | 17,297,000 | 2,878,000 | 14,250,000 | 42 6 |
| 1887 | 405 | 7,559,000 | 18,363,000 | 3,766,000 | 15,304,000 | 46 8 |
| 1888 | 425 | 7,999,000 | 19,152,000 | 3,562,000 | 16,131,000 | 42 4 |
| 1889 | 445 | 8,323,000 | 19,684,000 | 4,031,000 | 16,767,000 | 50 0 |
| 1890 | 414 | 7,904,000 | 19,214,000 | 4,472,000 | 16,168,000 | 60 11 |
| 1891 | 376 | 7,406,000 | 18,518,000 | 3,181,000 | 15,374,000 | 52 4 |
| 1892 | 362 | 6,709,000 | 16,344,000 | 3,780,000 | 13,860,000 | 51 1 |
| 1893 | 327 | 6,977,000 | 16,621,000 | 4,066,000 | 13,807,000 | 46 11 |
| 1894 | 325 | 7,427,000 | 17,804,000 | 4,414,000 | 14,885,000 | 46 0 |
| 1895 | 344 | 7,703,000 | 18,629,000 | 4,450,000 | 15,224,000 | 47 11 |
| 1896 | 373 | 8,660,000 | 21,204,000 | 5,438,000 | 17,114,000 | 47 10 |
| 1897 | 380 | 8,796,000 | 21,327,000 | 5,969,000 | 17,552,000 | 48 1 |
| 1898 | 358 | 8,610,000 | 20,958,000 | 5,468,000 | 17,196,000 | 52 6 |
| 1899 | 411 | 9,421,000 | 22,820,000 | 7,055,000 | 19,061,000 | 69 4 |
| 1900 | 403 | 8,959,000 | 22,101,000 | 6,298,000 | 18,742,000 | 84 0 |
| 1901 | 336 | 7,929,000 | 19,265,000 | 5,549,000 | 16,273,000 | 62 8 |
| 1902 | 348 | 8,679,000 | 20,928,000 | 6,440,000 | 17,649,000 | 64 9 |
| 1903 | 349 | 8,935,000 | 21,879,000 | 6,314,000 | 18,302,000 | 63 1 |
| 1904 | 327 | 8,694,000 | 21,146,000 | 6,101,000 | 17,535,000 | 58 5 |
| 1905 | 345 | 9,608,000 | 23,051,000 | 7,345,000 | 19,255,000 | 63 0 |
| 1906 | 368 | 10,183,000 | 24,670,000 | 7,823,000 | 20,863,000 | 69 11 |
| 1907 | 369 | 10,114,000 | 25,124,000 | 7,642,000 | 21,119,000 | 74 2 |
| 1908 | 322 | 9,057,000 | 22,735,000 | 6,057,000 | 18,742,000 | 63 5 |

## PRODUCTION AND EMPLOYMENT IN THE BRITISH IRON AND STEEL TRADES

Showing (1) Pig Iron Production, (2) Employment in the Iron and Steel Manufacture, and (3) Employment in the Metal, Engineering, and Shipbuilding Trades

| Year | Production of Pig Iron | | Persons Employed in the Iron and Steel Trades, including Dealers. Census Figures. | Persons Employed in the Metal, Engineering, and Shipbuilding Trades.* Census Figures. |
|---|---|---|---|---|
| | Total | Per Head of Population | | |
| | Tons | Cwts. | | |
| 1854 | 3,100,000 | 2·2 | 110,408 † | 504,968 † |
| 1855 | 3,200,000 | 2·4 | | |
| 1856 | 3,600,000 | 2·6 | | |
| 1857 | 3,700,000 | 2·6 | | |
| 1858 | 3,500,000 | 2·4 | | |
| 1859 | 3,700,000 | 2·6 | | |
| 1860 | 3,800,000 | 2·6 | | |
| 1861 | 3,700,000 | 2·6 | 149,366 | 669,814 |
| 1862 | 3,900,000 | 2·6 | | |
| 1863 | 4,500,000 | 3·0 | | |
| 1864 | 4,800,000 | 3·2 | | |
| 1865 | 4,800,000 | 3·2 | | |
| 1866 | 4,500,000 | 3·0 | | |
| 1867 | 4,800,000 | 3·2 | | |
| 1868 | 5,000,000 | 3·2 | | |
| 1869 | 5,400,000 | 3·4 | | |
| 1870 | 6,000,000 | 3·8 | | |
| 1871 | 6,600,000 | 4·2 | 223,448 | 789,230 |
| 1872 | 6,700,000 | 4·2 | | |
| 1873 | 6,600,000 | 4·2 | | |
| 1874 | 6,000,000 | 3·6 | | |
| 1875 | 6,400,000 | 4·0 | | |
| 1876 | 6,600,000 | 4·0 | | |
| 1877 | 6,600,000 | 4·0 | | |
| 1878 | 6,400,000 | 3·8 | | |
| 1879 | 6,000,000 | 3·4 | | |
| 1880 | 7,700,000 | 4·4 | | |
| 1881 | 8,100,000 | 4·6 | 241,346 | 900,954 |
| 1882 | 8,600,000 | 4·8 | | |
| 1883 | 8,500,000 | 4·8 | | |
| 1884 | 7,800,000 | 4·4 | | |
| 1885 | 7,400,000 | 4·2 | | |
| 1886 | 7,000,000 | 3·8 | | |
| 1887 | 7,600,000 | 4·2 | | |
| 1888 | 8,000,000 | 4·4 | | |
| 1889 | 8,300,000 | 4·4 | | |
| 1890 | 7,900,000 | 4·2 | | |
| 1891 | 7,400,000 | 4·0 | 245,847 | 1,056,724 |
| 1892 | 6,700,000 | 3·6 | | |
| 1893 | 7,000,000 | 3·6 | | |
| 1894 | 7,400,000 | 3·8 | | |
| 1895 | 7,700,000 | 4·0 | | |
| 1896 | 8,700,000 | 4·4 | | |
| 1897 | 8,800,000 | 4·4 | | |
| 1898 | 8,600,000 | 4·2 | | |
| 1899 | 9,400,000 | 4·6 | | |
| 1900 | 9,000,000 | 4·4 | Comparative | |
| 1901 | 7,900,000 | 3·8 | Figures | 1,435,835 |
| 1902 | 8,700,000 | 4·1 | cannot be given | |
| 1903 | 8,900,000 | 4·2 | | |
| 1904 | 8,600,000 | 4·0 | | |
| 1905 | 9,600,000 | 4·4 | | |
| 1906 | 10,200,000 | 4·6 | | |
| 1907 | 10,100,000 | 4·5 | | |
| 1908 | 9,000,000 | 4·0 | | |

* Not including workers in jewellery and precious metals, or watch and scientific and surgical instrument makers, but including workers in brass and other metals. † Census figures of 1851.

PIG IRON AND CRUDE STEEL OUTPUTS

(In Millions of Tons)

| Years | PIG IRON | | | | CRUDE STEEL | | | |
|---|---|---|---|---|---|---|---|---|
| | U.K. | France | Germany | U.S.A. | U.K. | France | Germany | U.S.A. |
| 1854 ... ... | 3·1 | 0·8 | Not known | 0·7 | Not known | 0·02 | Not known | Not known |
| Aver. 1855–9 ... | 3·5 | 0·9 | ,, | 0·7 | ,, | 0·02 | ,, | ,, |
| ,, 1860–4 ... | 4·1 | 1·1 | 0·7 | 0·8 | ,, | 0·04 | ,, | ,, |
| ,, 1865–9 ... | 4·9 | 1·2 | 1·1 | 1·3 | 0·2 | 0·06 | 0·2 | 0·03 |
| ,, 1870–4 ... | 6·4 | 1·2 | 1·8 | 2·2 | 0·5 | 0·13 | 0·3 | 0·14 |
| ,, 1875–9 ... | 6·4 | 1·4 | 2·0 | 2·2 | 0·9 | 0·3 | 0·4 | 0·6 |
| ,, 1880–4 ... | 8·1 | 1·9 | 3·2 | 4·2 | 1·8 | 0·4 | 0·8 | 1·6 |
| ,, 1885–9 ... | 7·7 | 1·6 | 4·0 | 6·0 | 3·0 | 0·5 | 1·1 | 2·8 |
| ,, 1890–4 ... | 7·3 | 2·0 | 4·8 | 8·1 | 3·2 | 0·8 | 2·8 | 4·3 |
| ,, 1895–9 ... | 8·6 | 2·3 | 6·7 | 10·6 | 4·2 | 1·3 | 5·1 | 7·6 |
| ,, 1900–4 ... | 8·6 | 2·6 | 8·9 | 16·4 | 4·9 | 1·7 | 7·3 | 13·4 |
| 1905 ... ... | 9·6 | 3·0 | 10·7 | 23·0 | 5·8 | 2·2 | 9·9 | 20·0 |
| 1906 ... ... | 10·2 | 3·3 | 12·1 | 25·3 | 6·5 | 2·4 | 11·0 | 23·4 |
| 1907 ... ... | 10·1 | 3·5 | 12·7 | 25·8 | 6·5 | 2·7 | 11·9 | 23·4 |
| 1908 ... ... | 9·1 | 3·3 | 11·6 | 15·9 | 5·3 | 2·7 | 11·0 | 14·0 |

IMPORTS OF IRON AND STEEL, IN ALL SHAPES.

| Year | Pig and Puddled Iron | Wrought Iron | Finished or partly manufactured Iron and Steel | Scrap Iron | Implements and Tools | Cutlery and Hardware | Scientific Instruments |
|---|---|---|---|---|---|---|---|
| | £ | £ | £ | £ | £ | £ | £ |
| 1854 | | 528,000 | | Not separately recorded before 1887 | Not separately recorded before 1900 | Not separately recorded before 1897 | Not separately recorded before 1897 |
| 1855 | | 542,000 | | | | | |
| 1856 | | 776,000 | | | | | |
| 1857 | | 690,000 | | | | | |
| 1858 | | 340,000 | | | | | |
| 1859 | | 576,000 | | | | | |
| 1860 | | 712,000 | | | | | |
| 1861 | | 595,000 | | | | | |
| 1862 | | 755,000 | | | | | |
| 1863 | | 807,000 | | | | | |
| 1864 | | 1,046,000 | | | | | |
| 1865 | | 1,049,000 | | | | | |
| 1866 | | 1,261,000 | | | | | |
| 1867 | | 1,259,000 | | | | | |
| 1868 | | 1,104,000 | | | | | |
| 1869 | | 1,117,000 | | | | | |
| 1870 | | 1,307,000 | | | | | |
| 1871 | | 1,589,000 | | | | | |
| 1872 | | 2,080,000 | | | | | |
| 1873 | | 1,996,000 | | | | | |
| 1874 | | 2,384,000 | | | | | |
| 1875 | | 2,743,000 | | | | | |
| 1876 | | 2,521,000 | | | | | |
| 1877 | | 2,515,000 | | | | | |
| 1878 | | 2,728,000 | | | | | |
| 1879 | | 2,600,000 | | | | | |
| 1880 | | 3,640,000 | | | | | |
| 1881 | | 3,705,000 | | | | | |
| 1882 | | 3,871,000 | | | | | |
| 1883 | | 4,107,000 | | | | | |
| 1884 | | 3,859,000 | | | | | |
| 1885 | | 3,581,000 | | | | | |
| 1886 | | 3,157,000 | | | | | |
| 1887 | 170,000 | 990,000 | 2,482,000 | 29,000 | | | |
| 1888 | 150,000 | 1,026,000 | 2,810,000 | 35,000 | | | |
| 1889 | 304,000 | 1,034,000 | 3,105,000 | 78,000 | | | |
| 1890 | 270,000 | 925,000 | 3,279,000 | 49,000 | | | |
| 1891 | 256,000 | 752,000 | 3,361,000 | 37,000 | | | |
| 1892 | 236,000 | 692,000 | 3,097,000 | 41,000 | | | |
| 1893 | 174,000 | 593,000 | 3,055,000 | 35,000 | | | |
| 1894 | 300,000 | 555,000 | 3,138,000 | 52,000 | | | |
| 1895 | 431,000 | 549,000 | 3,393,000 | 49,000 | | | |
| 1896 | 441,000 | 570,000 | 4,733,000 | 59,000 | | | |
| 1897 | 518,000 | 540,000 | 3,441,000 | 69,000 | | 711,000 | 99,000 |
| 1898 | 538,000 | 556,000 | 3,905,000 | 70,000 | | 895,000 | 207,000 |
| 1899 | 621,000 | 577,000 | 4,377,000 | 90,000 | | 1,114,000 | 238,000 |
| 1900 | 805,000 | 656,000 | 5,854,000 | 112,000 | 418,000 | 901,000 | 649,000 |
| 1901 | 792,000 | 735,000 | 6,034,000 | 122,000 | 415,000 | 1,152,000 | 711,000 |
| 1902 | 798,000 | 1,085,000 | 6,027,000 | 113,000 | 381,000 | 1,402,000 | 949,000 |
| 1903 | 577,000 | 1,113,000 | 6,972,000 | 57,000 | 596,000 | 1,451,000 | 759,000 |
| 1904 | 561,000 | 685,000 | 6,971,000 | 61,000 | 548,000 | 1,194,000 | 784,000 |
| 1905 | 591,000 | 666,000 | 7,332,000 | 72,000 | 339,000 | 1,072,000 | 849,000 |
| 1906 | 494,000 | 703,000 | 7,163,000 | 109,000 | 330,000 | 1,136,000 | 1,013,000 |
| 1907 | 558,000 | 572,000 | 6,085,000 | 83,000 | 400,000 | 1,160,000 | 1,087,000 |

INTO THE UNITED KINGDOM, 1854 TO 1907

| Electrical Goods Apparatus (not Machinery) | Machinery and Steam Engines | Ships and Boats | Cycles, &c. | Motor Cars and Motor Cycles | Total | Year |
|---|---|---|---|---|---|---|
| £ | £ | £ | £ | £ | £ | |
| Not separately recorded before 1897 | Prior to 1897 the figures refer to Sewing Machines only, other Machinery being included in the "Iron and Steel" Totals. | Not separately recorded before 1903 | Not separately recorded before 1897 | Not separately recorded before 1902 | | |
| | | | | | 528.000 | 1854 |
| | | | | | 542,000 | 1855 |
| | | | | | 776,000 | 1856 |
| | | | | | 690,000 | 1857 |
| | | | | | 340,000 | 1858 |
| | | | | | 576,000 | 1859 |
| | | | | | 712,000 | 1860 |
| | | | | | 595,000 | 1861 |
| | | | | | 755,000 | 1862 |
| | | | | | 807,000 | 1863 |
| | | | | | 1,046,000 | 1864 |
| | | | | | 1,049,000 | 1865 |
| | | | | | 1,261,000 | 1866 |
| | | | | | 1,259,000 | 1867 |
| | | | | | 1,104,000 | 1868 |
| | | | | | 1,117,000 | 1869 |
| | | | | | 1,307,000 | 1870 |
| | | | | | 1,589,000 | 1871 |
| | | | | | 2,080,000 | 1872 |
| | | | | | 1,996,000 | 1873 |
| | | | | | 2,384,000 | 1874 |
| | | | | | 2,743,000 | 1875 |
| | | | | | 2,521,000 | 1876 |
| | | | | | 2,515,000 | 1877 |
| | | | | | 2,728,000 | 1878 |
| | | | | | 2,600,000 | 1879 |
| | | | | | 3,640,000 | 1880 |
| | | | | | 3,705,000 | 1881 |
| | | | | | 3,871,000 | 1882 |
| | | | | | 4,107,000 | 1883 |
| | | | | | 3,859,000 | 1884 |
| | | | | | 3,581,000 | 1885 |
| | | | | | 3,157,000 | 1886 |
| | | | | | 3,691,000 | 1887 |
| | | | | | 4,021,000 | 1888 |
| | | | | | 4,521,000 | 1889 |
| | | | | | 4,523,000 | 1890 |
| | | | | | 4,406,000 | 1891 |
| | 255,000 | | | | 4,321,000 | 1892 |
| | 225,000 | | | | 4.082,000 | 1893 |
| | 213,000 | | | | 4,258,000 | 1894 |
| | 237,000 | | | | 4,659,000 | 1895 |
| | 303,000 | | | | 6,106,000 | 1896 |
| 242,000 | 2,371,000 | | 527,000 | | 8,518,000 | 1897 |
| 368,000 | 3,056,000 | | 613,000 | | 10,208,000 | 1898 |
| 614,000 | 3,673,000 | | 287,000 | | 11,591,000 | 1899 |
| 1,266,000 | 3,476.000 | | 195,000 | | 14,330,000 | 1900 |
| 849,000 | 3,063,000 | | 176,000 | | 14,949.000 | 1901 |
| 687,000 | 4,761,000 | | 144,000 | 1,103,000 | 17,410,000 | 1902 |
| 876,000 | 4,450.000 | 58,000 | 99,000 | 1,988,000 | 18,990,000 | 1903 |
| 846,000 | 4,312.000 | 26,000 | 83,000 | 2,472.000 | 18,543,000 | 1904 |
| 1,010,000 | 4,538,000 | 33,000 | 130,000 | 3,447,000 | 20,079,000 | 1905 |
| 1,188,000 | 5,127,000 | 28,000 | 158,000 | 4,452,000 | 21,901,000 | 1906 |
| 1,248,000 | 5,314,000 | 27,000 | 171,000 | 4,631,000 | 21,336,000 | 1907 |

## EXPORTS OF IRON AND STEEL IN ALL SHAPES,

| Year | Iron and Steel and Manufactures Thereof. | Scrap Iron | Cutlery | Hardware | Implements and Tools | Scientific Apparatus | Telegraph Cables, &c. |
|---|---|---|---|---|---|---|---|
| | £ | £ | £ | £ | £ | £ | £ |
| 1846 | 4,178,000 | Not recorded before 1851 | 2,181,000 | | Not recorded before 1851 | Not recorded before 1887 | Not recorded before 1853 |
| 1847 | 5,266,000 | | 2,342,000 | | | | |
| 1848 | 4,778,000 | | 1,860,000 | | | | |
| 1849 | 4,986,000 | | 2,201,000 | | | | |
| 1850 | 5,350,000 | | 2,641,000 | | | | |
| 1851 | 5,768,000 | 62,000 | 2,827,000 | | 59,000 | | |
| 1852 | 6,633,000 | 51,000 | 2,692,000 | | 59,000 | | |
| 1853 | 10,772,000 | 73,000 | 3,665,000 | | 77,000 | | 73,000 |
| 1854 | 11,615,000 | 60,000 | 3,868,000 | | 116,000 | | 82,000 |
| 1855 | 9,369,000 | 97,000 | 2,959,000 | | 112,000 | | 164,000 |
| 1856 | 12,830,000 | 136,000 | 3,748,000 | | 155,000 | | 80,000 |
| 1857 | 14,936,000 | 197,000 | 4,016,000 | | 191,000 | | 302,000 |
| 1858 | 12,486,000 | 95,000 | 3,278,000 | | 190,000 | | 225,000 |
| 1859 | 13,834,000 | 31,000 | 3,809,000 | | 193,000 | | 742,000 |
| 1860 | 13,673,000 | 17,000 | 3,771,000 | | 254,000 | | 252,000 |
| 1861 | 11,226,000 | 36,000 | 3,426,000 | | 248,000 | | 214,000 |
| 1862 | 12,858,000 * | 98,000 | 2,865,000 | | 292,000 | | 321,000 |
| 1863 | 14,833,000 | 58,000 | 3,341,000 | | 270,000 | | 317,000 |
| 1864 | 15,035,000 | 14,000 | 3,579,000 | | 261,000 | | 218,000 |
| 1865 | 15,427,000 | 13,000 | 3,762,000 | | 311,000 | | 149,000 |
| 1866 | 17,111,000 | 70,000 | 3,826,000 | | 279,000 | | 312,000 |
| 1867 | 17,375,000 | 188,000 | 3,425,000 | | 229,000 | | 210,000 |
| 1868 | 17,257,000 | 377,000 | 3,276,000 | | 270,000 | | 338,000 |
| 1869 | 21,865,000 | 487,000 | 3,737,000 | | 348,000 | | 1,010,000 |
| 1870 | 23,537,000 | 501,000 | 3,812,000 | | 326,000 | | 2,523,000 |
| 1871 | 25,483,000 | 666,000 | 4,023,000 | | 274,000 | | 1,518,000 |
| 1872 | 35,340,000 | 656,000 | 5,089,000 | | 365,000 | | 405,000 |
| 1873 | 37,332,000 | 399,000 | 4,938,000 | | 501,000 | | 2,359,000 |
| 1874 | 30,945,000 | 245,000 | 4,403,000 | | 414,000 | | 2,113,000 |
| 1875 | 25,644,000 | 103,000 | 4,264,000 | | 416,000 | | 1,168,000 |
| 1876 | 20,641,000 | 96,000 | 3,483,000 | | 413,000 | | 815,000 |
| 1877 | 20,013,000 | 101,000 | 3,338,000 | | 407,000 | | 1,246,000 |
| 1878 | 18,269,000 | 124,000 | 3,298,000 | | 421,000 | | 746,000 |
| 1879 | 18,616,000 | 801,000 | 3,028,000 | | 364,000 | | 2,501,000 |
| 1880 | 27,225,000 | 1,165,000 | 3,521,000 | | 378,000 | | 1,301,000 |
| 1881 | 27,103,000 | 488,000 | 3,881,000 | | 422,000 | | 1,984,000 |
| 1882 | 31,091,000 | 507,000 | 4,017,000 | | 591,000 | | 1,043,000 |
| 1883 | 28,252,000 | 338,000 | 3,756,000 | | 853,000 | | 1,238,000 |
| 1884 | 24,273,000 | 223,000 | 3,143,000 | | 994,000 | | 2,509,000 |
| 1885 | 21,449,000 | 261,000 | 2,852,000 | | 876,000 | | 770,000 |
| 1886 | 21,430,000 | 388,000 | 2,846,000 | | 829,000 | | 993,000 |
| 1887 | 24,164,000 | 828,000 | 2,921,000 | | 890,000 | 216,000 ‡ | 817,000 |
| 1888 | 26,020,000 | 397,000 | 3,168,000 | | 1,000,000 | 245,000 | 521,000 |
| 1889 | 28,710,000 | 432,000 | 2,982,000 | | 1,253,000 | 285,000 | 1,038,000 |
| 1890 | 31,063,000 | 502,000 | 2,764,000 | | 1,338,000 | 308,000 | 1,602,000 |
| 1891 | 26,523,000 | 354,000 | 2,528,000 | | 1,312,000 | 289,000 | 1,434,000 |
| 1892 | 21,438,000 | 328,000 | 2,195,000 | | 1,262,000 | 291,000 | 910,000 |
| 1893 | 20,258,000 | 334,000 | 2,047,000 | | 1,226,000 | 273,000 | 1,063,000 |
| 1894 | 18,467,000 | 221,000 | 1,834,000 | | 1,195,000 | 249,000 | 1,387,000 |
| 1895 | 19,428,000 | 252,000 | 1,856,000 | | 1,240,000 | 278,000 | 782,000 |
| 1896 | 23,463,000 | 339,000 | 2,122,000 | | 1,414,000 | 337,000 | 857,000 |
| 1897 | 24,405,000 | 236,000 | 2,104,000 | | 1,364,000 | 349,000 | 998,000 |
| 1898 | 22,392,000 | 238,000 | 556,000 | 1,430,000 | 1,315,000 | 404,000 | 985,000 |
| 1899 | 27,713,000 | 388,000 | 603,000 | 1,536,000 | 1,430,000 | 411,000 | 1,407,000 |
| 1900 | 31,623,000 | 369,000 | 639,000 | 1,500,000 | 1,491,000 | 448,000 | 2,801,000 |
| 1901 | 25,009,000 | 273,000 | 637,000 | 1,440,000 | 1,492,000 | 503,000 | 3,148,000 |
| 1902 | 28,877,000 | 326,000 | 660,000 | 1,518,000 | 1,572,000 | 533,000 | 2,839,000 |
| 1903 | 30,399,000 | 442,000 | 685,000 | 1,595,000 | 1,700,000 | 582,000 | 1,808,000 § |
| 1904 | 28,067,000 | 483,000 | 697,000 | 1,944,000 † | 1,652,000 | 539,000 | 866,000 |
| 1905 | 31,826,000 | 454,000 | 667,000 | 1,994,000 | 1,784,000 | 599,000 | 1,552,000 |
| 1906 | 39,841,000 | 577,000 | 707,000 | 2,357,000 | 2,079,000 | 662,000 | 1,648,000 |
| 1907 | 46,662,000 | 548,000 | 769,000 | 2,540,000 | 2,241,000 | 813,000 | 1,710,000 |

* Prior to 1862 certain items were included under "Hardware."

† The great increase in 1904 is only apparent. In that year "Hollow-ware" was for the first time included under "Hardware."

FROM THE UNITED KINGDOM, 1846 TO 1907

| Machinery and Engines | New Ships | Arms, &c. | Cycles | Motor Cars | Total | Year |
|---|---|---|---|---|---|---|
| £ | £ | £ | £ | £ | £ | |
| 1,117,000 | Not recorded before 1899 | Not recorded before 1851 | Not recorded before 1892 | Not recorded before 1902 | 7,476,000 | 1846 |
| 1,263.000 | | | | | 8,871,000 | 1847 |
| 818,000 | | | | | 7,456,000 | 1848 |
| 701,000 | | | | | 7,888,000 | 1849 |
| 1,042,000 | | | | | 9,033,000 | 1850 |
| 1,168 000 | | 219,000 | | | 10,103,000 | 1851 |
| 1.251,000 | | 185,000 | | | 10.871,000 | 1852 |
| 1,985,000 | | 273,000 | | | 16,918,000 | 1853 |
| 1,931,000 | | 211,000 | | | 17,883,000 | 1854 |
| 2,243,000 | | 163,000 | | | 15,107,000 | 1855 |
| 2,716,000 | | 289,000 | | | 19,954,000 | 1856 |
| 3,884,000 | | 448,000 | | | 23,974,000 | 1857 |
| 3,599,000 | | 325,000 | | | 20,198,000 | 1858 |
| 3,713,000 | | 168,000 | | | 22,490,000 | 1859 |
| 3,838,000 | | 359,000 | | | 22,164,000 | 1860 |
| 4,214,000 | | 515,000 | | | 19,879,000 | 1861 |
| 4.092,000 | | 1,574,000 | | | 22,100,000 | 1862 |
| 4,368,000 | | 856,000 | | | 24,043,000 | 1863 |
| 4,849,000 | | 349,000 | | | 24,305,000 | 1864 |
| 5,223,000 | | 425,000 | | | 25,310,000 | 1865 |
| 4.759.000 | | 350,000 | | | 26,707,000 | 1866 |
| 4,969,000 | | 496,000 | | | 26,912,000 | 1867 |
| 4,729,000 | | 796,000 | | | 27,043,000 | 1868 |
| 5,119,000 | | 365,000 | | | 32,921,000 | 1869 |
| 5 293,000 | | 871,000 | | | 36.863.000 | 1870 |
| 5,942,000 | | 874,000 | | | 38,780,000 | 1871 |
| 8,201,000 | | 479,000 | | | 50,535,000 | 1872 |
| 10,020,000 | | 515,000 | | | 56,064,000 | 1873 |
| 9,891,000 | | 378,000 | | | 48,389,000 | 1874 |
| 9,059,000 | | 653,000 | | | 41,307,000 | 1875 |
| 7,210,000 | | 271,000 | | | 32,929,000 | 1876 |
| 6,723,000 | | 264,000 | | | 32,092,000 | 1877 |
| 7,498,000 | | 303,000 | | | 30,659,000 | 1878 |
| 7 279,000 | | 258,000 | | | 32,847,000 | 1879 |
| 9,264,000 | | 307,000 | | | 43,161,000 | 1880 |
| 9,960,000 | | 318,000 | | | 44,156,000 | 1881 |
| 11,932,000 | | 323.000 | | | 49,504,000 | 1882 |
| 13,433,000 | | 361,000 | | | 48,231,000 | 1883 |
| 13,073,000 | | 391,000 | | | 44,605,000 | 1884 |
| 11,087,000 | | 384,000 | | | 37,679,000 | 1885 |
| 10,137,000 | | 306,000 | | | 36,929,000 | 1886 |
| 11,126,000 | | 784,000 | | | 41,746.000 | 1887 |
| 12,939,000 | | 931,000 | | | 45,221,000 | 1888 |
| 15,274,000 | | 834,000 | | | 50,815,000 | 1889 |
| 16,411,000 | | 980,000 | | | 54.068,000 | 1890 |
| 15,817,000 | | 740.000 | | | 48,697,000 | 1891 |
| 13,887,000 | | 610,000 | 916,000 | | 41,887,000 | 1892 |
| 13,917,009 | | 521,000 | 1,033,000 | | 40,672.000 | 1893 |
| 14,205,000 | | 667,000 | 1,201,000 | | 39,426.000 | 1894 |
| 15,150,000 | | 974,000 | 1,386,000 | | 41,346,000 | 1895 |
| 17,014,000 | | 866,000 | 1,856,000 | | 48,268,000 | 1896 |
| 16,256,000 | | 836,000 | 1,430,000 | | 47,978,000 | 1897 |
| 18,390,000 | | 1,092,000 | 961,000 | | 47,763,000 | 1898 |
| 19,653,000 | 9,197,000 | 811,000 | 662,000 | | 68,811,000 | 1899 |
| 19,620,000 | 8,588,000 | 695,000 | 530,000 | | 68,304,000 | 1900 |
| 17,812,000 | 9,149,000 | 824.000 | 577,000 | | 60,874,000 | 1901 |
| 18,755,000 | 5,872,000 | 603,000 | 718,000 | 172,000 | 62,445,000 | 1902 |
| 20,058,000 | 4,284,000 | 587.000 | 849,000 | 344,000 | 63,333,000 | 1903 |
| 21,065,000 | 4,455,000 | 622,000 | 740,000 | 359,000 | 61,489,000 | 1904 |
| 23,260,000 | 5,431,000 | 969,000 | 1,037,000 | 542,000 | 70.115,000 | 1905 |
| 26,772,000 | 8,644,000 | 1,060,000 | 1,140,000 | 869,000 | 86,349,000 | 1906 |
| 31,763,000 | 10,023,000 | 1,000,000 | 1,288,000 | 1,381,000 | 100,738,000 | 1907 |

‡ Prior to 1887 smaller quantities of Scientific Apparatus were exported.

§ Prior to 1903 this item included Telegraph Wire. In 1908 and after Telegraph Wire is included under "Iron and Steel."

IRON AND STEEL EXPORTS,

| Description | 1892 | 1893 | 1894 | 1895 | 1896 | 1897 |
|---|---|---|---|---|---|---|
| | £ | £ | £ | £ | £ | £ |
| Pig and puddled iron ... ... | 1,974,745 | 1,971,518 | 1,912,958 | 2,077,073 | 2,533,883 | 2,889,440 |
| Wrought, in bars, rods, &c. ... | 1,147,682 | 929,552 | 823,365 | 854,017 | 1,094,289 | 1,087,644 |
| Steel—bars, rods, angles, &c. ... | 1,043,167 | 1,602,836 | 1,014,514 | 1,189,038 | 1.425,827 | 1,498,791 |
| Railroad—Rails ... ... ... | 1,622,332 | 1,921,157 | 1,309,231 | 1,432,911 | 2,594,357 | 2,671,745 |
| Chairs and sleepers ... | 280,567 | 267,590 | 244,584 | 170,860 | 385,012 | 468,038 |
| Unenumerated... ... ... | 304,323 | 322,267 | 331,584 | 293,265 | 581,041 | 717,796 |
| Wheels and axles complete<br>Tyres and axles ... ... | | | | In years | previous | to 1903 |
| Hoops and strips ... ... ... | 380,169 | 324,467 | 348,041 | 338,165 | 408.500 | 334,616 |
| Tinned plates and sheets ... | 5,330,216 | 4,991,300 | 4.338,786 | 4,239,193 | 3,036,015 | 3.038,569 |
| Sheets, galv. and corrugated ... | 2,077,068 | 2,045,770 | 1,948,652 | 2,251.374 | 2,843,622 | 2,562,081 |
| Black plates for tinning ... | 1,550,185 | 1.563,253 | 1,582,530 | 338,346 | 477,999 | 569,899 |
| Other plates and sheets ... (including armour plates) | | | | 1,125,199 | 1,419.205 | 1,570,151 |
| Anchors, grapnels, chains, and cables ... ... ... ... | 315,896 | 278,976 | 274,011 | 275,760 | 345,184 | 331,573 |
| Tubes, pipes, &c. (wrought) ... | 652,421 | 599,995 | 567,290 | 686,591 | 989,876 | 976,054 |
| Pipes and fittings (cast) ... ... | | | | Not sepa | rately di | stinguish |
| Nails, screws, and rivets ... | 327,950 | 321,950 | 281,617 | 306,328 | 360,515 | 367,337 |
| Bolts and nuts... ... ...<br>Wrought-iron manufactures, unenumerated ... ...<br>Bedsteads ... ... ... | 1.910,766 | 1,564,909 | 1,440,678 | 1,551,158 | 1,959,897 | 2,073,976 |
| *Cast-iron manufactures, unenumerated ... ... ... | 1,155.255 | 999,195 | 868,394 | 907,770 | 1,064,255 | 1,726,760 |
| Cast steel ingots and bloom ... | 30,740 | 30,485 | 62,495 | 59,507 | 109,251 | 117,118 |
| †Wire and manufactures thereof | 793,915 | 647,461 | 620,536 | 711,188 | 903,995 | 867,640 |
| Girders, beams, joists, and pillars ... ... ... ...<br>Iron castings ... ... ...<br>Iron forgings ... ... ...<br>Steel castings ... ...<br>Steel forgings ... ... ...<br>Manufactures of steel, or steel & Iron combined unenumerated | 500,754 | 475,622 | 498,181 | 620,640 | 930,070 | 1,136,746 |
| Total exports, iron and steel ... (See note below) | 21,438,152 | 20,258,303 | 18,467,447 | 19,428,383 | 23,462,793 | 24,405,374 |

N.B.—The totals before and after 1902 are not strictly comparable. Prior to 1903
*e.g.*, telegraph wire, which

* Reduced in 1903–4 by transference of items to new headings.

IN DETAIL, 1892 TO 1907

| 1898 | 1899 | 1900 | 1901 | 1902 | 1903 | 1904 | 1905 | 1906 | 1907 |
|---|---|---|---|---|---|---|---|---|---|
| £ | £ | £ | £ | £ | £ | £ | £ | £ | £ |
| 2,739,093 | 4,785,244 | 5,994,306 | 2,630,526 | 3,571,185 | 3,360,430 | 2,369,210 | 3,096,955 | 5,824,616 | 7,222,781 |
| 993,973 | 1,229,088 | 1,543,143 | 1,041,534 | 1,027,478 | 999,025 | 882,863 | 1,002,762 | 1,213,027 | 1,367,805 |
| 1,563,930 | 1,882,566 | 2,073,858 | 1,511,193 | 1,766,233 | 1,917,469 | 1,604,014 | 2,081,654 | 2,704,106 | 3,159,201 |
| 2,173,665 | 2,311,200 | 2,366,785 | 2,736,264 | 3,173,203 | 3,212,700 | 2,544,289 | 2,731,854 | 2,591,363 | 2,832,811 |
| 311,207 | 308,625 | 270,723 | 241,987 | 332,299 | 251,083 | 238,754 | 406,756 | 383,052 | 543,057 |
| 526,773 | 507,649 | 554,559 | 656,302 | 649,249 | 738,647 | 750,222 | 743,960 | 854,874 | 682,677 |
| not incl | uded in | these | returns. | | 669,023 | 398,406 | 538,867 | 656,048 | 849,028 |
| | | | | | | 223,909 | 220,356 | 269,035 | 438,887 |
| 358,668 | 405,286 | 478,231 | 348,183 | 344,656 | 371,750 | 344,607 | 339,399 | 386,955 | 490,200 |
| 2,744,077 | 3,168,614 | 3,976,796 | 3,704,088 | 4,337,688 | 3,958,643 | 4,595,568 | 4,566,984 | 4,936,868 | 5,922,092 |
| 2,532,376 | 3,120,708 | 3,788,391 | 3,192,850 | 4,132,736 | 4,383,963 | 4,487,635 | 4,825,211 | 5,896,866 | 6,887,365 |
| 541,886 | 829,715 | 711,729 | 534,918 | 599,712 | 651,206 | 601,879 | 654,253 | 654,985 | 754,786 |
| 1,402,561 | 1,880,075 | 1,971,670 | 1,222,746 | 1,428,641 | 1,419,689 | 1,162,328 | 1,632,249 | 2,274,652 | 2,680,121 |
| 345,504 | 410,821 | 483,250 | 453,894 | 476,802 | 448,336 | 457,125 | 478,974 | 595,092 | 597,931 |
| 916,166 | 1,122,546 | 1,331,727 | 1,004,875 | 1,009,782 | 1,866,869 | 1,866,150 | 1,486,411 | 1,847,422 | 2,145,448 |
| ed prior | to 1905 | | | | | | 722,877 | 1,085,112 | 1,407,635 |
| 356,513 | 393,462 | 449,711 | 391,872 | 388,810 | 415,316 | 426,933 | 465,995 | 515,823 | 554,352 |
| 2,056,683 | 1,921,535 | 2,057,650 | 1,806,433 | 1,860,654 | 250,901 | 267,169 | 325,238 | 407,024 | 508,629 |
| | | | | | 1,716,128 | 1,082,199 | 924,404 | 987,244 | 1,096,891 |
| | 250,118 | 350,646 | 257,922 | 352,908 | 413,788 | 369,201 | 418,446 | 487,763 | 548,929 |
| 1,057,593 | 1,143,668 | 1,195,190 | 1,121,195 | 1,077,550 | 830,911 | 594,557 | 480,482 | 504,969 | 523,308 |
| 94,208 | 128,426 | 98,517 | 39,247 | 142,359 | 77,250 | 37,581 | 59,596 | 88,623 | 111,831 |
| 772,604 | 886,347 | 904,142 | 967,843 | 1,042,869 | 1,170,060 | 1,194,670 | 1,569,546 | 1,964,038 | 2,201,946 |
| | | | | | | 410,054 | 553,183 | 983,528 | 1,007,362 |
| 904,231 | 1,027,034 | 1,022,329 | 1,144,885 | 1,162,523 | 1,276,074 | 1,157,348 | 108,528 | 131,529 | 110,575 |
| | | | | | | | 13,164 | 20,273 | 23,756 |
| | | | | | | | 22,861 | 35,592 | 35,204 |
| | | | | | | | 80,820 | 62,099 | 92,304 |
| | | | | | | | 1,274,653 | 1,478,017 | 1,864,936 |
| 22,391,711 | 27,712,727 | 31,623,353 | 25,008,757 | 28,877,337 | 30,399,261 | 28,066,671 | 31,826,438 | 39,840,595 | 46,661,848 |

certain items then included did not appear under Iron and Steel in the Trade Returns.
was classed with cables.
† Prior to 1903 did not include telegraph wire.

## IRON AND STEEL IMPORTS IN DETAIL, 1892 TO 1907

| Description | 1892 | 1893 | 1894 | 1895 | 1896 | 1897 | 1898 | 1899 |
|---|---|---|---|---|---|---|---|---|
| | £ | £ | £ | £ | £ | £ | £ | £ |
| Pig & puddled iron | 235,681 | 174,038 | 299,739 | 431,272 | 441,244 | 517,686 | 537,690 | 620,851 |
| Wrought, in bars, rods, &c. ... ... | 692,259 | 593,033 | 555,558 | 549,534 | 570,412 | 539,669 | 556,549 | 577,358 |
| Steel, unwrought or part wrought ... | 62,486 | 90,506 | 76,810 | 95,003 | 157,746 | 276,131 | 252,512 | 434,020 |
| Girders, beams, joists, &c. ... ... | 502,574 | 419,383 | 428,230 | 436,384 | 467,385 | 484,504 | 645,893 | 631,832 |
| Rails ... ... ... ...<br>Ship, bridge, boiler, and other plates and sheets ... ...<br>Hoops and strips ...<br>Steel, bars, angles, &c. ... ... ... ...<br>Wire rods ... ...<br>Nails, screws, Rivets, bolts, and nuts ... ... ... ...<br>Steel castings and forgings ... ... ...<br>Unenumerated ... | 2,532,118 | 2,545,639 | 2,632,944 | 2,861,971 | *4,107,533 | 2,679,995 | 3,006,630 | 3,311,363 |
| Total imports, iron and steel... ... | 4,025,118 | 3,822,599 | 3,993,281 | 4,374,164 | 5,744,320 | 4,497,985 | 4,999,274 | 5,575,424 |

| Description | 1900 | 1901 | 1902 | 1903 | 1904 | 1905 | 1906 | 1907 |
|---|---|---|---|---|---|---|---|---|
| | £ | £ | £ | £ | £ | £ | £ | £ |
| Pig & puddled iron | 804,879 | 792,361 | 798,156 | 576,996 | 560,753 | 590,959 | 494,262 | 558,376 |
| Wrought in bars, rods, &c. ... ... | 656,014 | 734,912 | 1,084,613 | 1,113,550 | 684,717 | 666,015 | 702,708 | 571,717 |
| Steel, unwrought or part wrought ... | 1,218,175 | 1,106,365 | 1,415,335 | 1,308,025 | 2,267,653 | 2,615,206 | 2,221,108 | 1,748,013 |
| Girders, beams, joists, &c. ... ... | 705,995 | 828,604 | 820,517 | 933,256 | 776,888 | 738,836 | 865,719 | 574,980 |
| Rails ... ... ... ... | 313,312 | 412,829 | 332,872 | 470,791 | 243,906 | 196,858 | 74,040 | 107,999 |
| Ship, bridge, boiler, and other plates and sheets ... ... | | | | 550,289 | 492,514 | 497,993 | 611,508 | 448,793 |
| Hoops and strips ... | | | | 121,861 | 116,865 | 117,333 | 138,086 | 180,154 |
| Steel, bars, angles, &c. ... ... ... ... | | | | 932,449 | 484,512 | 317,667 | 379,167 | 195,956 |
| Wire rods ... ... ... | 3,616,421 | 3,686,421 | 3,458,432 | 155,566 | 173,367 | 295,800 | 299,467 | 278,480 |
| Nails, screws, rivets, bolts, and nuts ... ... ... ... | | | | 632,455 | 619,836 | 677,055 | 670,112 | 622,261 |
| Steel castings and forgings ... ... ... | | | | 1,867,243 | 1,795,761 | 218,262 | 221,985 | 142,423 |
| Unenumerated ... | | | | | | 1,657,612 | 1,681,590 | 1,786,027 |
| Total imports, iron and steel ... ... | 7,314,696 | 7,561,734 | 7,909,925 | 8,662,481 | 8,216,772 | 8,589,405 | 8,359,752 | 7,215,179 |

* In 1896 and previous years a certain amount of machinery was included in this item.

In 1906 the world's iron and steel production was as follows:

THE WORLD'S PIG IRON AND STEEL PRODUCTION, 1906

| Country | Pig Iron | | Steel | |
|---|---|---|---|---|
| | Tons | Per Cent. | Tons | Per Cent. |
| United States ... | 25,300,000 | 43 | 23,400,000 | 46 |
| Germany ... ... | 12,100,000 | 21 | 11,000,000 | 22 |
| United Kingdom ... | 10,200,000 | 17 | 6,500,000 | 13 |
| Total above and all other countries | 58,600,000 | 100 | 51,000,000 | 100 |

Thus Britain is no longer first in the iron and steel world. America wields a supremacy through natural resources which neither Britain nor Germany can hope to rival. As to Germany, it is a curious fact that it was the invention of the basic process by Sydney Thomas, an Englishman, which gave Germany the lead of England by enabling her to make practical use of her enormous native supplies of phosphoric iron ores.

I give a fuller comparison between the four leading countries in the table on page 145.

The chief feature is the extraordinary progress of the American figures. It should not be forgotten that America has great natural advantages over Germany and Britain, and that a large part of her iron goes to build the enormous lengths of railway line which her great territory demands.

The Census of Production, 1907, Preliminary Tables gives the output of British Iron and Steel works (smelting, founding, and rolling) as £105,597,000. In that year our imports were worth £6,836,000 and our exports £46,563,000. This puts foreign competition into its proper perspective.

Britain still easily holds supremacy in iron and steel exports. In recent years her commerce has been:

BRITISH COMMERCE IN IRON AND STEEL

(Not including Ships, Machinery, or Hardware)

| | Imports for Home Consumption (c.i.f.) | Exports of British Make (f.o.b.) |
|---|---|---|
| | £ | £ |
| 1900 (good year) ... ... | 6,858,000 ... | 31,620,000 |
| 1907 (good year) ... ... | 6,836,000 ... | 46,563,000 |
| 1908 (bad year) ... ... | 7,391,000 ... | 37,428,000 |

If to the products included in the above table there be added ships, engines, machines, cycles, motor-cars, arms, cutlery, hardware, tools, implements, needles, and every other thing made out of iron and steel, the export figures are swollen to the magnificent total of about £100,000,000 a year, while the total home production is probably worth as much as £170,000,000 a year. It will be seen that this great trade is in no sort of danger of being overwhelmed by imports.

In the tables on pages 146 to 152 a record is presented (1) of iron and steel imports and exports of all kinds, from pig iron to a cycle, from a girder to a ship, for the last sixty years, and (2) of iron and steel imports and exports, commonly so called, for the past fifteen years.

Generally, the British iron and steel industry was never better equipped than at the present time. It is true that it is now (1909), passing through a period of depression common to the entire world, but there is no doubt whatever that in the near future it will advance to new records of production.

The table on page 143 shows how the price of iron is appreciating. The average price of exported pig has not been less than 50s. per ton since 1897. The world has already creamed its cheapest iron supplies, and the next generation may be driven to use grades of ore which would not now pay for working.

**JOINERY**—Protectionists have spread the most erroneous and exaggerated ideas with regard to the imports of ready-made joinery into this country. It is represented that such imports are large and increasing; as a matter of fact they are are small and diminishing:

IMPORTS OF READY-MADE JOINERY

| | £ (c.i.f.) |
|---|---|
| 1887 ... ... ... ... ... ... | 488,000 |
| 1908 ... ... ... ... ... ... | 209,000 |

In the same twenty-one years the imports of timber have doubled. (*See* RAW MATERIALS IMPORTED.)

But even if the imports of joinery were larger, carpenters should remember that, if they were taxed, every other material of house-building would also be taxed, including cement, iron, nails, glass, &c. (*see* BUILDING). As a result of dearer materials fewer houses would be built, and there would be less and not more work for carpenters. Carpenters should not be misled by trade depression into believing that Free Trade is the cause of that depression. The trade depression of 1908-9 exists all over the world, and even more in Protectionist countries than in Free Trade Britain: it began, indeed, in America.

**JUTE**—About 250,000 tons of jute are imported for home consumption into the United Kingdom every year. There is a considerable external commerce in jute, yarn, and goods:

BRITISH COMMERCE IN JUTE MANUFACTURES

| | Imports for Home Consumption (c.i.f.) | Exports of British Make (f.o.b.) |
|---|---|---|
| | £ | £ |
| 1900 (good year) ... ... | 566,000 ... ... | 2,434,000 |
| 1907 (good year) ... ... | 784,000 ... ... | 4,109,000 |
| 1908 (bad year) ... ... | 760,000 ... ... | 2,859,000 |

The imports are chiefly from India, which is also the source of the raw material. Protectionists have not told us whether they would like to tax imports from India, or, if they do, how they could deny India the same "remedy" against British iron and cotton goods.

**LACE (COTTON)**—The British lace trade is a growing industry which is increasing its output both for the home market and for export.

BRITISH COMMERCE IN COTTON LACE

| | Imports for Home Consumption (c.i.f.) | Exports of British Make (f.o.b.) |
|---|---|---|
| | £ | £ |
| 1900 (good year) | not recorded | 2,671,000 |
| 1907 (good year) | 1,697,000 | 4,872,000 |
| 1908 (bad year) | 1,794,000 | 3,856,000 |

The trade holds its own at home and abroad, in spite of the ability exhibited by Continental manufacturers. It is amusing to note in this connection that the new American tariff allows American lace manufacturers to import lace machinery free of duty in order to give them a chance. This is another practical recognition of the virtues of Free Trade.

**LAND VALUES AND PROTECTION**—During the Napoleonic wars corn was dear, rents were high, and British landlords greatly profited. After the war they enacted the ill-advised Corn Laws (*which see*), in order to keep up the price of corn and the value of land. The landlords' opposition to Free Trade will, therefore, be easily understood. Free Trade, enabling the British people to benefit by the invention of the railway and the steamship to obtain the fruit of the world's best harvests, reduced agricultural rents and the market value of British agricultural land. The landed interest, although it does not now play the commanding part which it did before the industrial revolution was accomplished, is still a strong factor in the Unionist party, and it still looks to Protection as a means of raising agricultural land values by raising the price of food.

**LARD**—We import about 2,000,000 cwts. of lard every year, to the value of about £4,500,000, chiefly from the United States. This valuable supply would be taxed under Protection, in common with every other food. The Protectionists suggest a 5 per cent. duty, but this, of course, is to make a beginning.

**LEAD**—The growth of our imports of lead has been very satisfactory. In 1887 it was 126,000 tons, in 1908 it was 237,000 tons, in each case for home consumption. It should be noted that this import, valued in 1908 at £3,224,000, is classified in the Board of Trade Returns as a "manufacture" —as, strictly speaking, it is. These millions, like the others representing copper ingots, &c., are included in the total of £120,000,000 worth of manufactured articles imported for home consumption in 1908, which the Protectionists propose to tax in order, as they tell us, to "make work."

**LEATHER**—We have a considerable commerce in leather, for our trades using leather as a raw material are many and extensive. The following figures relate to undressed and dressed hides and to tanned or dressed goatskins and sheepskins:

BRITISH COMMERCE IN LEATHER

| | | Imports for Home Consumption (c.i.f.) | | Exports of British Make (f.o.b.) |
|---|---|---|---|---|
| | | £ | | £ |
| 1900 (good year) | ... | 7,195,000 | ... | 1,439,000 |
| 1907 (good year) | ... | 7,268,000 | ... | 2,632,000 |
| 1908 (bad year) | ... | 8,001,000 | ... | 2,218,000 |

Many varieties of leather, used for widely varying purposes, are included in these figures. It would obviously be possible, by means of prohibitive duties, to shut out all foreign leather, and to compel our leather trades to buy their leather from British makers only. Let us consider whether that would be good for the trades concerned, or for the nation at large. To give a monopoly to British leather makers would be to place such important trades as boot-making, bag-making, and harness and saddle-making, at the mercy of British leather makers, who would be in a position to charge whatever they pleased in a monopoly market. The case of leather neatly illustrates the case for Free Trade. The Free Trader holds that the Government should be impartial as between the leather maker and the leather user. Through that impartiality we carry on such branches of the leather trade as suit us, and our leather-using trades have the best and cheapest materials at their disposal.

The British leather trades have increased both their production and exports, showing that in certain branches they do well.

**LINEN**—The value of the production of the British linen trade will not be known before the results of the Census of Production are got out, but that the trade is a flourishing one is shown by the fact that, whereas in 1893 our imports of dressed and undressed flax were valued at £2,346,000, in 1907 they were valued at £3,354,000. Moreover, the following figures for external trade are given in the Board of Trade returns:

BRITISH COMMERCE IN LINEN MANUFACTURES

| Year | Linen Yarn | | Linen Goods | |
|---|---|---|---|---|
| | Imports for Home Consumption (c.i.f.) | Exports of British Make (f.o.b.) | Imports for Home Consumption (c.i.f.) | Exports of British Make (f.o.b.) |
| | £ | £ | £ | £ |
| 1900 (good year) ... | 914,000 | 934,000 | 550,000 | 5,225,000 |
| 1907 (good year) ... | 785,000 | 1,243,000 | 783,000 | 7,346,000 |
| 1908 (bad year) ... | 680,000 | 903,000 | 622,000 | 5,802,000 |

Not only are the exports very large and increasing, but the imports consist largely of yarn.

**LINOLEUM**—There is an exceedingly large home trade in oilcloth and linoleum, and a growing export trade:

BRITISH COMMERCE IN OILCLOTH

| | | Imports for Home Consumption (c.i.f.) | | Exports of British Make (f.o.b.) |
|---|---|---|---|---|
| | | £ | | £ |
| 1900 (good year) | ... | 120,000 | ... | 1,313,000 |
| 1907 (good year) | ... | 98,000 | ... | 2,381,000 |
| 1908 (bad year) | ... | 69,000 | ... | 1,996,000 |

The imports are few and diminishing, while the exports are growing rapidly.

**LIVING**—*See* Cost of Living.

**MACHINE BELTING**—The use of electric motors is diminishing the transmission of power by shaft and belt, but there is still a considerable manufacture of machine belting made of leather, cotton, and other materials. There is also an external trade, as will be seen by the following figures for 1908:

BELTING OF LEATHER

| | | | | £ |
|---|---|---|---|---|
| Imports for home consumption ... | ... | ... | ... | 51,000 |
| Exports of British make ... | ... | ... | ... | 480,000 |

BELTING OF COTTON, &c.

| | | | | |
|---|---|---|---|---|
| Imports for home consumption ... | ... | ... | ... | 68,000 |
| Exports of British make ... | ... | ... | ... | 552,000 |

Although the imports are so small, it would be folly to tax them, for to do so would be to give a quasi-monopoly to the home manufacturers, and thus to enable them to raise the price of what is a material of industry. A wise Government should refuse to countenance any attempt to deprive its manufacturers of access to the best and cheapest appliances in the world.

**MACHINERY**—(*See* Engineering).

**MAIZE**—We import very large quantities of this food stuff, the supplies of which were short and dear in 1908:

BRITISH IMPORTS OF MAIZE FOR HOME CONSUMPTION (C.I.F.)

| Year | Maize | | Maize Meal | |
|---|---|---|---|---|
| | Cwts. | £ | Cwts. | £ |
| 1906 | 48,685,000 | 11,973,000 | 616,000 | 195,000 |
| 1907 | 53,380,000 | 14,604,000 | 659,000 | 214,000 |
| 1908 | 33,841,000 | 10,388,000 | 450,000 | 159,000 |

It is noteworthy that Mr. Chamberlain, in his programme of October 6, 1903, said:

"I propose to put no tax whatever on maize, partly because maize is a food of some of the very poorest of the people, and partly also because it is a raw material for the farmers, who feed their pigs on it."

It is, of course, perfectly true that an import duty would raise the price of maize, and Mr. Chamberlain's exemption of maize shows that he himself perceives that the foreigner does *not* pay the import duty.

Mr. Chamberlain also showed that he was unaware of the fact that maize, although not produced in the United Kingdom, is really a competitive import. It competes with oats, of course, as an alternative food for animals.

**MANUFACTURES IMPORTED**—As is shown under IMPORTS (COMPARATIVE) every country is compelled, by the needs of its people, to import large quantities of manufactured articles. The reason for this is that no country in the world does everything equally well, and every country, therefore, benefits by changing some of its work for work done in other countries (*see* FREE TRADE). Even if duties are imposed, the importation of manufactures may be reduced, but it will certainly remain considerable, for the home manufacturers must import in order to get on with their work.

At the present time our imports of manufactured articles for home consumption are worth about £120,000,000 a year. The greater part of the goods represented by this sum are actually bought by British manufacturers for use as raw materials or plant to form the very basis of their industry. For example, in 1908 the following manufactures were imported :

Under metal, £300,000 worth of pig iron, chiefly charcoal iron from Sweden, which is invaluable to our manufacturers ; £8,500,000 worth of copper in ingots, &c. ; £3,000,000 worth of lead ; £350,000 worth of quicksilver ; over £6,000,000 worth of ingots of tin ; nearly £2,000,000 worth of crude zinc.

About £3,500,000 worth of special machinery was brought in, and several million pounds' worth of textile yarns, invaluable to our woollen and other manufacturers.

Chemicals accounted for about £8,500,000 of imports, and all these, of course, are indispensable raw materials. Leather, again, accounts for a further £8,000,000. The greater part of our £3,500,000 worth of glass imports is raw material, and so also is the £3,500,000 worth or so of paper imports.

Of oilseed cake about £2,000,000 a year is brought in, and of paraffin wax about £1,000,000 worth. Straw-plait accounts for about £600,000. Another £1,000,000 or so consists of stone.

These and other similar items account for the greater part of our imports of manufactures. In other words, when Protectionists propose to "make work" by taxing imports of manufactures, they propose to tax the materials without which many of our industries would be crippled.

A detailed examination of our imports of "manufactures," having regard to these facts, has been made by the Board of Trade and published in Blue Book Cd. 4954. The Board of Trade divided our manufactured imports into three classes :

(A) Articles completely manufactured, and ready for consumption (*e.g.*, watches, hats).

(B) Articles manufactured, but requiring to pass through some process of adaptation or combination before entering into consumption (*e.g.*, paper, leather).

(C) Articles partly manufactured (*e.g.*, yarns, pig iron).

Let us see how our imports of manufactures appear when thus analysed. The following are the official figures :

ANALYSIS OF BRITISH IMPORTS OF MANUFACTURED ARTICLES FOR HOME CONSUMPTION

| Year | Class A Manufactured Articles Ready for Consumption | Class B Manufactured Articles Imported as Materials | Class C Partly Manufactured Articles Imported as Materials | Total |
|---|---|---|---|---|
| | Million £ | Million £ | Million £ | Million £ |
| 1860 | 7·7 | 6·8 | 5·9 | 20·4 |
| 1870 | 15·5 | 20·4 | 9·5 | 45·4 |
| 1880 | 26·1 | 24·7 | 12·0 | 62·8 |
| 1890 | 30·6 | 27·8 | 15·1 | 73·5 |
| 1900 | 47·0 | 41·9 | 21·2 | 110·1 |
| 1901 | 50·5 | 39·1 | 19·8 | 109·4 |
| 1902 | 52·8 | 43·2 | 19·6 | 115·6 |
| 1903 | 52·9 | 44·1 | 19·3 | 116·3 |
| 1904 | 49·9 | 43·7 | 22·2 | 115·8 |
| 1905 | 50·9 | 47·8 | 22·7 | 121·4 |
| 1906 | 51·5 | 52·3 | 26·5 | 130·3 |
| 1907 | 49·7 | 50·6 | 27·6 | 127·9 |
| 1908 | 44·8 | 49·9 | 25·1 | 119·8 |

The bogey of competitive imports, thus examined in detail, resolves itself into an importation in 1908 of only £44,800,000 worth of manufactures ready for consumption, and of £75,000,000 worth of manufactured and partly manufactured articles for use as raw materials of industry.

Nor should it be forgotten that the imports in Class A, small as they are, are the *consumer's protection.* They guard him against the worst efforts of monopolists. The workman buying a tool or the housewife buying a pie-dish has as much right to the protection of Free Trade as the boot manufacturer who has need to buy leather.

**MARGARINE**—We import for home consumption over £2,000,000 worth a year of this foodstuff. The importation is diminishing, however. Even this food, it should be remembered, is included in Mr. Chamberlain's programme of food taxation. The tax proposed is 5 per cent. This for a beginning; there is no doubt whatever that the 5 per cent. would merely be a stepping-stone to higher duties.

**MEAT**—According to Mr. R. H. Hooker, of the Board of Agriculture, we raise at home rather more meat than we import, the foreign supply, however, tending to form an increasing proportion of the total supply. In 1908 the total British meat supply was 46,850,000 cwts., of which 25,313,000 cwts. were home-raised and 21,537,000 imported.

Mr. Chamberlain proposed a 5 per cent. duty on foreign meat only. Mr. Chamberlain's Tariff "Commission," however, clearly desire that both Colonial and foreign supplies should be taxed. In par. 394 of their Agricultural Report they throw over Mr. Chamberlain, and say that the duty on foreign meat should be a "general level" of 5 per cent., while the Colonial duty should be "subject to negotiation with the Colonies." There is no doubt whatever that this means a Colonial meat tax, and Free Traders cannot too clearly make it known that we have now to fight not only for untaxed foreign food but even for untaxed Colonial food.

The experience of Germany in regard to meat taxes must be recorded here.

The following table shows how the German meat duties have grown since 1879:

GROWTH OF GERMAN MEAT DUTIES

| | Customs Duty Per 100 kilogs | | English Equivalent Per cwt. | |
|---|---|---|---|---|
| | mks. | pf. | s. | d. |
| Tariff of 1879 ... ... ... | 12 | 00 | 6 | 0 |
| ,, ,, 1885 ... ... ... | 20 | 00 | 10 | 0 |
| Duty altered by treaty in 1892— | | | | |
| Fresh meat ... ... ... | 15 | 00 | 7 | 6 |
| Prepared meat ... ... | 17 | 00 | 8 | 6 |
| Tariff of 1906: | | | | |
| Fresh, including chilled ... | 27 | 00 | 13 | 6 |
| ,, frozen ... ... | 35 | 00 | 17 | 6 |
| Prepared simply ... ... | 35 | 00 | 17 | 6 |
| ,, for table ... ... | 75 | 00 | 37 | 5 |
| Fresh meat free from bone charged 10 per cent. extra. | | | | |

Such are the meat taxes which oppress the German working man and which are detested by German industrial Protectionists. The latter have been forced to adopt them by the German

Agrarian (landed and agricultural) party, just as here the landed interest forces the Protectionist party to put food taxes in the fiscal programme. (*See* GERMANY for the opinion of the German working man on this subject.)

**MERCANTILE SYSTEM**—The ancient mercantile system, which confounded the economic conceptions of Governments for centuries, and which attained its full development in the seventeenth century, is the parent of modern Protection. It harassed our trade and it abased our relations with our Colonies. Its crudities and absurdities were pulverised by Adam Smith in his famous "Wealth of Nations," published in 1776.

The conception of the mercantile system was that the wealth of a country increased by virtue of exporting much, importing little, and drawing the balance into the country in the form of gold and silver. Gold, in short, was ignorantly confounded with wealth. The same ideas clog the minds of Protectionists to-day. Many of the utterances of current Protectionist speeches might be taken from the ancient mercantilist writings. Protectionists still deplore the "excess of imports," blind to the fact that the two greatest mercantile nations, Britain and Germany, increasingly flourish as their excess of visible imports increases. They speak of gold as synonymous with wealth, blind to the fact that the three wealthiest nations, America, Britain, and Germany, are not great gold-producing nations.

Under the mercantile system a colony was considered a milch cow for the Mother Country. Colonies were forbidden to manufacture; it was considered their duty to furnish materials, and especially gold, to the Mother Country, and to no one else. The Colonial market was regarded as a close monopoly for the home manufacturer. In return Colonial products were given preferential duties at home. These ideas poisoned the wells of Colonial patriotism, and led to the loss of the North American Colonies. It is exactly the same conception which pervades Mr. Chamberlain's "Preference," which is spoken of by Protectionists of to-day as an infallible means of obtaining a British monopoly in Colonial markets.

**MILK**—To deal first with the preserved article, we have considerable imports of condensed milk. In 1908 £62,000 worth of unsweetened and £1,545,000 worth of sweetened condensed milk was imported. The sweetened article has to pay import duty on account not of the milk, but of the sugar which is in it, under the Tory sugar tax, half of which the Free Trade Government has remitted. Under the Chamberlain programme the milk also would be taxed at 5 per cent. (for a beginning).

It is far more important, however, to consider the case of fresh milk. Fresh milk must, of course, be produced at home. It is not possible, therefore, for a Protectionist Government to tax it directly; but let it not be forgotten that it would be taxed indirectly. British dairy farmers would be severely hit by Protection, for they would have to buy taxed foodstuffs, taxed manures, taxed machinery, taxed clothes, and taxed everything else. As a consequence, their cost of production would be greatly increased, and they could only recoup themselves by raising the price of milk.

**MILLING**—Milling is one of Mr. Chamberlain's "ruined" industries. On October 6, 1903, he spoke of "re-establishing the milling industry in this country."

The fact of the case is that the British milling industry was never so prosperous. Indeed, it has so beaten the American miller that in 1908 the United States Government sent a Special Commissioner over here to inquire by what means, if any, the American milling trade could recover the British market. Let the reader compare Mr. Chamberlain's talk about "re-establishing" with the following extracts from the official report of the American Commissioner referred to, Mr. M. W. Davis:

"Flour milling in the United Kingdom presents features of decided interest because of the progress and growth attained by this industry in recent years. . . . There are two quite distinct classes—the interior or country mills and the port mills. Both classes have increased greatly in capacity in the past ten years, but the most modern plants and the largest have naturally been established at ports having the best facilities. . . . The competition which has reduced the sale of American flour to about one-half the volume of former years, of course, comes from these modern coast mills."

To sum up, British millers actually produce eight-ninths of our total flour consumption. They grind, of course, all our British wheat, while of the wheat imports of 1908, 91,133,000 cwts. were brought in as grain, and only 12,970,000 cwts. as flour.

**MINING**—The number of persons employed in mining and quarrying in the United Kingdom had increased from 372,481 in 1851 to 906,541 in 1901; to-day it is over 1,000,000. The larger number of these people are heads of families, and it is probable that the number of men, women, and children who live by mining is therefore over 3,000,000. The whole of these persons stand to lose heavily by Protection. The greater number of them are coal miners, who cannot be provided with an import duty. On the other hand, the Protectionists threaten them with a revival of the coal export duty, the economic folly of which is exposed under COAL and SHIPPING, *which see.* And not only would the coal export duty hit the miner directly, but everything the miner buys would be raised in price by Protection, so that his real wages would be lowered.

The folly of Protection is neatly illustrated in the mining industry. We have far less iron ore than America and Germany, and import a great deal from Spain and other places. Spanish iron ore is imported at Middlesbrough and directly competes with the product of the Cleveland iron-miners. The Protectionists refuse to protect the Cleveland iron-miners against Spanish competition. Why? Because, they say, iron ore is a raw material. The Cleveland iron-miner knows very well, however, that when iron ore is got it is his manufactured article, embodying just as much labour as any other manufactured article, and more than most.

**MOST-FAVOURED-NATION CLAUSE**—It ought to be, but it is not, commonly known that we enjoy in practice the lowest import duties levied by every nation in the world. We have a very valuable series of commercial treaties with the world at large, each of which contains a clause to this effect:

"No other or higher duties shall be imposed on the importation into the dominions and possessions of Her Britannic Majesty of any article the growth, produce or manufacture of the dominions and possessions of His Majesty the Emperor of All the Russias, from whatever place arriving, and no other or higher duties shall be imposed on the importation into the dominions and possessions of His Majesty the Emperor of All the Russias of any article the growth, produce or manufacture of Her Britannic Majesty's dominions and possessions, from whatever place arriving, than are or shall be payable on the like article the growth, produce or manufacture of any other foreign country."

This is Article II. of our Treaty of Commerce with Russia, dated January 12, 1859. By virtue of it, if Russia grants lower duties to Germany or any other nation, we automatically enjoy those same lower duties. It is thus an automatic protection of our trade with Russia.

To illustrate this, in 1893 Russia, who had then just instituted a double scale tariff, applied her higher duties to German trade, and Germany retaliated by raising her duties against Russia 50 per cent. Russia retorted by raising her maximum duties 50 per cent., and by special tonnage dues on German shipping. The end of this tariff war, which caused great loss to Germany, came in February, 1894. Both countries made concessions; Russia granted many reductions of duties on manufactures to Germany. The articles affected included iron, brass, and copper goods, wire, cutlery, tools, engines, textiles, paper, earthenware, glass, cement, and furniture. Now for the value of our most-favoured-nation clause with

Russia. Under its terms we automatically came to enjoy all the tariff reductions granted by Russia to Germany. We took no part in the strife, but gained what there was of gain in the outcome. That is a concrete instance of how the thing works in practice.

America does not enjoy most-favoured-nation treatment by France. She has most of the maximum duties of the French tariff opposed to her while we enjoy the lower scale. Thus the French duties on locomotives are as follows:

FRENCH DUTIES ON LOCOMOTIVES.

| | Per 100 kilogs. |
|---|---|
| Maximum tariff ... ... ... ... | 20 francs |
| Minimum tariff ... ... ... ... | 15 „ |

If a British locomotive goes to France its importer is taxed 15 per cent. If an American locomotive goes to France its importer is taxed 20 per cent. This does not say much for the powers of retaliation conferred by that very "big revolver" the Dingley Tariff.

I desire to give an all-round view of this important subject, and I therefore point out that cases may occur in which the most-favoured-nation clause is only of nominal value. Let us suppose that nation A is a wine-producing country, and that she is granted lower duties on wine by nation B. Suppose also that we have a most-favoured-nation arrangement with nation B. That being the case, we should automatically benefit by the reduction in the wine duty granted to nation A. But we do not export wine, and therefore the concession of nation B. would be to us purely nominal. If, then, two nations make a treaty with each other, granting mutual concessions of duties on articles which we do not export, the most-favoured-nation clause does nothing for us. It remains to ask whether in practice the clause covers us generally, and the answer to this inquiry fortunately is in the affirmative. Foreign industrial nations manufacture a large variety of articles, and any arrangement between them for reductions of duty usually benefit us, as in the case of Germany and Russia already alluded to.

Another point of importance should be made here. Let us suppose that, following the unwise counsels of Tariff Reformers, we made a tariff and used it as a weapon in order to beat down the German tariff. Imagine that, as a result, we reduced the German duties by 50 per cent. Would it be very much of a triumph? Unfortunately it would not, for this reason. Other nations, *e.g.*, France, have most-favoured-nation clauses with Germany. As soon as we reduced the German duties, therefore, they would be reduced for France just as much as for ourselves. We should have fought, not for ourselves alone, but for the world at large. I doubt if our Protectionists commonly realise that any advantages gained by us in a tariff war with any country would be distributed under existing commercial treaties to our competitors.

It is an interesting fact in this connection that France and Germany have a perpetual most-favoured-nation arrangement. This was arrived at by the Treaty of Frankfort in 1871. By this treaty Germany and France bound themselves in perpetuity to give to each other all tariff favours granted by them to Britain, Belgium, Holland, Switzerland, Austria, and Russia. This linking up of the nations by commercial treaties is, of course, a most valuable world asset, making for peace and for freedom of commercial intercourse.

The United States of America and Britain long ago concluded a treaty containing a most-favoured-nation clause in terms quite as plain as the Russian one. Although there can be no possible doubt as to the meaning of the clause, America takes her own peculiar view of it—a view shared by no other nation in the world. America holds that when a concession is granted to nation A in return for some reciprocal advantage, nation B does not receive the concession, in spite of a most-favoured-nation clause, unless B also gives America a reciprocal advantage equivalent to that granted by A. This American view may some day cause trouble. At present it matters little, for so far America has only granted a few concessions to other nations of such small moment that the point is almost an academic one. America has granted to France, for example, lower rates of duty on wine, spirits, and works of art than she grants to us. We do not export wine, and the works of art duty we need not trouble about. As to spirits, however, we are concerned, as we export whisky, and British whisky is more highly taxed by America than French brandy because of the peculiar interpretation of the most-favoured-nation clause referred to. For long an argument has been proceeding between our Foreign Office and the United States on the point. So far we have been unable to secure from America the due observance of the proper and accepted meaning of "most favoured nation."

To return to the general question, as I before pointed out, existing facts show us that Protectionist nations have practically failed to gain advantages which we do not possess under Free Trade. What would be the position if we adopted Mr. Chamberlain's Glasgow programme of Tariff "Reform"? Our imports consist largely of food, and obviously we could not use the food taxes for bargaining, because under the Colonial preference they would be fixed bargains with the Colonies and therefore not negotiable. Again, another large part of our imports consists of raw materials, but no one suggests that these should be taxed, and therefore this part of our imports would not serve for purposes of retaliation. Indeed, the only imports which could be taken into account in retaliating would be manufactures. Now the imports of manufactures for home use by the three leading nations are: America, £131,000,000; Britain, £128,000,000; Germany, £88,000,000. These figures show us that our bargaining powers in this direction would not be superior to those of America or Germany. But America and Germany have not been able by the use of taxes on these imports to reduce each other's tariffs. How, then, could we succeed with a small tariff where these and other nations have failed with high tariffs?

**MOTOR-CARS**—The motor-car industry is still so young that our external trade in it was not recorded in the Board of Trade Returns until 1902. The following figures relate to motor-cars, motor-cycles, and parts thereof:

BRITISH COMMERCE IN MOTOR-CARS, MOTOR-CYCLES, AND PARTS

| | Imports for Home Consumption (c.i.f.) | Exports of British Make (f.o.b.) |
|---|---|---|
| | £ | £ |
| 1902 ... ... | ... 1,045,000 | ... 172,000 |
| 1907 (good year) | ... 4,242,000 | ... 1,378,000 |
| 1908 (bad year) | ... 3,806,000 | ... 1,320,000 |

The value of our British production in this new industry is not yet known, but the progress of the British motor-car is remarkable. All credit must be given to France for founding the trade, but our engineers have shown that they are capable of producing machines of the highest class, and they have given special attention to motors for commercial purposes. This case illustrates remarkably the undesirability of penalising consumers in order to give a monopoly market to the pioneers of a new industry. It is very questionable whether British motor-car makers would have made the progress they have if import duties had at one and the same time encouraged inefficiency, and made tools, machinery, and running costs dear.

**MUSICAL INSTRUMENTS**—Only since 1904 have the Board of Trade Returns recorded separately the external trade in pianofortes. The figures for 1904, 1907, and 1908 are:

BRITISH COMMERCE IN MUSICAL INSTRUMENTS

| | Pianofortes | | Other Instruments, including Parts | |
|---|---|---|---|---|
| | Imports for Home Consumption (c.i.f.) | Exports of British Make (f.o.b.) | Imports for Home Consumption (c.i.f.) | Exports of British Make (f.o.b.) |
| | £ | £ | £ | £ |
| 1904 ... | 621,000 | 137,000 | 470,000 | 126,000 |
| 1907 ... | 650,000 | 165,000 | 371,000 | 128,000 |
| 1908 ... | 579,000 | 149,000 | 368,000 | 113,000 |

The manufacture of pianofortes, reed-organs, and harmoniums, of which our imports of musical instruments chiefly consist, is not a matter in which this country is, or ever has been, supreme. Germany is easily first in pianoforte-making, and reed instruments have been almost entirely developed in France and the United States. The pianos imported are valued at the ports at an average of £30 each, but foreign makers are as prominent in the best as in the cheapest varieties. The figures in the right-hand columns include a considerable quantity of imports of pianoforte actions.

An import duty would not touch the sale of the foreign high-class pianofortes, and it is doubtful whether it would do much for the British cheap makes, since they are largely made out of imported actions. The duty, however, would diminish the consumption of what has become one of the commonest of luxuries. On the whole, Britain gains by exchanging some of her work for a form of manufacture in which the Germans have excelled.

**MUTTON**—At the present time we raise at home about 5,500,000 cwts. a year of mutton and lamb and import about 4,500,000 cwts. a year. The oversea supply is gaining on the home supply with the growth of the needs of our population. Our imported supplies of fresh mutton (including refrigerated) in 1908 were as follows:

| From | Cwts. | £ |
|---|---|---|
| Holland ... ... ... ... ... | 267,000 | 641,000 |
| Uruguay ... ... ... ... ... | 64,000 | 101,000 |
| Argentina ... ... ... ... ... | 1,557,000 | 2,513,000 |
| Australia ... ... ... ... ... | 636,000 | 1,195,000 |
| New Zealand ... ... ... ... | 1,738,000 | 3,453,000 |
| Total from above and other places... | 4,391,000 | £8,148,000 |

It will be seen that this valuable supply of fresh meat is secured at about 4d. a lb.

The greater part is imported from Australasia, Argentina coming next in order of importance. Mr. Chamberlain proposed to tax foreign mutton 5 per cent. (for a beginning), but

Mr. Chamberlain's Tariff "Commission" desires to tax both the Colonial and the foreign supplies. (*See* remarks under MEAT.)

**NAVIGATION LAWS**—The Navigation Laws of Britain dated from the fourteenth century and were abolished in 1849. They were designed to restrict the commerce of Britain and her Colonies, and participation in the British coasting trade, to British ships, with a view to encouraging British shipping. Adam Smith, in his "Wealth of Nations," defends the Navigation Laws because he considered it necessary to preserve our sailors and shipping as the chief defence of our shores.

The following figures are taken from the official returns:

TONNAGE OF VESSELS EMPLOYED IN OVERSEA TRADE

(Entered with Cargo at British Ports, 1849 and 1907)

| | British | Foreign | Total |
|---|---|---|---|
| 1849 ... | 4,390,000 ... | 1,681,000 ... | 6,071,000 |
| 1907 ... | 29,266,000 ... | 12,137,000 ... | 41,403,000 |

TONNAGE OF VESSELS EMPLOYED IN THE COASTING TRADE

(Entered with Cargo at British Ports, 1854 and 1907)

| | British | Foreign | Total |
|---|---|---|---|
| 1854 ... | 12,762,000 ... | 46,000 ... | 12,808,000 |
| 1907 ... | 30,731,000 ... | 344,000 ... | 31,075,000 |

The second table cannot be taken back to 1849 because statistics of foreign vessels engaged in the British coasting trade did not then exist. In 1854 foreign vessels were for the first time permitted to work on our coasts, it being a cardinal principle of the old Navigation Laws to forbid them such working. It will be seen that in 1907, as in 1854, the foreign tonnage engaged in the British coasting trade is a negligible quantity.

The first table shows that British ships are the chief carriers of our trade, more than two-thirds of the tonnage entering British ports in 1907 being British.

**NEW ZEALAND PREFERENCE**—The New Zealand Preferential Tariff came into force at the end of 1903. Its principle is to impose additional duties on foreign goods, by charging them a percentage extra upon the rates for British goods. Goods are arranged in three schedules. The first schedule covers cement only, and upon this the foreign duty is double the British duty. The second schedule covers boots, hardware, nails, iron pipes, pianos, glass, earthenware, &c., and upon these the foreign duty is 50 per cent. higher than the British duty. The third schedule covers goods which, when British, are on the free list, but which, when foreign, are charged to duty at 20 per cent. *ad valorem.*

The New Zealand Preference has more reality about it than either the Canadian or Australian Preferences, *which see*, but, unfortunately the New Zealand market is small. The following table gives a few specimens of the Preference :—

THE NEW ZEALAND TARIFF

| Goods | Duty Payable | | Imports, 1905 | |
|---|---|---|---|---|
| | If British | If Foreign | British | Foreign |
| | | | £ | £ |
| Boots ... ... | $22\frac{1}{2}$ p.c. | $33\frac{3}{4}$ p.c. | 197,000 | 66,000 |
| Hardware ... ... | 20 " | 30 " | 203,000 | 56,000 |
| Paper ... ... | Free | 20 " | 131,000 | 3,000 |

In the year 1905, of a total importation into New Zealand of £12,481,000 from all places, as much as £7,784,000 was from the United Kingdom, but it is difficult to say what the precise influence of the preference amounted to, as the proportions were much the same before 1903.

**OATS**—We have a considerable importation of oats, amounting in 1908 to 14,271,000 cwts. valued at £4,163,000, in addition to 500,000 cwts. of oatmeal valued at £416,000.

Oats, like the other cereals, come under the ban of the

Chamberlain food taxes, the suggested duty being 2s. per quarter, or, say, 6d. per cwt. (for a beginning). A tax on this important foodstuff would raise the price both of the home and the imported supply. The home crop of oats is about 20,000,000 quarters, or, say, 80,000,000 cwts.

The Tariff "Commission" desire to tax both foreign and Colonial oats.

**OILCLOTH**—*See* LINOLEUM.

**OILSEED CAKE**—We import every year over £2,000,000 worth of oilseed cake. In 1908 the figures were 332,000 tons, worth £2,118,000. Farmers find oilseed cake dear enough as it is. They will be interested to know that, as oilseed cake is a "manufactured article," classed as such in the Board of Trade Returns, it is included in the goods which Protectionists denounce as "robbing British workmen of work." Taxation of this important foodstuff would be a serious matter for the dairy farmers, who, in this and in other matters, stand to lose heavily by Protection.

**OVERSEA INVESTMENTS**—Britain—or, to speak more accurately, British investors—have exceedingly large investments in foreign countries and in our Colonies, which have been variously estimated at from £2,000,000,000 to £2,500,000,000. France, Germany, and America also have such investments, in each case exceeding £1,000,000,000. British oversea investments are about equally distributed between foreign countries and our Colonies, and probably more than half of them have been sunk in the building of railways.

At the beginning of the present fiscal controversy, in 1903–4, one of the commonest assertions made by Protectionists was that we were *living on our capital and selling out our foreign investments in order to pay for our imports.* Free Traders, in reply, pointed out that the Inland Revenue Commissioners showed plainly in their Annual Reports that we were not selling out. Somerset House gives the following figures:

PROFITS KNOWN TO BE DERIVED FROM OVERSEA INVESTMENTS

| | | |
|---|---|---|
| | | £ |
| In 1887 | ... ... ... ... ... | 44,508,000 |
| ,, 1897 | ... ... ... ... ... | 56,319,000 |
| ,, 1907 | ... ... ... ... ... | 79,560,000 |

These figures are in addition to other profits from abroad which cannot be distinguished, but which must amount to a considerable sum. The above figures, however, although incomplete, prove that we are *not* selling out our foreign investments.

Apparently we satisfied the Protectionists on the point, for in 1909 a curious thing happened. The Protectionist argument swung completely round. Protectionists began to assert the very opposite of what they asserted in 1903. They now say that the figures show that our oversea investments are increasing too rapidly. This is one of the most amusing changes of front which the fiscal agitation has produced, and it has produced many.

Oversea investments bring to our shores every year, as the above figures show, a large amount of imports, which goes to swell the wages fund and increase the wealth of the country. Whether or not every oversea investment is a good thing for the country whose citizen makes it is a different and a difficult point, but certain it is that the point is quite irrelevant to the fiscal question. The citizens of Protectionist countries are no more prevented from making foreign investments than British citizens, and *in proportion to their wealth* both France and Germany have probably more foreign investments than we have. The latest Protectionist "argument" on our oversea investments, indeed, is as worthless as the one which they first produced and then abandoned.

It should be added that it is not the fault of Protectionist writers and speakers if foreign investments have been rendered popular. On this head I will quote an article entitled "Politics and Prices" which appeared in the *Times* on November 26, 1909:

"The unpopularity of home investments is a stubborn

fact. . . . But how far is it due to the facts of the case and how far to the picturesque utterances of the politicians? When Mr. Chamberlain determined to alter the fiscal system of these islands he thereby found it necessary to maintain that British industries were dying; that if our present system is maintained disaster and destruction must be the ultimate fate of the Empire. The tune that he performed so ably has been repeated with variations by the whole host of his lieutenants and followers, and a chorus of Cassandras has sung our approaching doom in crashing and crushing harmony.

"The investing classes, being largely in sympathy with the party which has adopted Tariff Reform, takes all that it hears about the inevitable doom of the country as literally correct, naturally begins to prefer to put some of its money abroad, and so one of the causes of the comparative unpopularity of home investments arises from the necessity with which one of the great parties is faced, of proving that we are on the road to irretrievable ruin. . . .

"Let us . . . look at one of the many causes which, quite apart from politics, have produced this unpopularity of home investments. . . . The first and greatest of them is the simple fact that home investments were relatively too dear. After all that has been said about the doom of British industry and the destruction of British credit, Consols have only quite lately fallen to a point at which they yield 3 per cent. to the buyer. The lamentable condition of the Home Railway market has been a chronic theme for years. It has had no friends. . . . The market has been pilloried, beaten, and insulted, and is in the eyes of all who remember its former glories utterly discredited and down-trodden. Here then, at least, one would expect that any one eccentric enough to make a purchase would get a fair round yield for his money. . . . And yet, if he bought London and North-Western Ordinary to-day, he would earn, on the basis of the last two dividends, less than 4½ per cent. on his money; while, if he went to the foreign market, he could get a higher yield on a Japanese bond secured by a special hypothecation."

Concluding, the same writer says:

"Such is the prestige of home investments, impaired but still so pre-eminent, that they remain to a certain extent a fancy article, the holding of which involves some sacrifice. . . . And it may be some consolation to those of us who are not compelled by political exigencies to toll the passing-bell for our country's financial greatness to remember that quite reasonable economic influences have had something to do with these quite natural happenings, which are used so effectively by politicians of both parties."

The public are indebted to the *Times* for this outspoken criticism of the jeremiads of the Protectionists. As I show elsewhere under UNITED KINGDOM, British trade and British commercial prestige are being decried effectively the world over by British writers. This insane policy of crying "stinking fish" in every market must be working great harm to our trading interests.

**PAPER**—The use of paper has increased enormously since Mr. Gladstone made the great gift of untaxed paper to the British people in 1860–61. Paper is a most important raw material of industry, and for the most part a very cheaply manufactured article. The total value of the British production of paper is unknown, but the imports of materials for paper-making have grown enormously, from 340,000 tons in 1887 to 891,000 tons in 1907. The commerce in paper is as follows:

BRITISH COMMERCE IN PAPER, CHIEFLY UNPRINTED

| | Imported for Home Consumption (c.i.f.) | Exports of British Make (f.o.b.) |
|---|---|---|
| | £ | £ |
| 1900 (good year)... | 6,222,000 | 1,649,000 |
| 1907 (good year)... | 5,527,000 | 2,344,000 |
| 1908 (bad year) ... | 5,651,000 | 2,316,000 |

The home production is very great. In 1907 we imported 17,820,000 cwts. of paper materials for home consumption, as against an import of 8,640,000 cwts. of paper. Of the paper imported, 3,395,000 cwts. is printing paper, 224,000 cwts. is printed paper, 2,411,000 cwts. are packing papers, and the balance of over 3,000,000 cwts. consists of strawboard and millboard.

Ought we to tax paper imports? The answer must be a negative, for by taxing paper we should inflict serious injury upon profits and employment in the great printing trade, which employs far more men than the paper trade. A 10 per cent. tax on paper would mean throwing thousands of printers out of work, but it would not satisfy such paper-makers as are Protectionists, for as soon as they got 10 per cent. they would want 20 per cent. and use precisely the same arguments to get it.

**PATENT LAW AND PROTECTION**—Mr. Lloyd George altered the British Patent Law in such manner as to require that a patent should become void if the person to whom it was granted did not work the patent in the United Kingdom It was at first freely alleged that this was a policy of Protection, but this argument was pulverised in the High Court of Justice and less is now heard of it. A patent, of course, is the grant of a complete monopoly for a certain period, and all that Mr. Lloyd George did was to prevent that monopoly being used against British interests. He did not increase the monopoly; on the contrary he limited it. Under the law as it was, although this might be a most suitable country in which to carry on an industry, the patentee, under his State-given monopoly, could import his articles and charge what he liked for them. That, of course, was not Free Trade, and to require that the monopoly should not be abused was no derogation of Free Trade.

In the High Court of Justice, Chancery Division, on March 26, 1909, Mr. Justice Parker, *in re* Hatschek's Patent, commenting on the Lloyd George Act, said that the Act was not intended to be protective, and added:

"The policy of the section appears to me to be directed to securing fair play between foreign industries and the industries of this country, and *not to secure for the latter during the period of the patent a protection which they would not enjoy if no patent had been granted*, and which the legislature can always secure for them, either temporarily or permanently, if and when it considers fit."

## PAUPERISM IN THE UNITED KINGDOM

| Years | Total Number of Paupers | Ratio to Population | Amount Expended in Poor Relief | | |
|---|---|---|---|---|---|
| | | | Amount | Per Head per Pauper | Per Head per British Citizen |
| | Number | Per Cent. | Mill. £ | £ s. d. | £ s. d. |
| Aver. 1855–9 | 1,080,000 | 3·8 | 7·1 | 6 12 3 | 0 5 0 |
| ,, 1860–4 | 1,127,000 | 3·9 | 7·4 | 6 11 5 | 0 5 1 |
| ,, 1865–9 | 1,159,000 | 3·8 | 8·6 | 7 7 9 | 0 5 8 |
| ,, 1870–4 | 1,147,000 | 3·6 | 9·5 | 8 5 6 | 0 6 0 |
| ,, 1875–9 | 935,000 | 2·8 | 9·4 | 10 0 4 | 0 5 7 |
| ,, 1880–4 | 996,000 | 2·8 | 10·2 | 10 5 10 | 0 5 10 |
| ,, 1885–9 | 996,000 | 2·7 | 10·3 | 10 6 8 | 0 5 8 |
| ,, 1890–4 | 961,000 | 2·5 | 10·9 | 11 7 3 | 0 5 9 |
| ,, 1895–9 | 1,013,000 | 2·5 | 12·7 | 12 10 1 | 0 6 4 |
| ,, 1900–4 | 1,009,000 | 2·4 | 14·7 | 14 11 8 | 0 7 0 |
| 1905 | 1,094,000 | | 16·5 | | |
| 1906 | 1,114,000 | | 16·7 | | |
| 1907 | 1,103,000 | | 16·7 | | |
| 1908 | 1,110,000 | | 17·1 | | |
| Aver. 1905–8 | 1,105,000 | 2·5 | 16·7 | 15 3 3 | 0 7 8 |

**PAUPERISM**—The term "pauper" is a reproach to us all, and the best energies of the nation should be directed to the reform of the present Poor Law, and to such a wise treatment of distressed persons according to their needs as shall make the word "pauper" obsolete.

While our population has increased enormously, the number of paupers has considerably decreased in the last fifty years, so that the ratio of paupers to population has fallen very greatly. Thus, in England and Wales in 1855–9, the ratio to population was 4·7 per cent.; in 1895–9 it had fallen to 2·6 per cent.

For the United Kingdom as a whole the available statistics are printed on page 180. They show that pauperism has fallen from 3·8 per cent. in 1855–9 to 2·5 per cent. in 1905–8.

It must be obvious that if untaxed imports were actually a cause of pauperism, then pauperism would have grown enormously in the period, for in 1855–9 our imports for home consumption were £146,000,000, and in 1905–8 £519,000,000.

The increasing standard of British living has led to a greatly increased expenditure on paupers, as is shown by the details given. In 1855–9 Britain spent £6 12s. 3d. per annum on each of her 1,080,000 paupers; in 1905–8 she spent £15 3s. 3d. on each of her 1,105,000 paupers.

The pauperism statistics quoted refer to the one-day counts of persons relieved. The only figures we have showing the total number of individual paupers relieved during a year are given in a return made in 1892 at the instance of Mr. Ritchie (the late Lord Ritchie). This showed that the number of persons relieved *during 12 months* is about twice as great as the number relieved on one day. The one-day count of 1907 showed that there were 1,100,000 paupers relieved; we may take it, therefore, that there are probably about 2,200,000 paupers in the United Kingdom. It should not be forgotten, however, that this figure relates to many infirm persons, females, and children, and that the number of "able-bodied" men relieved on one day in the winter is about 50,000, a large proportion of whom are not able-bodied in the proper sense of the word.

So far as our pauperism statistics go, they show a great

decrease of distress in proportion to population, and the need for a complete change in our methods of dealing with distress.

**PAYNE TARIFF**—The new American Tariff, passed into law after bitter controversy in 1909, is known as the Payne Tariff, after Mr. Payne, Chairman of the Committee of Ways and Means of the American House of Representatives.

When the Payne Tariff is compared, schedule by schedule, with its predecessor, the Dingley Tariff, it is found that the reductions in duty are far more numerous than the increases of duty. Mr. Payne himself has claimed that taxes have been lowered on £800,000,000 worth of goods consumed; but this is probably a too sanguine estimate.

Certainly there have been great reductions in the metal duties. The tax on iron ore has been lowered from 40 cents to 15 cents per ton; the tax on pig iron from 4 dollars to 2½ dollars per ton, and so on.

On the other hand, the oppressive Dingley taxes on wool and woollens remain, and the duties on cottons have been actually raised. The taxes on timber have been reduced. The duty on wood-pulp remains, but the tax on cheap printing paper has been slightly amended for the better.

It is too early yet to judge how the various alterations will work out in practice, but no American is satisfied with his new tariff.

For the first time the Payne Tariff introduces the principle of maximum and minimum duties into American fiscal policy. The rates of which I have been speaking are to form a minimum tariff, applicable to nations which do not "discriminate" against American products. Section 2 of the Tariff Law provides that a maximum tariff is to be formed by adding 25 per cent. to the scheduled duties, and that this higher scale may be applied to nations which "unduly discriminate against the United States."

It remains to be seen how this section will be worked by the American executive. Presumably British goods will enjoy the minimum rates, but what of Germany, France, and other nations? France now actually discriminates against American goods, applying her maximum duties to many of them; it will be interesting to see the issue of Franco-American negotiations over the Payne Tariff.

The "drawback" provisions of the Dingley Tariff remain. (*See* DRAWBACKS.)

The passing of the tariff was greeted with a universal chorus of disapproval by the American Press and people. As the Washington correspondent of the *Mail* said in the *Daily Mail* of August 6, 1909, the Payne Tariff "has practically no admirers in either House of Congress." The *New York Evening Post* said: "Its reception by the Press is, at best, a damning with faint praise." No American likes the tariff, yet every American has got what he does not like. I add a few more American opinions:

*New York Times:* "Look for a moment at the heartless wrong done to the poor in respect of their clothing, especially their woollen clothing, which in our climate is an absolute necessary . . . the working classes get a lot of sham woollen cloths, made of cotton and shoddy, which are deficient in warmth, weak in weave, rotten in texture, and haven't one-tenth the wear in them of real woollen fabrics."

*New York Evening Post:* "The agents of the cotton interests are disguised as members of Congress. They commonly wear masks of partisan principles or goggles and false beards stamped with geographical labels. . . . When a tariff measure is under discussion the large contributors to the machine pull the wires that jerk the elected member."

*Boston Transcript:* "Since early in March there has been a tariff lobby at Washington that has filled most of the first-class hotels. One Senator said that he had no doubt a million dollars had been spent by this lobby. And not a cent of it in the interests of the consumer. . . . Many individual manufacturers sent men to look after rates in which they were specially interested, but the general plan was to have a group of men look after an entire schedule. One of the high-priced groups of men conducted the campaign for a duty on hides. This lobby was financed by the Cattle-growers' Association of the South-West. The lumber dealers started out by giving a banquet."

*Indianapolis News:* "It was simply a trade, a deal in taxes, which were to be paid by the people."

Upon the paper duties, which have long been a sore point with American newspapers, Mr. John Norris, Chairman of the Committee on Paper of the American Newspaper Publishers' Association, says:

"The paper-makers were in almost continuous touch with the finance committee for ten weeks, but the representative of the consumers could not get a hearing from the full committee until after eight weeks of application and continuous waiting in Washington. He finally obtained a hearing on June 9, 1909, after he had printed and issued a public complaint against the discrimination of the finance committee. He was allowed forty minutes to state the case, most of which time was consumed with interruptions and discussions of committee-men, but the intention of the finance committee to increase the House rate had been announced by at least one member of the committee seven weeks before that hearing."

Thus the chief lesson which is to be learned from the passage of the Payne Tariff is that it is exceedingly difficult to throw off Protection when once it has a country in its grip. Surely nothing could be more remarkable than that the American newspapers, in spite of the boasted power of the Press, should find themselves powerless to make proper representations before the American Finance Committee. We may gather from Mr. Norris's complaint how little power of representation is possessed by the average consumer when American tariffs are made.

The world's tariffs differ in many respects, as I point out under SCIENTIFIC TARIFF. In one respect only do they agree, and that is in that they give no satisfaction whatever to the nations which are saddled with them. Each tariff is moribund at its birth.

**PIANOFORTES**—*See* MUSICAL INSTRUMENTS

**POPULATION (INTERNATIONAL COMPARISON)**—On page 185 will be found a deeply interesting examination of the vital statistics of Britain, France, Germany and the

## POPULATION: COMPARATIVE STATISTICS

| Years | Estimated Population in Millions | | | | Birth Rate per 1,000 | | | Death Rate per 1,000 | | | Excess of Births + Excess of Deaths − | | |
|---|---|---|---|---|---|---|---|---|---|---|---|---|---|
| | U.K. | France | Germany | U.S.A. | U.K. | France | Germany | U.K. | France | Germany | U.K. | France | Germany |
| Annual Average 1855–9 | 28·2 | 36·3 | 33·2 | 28·9 | | | | | | | | | |
| 1860–4 | 29·2 | 37·4 | 34·9 | 32·7 | | | | | | | | | |
| 1865–9 | 30·4 | 38·2 | 37·1 | 36·2 | | | | | | | | | |
| 1870–4 | 31·9 | 36·7 | 41·3 | 40·6 | 34·1 | — | — | 21·3 | — | — | +408,000 | — | — |
| 1875–9 | 33·6 | 37·0 | 43·6 | 46·4 | 34·1 | 25·6 | 40·3 | 20·8 | 22·5 | 26·7 | +445,000 | +115,000 | +584,000 |
| 1880–4 | 35·2 | 37·7 | 45·7 | 52·5 | 32·4 | 24·7 | 37·6 | 19·5 | 22·4 | 26·1 | +453,000 | + 89,000 | +518,000 |
| 1885–9 | 36·6 | 38·2 | 47·7 | 58·7 | 30·8 | 23·5 | 37·1 | 18·7 | 21·8 | 24·9 | +442,000 | + 65,000 | +577,000 |
| 1890–4 | 38·1 | 38·4 | 50·3 | 65·1 | 29·6 | 22·4 | 36·1 | 18·8 | 22·5 | 23·6 | +409,000 | − 4,000 | +627,000 |
| 1895–9 | 40·0 | 38·6 | 53·6 | 71·6 | 28·9 | 22·0 | 35·9 | 17·8 | 21·7 | 21·2 | +444,000 | + 50,000 | +794,000 |
| 1900–4 | 42·0 | 39·0 | 57·7 | 79·0 | 27·9 | 21·4 | 34·7 | 16·8 | 20·0 | 20·2 | +466,000 | + 52,000 | +839,000 |
| 1905 | 43·2 | 39·2 | 60·3 | 83·1 | | | | | | | | | |
| 1906 | 43·7 | 39·2 | 61·2 | 84·2 | | | | | | | | | |
| 1907 | 44·1 | 39·2 | 62·1 | 85·8 | | | | | | | | | |
| 1908 | 44·5 | 39·3 | 62·9 | 87·2 | | | | | | | | | |
| Average 1905–8 | 43·9 | 39·2 | 61·6 | 85·1 | 26·5 | 20·3 | 32·4 | 15·4 | 19·7 | 18·4 | +488,000 | + 23,000 | +866,000 |

United States of America, based on the statistics compiled by the Board of Trade in Blue Book Cd. 4954.

It will be seen that since 1855–9 Britain has gained 16,000,000 people, France 3,000,000 people, Germany 29,000,000 people, and America 58,000,000 people.

In 1855–9 France had a big lead in point of population; she is now far behind ourselves.

In 1855–9 America was at parity with ourselves in this regard; in 1909 she has double our population.

A glance at the birth-rate figures will show how France has been beaten by superior German fecundity since 1870. It will show further how all the leading nations are losing their fertility. The menace to white civilisation implicate in these illuminating statistics demands the serious attention of every thinking man.

Happily the falling birth-rate is in part atoned for by a fall in the death-rate. It is interesting to observe that the British standard of life, as expressed in the death-rate, still maintains its lead, although German conditions have obviously improved very greatly of late.

The melancholy decline in the relative position of that gifted race the French is strikingly illustrated in the third set of figures. The existence of such statistics is a misfortune not merely for France, but for the world, which cannot afford to be without her ancient proportion of Frenchmen.

Comparisons between these four nations which ignore these vital statistics are obviously misleading.

**PORK**—Our imports of pork, fresh and salted, are worth only about £1,600,000 per annum, the chief part of our imports of pig-meat being in the form of bacon, *which see.* Our imports of pork, like all other meats, come under the Chamberlain tax of 5 per cent. (for a beginning). As has been pointed out under MEAT, the Tariff "Commission" desire to tax both Colonial and foreign supplies.

**POTTERS' CLAY**—Potters' clay (kaolin) is one of the few raw materials which we possess in abundance, Cornwall possessing some very fine deposits. It is also one of the few raw materials which we export in any quantity. In 1908 the exports of china and ball were 631,000 tons, which were exported for £668,000, or for over £1 per ton. Some Protectionists have suggested that we should place an export duty on this clay in order to handicap Continental earthenware producers; the insensate folly of the suggestion will be realised from the fact that our imports of raw materials are four or five times as great as our exports, and that if we placed an export duty on clay we should lay ourselves open to retaliation in kind in respect of many important materials.

**PREFERENCE**—The policy of the Colonial Preference is not a new gospel, as some modern Protectionists suppose and proclaim; it is as old as Protection itself, and as old as the mercantile system, *which see.* In the very heyday of the mercantile system, in 1660, in the glorious reign of Charles II., a heavy duty was imposed upon timber; a higher duty still being imposed upon foreign timber, the higher duties being known as aliens' rates. In 1661 timber imports from the North of Europe were absolutely prohibited, although this extreme Colonial preference was of the greatest injury to the British Navy. In 1840 the Select Committee of the House of Commons, which examined the import duties, condemned the Colonial Preference with no uncertain voice. Mr. Chamberlain's Preference proposals of 1902–3 are merely an attempt to revive an old and discredited system which was found out and thrown overboard, after long and bitter experience, sixty years ago.

In my "British Trade and the Zollverein Issue," published in 1902, I thus summarised the case against the Preference:

"1. Our self-governing Colonies can only offer us preferential trade with their small markets, in exchange for preferential trade in our market of 44,000,000 people.

"2. Two-thirds of our indispensable supplies of imported raw materials are derived from foreign countries, and we cannot give a preference on them without killing our industries.

"3. Three-fourths of our imported food supplies are derived

from foreign countries, and we cannot give a preference to the Colonies without a tax on food, which would be a cruel infliction upon our people.

"4. Three-fourths of our total commerce are transacted with foreign nations, and it is obviously unwise to adopt a policy which would strike at three-fourths of our trade.

"5. At present we enjoy most-favoured-nation treatment from all the world; this would be complicated and endangered by the Preference.

"6. As to present Colonial imports from foreign countries, the margin to be worked on by Preference is small, Colonial imports from foreign countries being made up largely of articles which we cannot supply."

These objections, which are as relevant to-day as when first I formulated them, are fatal to the policy of Preference.

**PRINTING**—The British printing industry is enormous. At the Census of 1901, 117,900 printers and lithographers were employed in England and Wales alone, as against only 34,650 in 1861. The greater part of the printing trade cannot be provided with import duties, for there are and can be but few imports of printed matter. The printing of newspapers and magazines and of most books, and all the binding and other operations connected therewith, must in almost all cases necessarily be done at home. On the other hand, Protectionists propose to tax paper and all the other manufactured materials, such as ink, machinery, metal, &c., used in printing processes. This fine industry, therefore, stands in great danger through the Protectionist agitation, and every printer should do his utmost to prevent the taxation of the printer's materials.

There is no question whatever that even a small tax on paper would compel newspaper proprietors either to raise the price of their papers, which would diminish consumption and employment, or to reduce the size of newspapers and so cut down wages bills. As to books, there would be a great check to consumption and output, with consequent great loss not only to printers, but to bookbinders, publishers, booksellers, and those who read.

**PROFITS**—*See* Income Tax.

**PROTECTION**—Protection is based on the conception that it is the duty of the State to protect its producers from foreign competition by the imposition of Customs duties in order to keep out or raise the price of imports. Free Traders oppose Protection, not because they do not believe that Governments should have regard for their producers, but because they believe the means of "protection" advocated by Protectionists, viz., the imposition of Customs duties, to be injurious to the best interests of the nation, uncertain in its application and results, and calculated to promote private monopolies.

In order to do full justice to the case for Protection, I take the following definition of its object and method from a speech made by Mr. Balfour at Edinburgh on October 3, 1904:

> "*The object of Protection is to encourage home industry. The means by which it attains that object is by* the manipulation of a fiscal system to raise home prices. *If the home prices are not raised the industry is not encouraged. If the industry is encouraged, it is by the raising of prices. That is, in a nutshell, Protection properly understood.*"

I do not think that Protection was ever more lucidly defined than in these brief, precise sentences.

The readers should observe that Mr. Balfour states (1) the object of Protection and (2) the method of Protection. The object of Protection is the object of us all. We all desire, whatever our political convictions, to "encourage home industries." It is when we come to the *method* of encouragement that Free Traders and Protectionists part company. As Mr. Balfour says, the method by which Protection seeks to attain its object is "by the manipulation of a fiscal system to raise home prices." The Free Trader believes that there are many sound economic methods by which home industries may be encouraged, but he does not believe in encouragement by means of Protective Customs duties.

And the reason why the Free Trader objects to the Protectionist method is partly indicated in Mr. Balfour's definition. The Free Trader knows that it is quite possible for a nation to encourage an industry in which foreign competition exists by means of a Protective Customs duty. Indeed, it is most obvious that if A is in competition in the British market with a foreign competitor, it is a good thing for A personally if his Government will consent either to shut out the foreign goods altogether or to raise their price by means of a duty. If the Government will be so obliging to A, he is enabled to make more profit, and his particular trade is encouraged. But what of the unfortunate people out of whom A has been given the means of making monopoly profits? Let us suppose that A is a leather manufacturer. The Government has "encouraged" him by a leather duty to "raise home prices." But what do the raised home prices mean to A's customers, and who are A's customers? Leather is not bought by the housewife or by the man in the street. Leather is bought by the following amongst other trades:

Boot and shoe makers.
Saddlery and harness makers.
Machine belt makers.
Bookbinders.
Upholsterers.
Bag and trunk makers.
Fancy leather goods makers.
Cotton spinners.
Glove makers.
Hat makers.

To all these trades leather is an indispensable raw material of industry. The Government decides to raise the price of leather in order to encourage the leather-maker. In doing so, it strikes a blow at all the above trades and many others. The very method which helps the leather trade hurts many other trades which employ far more people than the leather-making trade itself.

Or let us suppose that it is the paper manufacture which a Protectionist Government decides to "encourage" by the "manipulation of a fiscal system to raise home prices." To raise the price of paper is most obviously to encourage the paper manufacturers, for, although the consumption of paper must fall as its price rises, it is quite possible for more profit to be got out of a decreased sale within certain limits. But who are the paper-makers' customers? Paper is the raw material of:

Printers,
Publishers,
Lithographers,
All trades which use paper bags, wrappers, &c.,
Photographers,
Newspaper proprietors, &c.

An import duty on paper would seriously injure these important trades, which, of course, employ many times the amount of labour occupied by the paper trade itself. When the *Western Morning News*, a Protectionist newspaper, was found in 1908 to be using foreign paper, it ingenuously explained that it bought foreign paper to "protect" British industry. It explained that owing to "ring" prices for British paper it was compelled to avail itself of Free Trade. The *Western Morning News* said:

"The fact is that up to about 15 months ago all the paper used in printing the several journals published in this office was of British make. Something very like a 'ring' amongst British paper-makers at that time put up the prices of British-made paper to such an extent that it was impossible to continue to buy from them without a very serious addition to the cost of production of the paper. . . . English newspaper proprietors, therefore, in order to *protect* themselves, were forced to import paper from abroad so long as the operations of the paper-makers' combination continued to maintain the price of British-made paper at a prohibitive price."

Nothing could be more illuminating than this confession that Free Trade is the true "protection" of the paper-user. Given an import duty to "encourage" British paper-makers, and the *Western Morning News* would be robbed of the method by which, as it now confesses, it "protects" itself.

In view of these all-important, practical, common-sense

considerations, let us re-write Mr. Balfour's definition of Protection in order to make it a complete statement in brief of the case for Free Trade:

> "*The object of Protection is to encourage home industries. The means by which it attains that object is by the manipulation of a fiscal system to raise home prices. If by this system the home prices in a particular industry are raised, the effect is obviously to discourage all the other industries which use its products as materials. As only the minority of trades encounter foreign competition, and as many of the trades in that minority produce articles which are raw materials of other trades, it follows that the method of manipulation of a fiscal system to raise home prices must be rejected as futile for the encouragement of British industry as a whole.*"

The concluding part of this expansion of Mr. Balfour's definition, like the remainder, will bear the closest investigation. The point is of the first importance. The highest type of Protectionist, the man who has no axe to grind and no trade in which he is personally interested to gain monopoly for, is the man who believes it to be possible to modify national production in the national interest by controlling external trade. But external trade is the minor and not the major part of the nation's activities. External trade should be properly regarded as the feeder of home trade. A moment's thought will show that by far the greater number of British workers are employed in trades and industries which are independent of foreign competition. What, then, becomes of the belief of the worthy type of Protectionist that by the expedient of import duties national production as a whole can be made healthier or more symmetrical? How, by a system which at the most can affect the minority of trades by enabling them to charge higher prices to other trades, can an improved or larger national product be arrived at?

Few people realise what a small proportion of our population could be "benefited" by Protection

In 1901, the date of the last Census, there were about 42,000,000 men, women, and children in the United Kingdom.

Of these about 18,260,000 were engaged in occupations for gain, the remaining 23,740,000, of course, being chiefly women and children.

Let us see how these 18,260,000 persons were employed.

Following the Census classifications, the first six categories are: (1) General and Local Government; (2) Defence; (3) Professions; (4) Domestic Service; (5) Commercial Occupations; (6) Conveyance of Men and Goods. Clearly these six categories of employments do not suffer from foreign competition. Prime ministers, town clerks, soldiers, sailors, lawyers, schoolmasters, doctors, bankers, railwaymen, dockers, porters, &c., are not subject to foreign competition. They cannot be provided with a tariff to give them "lower income tax and work for all." On the contrary, an import tariff, by restricting trade, would injure merchants, agents, clerks, dockers, porters, &c., directly in their avocations; while it would affect them indirectly by raising the price of food and other commodities. No one would suffer more in these respects than the London clerk, who is usually a Unionist because it is so "respectable."

Now these six categories alone account for 5,600,000 people out of the 18,260,000 engaged in occupations.

The next categories are agriculture, 2,262,000 persons; fishing, 62,000 persons; mining, 944,000 persons.

The last two of these are not offered anything by the Tariff Reformers. The fishing industry is protected by Nature, and Protectionists aver that they will not tax raw materials, so that a man who mines iron ore is unkindly refused a duty. As for coal, we do not import that commodity. There remain the 2,262,000 persons employed in "agriculture." Of these, 245,000 are gardeners, florists, &c., who are practically untouched by foreign competition. Of the remaining 2,000,000 or so, a very large number are dairy farmers, market gardeners, &c., who would be directly injured by corn and manure duties, and who cannot very well be provided with duties themselves. It is impossible to "protect" fresh milk, and English Cheddar cheese is not really competed with by the inferior Canadian or American article. If we put it that 500,000 out of the 2,262,000 agricultural persons cannot be "protected," while they may, on the other hand, be injured, we shall be stating too much for Protection. As a matter of fact, the Chamberlain Glasgow tariff was useless to the British farming interest.

We pass to metals, machinery (1,475,000); jewellery, instruments, &c. (168,000); and building construction (1,336,000).

The first two of these may be provided with duties; the third cannot. Customs duties may be levied on iron, or engines, or watches, or jewels, but houses cannot be imported. In taking it that the 1,643,000 workers engaged in the first two categories of employment can be protected, however, we are over-estimating, since the figures include many dealers and many workers in trades in which importation is, in practice, impossible.

Next we come to wood (308,000); bricks, glass, china (190,000); chemicals, oils, &c. (150,000); skins, leather, &c. (118,000); paper, printing, &c. (334,000); textiles (747,000).

The 308,000 wood, furniture, &c., workers are only in a negligible degree open to foreign competition. As to bricks, tiles, china, glass, &c., bricks are rarely imported, and at most 150,000 of the 190,000 could be protected. In including all the 150,000 chemical, &c., workers as food for Protection, I grant too much to Protection. As to paper, printing, book-binding, &c., if we take it that one-half the workers could be provided with duties we also say too much for Protection. The greater part of printing, book-binding, &c., must necessarily be done at home, as I have already pointed out.

As to textiles, we have few cotton imports, and that disposes of 546,000 of the 1,462,000 textile workers of the 1901 Census. The 1,462,000 also includes drapers, and others who cannot be protected. If we put it that 747,000 out of 1,462,000 textile workers can be protected, we do more than justice to the case for Protection.

There remain 1,396,000 workers and dealers in dress; 1,301,000 workers in food, drink, &c.; 79,000 gas, water, &c., workers; and 1,075,000 general labourers, dealers, &c., who obviously cannot be protected by Customs duties.

The facts we have broadly reviewed are summed up in the following table:

CUSTOMS DUTIES AND OCCUPATIONS

| | Might be "Protected" | Could not be "Protected" |
|---|---|---|
| Government | — | 254,000 |
| Defence | — | 204,000 |
| Professions | — | 733,000 |
| Domestic offices | — | 2,199,000 |
| Commercial | — | 712,000 |
| Conveyance | — | 1,498,000 |
| Agriculture | 1,762,000 | 500,000 |
| Fishing | — | 62,000 |
| Mining | — | 944,000 |
| Metals, machinery, &c. | 1,475,000 | — |
| Jewels, implements, &c. | 168,000 | — |
| Building, &c. | — | 1,336,000 |
| Wood, furniture, &c. | — | 308,000 |
| Brick, cement, pottery, glass | 150,000 | 40,000 |
| Chemicals, oils, &c. | 150,000 | — |
| Skins, leather, &c. | 118,000 | — |
| Paper, printing, &c. | 167,000 | 167,000 |
| Textiles | 747,000 | 715,000 |
| Dress | — | 1,396,000 |
| Food, lodging | — | 1,301,000 |
| Gas, water, &c. | — | 79,000 |
| General workers, dealers | — | 1,075,000 |
| Total | 4,737,000 | 13,523,000 |

It will be seen that of 18,260,000 persons, only 4,737,000 could be "protected"; while 13,523,000 could make no claim on the tariff makers.

If we distribute the unoccupied and dependent women and children between the two groups in the same ratio we get:

| | Might be "Protected" | Could not be "Protected" |
|---|---|---|
| Occupied persons | 4,737,000 | 13,523,000 |
| Dependent unoccupied persons | 6,158,000 | 17,582,000 |
| Total | 10,895,000 | 31,105,000 |

Broadly, we see that of 42,000,000 people, in 1901, 10,895,000 workers and their dependents might be "protected," while 31,105,000 could not, because of the nature of their occupations, be "protected." So that only one-fourth of the entire population of the country is directly interested in the framing of a protective tariff. *Three-fourths of us are engaged in occupations which cannot be provided with Protective duties.*

I must not be understood to admit that even the 10,895,000 would really gain anything by Protection. I have simply made a broad attempt to show how many people we could *attempt* to benefit by Customs duties, and I submit that its conclusions are worth grave consideration.

There is only one way in which a nation can achieve industrial and commercial success, and that is by efficiency. Front rank in competitive industry can only be achieved by nations of natural aptitude gifted with certain indispensable natural resources—chiefly coal—whose peoples consent to the discipline of education.

If a nation has sufficient natural resources, natural aptitude and science, it cannot need Protection, any more than a strong man needs protection against the assaults of a child. If, on the other hand, a nation has not native stores of energy, natural aptitude, and scientific training, then Protective duties cannot give it success. Protective duties are futile either to give a nation what it does not possess in the way of resources or aptitude, or to give its people the training which ought to be theirs.

To take concrete cases, Britain, America, and Germany are the three supreme industrial nations. Why? Not primarily because of Free Frade or Protection. Britain has Free Trade, America has High Protection; Germany has a tariff which, as compared with ours, is Protective, but which, as compared with that of America, may be termed a system of Free Trade. Yet all three nations are prosperous and progressive. That is the first lesson the fiscal inquirer should learn. America is great because she is the naturally richest country in the world, the greatest coal country, the greatest iron country, the greatest copper country, the greatest lead country, the greatest oil country, the greatest cotton country. No fiscal policy, however outrageous, could alter these facts, even if it went the length of blocking up the ports. If American harbours were destroyed, America would remain the richest industrial country in the world.

Britain and Germany, as compared with America, are poor in natural gifts, but each is rich in gifts as compared with any fourth nation. Germany and Britain are both great coal countries, and coal, because it draws industries to it, is the main secret of British and German success. Britain has this advantage over Germany, that her absolute Free Trade, making her a great Free Port, gives her the lion's share of the world's shipping and enables her to work with her coal every known raw and manufactured material in the fullest measure. Germany, with her several free ports, her free trade for shipbuilders, her considerable free list, and many small or moderate duties, recognises in part the virtues of Free Trade, but her industries are handicapped by lack of full access to foreign material. On the other hand, Germany has these enormous advantages over Britain, that her people are much better educated and disciplined, that her captains of industry are scientific, and that she has national railways.

This statement, although broad, will stand careful examination. And understood it will prevent any man from entertaining the futility of a system of Protective Customs duties, or from believing that Germany and America are great through Protection.

If the conception of Protection is worthless, what can we say of it in practice?

The theory is to make a scientific tariff in order to develop and protect a country or Empire. The practice is to set by the ears a vast number of conflicting personal interests, each of which strives, when the tariff is made, to get the most out of it, regardless of the welfare of the others.

What is a Protectionist Government to do? How can it frame a scientific tariff? Upon whom does it rely for its majority? How is it to acquire such intimate knowledge of a thousand complicated trades as to be able to do justice to each? What Committee or Commission can weigh such an infinity of detail in the balance?

To ask these questions is to answer them. No individualist Government, divorced from the actual direct control of industry and commerce, can be equal to the task. The last German tariff, after a hundred and one impotent sittings in Committee, in which conflicting interests squabbled and intrigued, was passed, largely undiscussed, by a gross abuse of the closure, carried by a most improper bargain between certain of the German political parties. The American Tariff of 1909 only passed the American Senate by 47 votes to 31 and is detested by every one who had anything to do with it. There is no need for me to recall here the disgraceful intrigues, the wire-pulling, the lobbying, and the corruption which made this fiscal monster; the American cables have recounted the details, and they are fresh in the reader's recollection.

What guarantee have we that a British Tariff would have more wisdom in it? We can answer that question conclusively by reference to the extraordinary changes which have characterised the Tariff agitation itself in the United Kingdom in 1903–1909.

Mr. Chamberlain's practical programme of October 6, 1903, was carefully thought out; but what has become of it? Mr. Chamberlain proposed small duties—2s. a quarter on corn, 5 per cent. on meats, 5 per cent. on dairy produce, and an average 10 per cent. on manufactures. *It was a cardinal point of his policy that Colonial food should remain untaxed.* Even as to foreign food, bacon and maize were to remain untaxed. Raw materials were not to be taxed. Duties were in no case to be large.

All these points have gone by the board. Mr. Chamberlain's own Tariff "Commission" have decided that Colonial food must be taxed, that bacon and maize are to be taxed; that hops, a raw material of industry, must be taxed; that fruit and vegetables must be taxed; and as for small duties on manufactures, a large number of Protectionist manufacturers who gave evidence before the Tariff "Commission" demanded high duties and alleged that small duties would be useless. It is amusing to note that the Agricultural "Report" said that imports of manures and feeding-stuffs ought to be free, but, of course, manure manufacturers would not agree to that. In the Engineering "Report," we find Protectionist engineers demanding taxes on agricultural machinery for the discomfiture of the farmers. From such details as these we can imagine what sort of pressure would be brought to bear upon a Protectionist Chancellor of the Exchequer by conflicting interests. Under such circumstances the life of a member of Parliament would not be worth living. One can imagine the daily bombardment of letters, circulars, pamphlets, and deputations, making the most contradictory assertions in support of, or in opposition to, any duties proposed, and one can imagine the wearied M.P. rejoicing at last to see the sordid discussion ended by the closure, and any decision, no matter what, arrived at.

**PROTECTION A SOCIALISM**—In his speech at Birmingham on September 22, 1909, Mr. Balfour spoke of "Socialism and Tariff Reform" as being "alternatives"; and, in spite of the obvious rapid progress of Socialism in Germany and other protected countries, many Protectionists blindly urge the adoption of "Tariff Reform" as a means of combating Socialism. The point is worth discussion.

If we put Protection at its highest, and brush aside for the moment what in practice Protectionists will never be able to brush aside, the advancement of sectional interests at the expense of the State, what does it assert? It asserts an entirely admirable principle, that it is the duty of the State to interfere actively in the economic development of the nation, and it believes that a healthy and symmetrical economic development can be secured by moulding productive powers through changing the currents and nature of external trade. This is a fair statement of the object of Protection as seen and aimed at by the sincere and unselfish Tariff Reformer who has no special interest to serve.

But this object and aim, it will be perceived, are the object and aim of Socialism. The conception of Protection is a Socialistic conception which amounts to a denial of individual liberty and a denial of liberty in the individualistic use of capital.

A citizen desires to buy boots. Individual liberty grants him the right to buy the best and cheapest boots in the world. Protection enters the plea that the exercise of individualism in such a manner is incompatible with the prosperity of the British boot trade, and asserts that it is the duty of the State to impose such a Customs duty on imported boots as shall make it difficult or impossible for the boot buyer to purchase other than British-made boots. By this means, the Protectionist alleges, the British boot trade would be encouraged and maintained.

A British boot manufacturer desires to buy leather. As a capitalist he has set up an expensive factory and plant. As a man of business he desires access to the cheapest and best raw materials in the world. His chief raw material is leather. Individualism gives him liberty to buy leather in the cheapest market. Protection denies him the right to use his capital to the best advantage, and asserts that a Customs duty must be imposed on imported leather in order to encourage and maintain the British leather industry.

Faced with the conflict of individual interests, implicit in our complicated and inter-dependent industries, the Protectionist asserts that the State should control national development and modify the relations of the various industrial factors by a "scientific tariff," which shall have regard to the sustenance and maintenance of all important and suitable industries. The doctrine of the "scientific tariff" is a State control of industry which denies that successful industry is compatible with individual liberty, and which sets up a committee of experts to decide what sort of economic development is necessary for the country's prosperity, and what industries, in what degree, shall be developed.

Protection is thus a form of Socialism which sets the State the impossible task of controlling trade by the indirect, clumsy and wasteful method of taxing imports. It is a Socialism which has all the vices of State interference without any of its virtues. A Socialist Government would carry on such trades and industries as it thought essential for the welfare of the nation, and its own departmental committees would be entrusted with the work of economic development. Like the Post Office Department, the committees would report upon such measures as were necessary for their work, and the democratic Government would have to decide, in the general interest, upon the degree and nature of various developments. Such a Government might well fall into error, and might well be deceived and misled by its servants, but at least there would be no private combinations of capitalists who could profit by its measures. A Protectionist Government, on the other hand, having no direct control of industry, is compelled to frame a Customs tariff setting up indirect control, while resigning the powers of monopoly to private hands. Thus, if Socialism is stupid and impossible, Protection is a particularly stupid and impossible method of embodying the Socialist conception.

Mr. Balfour is not entitled to argue that "Tariff Reform" is an alternative to Socialism. He is only entitled to argue that a Socialism which relies upon State control through Customs duties is superior to a Socialism which relies upon the public ownership of capital. He is entitled to urge that Protection is a Socialism which gives play to the motive of private gain in a degree superior to that which would obtain if the machines were owned by the State instead of by private monopolists.

But the Protectionist should seriously consider his position before claiming such a virtue for his Socialism. Can the capitalist be relied upon to make patriotic use of the means of modification presented to him by the practice of Protection? Is the capitalist a good partner in the scheme of State control of industry? For answer let us go no further than Mr. Balfour's own speech of September 22, 1909. In a remarkable passage he said:

"You have capital, mobile capital, international capital, ready to move to America, to Germany, to England, wherever it may be that it can get the best investment. There is not that inequality of opportunity between those countries which was the whole basis of the original economic doctrine of Free Trade. Now, what I want you to notice is this. The condition of things which I have just explained matters very little to the capitalist. If he gets his interest, it matters little to him whether he gets it by giving employment in America, giving employment in Britain, or giving employment in Germany. To him it is all one. It is not one to the workers of this country." (Cheers.)

Such is the capitalistic partner as seen by the leader of modern British Conservatism. He is seen as a creature indifferent to the welfare of his country, indifferent to the lot of the pawns of industry, indifferent to any and every consideration save one—that he gets his interest. He is not an Englishman; he is a capitalist. "To him it is all one" whether Britain sinks or swims. Yet the limner of this pitiful picture of an economic man, which is doubtless exaggerated, but certainly not without truth in some cases, asks the nation to rely upon a Socialism in which the Government is to develop national resources by modulating imports, for the rest entrusting the carrying out of the collective conception to creatures postulated to be without country and without heart.

There is no logical nexus between the negative policy of Free Trade and *laissez faire*, for objection to Protective import duties does not demand that we should reject the principle of State action. An opponent of Protective import duties may be either an individualist who objects to any and every form of State action, or a Socialist who objects to that particular form of State action. On the other hand, a Protectionist is obviously committed to the principle of State action, and Mr. Balfour can only claim that he wears his Socialism with a difference.

**PROTECTION AND REVENUE**—*See* REVENUE FROM PROTECTION.

**QUARRYING**—In their appeals to quarrymen Protectionists alternate between two policies, and it is high time they told us which they intend to pursue. Mr. Chamberlain distinctly pledged himself not to tax raw materials, and this pledge has been reiterated again and again, so plainly that it would be distinctly dishonourable to abandon it. Yet we find Protectionists making local appeals to quarrymen and promising them import duties upon such products as stone, slate, and granite. If these things are not raw materials, then there are no raw materials. Free Traders point out to quarrymen that to tax imports of raw material would be to strike a deadly blow at the prosperity of this country; they cannot, therefore, countenance any attempt to tax foreign stone, slate, or granite. They cannot, for the sake of buying quarrymen's votes, make promises which can only be fulfilled by betraying the best interests of the country. They also point out to quarrymen that if duties were granted on quarried products there would have to be duties on all other products also, so that quarrymen would not gain by import duties.

**RAILWAY RETURNS**—Since the greater part of the productions of a country are necessarily carried on its railways, the railway returns afford an excellent test of the growth of the bulk of trade:

UNITED KINGDOM: GROSS RAILWAY RECEIPTS

| | Passenger Traffic Receipts | Goods Traffic |
|---|---|---|
| | £ | £ |
| 1893 | 35,800,000 | 40,900,000 |
| 1897 | 40,500,000 | 47,800,000 |
| 1903 | 47,900,000 | 55,100,000 |
| 1907 | 50,900,000 | 61,200,000 |

These figures, of course, are absolutely conclusive against the Protectionist tales of declining trade.

**RAILWAYS**—Not individuals, but a system, is chiefly to blame for what is universally admitted to be the present uneconomic position of British railway undertakings. It is not that railway directors or railway managers had, or have, a double dose of original sin. True it is that they ride the public hard, but they have been placed in the saddle by the House of Commons itself. The present technical and financial condition of our railways has its roots in the policy of *laissez faire* which for so long consistently resigned everything connected with British trade and industry to unregulated haphazard development. In all the years since the Stockton-Darlington Railway opened in 1825 it has never been realised in the United Kingdom that the railway problem is a national one, needing national direction fully as much as the Army or the Navy.

In ultimate analysis, trade and industry resolve themselves into movement. To manufacture is to move particles of matter into new and useful positions. A railway, by readily enabling us to bring particles of matter together usefully, is an instrument of industry. It is a tool fully as much as a chisel or a plane is a tool. And, since the rapid movement of persons enables them to choose favourable positions in which to live and make their homes, railways have, or may have, a profound effect upon the social life of nations. A railway is at the back of home-making as much as it is at the back of trade and industry. The nature of the ownership of such a prime instrument is, therefore, a matter of deep national concern, for the owners, by their action or inaction, can in effect determine how a nation shall develop under modern conditions. They can determine in what measure a nation shall make use of its natural advantages. They can determine whether towns shall be healthy or unhealthy. They can determine not only the trade but the welfare of a people.

Through the inadequate manner in which geography is taught in our schools, few of our people realise the tremendous natural advantages which they possess. Here we are at the gates of Europe, living on islands no part of which is far removed from the sea. Yet, by allowing our internal transport system to become cumbrous, inefficient, and dear, we have robbed ourselves of a great part of our natural transport efficiency. The United Kingdom has handicapped itself in the use of its own inventions, while Germany, possessed with the feeling of national organisation, has a railway system, coherent and economical, which has atoned, or largely atoned, for her unfortunate lack of coast-line. As Mr. J. Stephen Jeans puts it in his treatise on the British iron trade:

"It would naturally be supposed that, in a small country like Great Britain, with no point of its area more than a hundred miles or so from a seaport, the cost of transport would be much less than in countries which, like Germany and the United States, are differently situated. Geographical conditions should be entirely favourable to this country. But the natural advantages of our geographical position are not realised as they should be, because of the relatively high railway rates enforced and the absence of competition."

Britain has her coal and iron near the water. She has great coalfields watered by the sea. Germany has neither our ports nor our coast-line. We have neglected our advantages, and partly nullified them by neglecting the economic development of transport. Germany, on the other hand, has wisely and patriotically done her best, by thoughtful and coherent railway and canal development, to atone for her natural disadvantages. So conspicuously has she succeeded that in 1909 it may be said that, through the wonderful facilities placed at the disposal of her traders, she has largely compensated herself for her lack of access to the sea, and that she possesses more *internal* Free Trade than Great Britain. (*See* GERMANY.)

### THE CAPITAL TROUBLE

The present deplorable position of the British railways arises from (1) over-capitalisation, and (2) economic waste through competition and the existence of unnecessary units of management and service.

To take first the question of capital, the burden of over-capitalisation is so great that, even if the follies of competition did not exist, the position of British railways would be exceedingly unfavourable. This should be clearly borne in mind, for even if the economic waste were got rid of the capital burden would remain to oppress the railways, and through them to oppress our trade and industries.

The capitals of British railway companies in 1906 were in the aggregate:

BRITISH RAILWAY CAPITAL IN 1906

| | £ |
|---|---|
| Ordinary Stock ... ... ... ... | 486,700,000 |
| Preferred and Guaranteed Stock ... | 458,500,000 |
| Debentures and Loans ... ... ... | 341,700,000 |
| | £1,286,900,000 |

This enormous sum, almost twice as great as the British National Debt, is probably three times as great as it ought to be. Much of it is purely nominal. The Board of Trade give us the following analysis:

NOMINAL ADDITIONS TO BRITISH RAILWAY CAPITALS

| | Stock | Nominal Additions | | Amount of Stock without Nominal Additions |
|---|---|---|---|---|
| | | Amount | Per Cent. | |
| | Million £ | Million £ | | Million £ |
| Ordinary ... | 486·7 | 90·0 | 18½ | 396·7 |
| Preferred ... | 458·5 | 61·0 | 13½ | 397·5 |
| Debentures ... | 341·7 | 44·3 | 13 | 297·4 |
| Total ... | 1,286·9 | 195·3 | 15 | 1,091·6 |

This table is of very great interest and importance. The watered capital, in point of nominal additions alone, amounts to nearly £200,000,000. Deducting this, British railway capital is reduced to £1,091,600,000 at a stroke.

The importance of the nominal additions lies in this. The net profits of the British railways in 1906 amounted to £44,500,000, a sum equal to one-third of our Imperial revenue, and furnished from the same source as our Imperial revenue—the pockets of the British people. Although this sum is so enormous, it suffices to pay an all-round return of rather less than 3½ per cent. on the nominal capital of £1,286,000,000. But, as the Board of Trade point out, the £44,500,000 is equal to over 4 per cent. on the capital of £1,091,000,000.

How, then, was the nearly £200,000,000 of nominal capital,

which gives such a false appearance to railway figures, made? It was done by a ridiculously simple process. The companies have from time to time gone to Parliament, in which railway interests have always been so largely and directly represented by directors and shareholders, and obtained powers to take £100 of capital and call it £200 or more. Mr. McDermott, editor of the *Railway News*, in his handbook on railways, thus comments on the process:

> "The adoption of 'watering' by duplicating stocks is largely responsible for the unfavourable appearance in recent years of the aggregate statistics of the railways of the United Kingdom in the matter of a return upon the capital invested."

With regard to the practical details of this interesting process, which amounts to financial jugglery, let me give an illustration. The railway authority referred to, who, be it remembered, is the editor of a railway shareholders' paper, says:

> "The Taff Vale Railway, which had earned and distributed dividends as high as 18 per cent., carried the principle [of watering] still further. . . . Permission was obtained by the Act of 1889 to issue £250 of new stock for each original £100."

But it should not be imagined that this particular £200,000,000 of openly watered capital accounts for the whole, or anything like the whole, of the water which masquerades as British railway capital.

In the first place, British landlords, greed meeting greed, charged railway promoters the most outrageous sums for land. In the early days railway Bills were deliberately fought in a Parliament (then composed of *two* Houses of landlords) at enormous expense until the promoters gave way and paid ransom. Mr. William Galt, who, in the middle of the nineteenth century, vainly endeavoured to persuade his countrymen to nationalise the railways, tells of £120,000 being given to one noble lord as the price of the withdrawal of his opposition to a railway Bill. The reader has got to realise that that £120,000 still figures in railway capital, and forms part of the £1,286,900,000 above referred to.

The following examples will show the cost per mile for land on the early railways:

| | Per Mile £ |
|---|---|
| London and South-Western ... ... ... | 4,000 |
| London and Birmingham (now part of the London and North-Western) ... ... ... | 6,300 |
| Great Western ... ... ... ... ... | 6,300 |
| London and Brighton ... ... ... ... | 8,000 |

Apart from the pillage of the landowners, railway speculators —inspired, of course, by the same motives as the landowners —piled up Parliamentary costs by fighting for the control of routes. The following examples will show the enormous costs of introducing and fighting railway Bills in the House of Commons:

| | Per Mile £ |
|---|---|
| London and South-Western ... ... ... | 650 |
| London and Birmingham ... ... ... | 650 |
| Great Western ... ... ... ... ... | 1,000 |
| London and Brighton ... ... ... ... | 3,000 |

Again the reader has got to realise, or try to realise, that these extraordinary sums still figure on railway stock certificates to-day, and form part of the £1,286,900,000 of so-called British railway capital.

To proceed, another variety of "water" was created by a process thus described by Galt in 1864:

"The general demand for railways has called into existence a new class of speculators, who unite in their own persons the several functions of promoters, contractors, shareholders in the first instance, and lessees when necessary—men of great wealth, enterprise, experience, and energy, in every way fully competent to carry out whatever they undertake, always on the look-out for business wherever they can see there is work to be done and the likelihood of a profitable investment. This class is the scourge of the railway interest; in former times they were unknown. Railway companies then only contended with each other; now two or three individuals form a company, and run up an opposition line with or without assistance from others, as the case may be; and when the line is finished they sell it, lease it, or work it in opposition to an old line till they can get their own price, and having cleared a small fortune by the transaction, they are off to fresh fields and pastures new in search of some other enterprise."

A further large sum has been added to the fictitious capital by the issue of railway stocks at large discounts—a fact only partly balanced by certain premium issues.

Again, profits were improperly swollen year after year by the unbusinesslike process of charging against capital large sums which were properly chargeable against revenue. Perhaps the classical instance of this form of watering was the charging of tarpaulins to capital account.

Finally, for generations promotion moneys of the most scandalous character—fees, bribes, commissions, advertisement charges, &c.—have added their quota to the "water" which to-day bulks as £1,286,900,000 of railway capital. In the second railway mania alone, newspapers and bogus railway papers, which sprang up like mushrooms, netted enormous sums from railway promoters.

It is not possible to estimate precisely, as in the case of the stock openly watered with the consent of Parliament, how much water has been added from the previously mentioned and other causes to British railway capital through the resignation of railway construction to promoters and speculators at the best selfish and at the worst dishonest. But there can be no question that it far exceeds in amount the £200,000,000 of manipulation stocks. If the British railways had been constructed by a central authority possessing compulsory powers there can be no question that a very much better railway system than we possess could have been made for £400,000,000. That is to say, railway profits are so enormous at the present time that they represent something like 12 per cent. upon the real capital employed. When the railways talk of their small dividends they, in effect, condemn the methods by which they were brought into existence.

Now let us look at the receipts and expenses of the railway companies:

BRITISH RAILWAY RECEIPTS AND EXPENSES, 1906

| | £ |
|---|---|
| Received from the British public: | |
| (a) From passengers ... ... ... | 49,900,000 |
| (b) From goods' traffic ... ... ... | 58,400,000 |
| (c) From boats, canals, harbours, &c.... | 4,800,000 |
| (d) From rents, hotels, &c. ... ... | 4,100.000 |
| | 117,200,000 |
| Working expenses (including rates only £5,000,000) ... ... ... ... | 72,700,000 |
| Net profit for the year... ... | £44,500,000 |

Yet this princely profit, as we have seen, pays only 3½ per cent. on the fictitious capital. Let us contrast the case of the Prussian State railways.

BRITISH AND PRUSSIAN RAILWAYS CONTRASTED

| | United Kingdom | Prussia |
|---|---|---|
| Mileage ... ... ... | 23,000 | 21,000 |
| Capital employed ... | £1,286,900,000 | £437,700,000 |
| Net profits ... ... | £44,500,000 | £33,500,000 |
| Net profit per cent. of capital employed ... | 3·4 | 7·5 |

I shall have occasion to return to the Prussian railway system presently. In the meantime the reader cannot fail to be struck with these extraordinary figures. The Prussian State railways make a yearly profit of £33,500,000 upon a capital of only £437,700,000. They make 7·5 per cent. when we make only 3·4 per cent. Yet German traders enjoy lower railway rates than we do. *Out of higher charges British railways make a lower rate of profit.* The reader has been given the explanation.

### Railway Waste

Competition in the railway industry is obviously and inherently unnecessary, uneconomical, and absurd. The history of British railway development, down to the latest amalgamations and rumours of amalgamation, is largely concerned with the elimination of competitive waste and unnecessary managements and duplications of service. Small companies serving the same district, in part competing with each other, and each burdened with a separate staff of officials, and with separate offices and depôts, have joined up and created the great trunk lines as we know them. Thus the London and North-Western Railway has been formed from, amongst other lines, the "Manchester and Birmingham," "London and Birmingham," and the "Grand Junction," while the "Grand Junction" was itself the amalgamation of five companies. Again, the Midland amalgamated the "North Midland," "Midland Counties," "Birmingham and Derby," "Bristol and Gloucester," and other lines. By such combinations, strictly economic processes, the number of companies has been reduced until at the present time by far the greater part of our railway system is owned by only twenty-seven companies, which between them employ 90 per cent. of all the railway servants of the United Kingdom. These twenty-seven great companies are now actively negotiating with each other to reduce some of the follies of competitive waste which remain.

Although the economic folly of railway competition is so obvious, Parliament for long blindly clung to the fetish of competition as the protector of the public against railway extortions. In 1872 a Joint Select Committee of both Houses of Parliament pointed out:

"That Committees and Commissions carefully chosen have for the last thirty years clung to one form of competition after another; that it has nevertheless become more and more evident that competition must fail to do for railways what it does for ordinary trade, and that no means has yet been devised by which competition can be permanently maintained.

"That, in spite of the recommendations of these authorities, combination and amalgamation have proceeded at the instance of the companies without check and almost without regulation. United systems now exist, constituting by their magnitude and by their exclusive possession of whole districts monopolies to which the earlier authorities would have been most strongly opposed. *Nor is there any reason to suppose that the progress of combination has ceased or that it will cease until Great Britain is divided between a small number of great companies.*"

It will be seen that the 1872 Committee were true prophets. Their report went on to consider competition in detail. They recorded that competition by sea was in places effective, as it still is; that canal competition was weakening—it has since become even weaker. As to competition between railways, they said:

"There is little real competition in point of charges between railway companies, and its continuance cannot be relied upon. There is at the present time considerable competition in point of facilities, but the security for its permanence is uncertain."

"Self-interest," the Committee went on to say, "still is and will continue to be the leading motive of railway companies." But, unfortunately, the Committee, while recognising that "the management of railways differs from that of an ordinary trade or manufacture, and approximates in some degree to the business of a public department," and while also recognising that the question of public ownership "may possibly arise" through "the progress of combination," did not themselves face the question of nationalisation, but contented themselves with suggesting palliatives of the system of private ownership. Some of their suggestions have since been carried into effect.

Unfortunately, then as now, we had not a Parliament or a statesman prepared to grapple with this question as the Germans grappled with it. And as the years pass the difficulties increase.

The public suffers and pays for all the follies of competitive waste without securing any of the advantages of competition. One may travel by five different routes between London and Manchester. Many unnecessary trains are run between these places daily, and the public pay to run them. In the last resort it is the man at the ticket-office window, or the trader sending goods, who pays for the unnecessary services. The fare by each of the five London–Manchester routes is precisely the same—15s. 5½d. third class—an obviously "arranged" price. Or one can travel by three different routes between London and Birmingham, and again the fare by each route is the same—9s. 5d. Or one can travel by two routes from London to Jersey. The routes are "competitive," but the fare, strange to say, is the same—33s. Seventy-five trains are run, or were run until recently, between London and Sheffield daily by three companies, many arriving about the same time or within a few minutes of each other, three-parts empty. The work could well be done by sixty trains or less, and those who use the seventy-five trains pay to run them when they need only pay to run sixty. They pay also, of course, shares of the wasteful management expenses, advertising, and other charges.

Very tardily the companies themselves appear to be awakening to the follies of unnecessary train-running. *The Times* of September 22, 1908, contains the following paragraph:

"We are able to announce that after November 1st the London and North-Western, Midland, and Great Northern Railway Companies will cease to run competitive midnight trains from London to Inverness, and will concentrate on one train each night. At present three expresses leave Euston, St. Pancras, and King's Cross respectively each night for the North at intervals between 11.30 p.m. and midnight. As a rule the trains are half empty; except at certain times during the holiday season, the passengers might easily be accommodated in one train. The companies concerned have now realised that the three trains are a needless expense. It has been decided, therefore, that in future each company shall despatch two trains a week—and no more. After November 1st the Inverness express will probably depart from Euston on Tuesdays and Thursdays, from St. Pancras on Wednesdays and Saturdays, and from King's Cross on Mondays and Fridays.

"One of the advantages which is expected to follow from the

'grouping' of the principal English railway companies is, of course, the abandonment of duplicated trains running to the same places at or about the same time of the day. Passengers will be able to use their return tickets on any of the lines of the allied companies. Whether the new departure which is announced with regard to the Scottish trains foreshadows an Anglo-Scottish working arrangement in the near future remains to be seen. By some railway officials, at any rate, such an agreement is regarded as extremely likely to take place sooner or later."

Thus one particularly obvious folly ceases, but such obvious follies are to be counted by thousands up and down the railways of the country.

The number of railway directors can only be expressed in four figures. It is an army of waste. They are dummy figures for the most part, who know little of railway management. They draw a large sum of money and give the nation nothing in return. They are not merely useless, they are worse than useless. Their work could be done by a single Railway Board.

The uneconomic division of what ought to be a single national railway system demands, of course, a Railway Clearing House, with an army of 4,000 clerks, to adjust accounts between companies which ought not to exist. From an economic point of view these 4,000 men are unemployed, for they are doing work which ought not to need doing.

Each company is necessarily in trade with every other company. Not only has a central Clearing House to adjust matters, but a large part of the time of the clerks and officers of each company is taken up with the inter-company trading which nationalisation would sweep away.

Take, again, the competition for freights. Each great centre of trade has its competitive railway offices wasting rent, rates, light, salaries, wages, and printing. One great town has eight railway shops in one street; in many towns thousands of pounds per annum per town are wasted in this way.

Here is an account got out by Mr. P. W. Wilson, M.P., of

the amounts spent by seven of the largest companies on duplicated services :

GENERAL MANAGEMENT AND SUPERINTENDENCE

| Company | General Manager | Superintendent of the Line | Locomotive Superintendent | Engines, No. of |
|---|---|---|---|---|
| | £ | £ | £ | |
| North-Western ... | 64,456 | 40,999 | 40,922 | 2,590 |
| Midland ... ... | 48,112 | 25,653 | 24,308 | 2,790 |
| Great Western ... | 49,430 | 33,784 | 18,379 | 2,509 |
| North-Eastern ... | 35,500 | 23,434 | 25,318 | 2,000 |
| South-Western ... | 20,980 | 10,254 | 5,375 | 746 |
| Great Eastern ... | 32,769 | 3,312 | 7,205 | 1,085 |
| Great Northern ... | 31,358 | 12,269 | 8,679 | 1,279 |
| | £282,600 | £149,696 | £130,186 | 12,999 |

Thus nearly £600,000 is spent by only seven companies on services which, if consolidated, could probably be carried out efficiently for less than one-half the money. It is amusing to note that 12,999 locomotive engines demand the attention of seven locomotive superintendents, each, of course, with his staff of officials, offices, clerks, &c. If we got out the same particulars for each of our many railway companies an enormous wastage would be revealed.

The British public are familiar with the duplication of railway stations and termini. The same sort of thing used to obtain in Germany before nationalisation. One may now see in a great German town a palatial railway terminus which has been paid for out of the sale of the sites of the old inefficient competitive termini which it replaced. One wonders how long it will be before King's Cross, St. Pancras, Euston, and Marylebone are turned into one magnificent and convenient railway palace; how long the dirt and inconvenience of a terminus like King's Cross are to remain as a reproach against our business ability and common sense.

Or take the question of advertising. The railway companies are now spending enormous sums on advertising, each advertising its resorts and alleged facilities against the other, and doing it in the most wasteful way. Here is an illustration. At Christmas, 1907, the Great Northern inserted in papers of general circulation an expensive advertisement, which ran:

"G.N.R. EXPRESS DELIVERY OF CHRISTMAS PARCELS

"For particulars of rates and arrangements for collection and delivery, apply any G.N. office or Chief Passenger Agent, King's Cross Station."

As the Great Northern Railway only serve certain districts, to advertise in papers circulating all over the United Kingdom is clearly to waste money. It may be added that the man who sent a Christmas parcel by a railway and not by the State Parcels Post would be very ill-advised. The State has to use the private railways, but its fine collecting and delivery system triumphs in spite of the railways.

If it be thought that what has been said above is an exaggerated picture of railway waste, let the reader ponder what Lord Allerton, Chairman of the Great Northern, said to his shareholders on December 20, 1907, on the occasion of their meeting to "agree" with the Great Central Railway:

"If you go through the streets of London you will see—say, in Shaftesbury Avenue—the G.N.R. have opened a receiving office, and you will see a minute afterwards that the Great Central have opened a receiving office on the other side of the street. . . . Take the case of capital expenditure. Why, there is a mine of wealth there. During the past few years there has been, I will say, hundreds of thousands of pounds spent in capital expenditure by the two companies which might have been saved if this agreement had been made so many years ago, such as in reaching collieries and in what is called protecting the traffic, by making fresh branches, all to be worked over to the same point for the same traffic. All this necessitates engines and trains where very often one would do. The lines are blocked, your lines are crowded, trains are delayed, which lead to all sorts of waste and extravagance, and if it were only for the purpose of saving the enormous waste which necessarily goes on now—I say it would have been well worth your while to have made this agreement with the Great Central many years ago." (Loud applause.)

Lord Allerton then went on to direct his hearers' attention to the "intertwining" and "interweaving" of the two lines, and said:

"You can hardly conceive the disadvantages that exist by two unnecessary and separate train services, not always taking the shortest road, not always making connection at a particular junction so that trains may meet, and very often making the arrangements such that they shall not meet. I know, as a matter of fact, that this is the case."

The Great Northern Chairman then dropped into anecdote, and gave his shareholders the following gem:

"I complained one day at Doncaster—and I hope the Great Central won't be cross with me about this observation—but I was trying to get to a place called Frodingham. You can only get there by going round at Retford, or going by the Central by Doncaster; and I said to the stationmaster—I am afraid in a tone which was not pleasant—'Why on earth don't you agree with the Great Central to make these trains fit?' 'Well, sir,' he said, 'we have altered ours three times in order to make them fit, and every time we have altered them they have altered theirs.' (Laughter.) This is the way in which the public is inconvenienced."

Lord Allerton spoke truly and without exaggeration. Indeed, it would be difficult to imagine any absurdity more exaggerated than the commonplaces of the British railway service. What the British public should deduce from his speech is this: If an agreement between two railway companies is desirable, to prevent economic waste, then *a fortiori* is a combination of all the railways desirable.

Between unnecessary trains, directors, managers, clerks, canvassers, offices, stations, trucks, carriages, engines, advertisements, posters, handbills, time tables, and stationery our railway companies perforce waste many millions every year. The waste, it is clear, can only be eliminated by amalgamation. The more amalgamation the more monopoly, and private individuals cannot safely be allowed to exercise monopoly. Parliament, whose fault it is primarily that the present chaos exists, must perform for the nation what the companies are doing slowly and clumsily in their own private interest. It must amalgamate all the systems into one economic unit, and work that unit in the interest of the people at large.

### Railways and the British Trader

The British trader has a long list of grievances against our railway companies. It is impossible to state the case more than broadly in a general survey such as this, but we may note:

1. The rates charged by British railway companies for the conveyance of goods and minerals are generally in excess of those enjoyed by the British traders' foreign competitors. It follows that British railways act generally in stimulation of foreign competition. In effect they levy a heavy tax upon every trader who purchases or sells minerals or materials.

2. Apart from the general handicap expressed in (1) our railways actually give preferential rates to foreign merchandise (*e.g.*, potatoes) in such manner as to injure British industry.

3. British agriculture is injuriously affected by lack of facilities and high rates.

4. In regard to special charges, such as for cartage, siding rents, demurrage, &c., the companies are practically out of control of the law as it stands, and in regard to these matters they are often unreasonable and tyrannical.

5. The companies, by exacting their high legal maximum rates if traders do not submit, normally obtain freights at "owners' risk," thereby escaping all liability for the damage they inflict.

6. The companies have, in practice, frustrated the intention of Parliament that any trader should be able to demand quotation of through rates.

7. The companies refuse to take consignments of live stock unless the consignor accepts in writing the condition that the railway shall not be responsible for loss.

8. Owing to the long purse of the companies, and their experience in fighting technical points, it is the height of folly for a trader to take action against the companies. Moreover, the railways do not hesitate to resort to retaliation if a litigant is successful against them.

9. No trader is safe from having his trade injured by the grant of preferential railway rates to his rival.

### Success of Railway Nationalisation Abroad

Nothing is more striking than the success which has attended the policy of nationalisation in connection with foreign and Colonial railway systems. The Parliamentary Return No. 331 of 1908, which was made on my motion, shows that the great majority of countries both own and work the whole or the greater part of their railway systems. In the British Empire the Mother Country is almost the only part which has not adopted nationalisation. In Europe, Austria-Hungary, Belgium, Denmark, France, the various States of the German Empire, Italy, Norway, Portugal, Russia, Sweden, Switzerland, and even Turkey, have in whole or part State railways. Elsewhere Japan has recently followed what is the almost universal plan. Britain and America apart, the chief countries of the world give a clear verdict for nationalisation.

The report gives, as far as can be ascertained, the financial results of the policy. But it should be clearly remembered that it is not necessarily the duty of a Government to make profit on its railways at all. Profit may arise, and usually does arise, but the first consideration is service to the nation. That, of course, is the point which differentiates the public from the private railway.

Germany may fairly claim to have achieved both tho ends of revenue and public benefit. It was never imagined when Prussia began her policy of railway nationalisation that profits would be made. The object aimed at was national benefit. The interests of the travelling public were to be served. Trade was to gain, rates were to be simplified, and and so forth. In accomplishing these things the Prussians found that revenues grew so rapidly with improving management that profit arose, and the figures of recent years have been extraordinarily good.

In 1904, while the receipts were £78,663,330, the expenses were only £47,553,497, showing a net profit of £31,109,833, or 7·19 per cent. on the capital employed.

In 1905 the figures were even better. The receipts came to £85,021,612, while the expenses amounted to £51,541,802, showing a net profit of £33,479,810, or 7·54 per cent. on the capital employed.

Now, if these figures had been obtained by excessive fares or freights Prussia would have gained revenue and lost really national profit, but all available evidence goes to show that profits have been made even while enlarged facilities have been given. Thus our attaché at Berlin, in a recent report, said:

> "The improvement has not been brought about by starving the country, but in spite, or, far more likely, in consequence, of reduction in rates, an increase in wages and improvements in the passenger service, while at the same time an amount of capital has been invested in new railways, many of which are secondary lines."

Another observer, Professor Gustav Cohn, says:

> "Considerable reductions have been made in the rates of travel, more especially in the goods traffic, and it is precisely and exclusively in this department that the surplus has been earned. A number of new lines have been constructed which have diminished the net profit of the whole system; the rolling stock, &c., has been much improved, and new stations have been built, the extraordinary magnificence of some of which no other country can produce the parallel."

It is impossible here to set out the scale of German goods traffic in detail, but especial attention should be given to the "preferential rates." They are used not only as bounties to assist certain districts to compete with foreign countries in Germany itself, and as export bounties to encourage foreign trade, but to assist districts when in special distress. Such a policy costs money, and it is in spite of that cost that the Prussian State railways pay a net profit of 7½ per cent. The export bounties may be illustrated from the Levant trade. In order to favour German exporters, a special Levant tariff was introduced in 1890. As a consequence our exporters suffered.

To illustrate another point, in 1891 the German harvest was very bad. Accordingly, the rates on all kinds of grain were specially cheapened to relieve the consequent distress. But, in spite of this policy, high railway profits were made in 1891.

With regard to general facilities, there can be no question that the Prussian railway administration has achieved a simplicity in its goods traffic and rates to which the British trader is unhappily a stranger.

It should be added that the other States of Germany also own their own railways, in every case with profitable results. In 1905 the Report shows that the railways of the German Empire, including Prussia, made a net profit of nearly £43,000,000.

To pass from bureaucratic Germany to democratic Switzerland; the Swiss people sanctioned nationalisation in 1898 by a referendum, and by a majority of two to one. Nationalisation is thus quite recent, but already the financial results, the Report says, are quite satisfactory. Not only are the profits paying interest, but they are paying off the capital in such fashion that in sixty years the whole will be repaid. But again it is to be observed that the question of profit is the smallest part of the business, for goods rates have been reduced and the railway service has been improved. The net profit in 1905 amounted to £1,620,816. As already pointed out, the railwayman's hours and wages have been improved, and they have been granted Old Age Pensions and other benefits.

Belgium furnishes another instance of successful working in spite of fares which, to a British traveller, appear incredibly low, and in spite of low railway freights. The working expenses and pensions of the Belgian State railways in 1905 were £3,706,362 less than the gross receipts, so that not only were all interest charges met but a large amount of capital repaid.

Austria, on the other hand, is an instance in which, while a considerable profit is made on the working, that profit is not large enough to meet all the charges for interest and sinking fund, but it should not be forgotten that in Austria, as in Germany, profit has not so much been aimed at as public benefit.

To sum up, there is as little inclination in the world at large to revert from public railways to private railways as there is in British towns to revert from public tramways to private tramways, and for the same good reasons.

### Is Nationalisation Practicable in Britain?

Is nationalisation practicable for us? The British railway muddle has been made; can we win our way through State purchase and control to an economic railway position?

Nationalisation, obviously, could not at once dry up the oceans of "water" which, as we have seen, exist in British railway capitals to-day. A moment's thought, however, will show that it is equally obvious that:

1. Public credit being higher than private railway credit, a great saving in interest could at once be effected by public ownership.
2. The institution of a sinking fund derived from the large sums that would be saved by the abolition of the follies of railway waste would, year by year, diminish the railway capital burden.

The finance of the question presents no insuperable difficulty. It would be both practicable and equitable to pay out British railway shareholders as the late Lord Goschen converted the National Debt. Goschen's conversion scheme dealt with nearly £600,000,000 of Consols. And it would be but little more difficult to deal with twice that amount of railway stock on some such lines as the following:—

Taking the present profit—£44,500,000—at 25 years' purchase, we get £1,112,000,000, to which let us add, say, £40,000,000 for non-dividend stocks, making £1,152,000,000.

If the railway shareholders were paid this sum in Government stock at par, bearing $3\frac{1}{2}$ per cent. interest for ten years and 3 per cent. interest thereafter, the immediate payment of interest would amount to £40,000,000 per annum, which, after ten years, would be reduced to about £34,000,000 per annum.

Immediately, therefore, charges could be reduced, even if there were no economy from combination. But large economies would be certain, and out of them would proceed reduction of fares and freight rates and increase of facilities which, in their turn, would produce a vast increase of both passenger and goods traffic and a consequent swelling of profits.

In Britain, as in Germany, the service of the public interest would bring in its train a handsome addition to the Imperial revenue.

A discussion of the relation of railways to Free Trade will be found under Free Trade.

**RAW MATERIALS IMPORTED**—The imports of raw materials of industry into the United Kingdom have grown enormously, and the following figures will repay careful attention:

UNITED KINGDOM: IMPORTS OF RAW MATERIALS FOR HOME CONSUMPTION

| | 1887 | 1907 |
|---|---|---|
| Iron ore (tons) ... ... | 3,759,000 ... | 7,633,000 |
| Copper (tons) ... ... ... | 186,000 ... | 240,000 |
| Lead (tons) ... ... ... | 126,000 ... | 205,000 |
| Zinc (tons) ... ... ... | 57,000 ... | 89,000 |
| Tin, crude (cwts.) ... ... | 280,000 ... | 340,000 |
| Cotton (cwts.) ... ... ... | 13,382,000 ... | 18,364,000 |
| Wool, hair, &c. (including home-grown) (lb.) ... | 514,600,000 ... | 850,300,000 |
| Timber (loads)... ... ... | 5,654,000 ... | 9,622,000 |
| Furniture woods (tons) ... | 95,000 ... | 260,000 |
| Paper materials (tons) ... | 340,000 ... | 891,000 |
| Paper (cwts.) ... ... ... | 1,692,000 ... | 8,741,000 |
| Hides (cwts.) ... ... ... | 662,000 ... | 639,000 |

Here is most conclusive proof of how the industries of the United Kingdom have grown in only twenty years.

**RAW MATERIALS IMPORTED (SOURCES OF)**—Our enormous imports of raw materials are drawn chiefly from foreign countries.

BRITISH IMPORTS OF RAW MATERIALS, 1908

| | £ |
|---|---|
| From foreign countries ... ... ... ... | 145,548,000 |
| From British possessions ... ... ... ... | 57,907,000 |
| Total imports ... ... ... ... ... | 203,455,000 |
| Re-exported ... ... ... ... ... | 45,310,000 |
| Net imports for home consumption ... | 158,145,000 |

It will be seen that over two-thirds of our indispensable imported raw materials are drawn from foreign countries; these are the chief "dumpings" we receive. (*See* remarks under PREFERENCE.)

The above figures relate to the Board of Trade "Raw Materials" classification. In addition, of course, we import an enormous quantity of "manufactures" which are materials, such as copper, tin, zinc, yarns, straw plait, &c. (*See* MANUFACTURES, IMPORTED.)

**RECIPROCITY**—"Reciprocity" was a term coined by Protectionists because, when it was invented in the seventies, the very name of Protection was so discredited by British experience that Protectionists were compelled to assume an alias. The same motive led to the coining of the names "Fair Trade" and "Tariff Reform." By "Reciprocity" is meant the Protectionist belief that if a Protectionist country puts a duty on British wool, as America does, we should put a duty on American wool, to pay them back. The Free Trader points out that because America is foolish it is no reason why we should imitate her folly. We are not Free Traders to oblige other nations, but to please and benefit ourselves.

**RE-EXPORTS**—This is a term used to denote our exports of imported goods, as distinguished from our exports of British productions. (*See* Entrepôt Trade.)

**RETALIATION**—This is another of the terms under which Protection disguises itself. Sometimes the Protectionist tells you that he wishes for import duties in order to keep out foreign goods, *i.e.*, he desires Protection for the sake of Protection. At other times, he argues that he desires import duties in order to retaliate upon, and break down, foreign import duties, *i.e.*, that he desires import duties merely in order to take them off again when, by retaliation and negotiation, he has reduced foreign duties. It is a delightful example of the confusion of thought which permeates Protectionist reasoning.

As a matter of fact, experience clearly shows that the imposition of import duties does not break down foreign tariffs; on the contrary, it builds them up. Thus the last German tariff, instead of breaking down the tariffs of Germany's neighbours, led to the imposition of higher duties upon German goods by nearly all the Continental countries.

Of course, Free Traders have never renounced the right to retaliate in case of an attempt deliberately to damage British trade, but generally the Free Trader holds with Sir Robert Peel, who declared, after long and vain trial of Retaliation, that "we will consider our own interests and meet hostile tariffs with Free Imports."

**REVENUE FROM PROTECTION**—The raising of revenue by means of Customs duties protective in aim, expresses a confusion of thought and intention which was dwelt upon in the Report of the Select Committee of the House of Commons which in 1840 examined in detail and condemned the system which was then called "Protection," and which now masquerades as "Tariff Reform." The following passages from the Report of 1840 may be usefully noted in this connection:

"The tariff often aims at incompatible ends; *the duties are sometimes meant to be both productive of revenue and for protective objects*, which are frequently inconsistent with each other; hence they sometimes operate to the complete exclusion of foreign produce, and in so far no revenue can, of course, be received, and sometimes when the duty is inordinately high, the amount of revenue becomes, in consequence, trifling. They do not make the receipt of revenue the main consideration, but allow that primary object of fiscal regulations to be thwarted by an attempt to *protect a great variety of particular interests at the expense of the revenue and of commercial intercourse with other countries*. . . . The same principle of preference is largely applied by the various discriminating duties to the produce of our Colonies, *by which exclusive advantages are given to the Colonial interests at the expense of the Mother Country*."

In 1909, as in 1840, Protectionists urge the value of import duties in restriction of imports, even while they represent that a great and growing revenue is to be obtained by taxing imports. At every street corner Protectionist stump orators urge the British workman to "make work" by shutting out the imports which are alleged to deprive him of a job, even while an expanding return to the Treasury from the collection of import duties is advocated as an alternative to super-tax and death duty, and while by implication the continued growth of work-destroying imports is confessed.

On the morrow of the pronouncement by Mr. Chamberlain at Glasgow on October 6, 1903, I worked out a calculation of the revenue effect of Mr. Chamberlain's fiscal programme of 2s. per quarter on corn except maize, 5 per cent. on meat except bacon, 5 per cent. on dairy produce, and an average 10 per cent. on manufactures. Although information as to our home production of meat, &c., was not then as good as it is now, the estimates which I then made and published remain substantially reliable. I have thought it well, however, to re-work the figures, bringing them up to date, and utilising the valuable estimates of production of certain foods which have since been made. The quaint exclusion of maize and bacon from taxation has now been abandoned by the Protectionist party, and this factor slightly modifies the result.

I begin with corn, upon the foreign imports of which Mr. Chamberlain proposed to levy a duty of 2s. per quarter, or, say, 6d. per cwt. It should be remarked that Mr. Chamberlain's Tariff "Commission" have rejected what was a cardinal point of Mr. Chamberlain's policy, *that Colonial food should remain untaxed.* They have whittled down the Preference by proposing differential duties of 2s. per quarter on foreign corn and 1s. per quarter on Colonial corn—a fact which has not yet been brought home either to the British elector or to the Colonial corn producer. Cementing the Empire by means of a shilling duty where no duty now exists is by way of being a humorous proposition. However, I must not neglect this point in my calculations, since it obviously raises the gain to the British Treasury while it reduces the gain to the "cemented" Colonist.

Taking the figures of 1907, our supplies of corn, expressed in cwts., were roundly as follows :

BRITISH SUPPLIES OF CORN IN 1907

(In Millions of Cwts.)

| Corn | Home Supply | Foreign Supply | Colonial Supply | Total |
|---|---|---|---|---|
| Wheat (flour imports being expressed in equivalent weight of grain) ... ... | 28·2 | 73·8 | 41·8 | 143·8 |
| Barley ... ... | 33·1 | 17·6 | 2·0 | 52·7 |
| Oats ... ... ... | 91·8 | 8·9 | 1·6 | 102·3 |
| Maize ... ... | — | 50·4 | 2·9 | 53·3 |
| Rye ... ... ... | — | 0·8 | 0·1 | 0·9 |
| Buckwheat ... ... | — | 0·1 | — | 0·1 |
| Peas ... ... ... | 2·4 | 0·8 | 0·5 | 3·7 |
| Beans ... ... | 5·3 | 0·6 | 0·2 | 6·1 |
| Locust beans ... | — | 0·4 | 0·6 | 1·0 |
| Total ... ... | 160·8 | 153·4 | 49·7 | 363·9 |

Now let us apply to these facts the amended Chamberlain programme of 6d. per cwt. on foreign corn and 3d. per cwt. on Colonial corn. The British Treasury would undoubtedly get its revenue; the British Colonist would get 3d. per cwt. on his small supply; the British consumer would no less certainly have to pay the higher rate of tax, 6d. per cwt. on the entire supply of foreign, Colonial, and home-grown corn. Thus we get:

REVENUE FROM AND INCIDENCE OF THE CORN DUTIES

| Supply | | Duty Received by Treasury | Tax on Consumer | Colonists' Gain |
|---|---|---|---|---|
| | Cwts. | £ | £ | £ |
| Foreign (duty 6d.) | 153,000,000 | 3,800,000 | 3,800,000 | — |
| Colonial (duty 3d.) | 50,000,000 | 600,000 | 1,200,000 | 600,000 |
| Home ... ... | 161,000,000 | — | 4,000,000 | — |
| Total ... ... | 364,000,000 | 4,400,000 | 9,000,000 | 600,000 |

The result, it will be seen, is that the consumer is called upon to pay £9,000,000, in order that the Treasury may receive £4,400,000, and to give British Colonists a beggarly £600,000.

I have neglected the taxation of rice, tapioca, &c., which would also be taxed under the Chamberlain proposals, in order to simplify the subject.

I next consider the duties on meats. Mr. Chamberlain's proposal was 5 per cent. on foreign meat, and no duty on Colonial meat. Mr. Chamberlain's Tariff "Commission" delicately suggest that the duty on Colonial meat should be *subject to negotiation with the Colonies*, which, I take it, may mean many things, but certainly *does not mean untaxed Colonial meat.* I will take the liberty of supposing that, as in the case of corn, the Colonial duty would be half the foreign duty, *i.e.*, 2½ per cent.

In 1907 we imported £38,000,000 worth of foreign meat

and £14,000,000 worth of Colonial meat. According to the careful estimates of Mr. Hooker, of the Board of Agriculture, our home supply of meat is roundly as follows:

BRITISH HOME-GROWN MEAT

| | Mill. Cwts. |
|---|---|
| Beef ... ... ... ... ... ... ... | 13·1 |
| Veal ... ... ... ... ... ... ... | 0·8 |
| Mutton ... ... ... ... ... ... ... | 4·9 |
| Lamb ... ... ... ... ... ... ... | 0·7 |
| Pig meat ... ... ... ... ... ... | 5·8 |
| Total ... ... ... ... ... ... | 25·3 |

Our home-grown meat, 25,000,000 cwts., contrasts with about 22,000,000 cwts. imported from abroad. Few people are aware how large a proportion of our food is still raised at home. I assume that our home supply of meat is worth about £60,000,000 per annum against the £45,000,000 worth we import.

I now apply to these facts the 5 per cent. duty on foreign meat and the 2½ per cent. duty on Colonial meat, and we get:

REVENUE FROM AND INCIDENCE OF THE MEAT DUTIES

| Supply | | Duty Received by Treasury | Tax on Consumer | Colonists' Gain |
|---|---|---|---|---|
| | £ | £ | £ | £ |
| Foreign (duty 5 per cent.) | 38,000,000 | 1,900,000 | 1,900,000 | — |
| Colonial (duty 2½ per cent.) | 14,000,000 | 350,000 | 700,000 | 350,000 |
| Home ... ... ... | 60,000,000 | — | 3,000,000 | — |
| Total ... ... ... | 112,000,000 | 2,250,000 | 5,600,000 | 350,000 |

The result in the case of meat is that the consumer is called upon to pay £5,600,000, in order that the Treasury may raise £2,250,000, and that the Colonial meat producer may receive the negligible gift of £350,000.

Coming to dairy produce, Mr. Chamberlain's suggested duty was 5 per cent.; and again we find Mr. Chamberlain's Tariff "Commission" stating that the Colonial duty must be "*subject to negotiation with the Colonies"*—it is a pretty and a suggestive phrase. I again interpret this to mean at least 2½ per cent. on Colonial dairy produce, but, when the tiger has once tasted blood, the minimum Colonial duty will be worked up as the Canadians have worked up their minimum "preferential" tariff.

In 1907 our imports of dairy produce were as follows:

BRITISH IMPORTS OF DAIRY PRODUCE, 1907

| | Foreign Million £ | | Colonial Million £ |
|---|---|---|---|
| Butter ... ... ... | 17·6 | ... | 4·8 |
| Cheese ... ... ... | 1·3 | ... | 5·6 |
| Milk ... ... ... | 1·6 | ... | — |
| Eggs ... ... ... | 7·1 | ... | — |
| | 27·6 | | 10·4 |

Our home supplies have been investigated in part by a special Committee of the Royal Statistical Society, who have estimated that in the average of the five years ended June, 1903, we produced at home 68,300 tons of cheese, 156,250 tons of butter, and 620,000,000 gallons of milk used as milk. At £70 a ton the cheese is worth £4,781,000; at £110 a ton the butter is worth £17,187,000; at ninepence a gallon the milk is worth £23,250,000. These three items alone aggregate over £45,000,000 a year, to say nothing of eggs.

Applying to these facts the 5 per cent. duty on foreign stuff and the 2½ per cent. duty on Colonial stuff we get:

REVENUE FROM AND INCIDENCE OF THE DAIRY PRODUCE DUTIES

| Supply | | Duty Received by Treasury | Tax on Consumer | Colonists' Gain |
|---|---|---|---|---|
| | £ | £ | £ | £ |
| Foreign (duty 5 per cent.) | 28,000,000 | 1,400,000 | 1,400,000 | — |
| Colonial (duty 2½ per cent.) | 10,000,000 | 250,000 | 500,000 | 250,000 |
| Home ... ... ... | 45,000,000 | — | 2,200,000 | — |
| Total ... ... ... | 83,000,000 | 1,650,000 | 4,100,000 | 250,000 |

Although imports of fresh milk are practically non-existent it is difficult to see how a rise in the price of milk could be avoided, for the milk-producer would have to pay more for his feeding-stuffs, and manures, and every necessary of his business and life.

The case as to dairy produce, it will be seen, is that the consumer would have to pay £4,100,000 in order that the Treasury might gain only £1,650,000, and to give Colonial butter and cheese producers the small sum of £250,000.

To sum up the revenue effect and incidence of the Chamberlain food duties as amended by the Tariff "Commission," we get the following figures :

REVENUE FROM AND INCIDENCE OF THE PROPOSED DUTIES ON CORN, MEAT, AND DAIRY PRODUCE

| | Duty Received by Treasury | Tax on Consumer | Colonists' Gain |
|---|---|---|---|
| | £ | £ | £ |
| Corn ... ... | 4,400,000 | 9,000,000 | 600,000 |
| Meat ... ... | 2,250,000 | 5,600,000 | 350,000 |
| Dairy produce ... | 1,650,000 | 4,100,000 | 250,000 |
| Total ... ... | 8,300,000 | 18,700,000 | 1,200,000 |

The total result is that the British consumer would have to pay nearly £19,000,000 a year in order to put about £8,000,000 into the British Treasury and to benefit Colonial food producers by only £1,200,000 a year. In considering the last figure it should be remembered that Colonial Preference, and Colonial Preference only, was the starting-point of Mr. Chamberlain's fiscal propaganda. Now openly, and without shame, the Tariff "Commission" whittle away the Colonial gain to a mere £1,000,000 a year. I wonder how many Colonists are aware of the proposal to tax their exports to this country.

I ought to point out in passing that my tables do not exhaust the duties proposed by the Tariff "Commission," who have added to Mr. Chamberlain's programme duties on foreign and

Colonial fruit, potatoes, hops, and vegetables. Even Canadian apples are to be taxed under the new Imperialism.

We now come to a more difficult part of the inquiry, viz., the revenue effect of Mr. Chamberlain's "average 10 per cent. duty on imported manufactures." The mask has been thrown off with regard to Colonial manufactures, our imports of which are worth about £20,000,000 per annum, and there is no longer doubt that it is the intention of the Protectionists, if they get the chance, to tax Colonial manufactures as well as Colonial food. In 1907 our imports of foreign and Colonial manufactures for home consumption were worth £128,000,000 per annum, taking as "manufactures" the articles classified by the Board of Trade as "articles wholly or mainly manufactured."

Now, there is little doubt that the application to these imports of an all-round *ad valorem* duty of 5 per cent. or 10 per cent. would check importation but little. I believe that Mr. F. E. Smith, M.P., has said somewhere that he thinks a 10 per cent. duty would reduce imports by 50 per cent.; it is a preposterous suggestion. The German tariff on manufactures averages much more than 10 per cent., and the American tariff is higher still; yet both countries import about £100,000,000 worth of manufactures a year, if we classify them in the same way as ours are classified. Any statement on the subject of the possible decline in importation through an import duty must be necessarily speculative; but I have little doubt myself that if we applied a flat 10 per cent. rate to imports of the class named, their importation would not decline by more than 10 per cent. or 15 per cent. If we assume the reduction to be 15 per cent., imports of manufactures would be reduced to £109,000,000 per annum from all sources, foreign and Colonial. (It cannot too clearly be borne in mind that my figures relate to imports for home consumption.) Ten per cent. levied on £109,000,000 of imports would yield nearly £11,000,000 of revenue.

But the moment we come to grips with the details of our imports of manufactures, the sheer impossibility of levying 10 per cent., or anything like it, on many of the articles included in the £128,000,000 of imported foreign and Colonial manufactures, reveals itself. Take, for example, the Tariff "Commission's" report on the iron and steel trades issued in 1904. In paragraph 88 they suggest the following provisional scale of duties:

SCALE OF IRON AND STEEL DUTIES PROPOSED BY THE TARIFF "COMMISSION"

| | |
|---|---|
| Pig iron .. ... ... ... ... | 5 per cent. |
| Iron and steel bars, ingots, blooms, billets, &c., rails, girders, &c. ... | 6¼ per cent. |
| Wire rods and plates ... ... | 7½ per cent. |
| Sheets ... ... ... ... ... | 10 per cent. |
| Nails, screws, rivets, bolts, tyres, railway wheels and axles, crucible steel, &c. ... ... ... ... | Not to exceed 10 per cent. |

This, of course, amounts, not to an average 10 per cent., but to a much lower average, and it would be difficult to gain even a hearing for a higher scale.

But let us consider the following great categories included in the £128,000,000 of foreign and Colonial manufactures:

IMPORTS FOR HOME CONSUMPTION IN 1907

| | £ |
|---|---|
| B. Other metals: Copper, lead, zinc, tin, &c., chiefly in unwrought form ... | 22,000,000 |
| J. Chemicals, dyes, &c. ... ... ... | 10,000,000 |
| K. Leather, chiefly unwrought ... ... | 9,000,000 |
| M. Paper... ... ... ... ... ... | 5,500,000 |
| Total ... ... ... ... | £46,500,000 |

Here, in four categories of the trade returns, is revealed £46,500,000 worth of indispensable manufacturing materials upon which no Government could propose a 10 per cent. duty without suffering defeat in the House of Commons. On much of the stuff included in these items not even 5 per cent. could be levied without arousing a storm of opposition. The greater part of it would have to be put on the free list.

The fact is that most Protectionists believe that our £128,000,000 worth of imported foreign and Colonial manufactures consist of such things as are retailed in the shops, from hats to boots, and from watches to musical instruments. This belief is ludicrously at variance with the facts, for the greater part of our imports of manufactures consist of manufacturers' materials upon which British work is done, and without which British work could not be done. That is why I believe that a 10 per cent. all-round import duty would reduce consumption so little. Manufacturers must continue to import their materials, and the fall in importation of 10 to 15 per cent. which I think would ensue would not mean that the articles would be made at home instead of being imported, but would simply mean a reduction in general trade and output caused by appreciation in price.

The four categories named by no means exhaust the manufacturers' materials contained in the £128,000,000; indeed, of that total only about £50,000,000 worth consists of articles imported ready for retail consumption (*see* MANUFACTURES, IMPORTED, p. 162).

That is why it is that while a 10 per cent. all-round *ad valorem* duty would yield about £11,000,000, such a revenue could not be obtained in practice. Ten per cent. on the articles imported ready for retailing, after allowing for 15 per cent. reduction of volume, would yield only £4,000,000, and from the remaining £78,000,000 worth or so of manufactures, material, and plant, a Protectionist Government, if elected to-morrow, would find it difficult to obtain more than a few millions more. If they raised an average 5 per cent. on the £78,000,000, allowing for a reduction of 15 per cent. in imports, they would get about £3,500,000.

So that, on an importation of manufactures assumed to be reduced from £128,000,000 to £109,000,000 by the import duty, a Protectionist Government might get £4,000,000 from the articles ready for retail consumption, and £3,500,000 from the manufactured materials and plant; total, £7,500,000.

What of the consumer? The £7,500,000 is what the Government would get. What would the consumer pay in order to give this £7,500,000 to the Government?

The value of our home production of manufactures is unknown, but probably we produce about £900,000,000 worth a year. I imagine further that our annual production of manufactures *finished ready for retail* is about £500,000,000. I hardly see, therefore, how even such moderate duties as I have discussed could cost the consumer less than £50,000,000 per annum. Even if we neglect the duties on manufactured materials and plant, and confine ourselves to 10 per cent. levied on imported retail goods, we can hardly suppose that the general tax on the consumer, through price, on both imported supplies and native productions, could be less than this figure. In the nature of the case it is impossible to do more than make intelligent speculations, but in my opinion the figure named is the most conservative that we can entertain as reasonable. But the reader has the chief facts of the case before him, and can form a judgment for himself.

I sum up my tentative conclusions on this head in tabular form.

REVENUE FROM AND INCIDENCE OF DUTY ON MANUFACTURES

| Supply | | Duty Received by Treasury | Tax on Consumer | Colonists' Gain |
|---|---|---|---|---|
| | £ | £ | £ | £ |
| Foreign and Colonial imports reduced to | 109,000,000 | 7,500,000 | 7,500,000 | — |
| Home ... ... | 900,000,000 | — | 50,000,000 | — |
| Total ... | 1,009,000,000 | 7,500,000 | 57,500,000 | — |

In practice, of course, this great tax on the consumer would operate in a reduction of spending power, a consequent fall in production, and in a transfer of wealth from unprotected to protected interests—*i.e.*, from the many to the few.

If we now sum up this survey of the subject, we get the following figures:

REVENUE FROM AND INCIDENCE OF THE PROPOSED DUTIES ON FOOD AND MANUFACTURES

| | Duty Received by Treasury | Tax on Consumer | Colonists' Gain |
|---|---|---|---|
| | £ | £ | £ |
| Food ... ... | 8,300,000 | 18,700,000 | 1,200,000 |
| Manufactures... | 7,500,000 | 57,500,000 | — |
| Total ... | 15,800,000 | 76,200,000 | 1,200,000 |

The general result is thus exhibited as a tax on consumers amounting to £76,000,000 a year, nearly the whole of which would go into private pockets. The Treasury would receive less than £16,000,000, while the British Colonist, who played the part of a stalking-horse at the beginning of the Protectionist campaign, would find himself fobbed off with a trumpery £1,000,000 of preferential gain on his food supplies, while smarting under the infliction of British duties on manufactures, levied upon him in the name of an Imperial policy. It has been a short step from Mr. Chamberlain's original call on the British people to make "sacrifices" in the name of Empire to the Tariff "Commission's" proposal to tax Imperial products.

Now let us consider the revenue of nearly £16,000,000 which the amended Chamberlain programme might conceivably produce. Mr. Chamberlain pledged himself, and his followers are honourably pledged, to remit taxes on tea, sugar, &c., to set off the £8,000,000 or so raised by the taxation of bread, meat, and dairy produce. *Therefore, that item cannot be considered as an addition to the revenue.*

So important is this point that I think it well to put on record here the nature of the honourable pledges which have been given to the British people by Mr. Chamberlain and his followers, that, whatever happens in the near or distant future, there may be something more than a newspaper record of the nature of the Protectionist campaign.

Speaking at the Constitutional Club, London, on June 26, 1903, Mr. Chamberlain said:

"If an increased cost on bread is met by an approximate decrease on some other articles, either for consumption, or that are necessary for the comfort of his life, then in that case, although the cost of bread might be raised, the cost of living will not be increased in the slightest degree."

At Glasgow, on October 6, 1903, Mr. Chamberlain, in the opening speech of his campaign, gave the pledge in most definite terms, accompanied by an accusation against his opponents that they were concealing the fact that he had made the pledge. This is what Mr. Chamberlain said:

"If you wish to have a preference, if you desire to gain this increase of trade, if you want to prevent separation, you must put a tax on food. Now there is the murder—the murder is out. . . . This statement, which they quote, is true, but it is only half the truth, and they never give you the other half. YOU NEVER SEE ATTACHED TO THIS STATEMENT, THAT YOU MUST TAX FOOD, THE OTHER WORDS THAT I HAVE USED IN REFERENCE TO THIS SUBJECT, THAT NOTHING THAT I PROPOSE WOULD ADD ONE FARTHING TO THE COST OF LIVING OF THE WORKING MAN, OR OF ANY FAMILY IN THIS COUNTRY. . . . You have heard it said that I propose to put a duty of 5s. or 10s. a quarter on wheat. I propose to put a low duty on foreign corn, no duty at all on the corn coming from our British possessions. But I propose to put a low duty on foreign corn, not exceeding 2s. a quarter. I propose to put no tax whatever on maize. . . . I propose to put a small tax of about 5 per cent. on foreign meat and dairy produce. I propose to exclude bacon, because, once more, bacon is a popular food to some of the poorest of the population. . . . BUT I PROPOSE ALSO SOME GREAT REMISSIONS; I PROPOSE TO TAKE OFF THREE-FOURTHS OF THE DUTY ON TEA, AND HALF OF THE WHOLE DUTY ON SUGAR, WITH A CORRESPONDING REDUCTION ON COCOA AND COFFEE."

Mr. Chamberlain then went on to say that he had worked out workmen's budgets, and that he was quite sure that his remissions would more than balance his new taxes. He finished his argument by saying:

"You will see, if you follow me, that on the assumption that you pay the whole of the new taxes yourselves, the agricultural labourer would be half a farthing per week to the better, and the artisan would be exactly the same."

At Newcastle, on October 20, 1903, Mr. Chamberlain said:

"I am not asking you to raise the amount of taxes in this country. I am asking you to transfer them from one pocket to another."

The official propaganda of the Tariff Reform League repeated these pledges again and again. For example, their leaflet 104 says:

"Instead of putting the duties on tea, coffee, sugar, and tobacco, we can put them on foreign corn, foreign meat, and foreign butter."

So that the £8,000,000 of revenue from new food duties is not gain to the Treasury, for the Protectionists are under pledge to give it back by remissions of old taxes. At the same time we must remember that as the taxes on tea, sugar, or tobacco remitted are Free Trade taxes, the consumer would not be recouped by cancelling £8,000,000 of them against £8,000,000 of new Protective taxes on bread and meat. As we have seen, the latter would cost the consumer nearly £19,000,000, so that after the remission of old taxes the consumer would be £11,000,000 to the bad.

There remains only the £7,500,000 revenue from taxes on manufactures. This would be diminished by the serious cost of collection, which could hardly be less than £1,000,000, reducing the net revenue from the whole protective scheme to £6,500,000 a year. In order to give this small additional revenue to the Government, the consumer, as will be seen, would pay some £76,000,000, if not more.

As for "making work" through the taxation of imported goods, this has been disposed of in passing. Mr. F. E. Smith, I suppose, felt himself called upon to promise a reduction of 50 per cent. in the imports of manufactures, through a small import duty, in order to make out a case for "more work." I have noticed that the *Daily Mail* has seized upon a statement of mine, similar to that in this article, that a small import duty on manufactures would yield revenue, as a triumphant vindication of "Tariff Reform." The *Daily Mail* should have thought twice before admitting that, under the Chamberlain programme, manufactures would continue to come in only slightly diminished in volume. It is really high time that Protectionists made up their minds whether they want growing revenue from an increasing volume of imports as an "alternative" to Mr. Lloyd George's Budget, or a diminution of the imports which, they declare, cause poverty and distress in the British Isles.

* * *

After the manuscript of this book went to the printer, the *Birmingham Daily Post* published (on December 8, 1909) an article which, it is believed, is inspired by Mr. Chamberlain, and which may be taken to represent the official amendment of the Glasgow programme above referred to. The essential parts of the article are as follows:

"It is proposed to establish a general tariff, placing duties on practically all goods which are not deemed to be raw materials, with the object, first, of raising revenue; secondly, of giving the turn of the market to the home producer when in competition with a foreign rival; thirdly, of making preferential agreements with the Colonies; fourthly, of securing better terms of entry into foreign countries which now exclude us by prohibitive duties; and finally, of giving such encouragement to home producers that the evils of unemployment will be substantially mitigated.

"The tariff is to be of the simplest possible form, and is not to be 'protective' in the sense in which that word is understood in Germany or the United States. There is no intention, we believe, of having multifarious rates which throw open the door for Parliamentary intrigue or lobbying. There will be three rates of duty only, giving an average of about 10 per cent. The plan which we believe to be at present favoured is to allow raw materials to come in free, to place a duty of 5 per cent. on goods on which little labour has been spent, 10 per cent. on goods more nearly approaching the finished state, and 15 per cent. on completely manufactured articles.

There will be no variations from this scale, unless some very exceptional case can be proved.

"Thus the work of classification will be greatly simplified. Each article will almost naturally fall into its proper class, and, even when there is doubt, no great difficulty can arise. Just as there are to be three rates of duty, so there will be three scales in each rate.

"A tariff framed on the basis indicated above is calculated to produce a revenue of from £16,000,000 to £20,000,000, and at the same time to give an immense impulse to home trade and home employment. The cost of collection is put down at a maximum of £250,000—a marked contrast to the extravagant estimates of Free Trade speakers, who know little or nothing about the business of a Customs Department. It is admitted, however, that neither the full revenue nor the full cost of collection is certain to be in operation during the first year of a Unionist Administration.

"To take an example by way of illustration—if an article is deemed to come under the 10 per cent. rate, that will be the standard duty applicable to foreigners who are commercially 'friendly.' But there will be a lower duty—possibly 7½ per cent.—to be charged on Colonial produce, and a higher duty—possibly 12½ or 15 per cent.—to be charged on the produce of countries which seek unduly to penalise British goods.

"The figures we give are intended only to be illustrative. They may be varied in the actual working out of the tariff. Corn, according to present views, is to be liable to a duty of 2s. a quarter when coming from a foreign country. The chief object of this duty, of course, is to make it possible to give a valuable preference to the Colonies—Canada and Australia in particular.

"Mr. Chamberlain proposed to remit the whole of the duty to the Colonies. There is, however, a possibility of this arrangement being modified by asking the Colonies to agree to a substantial preference which will not free them from the whole of the duty. The chief aim of any modification would, of course, be to increase the revenue, and at the same time to lend some encouragement to wheat-growing at home.

"Flour will have to pay a higher duty, in consideration of the fact that it has had labour spent upon it, and to the very desirable end of promoting the grinding of corn in this country. It is manifestly better that we should import corn and mill it at home (thus employing our own labour) rather than import flour which has been prepared by other labour.

"Another modification excludes bacon and maize from the free list. It is recognised that Mr. Chamberlain was mistaken in treating these articles on an exceptional basis, and we do not doubt that he himself is sympathetic with present intentions with regard to them. Such important raw materials as cotton and wool will, of course, come in free.

"An immense amount of work has already been done with a view of producing a Tariff Reform Budget at comparatively short notice, and if the Unionist Party are returned to power next January every possible effort will be made to embody the new duties in the Budget of 1910. If this is found to be impracticable we may expect to see a 'beginning' which will take the form of giving tangible proof of the intention to give Colonial preference worth having to the Colonies, and of placing duties on certain articles which can conveniently be selected. In this event the full Tariff Reform Budget would make its appearance in 1911, with this exception, that the maximum duty would remain in abeyance for two years, so as to give time for the friendly negotiations of commercial agreement with foreign Powers."

This new manifesto, it will be found, is anticipated in its main features by the above article. Indeed, my estimate above of about £16,000,000 of conceivable revenue closely tallies with the Protectionists' own estimate of "£16,000,000 to £20,000,000." The reader's special attention, however, is directed to the fact that, in addition to the many alterations of principle and practice referred to in the above article, the Protectionists appear from the *Birmingham Post* announcement to be *deliberately backing out of the honourable pledges to remit old Free Trade revenue taxes.*

The "Preference" for Colonial manufactures, it may be noted, contains the same elements of make-believe as the Colonial Preferences examined elsewhere under AUSTRALIAN PREFERENCE and CANADIAN PREFERENCE. As soon as a Colony was found to be exporting freely a particular manufacture to this country, the Protectionists, following the Colonial example, would endeavour to raise the preferential "*minimum*," making that the actual and real degree of Protection required.

In negotiating with foreign countries in connection with a

tripartite tariff, foreign countries could not be expected to grant us most-favoured-nation treatment unless we put them on terms as favourable as our Colonies. For example, we should risk being put on the higher scale of the new American tariff (*see* PAYNE TARIFF) if we accorded to Canadian bootmakers lower duties than to American bootmakers.

**RURAL DEPOPULATION**—Nothing is commoner than the conception that rural depopulation is a phenomenon peculiar to Britain. As a matter of fact it is common to every country, and is a symbol of the effect of the application of science and machinery to agriculture. An ever-decreasing proportion of the world's population is needed to grow the world's food; consequently there is a continuous setting free of workers to engage in industrial pursuits and a growth of town populations at the expense of rural populations. "Back to the land," in brief, is an economic impossibility.

The facts as to rural depopulation in the United Kingdom are as follows:

UNITED KINGDOM: THE MOVEMENT TO THE TOWNS

| Census of— | Total Population | Urban Population | Proportion of Urban to Total Population |
|---|---|---|---|
| | Millions | Millions | Per Cent. |
| 1861 | 28·9 | 13·7 | 47·3 |
| 1871 | 31·5 | 17·2 | 54·5 |
| 1881 | 34·9 | 21·2 | 60·7 |
| 1891 | 37·7 | 24·8 | 65·6 |
| 1901 | 41·5 | 29·6 | 71·3 |

In England and Wales alone, in 1901, the proportion of the town to the rural population reached 77 per cent. It is now probably over 80 per cent.

Turning to France, the facts are as follows:

FRANCE: THE MOVEMENT TO THE TOWNS

| Census of— | Total Population | Urban Population | Proportion of Urban to Total Population |
|---|---|---|---|
| | Millions | Millions | Per Cent. |
| 1861 | 37·4 | 10·8 | 28·9 |
| 1866 | 38·1 | 11·6 | 30·5 |
| 1872 | 36·1 | 11·2 | 31·1 |
| 1876 | 36·9 | 12·0 | 32·4 |
| 1881 | 37·7 | 13·1 | 34·8 |
| 1886 | 38·2 | 13·8 | 36·0 |
| 1891 | 38·3 | 14·3 | 37·3 |
| 1896 | 38·5 | 15·0 | 39·0 |
| 1901 | 39·0 | 16·0 | 40·9 |
| 1906 | 39·2 | 16·5 | 42·1 |

In the land of so many small holders the movement to the towns is pronounced. In 1906 42 per cent. of the French population had become town-dwellers, and this in spite of the superior fecundity of the rural French population.

The figures for Germany are as follows:

GERMANY: THE MOVEMENT TO THE TOWNS

| Census of— | Total Population | Urban Population | Proportion of Urban to Total Population |
|---|---|---|---|
| | Million | Millions | Per Cent. |
| 1871 | 41·0 | 14·8 | 36·1 |
| 1875 | 42·7 | 16·6 | 39·0 |
| 1880 | 45·2 | 18·7 | 41·4 |
| 1885 | 46·8 | 20·5 | 43·7 |
| 1890 | 49·4 | 23·2 | 47·0 |
| 1895 | 52·3 | 26·3 | 50·2 |
| 1900 | 56·4 | 30·6 | 54·3 |
| 1905 | 60·6 | 34·8 | 57·4 |

German industrialisation has thus proceeded far, and at the present time over 60 per cent. of her people are living in the towns.

Even in the United States, whereas at the Census of 1860

only 16 per cent. were in the towns, in 1900 the Census showed that 33 per cent. had become urban dwellers.

Thus in all countries the towns are needing the increasing attention of Governments which desire to preserve the national health and welfare.

**RUSSIA**—Russia is noteworthy for one of the most ridiculous Protective tariffs in the world. Her duties on manufactured articles average about 130 per cent. *ad valorem.* Yet, strange to say, Protectionists never boast about Russia as an example of what Protection can do for a country. Inquiry will show that they are wise not to do so. The commerce of Russia is small and unprogressive, although she is rich in point of natural resources. In spite of her absurd tariff, she imports £35,000,000 a year of manufactured articles, while her exports of this character are worth only about £10,000,000 a year.

**SACKS**—*See* BAGS.

**SADDLERY AND HARNESS**—There are no recorded imports into this country of saddlery and harness, but the exports of British make are as follows:

BRITISH EXPORTS OF SADDLERY AND HARNESS (f.o.b.)

| | £ |
|---|---|
| 1900 ... ... ... ... ... ... | 477,000 |
| 1907 ... ... ... ... ... ... | 578,000 |
| 1908 ... ... ... ... ... ... | 433,000 |

While saddlery and harness cannot be "protected," since there are no imports to tax, the trade would suffer severely under Protection through the taxation of leather, metal, and other raw materials used in the industry.

**ST. ALDWYN, LORD**—After the South African War Lord St. Aldwyn (then Sir Michael Hicks-Beach), as Chancellor of the Exchequer in the Unionist Government, imposed, on April 15, 1902, a corn duty of one shilling per quarter. In the following year Mr. Ritchie (the late Lord Ritchie), who succeeded Sir Michael Hicks-Beach as Chancellor, repealed this shilling corn duty with Sir Michael Hicks-Beach's approval.

As it is sometimes said that a small corn duty cannot be felt by the consumer, the following extract from a speech which Lord St. Aldwyn made at Manchester on November 5, 1900, is worth attention:

"I thought that my duty last year on corn was so small that it would not increase the price of bread. I made a mistake. I found that in not a few cases it had the effect of giving an excuse to the bakers to raise the price of bread, and therefore I must confess that I believe that doubling that duty, and also adding new duties upon meat and dairy produce, must increase the cost of the food of the working classes. Well, I do not think it is necessary to pursue this argument, for if those who make these proposals do not believe that they would, why do they not tax maize and bacon, and why do they propose to reduce the duties on tea and sugar?"

**SAVINGS**—The deposits in United Kingdom Savings Banks increased from £77,000,000 in 1880 to £198,000,000 in 1903. It is quite impossible to compare these figures justly with the available savings banks statistics of other countries, because the savings statistics of different nations do not refer to the same class of people, or to the same class of institution, or to the same conditions of deposit. This is clearly pointed out by the Board of Trade in the second Fiscal Blue Book (Cd. 2337, Price 3s. 6d.). The Board of Trade say:

"If we confine our comparison to a single class of institution, *e.g.*, savings banks, it is vitiated by the fact that the conditions of deposit, *e.g.*, maximum limits of deposit, rate of interest, &c., differ in different countries, and the degrees to which savings banks are exposed to the competition of other modes of thrift and other classes of provident institutions also vary very greatly."

Protectionists, in spite of this common-sense warning, continue to circulate (*see*, for example, Tariff Reform League leaflet No 145) comparisons of the savings banks returns of Germany and England, those of Germany being three times as great as those of Britain. It is deplorable that such methods should be adopted. The German savings banks are municipal institutions which pay a higher rate of interest (our Post Office pays only 2½ per cent.) allow of larger deposits, and attract the savings of the middle classes. Let the reader imagine what would happen here if all our municipalities opened savings banks, paying 3 to 3½ per cent. interest as in Germany, and allowing of quite large deposits. The obvious result would be that enormous sums would be deposited not only by the working classes, but by tradesmen and other members of the middle class.

**SCIENTIFIC TARIFF**—The scientific tariff is the ideal cherished by fair-minded or ill-informed Protectionists who have visions of a great and good Government considering in detail the industries of the country and beneficently imposing such duties, and only such duties, as shall be for the general good.

In practice, alas! the scientific tariff is never arrived at, as is proved by the fact that there are no two tariffs in the world which agree on any point of principle or practice. Take the broad matter of the level of duties. Ought they to be high or low? In 1903 the Board of Trade calculated the average height of the duties of Protectionist countries on manufactured articles. What did they find? The height of the duties of the chief Protectionist nations varied as follows:

| Country | Per Cent. | Country | Per Cent. |
|---|---|---|---|
| Russia ... ... ... | 131 | Italy ... ... ... | 27 |
| United States ... ... | 73 | Germany... ... ... | 25 |
| Austria-Hungary ... | 35 | Belgium ... ... ... | 13 |
| France ... ... ... | 34 | | |

Which of these is the scientific tariff? If Russia is right, America must be wrong. If America is right, Germany must be very unscientific.

The fact is that tariffs are arranged by would-be monopolists scrambling for gain, and there is no tariff in the world that satisfies those who have it. For instance, the United States, on August 5, 1909, passed a new tariff, the last one being dated 1897. The Washington correspondent of the *Daily Mail* in its issue of August 6, 1909, says that the new tariff Act "*has practically no admirers in either House of Congress.*" The Bill only passed the Senate by 47 votes to 31. It was much the same with the last German tariff, passed in 1903. It was only carried through the Reichstag by a gross abuse of the closure; large parts of it were never discussed.

So it would be here. Every Member of Parliament would be bombarded with deputations, addresses, pamphlets, and letters, of which he could not find time to attend to one-hundredth part, and in relation to any particular trade—it may be the reader's trade—he would find himself driven by desperation to vote with his party to save his Government from defeat and dissolution. That is the truth about the making of a scientific tariff. (*See* PROTECTION and FREE TRADE.)

The practical working of the scientific tariff when at last made should also be considered. It is well that a generation which has never known the joys of a scientific tariff should be reminded of this exceedingly important side of the fiscal question. We have all heard of the unfortunate Customs official who, when confronted with a fine specimen of an Egyptian mummy, found it difficult to make up his mind whether he should tax it as preserved meat or let it through duty free as what Mark Twain would call a "healthy corpse," but it is rarely that the anxious importer is able to extract humour from the vagaries of a "scientific tariff."

How the operation of the American Customs law is regarded may be illustrated by an article by a Protectionist writer. The *Iron Age* of New York is a fiercely Protectionist journal. Its attitude on the Dingley Tariff is what is known in the wonderful American language as "stand pat." In a recent issue, dealing with the difficulties likely to arise in regard to freight classifications, it asks if these are to become as irksome as the Custom duties, and says:

"Readers of the *Iron Age* are familiar with some of those fierce controversies that grow out of a single word or phrase in the Customs tariff. In many cases a single lawsuit has cost 25,000 dollars or more to the citizen, firm, or company interested. This hair-splitting litigation has been very profitable to the lawyers, and some decisions of the highest Courts have caused wonder and bewilderment to the unfortunate business man who foots the bills."

And the American writer goes on to call the Customs law "a happy hunting-ground for the legal fraternity."

How could it be otherwise? Modern commerce has to deal with articles whose varieties are infinite. You can make your scientific tariff as complex as you please. You can provide for mixtures of textiles or of metals. You can make long lists of duties in regard to every sort of article likely to be imported into a civilised country. And when you have finished, some new production promptly arises which defies classification. And if you could revise your scientific tariff every day the hitherto unthought of would still come along demanding an impossible classification.

The experienced Customs official grows callous in the art of extortion. He adopts a simple and a golden rule. Question to be decided: Should a new machine or appliance be placed in category No. 2,026A and charged 10 per cent., or in category No. 1,628B, and be charged 45 per cent.? Answer: The higher of these two duties being 45 per cent., charge 45 per cent. for safety. Charge made accordingly. Exit importer to appeal against decision, and in the meantime to wonder how he is to price the machine until the appeal is heard.

How the thing works in America may be gauged from the following chronicle of recent cases.

When "ping-pong" came in, the Customs appraisers, being humorists, insisted that the ping-pong balls were "articles of which collodion is the component material in chief value." The importers, having no sense of humour, protested that ping-pong balls were "toys," and therefore subject to a smaller duty than as "articles of which collodion, &c." Result: an appeal to the United States Circuit Court. After the usual law's delay, Judge Wheeler decided that the balls were "toys."

Classification may make a considerable difference in the case of important materials. Thus under the Dingley Tariff printing paper, under paragraph 396, was dutiable at half a cent per lb., whereas writing paper was dutiable at 2 cents per lb., plus 10 per cent. *ad valorem.* Not long ago an American firm imported some hand-made printing paper for book printing. For this rash act they were charged at the rate of 2 cents. per lb., plus 10 per cent., by the Customs appraisers under the golden rule already referred to. The importers appealed, and the Customs appraisers' decision was reversed by the Circuit Court Judge; but what was done in the meantime with the taxed paper I do not know.

By the way, if, as Tariff "Reformers" allege, the foreign exporter and not the importer, pays the import duty, why should an American importer thus take the trouble to get the foreigner's taxes reduced?

The Dingley Tariff, of course, taxes a large variety of raw materials, and when Custom law uncertainty attaches to these there is a great hindrance to trade. Here is an extract from a recent issue of an American Protectionist paper:

> "The Customs status of pickled sheepskins was investigated five years ago and decided. A few weeks ago a duty of 20 per cent. was clapped upon them by a collector, who was sustained and perhaps instructed by an Executive order. The Executive ought not to make such a change as this. What a statute means ought to be found out before it is seven years' old, and Congress can make any change that may be necessary, but to make the matter still further complicated, a Senator asked the President to interfere, and the Executive was suspended and then revoked."

While this dispute was in progress trade, which waits for no man, went astray.

Another case. Some leather watch-chains were imported.

The importers declared them, not unnaturally, as "manufactures of leather" subject to a duty of only 35 per cent. *ad valorem*. The appraisers held that they were "jewellery," and as such subject to a duty of 60 per cent. *ad valorem*. The Circuit Court finally decided in favour of the importers.

In some cases an article is found clearly to fit two categories. Thus a willow chip basket is both a "willow manufacture" and a "chip manufacture." It cost a good many dollars in New York under the Dingley Tariff to decide under which heading it should be placed. I forget which way the arbitrary decision went.

Finally, let me show what our own Customs can do in the way of tariff humour. Recently a bad habit has sprung up of doctoring leather with powdered sugar in order to give it weight. Now the Australian Government, being anxious to preserve the good name of Australian leather, provided in its Commerce Act that leather exported must bear a label stating how much weighting material it contained. Accordingly there appeared at the British Custom House bales of leather declaring on their honour as bales that the leather in them contained "not more than 5 per cent. of crystal sugar." Now, as the reader knows, sugar and all articles containing sugar are now taxed. So these bales of leather were held up by our Customs as "confectionery" until the duty was paid.

A batch of recent (1908) Canadian Customs decisions neatly illustrates the injury to trade which arises from the practical working of tariffs. The Canadian Board of Customs decided that the following articles were dutiable at the rates mentioned:

1. Mills for grinding clay or other substances, whether for use in connection with steel converters or otherwise, 25 per cent.
2. Zinc rods, 25 per cent.
3. Mimeographs, 25 per cent.
4. Kremoline used in the confectionery trade, 25 per cent.
5. Refined cocoanut oil, 20 per cent.
6. Stereotyping outfits, such as casting mould, cutting-off cylinder, and imposing press, imported along with printing press, 10 per cent.

7. Electric motor and rheostat for use in connection with a printing press, 25 per cent.
8. Keystone rig and equipment for drilling wells, 25 per cent.
9. Pooer's well machine, 25 per cent.
10. Microscopes valued at not less than 100 dollars to be used in good faith in surgery, free as surgical instruments.
11. Soldering flux, 20 per cent.
12. Lithographic presses, 10 per cent.

Nearly all these decisions are calculated to injure Canadian work and employment. Items 1, 4, 6, 7, 8, 9, and 12 are taxes on machinery—on articles which are needed to equip Canada for industry. Items 2, 3, 5, and 11 are taxes on raw materials. It will be seen that even such a material as soldering flux is taxed 20 per cent. Item 10 exhibits the only gleam of common sense in the list, but even here, apparently, the student's microscope would not escape taxation.

**SHIPBUILDING**—In shipbuilding Britain possesess a remarkable supremacy:

THE WORLD'S SHIPBUILDING (EXCLUDING WARSHIPS)

(Lloyd's Figures)

| Country | 1906 | 1907 | 1908 |
|---|---|---|---|
| United Kingdom ... ... ... | 1,828,000 | 1,608,000 | 930,000 |
| Germany ... ... ... ... | 318,000 | 275,000 | 208,000 |
| United States ... ... ... ... | 441,000 | 475,000 | 304,000 |
| Holland ... ... ... ... ... | 67,000 | 69,000 | 59,000 |
| All the world, including the above ... | 2,920,000 | 2,778,000 | 1,833,000 |

(Warships are excluded from the above figures; in 1906, for example, including warships, Britain launched 1,936,793 tons.)

In 1908, as in 1893 and 1897, there was world depression in

## SHIPBUILDING

Tonnage built in British shipyards, 1860 to 1908. (Exclusive of vessels built for the British Navy)

| Year | Built for British Owners | | | Built for Export | | | Total Built for Home and Export, Sail and Steam |
|---|---|---|---|---|---|---|---|
| | Sailing | Steam | Total | Sailing | Steam | Total | |
| | Tons | Tons | Tons | Tons | Tons | Tons | Tons |
| 1860 | 158,172 | 53,796 | 211,968 | — | 13,903 | 13,903 | 225,871 |
| 1861 | 129,970 | 70,869 | 200,839 | 232 | 7.255 | 7,487 | 208,326 |
| 1862 | 164,061 | 77,338 | 241,399 | — | 20.533 | 20,533 | 261,932 |
| 1863 | 253,036 | 107,951 | 360,987 | 1,084 | 16,236 | 17,320 | 378,307 |
| 1864 | 272,499 | 159,374 | 431,873 | 2,279 | 26,681 | 28.960 | 460,833 |
| 1865 | 235,555 | 179,649 | 415,204 | 949 | 32,016 | 32,965 | 448.169 |
| 1866 | 207.678 | 133,511 | 341,189 | 3,641 | 34,709 | 38,350 | 379.539 |
| 1867 | 174.507 | 94,573 | 269,080 | 4,994 | 31,905 | 36,899 | 305.979 |
| 1868 | 237,687 | 78,510 | 316.197 | 8,671 | 37.460 | 46,131 | 362.328 |
| 1869 | 230,762 | 123,525 | 354,287 | 11,800 | 22,005 | 33,805 | 388,092 |
| 1870 | 117,032 | 225,674 | 342,706 | 9,429 | 42.222 | 51,651 | 394,357 |
| 1871 | 56,545 | 297,810 | 354,355 | 3,715 | 32,988 | 36,703 | 391,058 |
| 1872 | 54,967 | 338,004 | 392,971 | 3,790 | 77,957 | 81,747 | 474,718 |
| 1873 | 88.532 | 282,134 | 370,666 | 1,094 | 81,783 | 82.877 | 453,543 |
| 1874 | 187,313 | 333,890 | 521,203 | 1,781 | 80,883 | 82,664 | 603,867 |
| 1875 | 241,646 | 178,905 | 420,551 | 3,711 | 47,796 | 51,507 | 472.058 |
| 1876 | 236,890 | 123,475 | 360,365 | 4,198 | 13,457 | 17,655 | 378.020 |
| 1877 | 212.320 | 221,330 | 433,650 | 2,194 | 15,075 | 17,269 | 450.919 |
| 1878 | 141,165 | 287,080 | 428,245 | 7,108 | 35.366 | 42,474 | 470,718 |
| 1879 | 59,115 | 297,720 | 356,835 | 2,464 | 46,692 | 49,156 | 405,991 |
| 1880 | 57,480 | 346,361 | 403,841 | 585 | 68,470 | 69,055 | 472,896 |
| 1881 | 92,420 | 408,764 | 501,184 | 1,348 | 106.346 | 107,694 | 608,878 |
| 1882 | 145.700 | 521,575 | 667,275 | 2,139 | 113,637 | 115,776 | 783,051 |
| 1883 | 146,818 | 621,758 | 768,576 | 1,272 | 122,368 | 123.640 | 892,216 |
| 1884 | 162,234 | 335,208 | 497.442 | 10,945 | 79,887 | 90,832 | 588,274 |
| 1885 | 208,411 | 196.975 | 405,386 | 10,683 | 24,943 | 35,626 | 441,012 |
| 1886 | 138,362 | 154,638 | 293,000 | 6,887 | 31,641 | 38,528 | 331,528 |
| 1887 | 81,279 | 225,440 | 306,719 | 5,848 | 64,631 | 70,479 | 377.198 |
| 1888 | 75,696 | 407,445 | 483,141 | 20,697 | 70.109 | 90,806 | 573,947 |
| 1889 | 117,481 | 554,024 | 671,505 | 19,666 | 163.558 | 183,244 | 854,729 |
| 1890 | 123,224 | 528,789 | 652.013 | 25.468 | 135.157 | 160,625 | 812.638 |
| 1891 | 191.917 | 478.682 | 670,599 | 37,693 | 101,201 | 138,894 | 809.493 |
| 1892 | 258,700 | 434,091 | 692,791 | 28.372 | 80,385 | 108,757 | 801,548 |
| 1893 | 114.895 | 380,393 | 495 288 | 8,979 | 80,407 | 89,386 | 584,674 |
| 1894 | 89.156 | 485,460 | 574,616 | 10,472 | 84,404 | 94,876 | 669,492 |
| 1895 | 54,155 | 465,467 | 519,622 | 10.562 | 117,450 | 128,012 | 647,634 |
| 1896 | 57,467 | 462,503 | 519.970 | 15,824 | 201,020 | 216,844 | 736,814 |
| 1897 | 66,729 | 415,538 | 482,267 | 22,971 | 139,459 | 162,430 | 644,697 |
| 1898 | 41.839 | 654,158 | 695,997 | 3,051 | 171,560 | 174,611 | 870,608 |
| 1899 | 45,510 | 703,904 | 749,414 | 4.973 | 194,623 | 199,596 | 949,010 |
| 1900 | 38,576 | 698,330 | 736,906 | 7,546 | 199,815 | 207,361 | 944,267 |
| 1901 | 54,967 | 720,714 | 775 681 | 6,696 | 200,756 | 207,452 | 983,133 |
| 1902 | 64,811 | 735,563 | 800,374 | 16,253 | 133,798 | 150,051 | 950,425 |
| 1903 | 42,311 | 586,758 | 629,069 | 14,097 | 115,211 | 129,308 | 758,377 |
| 1904 | 33,749 | 701,635 | 735,384 | 17,979 | 130,896 | 148,875 | 884,259 |
| 1905 | 30,374 | 821,059 | 851,433 | 7,716 | 189,299 | 197.015 | 1,048.448 |
| 1906 | 31,902 | 890,280 | 922,182 | 17.181 | 217,408 | 234,589 | 1,156,771 |
| 1907 | 24,274 | 716,538 | 740,812 | 15,516 | 280,639 | 296,155 | 1,036,967 |
| 1908 | 26,621 | 386,431 | 413,052 | 10,771 | 169,390 | 180,161 | 593,213 |

shipbuilding, but whether in good years or in bad years, Britain is easily first.

In the table on page 252 the progress of British shipbuilding since 1860 is exhibited; its eloquent figures may be left to speak for themselves. I pass to the consideration of the factors of successful shipbuilding.

We have seen that Britain builds about two out of every three tons of the ships built in all the world, and that no other nation as much as approaches her in output. Can this continue?

Shipbuilding, now that wooden walls are practically obsolete, must be regarded as a combination of several branches of the iron, steel, and engineering industries. If we want to know which countries are naturally fitted to shine in shipbuilding, therefore, we must inquire which nations, possessing ports, possess also the indispensable base of successful modern industry—coal. These countries are Britain, America, and Germany. Between them these three nations output eight of every ten tons of coal produced in all the world. As I have pointed out under COAL, that is the real secret of the industrial supremacy of these three countries. Possessing such a proportion of the world's coal, it follows naturally that these three countries between them produce eight tons out of every ten tons of the world's iron, for iron production is dependent upon coal production. It follows also that these three countries are also chiefly fitted to produce the world's ships, and, as the above table shows, they do actually produce between them more than eight tons out of every ten of the whole. The other nations are not in the running.

But of the three great coal countries, Britain easily outdistances the other two. Why is this? So far as natural resources go, America should be easily first. She has an overwhelmingly great iron and steel industry, and has two fine seaboards in a commanding geographical position. Germany has resources in every respect inferior to those of America, and in some respects inferior to our own in this connection. Britain, superior in advantages to Germany, is far inferior to the United States. The explanation of America's backward position in shipbuilding is to be found in her Protective duties, which hit her both in shipping and in shipbuilding. Alone of the three, we have the sense to deal freely in the world's commodities, and thus to secure the world's carrying trade. Thus our shipping stimulates our shipbuilding. We may go further, and say that Germany's duties, and even more America's duties, operate as a stimulant to our mercantile marine, and therefore to our shipbuilders. Germany, with her free ports and her much more liberal fiscal policy, has a much greater ocean shipping than that of America, although under natural conditions her mercantile marine would be much smaller than that of our other great rival. The natural position of the three countries in point of ships should be (1) America, (2) Britain, (3) Germany. The actual position is Britain first and the others nowhere. Apart from any other consideration, this alone should determine every British citizen to remain a Free Trader.

As far as shipbuilding is concerned, Germany is a Free Trade country. She practically recognises the value of free imports to manufacturers by admitting free of duty all articles required in the construction of ships. The German conditions are practical, and her shipbuilders are on level terms with ours in point of Free Trade. We need not be surprised, therefore, that German shipbuilders are doing well. Looking to the future, we must expect Germany to lessen the great gulf shown in the above table. It should impress Tariff "Reformers" that Germany, desiring above all to increase her ships, should adopt Free Trade in shipbuilding materials as a means to achieve her end. I do not know how it is to be contended that a policy which is thus confessed desirable for the builder of ships should not be good also for the builder of houses. In respect of fiscal policy, the respective positions of Britain and Germany as shipbuilders should be clearly realised. Both enjoy Free Imports in shipbuilding materials. Britain, however, has the advantage of the stimulation of a larger mercantile marine built up by a general system of Free Trade.

A few years ago Mr. C. H. Cramp, the leading shipbuilder of the United States, gave the following bitter evidence before a Shipping Committee of the United States Senate:

"The enormous revenue represented by the freight and passenger tolls on our commerce and travel is constantly drained out of this country into British, German, and French pockets, in the order named, but mainly British; while the vast industrial increment represented by the necessary shipbuilding inures almost wholly to Great Britain.

"The foreign shipowner who carries oversea commerce makes us pay the freight both ways.

"For our exports we get the foreign market price less the freight.

"For our imports we pay the foreign market price, plus the freight.

"The English steamship is a foreign product, and its earnings, which we pay, are a foreign profit.

"Add to this the fact, equally important, that the carrier of commerce controls its exchanges, and the condition of commercial, financial, and industrial subjugation is complete.

"The United States is by far the most valuable of all the dependencies of Great Britain."

All this is literally true. British Free Trade plus American Protection puts American resources at our disposal and compels America to employ British ships to do American work.

It is true that the American tariff has a provision that shipbuilding materials may be imported free into the United States, but as the United States Merchant Marine Commission pointed out, this provision is nullified by the proviso that any ship built of foreign material which engages in coast trade must at once pay up the import duty. As a result, America, unlike Germany, does not enjoy Free Trade in shipbuilding.

What I have said above relates exclusively to the mercantile marine. When we come to consider warships, other factors have to be considered. Purely economic considerations do not alone operate in the building of navies. Nevertheless, the ruling factor is still the possession of coal, and therefore of a great iron and steel industry. The three countries which by Nature's favour produce nearly the whole of the world's iron and steel are the three countries which are able to sustain great navies. Britain, Germany, and America alone possess the economic power to back and to sustain enormous fleets of steel vessels. If either of these cares to devote herself to specialising in the production of engines of war she can wield mighty weapons, but I cannot see how either Britain or Germany, if they strained their iron and steel resources to the utmost, could ultimately sustain a two-Power standard navy if one of the other two Powers was America.

**SHIPPING**—The overwhelming maritime supremacy of the United Kingdom is shown by the following figures, compiled by the Board of Trade:

OCEAN TONNAGE OF THE LEADING MARITIME NATIONS, 1907

| | Tons. |
|---|---|
| United Kingdom ... ... ... ... | 11,485,000 |
| Germany... ... ... ... ... ... | 2,790,000 |
| United States ... ... ... ... ... | 871,000 |
| Japan ... ... ... ... ... ... | 1,481,000 |
| Norway ... ... ... ... ... ... | 1,458,000 |
| France ... ... ... ... ... ... | 1,403,000 |
| Italy ... ... ... ... ... ... | 901,000 |
| Total, above and all other countries, about ... ... ... ... ... | 26,000,000 |

Thus, taking steam and sailing vessels together, and old and new tonnage together, the United Kingdom owns nearly one-half of the sea-going ships of the entire world. If, however, it is taken into consideration that over 10,000,000 of our tons are steam tons, and that our tonnage is incomparably newer and better than that of the world at large, it will be seen that the above figures do less than justice to our supremacy. We own in effective tonnage more than one-half of the world's ocean shipping.

The table on page 257 is taken from Blue Book Cd. 4954.

If the reader will consider the positions on the map occupied by these four countries, and their relative shipping opportunities, he will see that it is not merely arguing *post hoc ergo propter hoc* to attribute our extraordinary maritime supremacy to the influence of Free Trade.

Britain, undoubtedly, occupies a favourable geographical position, and she ought to be a great shipping country.

Germany has very little coast line, and is severely handicapped by Nature as a shipping nation.

France is for all practical purposes as well favoured as ourselves in this regard.

The United States of America has a magnificent seaboard facing the two great oceans, a position which ought by this

GROWTH OF OVERSEA SHIPPING (STEAM AND SAIL)

(Figures in Millions of Tons)

| | United Kingdom | German Empire | France | United States |
|---|---|---|---|---|
| | Net Tons | Net Tons | Net Tons | Gross Tons |
| Average 1855-9... ... ... | 4·5 | — | 1·0 | 2·5 |
| ,, 1860-4... ... ... | 5·1 | — | 1·0 | 2·2 |
| ,, 1865-9... ... ... | 5·8 | — | 1·0 | 1·6 |
| ,, 1870-4... ... ... | 5·7 | 1·0 | 1·1 | 1·4 |
| ,, 1875-9... ... ... | 6·3 | 1·1 | 1·0 | 1·6 |
| ,, 1880-4... ... ... | 6·9 | 1·2 | 1·0 | 1·3 |
| ,, 1885-9... ... ... | 7·5 | 1·3 | 1·0 | 1·1 |
| ,, 1890-4... ... ... | 8·5 | 1·5 | 0·9 | 1·0 |
| ,, 1895-9... ... ... | 9·0 | 1·6 | 0·9 | 0·8 |
| ,, 1900-4... ... ... | 9·9 | 2·2 | 1·2 | 0·9 |
| 1905 ... ... ... ... | 10·7 | 2·5 | 1·4 | 0·9 |
| 1906 ... ... ... ... | 11·2 | 2·6 | 1·4 | 0·9 |
| 1907 ... ... ... ... | 11·5 | 2·8 | 1·4 | 0·9 |
| 1908 ... ... ... ... | 11·5 | 2·8 | Not known | 0·9 |

time to have placed her at least on a level with ourselves in point of shipping, especially as she has such wonderful stores of native material to ship.

Yet mark the comparative progress of these four nations.

Britain, admittedly favoured by Nature, has made such use of her position that she is not merely pre-eminent over any single country, but pre-eminent over the rest of the world.

Germany, not favoured by Nature, has beaten France and the United States put together in hollow fashion because she has adopted a Free Port policy for such ports as she possesses, and because she has stimulated her shipbuilders by giving them Free Trade in shipbuilding materials.

France, side by side with ourselves at the gates of Europe, has a practically stationary shipping.

The United States has seen her oversea shipping dwindle and dwindle, until months, or even years, may elapse at a great world port without sight of a ship flying the Stars and Stripes.

Of the ships which pass Gibraltar, fully 60 per cent. are British. Here are the official records of the Suez Canal traffic:

SUEZ CANAL TRAFFIC, 1908

(In Millions of Tons)

| | |
|---|---|
| British | 11·5 |
| German | 3·3 |
| French | 1·2 |
| Dutch | 1·0 |
| Austro-Hungarian | 0·5 |
| Russian | 0·3 |
| Japanese | 0·4 |
| Italian | 0·3 |
| Total above and other | 19·2 |

The Protectionists would menace British shipping in two ways. First, they would restrict imports, and second, they would restrict exports. The first point is widely understood; I doubt if the second is much known. A coal export duty figures largely in Tory speeches; I wonder how many of those who talk glibly of such a tax realise that it is a blow at our shipping. The point is this. Our imports, chiefly consisting of food and materials, are bulky. Our exports, chiefly consisting of manufactures in point of value, have little bulk. If, therefore, we had no bulky outward freight to balance the bulky imports, ships would be constantly coming to our shores loaded with food and material, and clearing largely in ballast for want of a bulky outward cargo. Our coal exports (which, be it remembered, are chiefly for the use of our own ships abroad) afford a bulky outward cargo, and thus make our shipping profitable both ways. This, of course, is of great importance to other interests beside the shipping interest, for if our ships lacked bulky outward freights, the inward cargoes could only be carried at heavier charges, and consequently our food and raw materials would cost us more.

Ignoring these common-sense considerations, Protectionists talk loosely about our coal exports and promise kindly to favour the British nation with a tax to restrict exports of coal.

**SILK**—Silk is one of the few lines of manufacture in which imports exceed exports in this country. In all other branches of the textile trade the home market is mainly or almost entirely supplied by the home manufacturers; in silk, on the other hand, the home market is mainly supplied by the foreign manufacturer. It is necessary to point this out clearly in order that it may be realised that the silk manufacture is not one in which, on the whole, British manufacturing genius has asserted itself. The figures for external trade are:

BRITISH COMMERCE IN SILK MANUFACTURES

| | Imports for Home Consumption (c.i.f.) | Exports of British Make (f.o.b.) |
|---|---|---|
| | £ | £ |
| 1900 (good year) ... ... | 13,386,000 ... | 1,638,000 |
| 1907 (good year) ... ... | 10,927,000 ... | 2,010,000 |
| 1908 (bad year) ... ... | 9,898,000 ... | 1,335,000 |

There is a striking diminution in the consumption of imported silk.

The spun silk branch of the silk trade has been entirely built up in this country in the last fifty years.

It is undoubtedly the fact that British consumers, by going without cheap silk, could make the British silk industry much larger than it is. Happily, there are many engaged in the silk trade who do not desire to be made thus parasitic upon the community.

**SLATES**—*See* QUARRYING.

**SMALL ARMS**—*See* Arms.

**SOAP**—The British soap industry is chiefly concerned with the home market. There is also a considerable export trade, worth, in 1908, £1,399,000. The imports are smaller, being worth about £500,000. The leading British soap manufacturers are Free Traders, and even Protectionists do not pretend that soap-making is a "ruined industry."

**SOUTH AFRICAN PREFERENCE**—The preferential tariff of the South African Colonies (Customs Union) hardly merits description. The chief classes of goods imported into South Africa are dutiable at 10 per cent. *ad valorem*, and when the imports are British one-fourth of this 10 per cent. is remitted, so that the preference amounts to a mere 2½ per cent. In 1906 certain duties were raised in such manner that, after deduction of the "Preference," the duty remains at the same level, or is even higher, than before. This stroke of humour is quite on a par with that achieved in connection with the Australian Preference, *which see.*

**STEEL**—*See* Iron and Steel.

**STONES**—*See* Quarrying.

**STRAW HATS**—*See* Hats.

**SUGAR**—As sugar is not produced in the United Kingdom, any import duty levied upon it, large or small, is simply a revenue duty, *i.e.*, no private interest can benefit by reason of the tax, and every penny of the tax collected, save only the cost of collection, goes into the Treasury. Sugar was taxed from 1660 until 1874, when the duty was entirely abolished by the Liberals. The present sugar duty we owe to the Unionist Government, who taxed sugar at 4s. 2d. per cwt. on April 19, 1901. Mr. Chamberlain promised to remit one-half of this duty in exchange for a tax on bread, but the Free Trade Government, elected in 1906, has carried out Mr. Chamberlain's promise *without* putting a tax on bread.

Our imports of sugar are very large; in 1908 they were valued at nearly £20,000,000 for home consumption.

**SWEATING**—The existence of sweating in the United Kingdom has been used by Protectionists as a weapon against Free Trade. It has been asserted, indeed, that sweating in Britain is caused by Free Trade. The absurdity of this can be easily demonstrated. In 1906 an exhibition of articles made by sweated workers was given in Berlin and attracted much attention at home and abroad. This exhibition led to the organisation of a similar exhibition here, and the National Anti-Sweating League was formed by its promoters, of whom I was one, in order to combat the evil and to secure a minimum wage for sweated workers, an effort which led to the Trades Boards Bill passing into law in 1909. Thus, so far from sweating not existing under Protection, the British Sweating Exhibition of 1906 was actually suggested by what was being done in a leading Protectionist country.

It is impossible by means of import duties to keep out sweated goods; the reason for this is that the fact that an article is low in price by no means proves that it is produced by sweated labour; in fact, the cheapest goods are made by high-priced and efficient labour exercised upon the best machinery and appliances. For example, a halfpenny newspaper appears to be "dirt cheap"; yet it is produced by highly-paid labour; sweated workers could not produce it.

**TARIFF "COMMISSION"**—The Tariff "Commission" is simply a private committee of Protectionists formed by Mr. Chamberlain to further the cause of Protection in this country. The use of the title "Commission" is unwarrantable, since, by the common usage of all the world, that word is reserved in its application to bodies or committees of inquiry or control set up by the official authority of States. The assumption of the title "Commission" in this instance sends abroad, apparently with British official authority, "reports" which are merely partisan documents calculated to work the gravest mischief to the interests of British trade. (*See* UNITED KINGDOM.)

It is noteworthy that the Tariff "Commission" has thrown overboard Mr. Chamberlain's suggestion that only foreign food should be taxed. Thus, Mr. Chamberlain proposed a 2s. tax on foreign corn and free entry for Colonial corn. The Tariff Commission suggests 2s. on foreign corn and 1s. on Colonial corn.

The Tariff "Commission's" reports show, as might be expected, the greatest diversity of opinion amongst Protectionists as to what they want. It is particularly noticeable that many Protectionist manufacturers say that Mr. Chamberlain's small duties would be quite useless, and that they want high duties. It is due to the "Commission" to say that it has published a certain amount of evidence from Free Trade manufacturers who crushingly condemn Protection.

**TARIFF REFORM**—"Tariff Reform" is a term which, in the mouths of Protectionists, abuses language, ignores history, and defies fact. If the reader will refer to the official history of British Customs tariffs published as a Blue Book in 1897, he will find on page 39 the following heading:

"TARIFF REFORM, 1842–1860,"

and under that heading he will find details of the true Tariff Reform. Says the official historian on the page referred to:

"The great Free Trade Acts of 1845 and 1846 were the largest measures of Tariff Reform which had so far been submitted to Parliament. The Act 8 Vic. c. 12 repealed the duty on more than 400 minor articles which brought in only small amounts of revenue and fettered commercial exchange to little purpose. . . ."

Free Trade IS Tariff Reform, and it is simply political impudence for Protectionists to call themselves Tariff

"Reformers." They are Protectionists, and what Protection means is explained elsewhere under PROTECTION, SCIENTIFIC TARIFF, CHAMBERLAIN PROGRAMME, &c.

**TEA**—We import over about £9,000,000 worth of tea per annum. As tea cannot be grown here, the import tax on tea is not a Protectionist tax, but merely a revenue duty, for it cannot create a private vested interest, and every penny of the tax, save only the cost of collection, goes to the State and not into private pockets. Mr. Chamberlain promised to reduce the tax on tea in exchange for his new suggested taxes on bread and meat and dairy produce, but the Free Trade Government elected in 1906 reduced the tea duty, which was left by the Tories at 6d., to 5d. per pound on May 14, 1906.

**TIMBER**—We have enormous imports of timber; as is shown under RAW MATERIALS, the imports increased from 5,654,000 loads in 1887 to 9,622,000 loads in 1907. There is, of course, danger that our imports of timber might be taxed in order to give a preference to the Colonies. How confused are the minds of the leaders of the Unionist party on the point is illustrated by the fact that Mr. George Wyndham, in a speech made at Liverpool on December 9, 1908, actually suggested a timber duty, which would be a ruinous step.

What we want in addition to free imports of timber is State afforestation, and no doubt this will be proceeded with under the present Government's National Development scheme. That scheme, by the way, illustrates Government interference of the right kind—a kind which develops industry and promotes trade without raising prices and costs of production.

**TIN**—Our imports of tin ore and crude tin are great and growing. (*See* RAW MATERIALS.) Tin, of course, is an indispensable raw material, and our modern Protectionists have promised that they will not tax raw materials. There is, however, nothing to prevent a tin tax if we once embark upon Protection. Already the Protectionists are promising protective duties to slate producers and granite producers, and if these are protected why should not the tin miners of Cornwall also be protected? Our imported tin comes chiefly from the Straits Settlements, being produced in the Malay Protectorate. In 1903 a Cornish tin mine owner wrote to the *Times* advocating a tax on Straits tin and arguing that it was not really produced in the British Empire because the Federated States are only a British Protectorate. Here is another instance to show that nothing is safe from taxation under Protection, not even a raw material like tin, the taxation of which would severely injure the tinplate and other trades.

At the general election of 1906, I am informed, the Tory candidate for the Camborne Division of Cornwall promised the tin miners a duty on tin, from whatever source derived! That is how taxes on raw materials find their way into "scientific tariffs."

**TINPLATES**—The tinplate trade remarkably illustrates the value of Free Imports in fighting foreign tariffs. By means of the McKinley and Dingley Tariffs the United States largely reduced our exports of tinplates to America. Before the McKinley tariff of 1891, 76 per cent. of our export tinplate trade was with America, and the American tinplate duties were therefore felt severely in South Wales, but only for a little while. So great was the recuperative power of the trade through its access to cheap material that at the present time, twelve years after the application of the Dingley Tariff, the British tinplate industry is larger than ever; in 1907 it had a record output. Instead of depending upon a single market, South Wales now exports tinplates to all parts of the world, and the American trade is now only about 20 per cent. of the total export trade.

The wonderful recovery of the export trade is shown by the Board of Trade Returns. Our average export of tinplates in the four years before the McKinley Tariff of 1891 was £5,682,000. After the operation of the McKinley and Dingley Tariffs, this figure was reduced to about £3,500,000 a year. In 1907 the exports had again risen to £5,917,000.

The Board of Trade record of tinplate and steel sheet works in the United Kingdom must be added.

EMPLOYMENT AT TINPLATE AND STEEL SHEET WORKS

(Number of Mills Working: Mean of End-monthly Returns for each Year)

| | Number |
|---|---|
| 1897 | 323 |
| 1898 | 322 |
| 1899 | 381 |
| 1900 | 384 |
| 1901 | 343 |
| 1902 | 398 |
| 1903 | 371 |
| 1904 | 385 |
| 1905 | 426 |
| 1906 | 421 |
| 1907 | 444 |
| 1908 | 440 |

The tinplate trade used to furnish, after the McKinley Tariff, favourite "anecdotes" for Protectionist platforms. The above figures will explain to the reader why it has been impossible to continue to point Protectionist morals in this connection.

In 1907, according to the Census of Production Preliminary Tables, the gross output of our tinplate works was worth as much as £9,350,000.

**TOBACCO**—Tobacco is a product, not produced at home, upon which we levy an import duty for revenue purposes. Before the present year the duty was 3s. per lb., which is about six times the value of the tobacco itself; Mr. Lloyd George has raised this to 3s. 8d. per lb. Higher duties are, of course, imposed upon manufactured tobacco, not to protect tobacco makers, but in order to levy an equivalent duty upon the corresponding amount of unmanufactured tobacco used in making the manufactured article.

Although the tobacco import duty is not a Protective tax, it illustrates how, through import duties, the consumer is made to pay without the degree of the tax being revealed to him. It is probable that if every tobacconist's shop bore a large placard pointing out to the public that it sold not tobacco, but taxes, the consumption of tobacco would not be so great. Under Protection every article in common use would have concealed in its price a tax which, unlike the tobacco tax, would not go to the Government, but to some private interest.

**TOOLS**—In addition to the very large production for the home market, we have a considerable export trade in tools and implements. There are also some imports.

BRITISH COMMERCE IN TOOLS AND IMPLEMENTS

(Not Machine Tools)

| | Imports for Home Consumption (c.i.f.) £ | Exports of British Make (f.o.b.) £ |
|---|---|---|
| 1900 (good year) ... ... ... | 325,000 ... ... | 1,491,000 |
| 1907 (good year) ... ... ... | 319,000 ... ... | 2,243,000 |
| 1908 (bad year) ... ... ... | 248,000 ... ... | 2,028,000 |

Imports of tools ought on no account to be taxed. The imports are diminishing, which seems to show that in some of the tools in which the Americans made such striking improvements we are doing better. In any case, it would be the height of folly to make tools dearer by taxation. If British work is to be efficient, it must have the best tools at the best price, wherever made.

**TRADE CYCLES**—The most unobservant person must have noticed that trade has a certain rhythmical fluctuation. Close observation shows that periods of good and bad trade alternate with remarkable regularity. If a curve is drawn accurately representing the trade of any country, it will be found that the curve moves upwards and downwards instead of progressing steadily. This movement from a position of good trade downwards to a position of bad trade and upwards again to trade recovery is sometimes called a "cycle of trade," and the cycle is usually completed in about ten years. Thus, in 1881–2 trade was good. It declined and became very bad in 1885–6. It then recovered, and in 1890 was very good again. Depression then set in, and in 1893–4 trade was again bad.

Then came recovery, and in 1899–1900 trade was very good. Again came depression, followed by recovery and good trade in 1907, when again there ensued depression and the bad trade of 1908–9. Recovery is, as I write (late in 1909), making itself evident, and in a year or two trade will be very good again. It will be seen that the top points of the trade cycles are separated by about ten years.

As regularly as the times of depression come round, Protectionists are found preaching that it is Free Trade that is the cause of bad trade. This is an ignorant representation, for these cycles of trade, which are inherent in the competitive system of industry (in which supply regularly overtakes demand and causes depression), are common to all nations. Thus the depression of the present time, which is suffered by all the world more or less, first made its appearance in October, 1907, in the United States, which has suffered much more heavily than Britain.

**TRUSTS**—The word "Trust" was originally used to describe a combination or pooling of the interests of a number of producers worked through a single Board of Control representing all the units of the combination. The term is now used broadly to describe any large combination of producers, in whatever form combined, whether by the merging of all the producers in one great company, or whether the units retain their individuality and work by joint agreement. Many different forms of combination, and many different names, such as "Trust," "Pool," "Combine," "Merger," "Syndicate," or "Kartell," all express the same idea, viz., the abolition of competition amongst a group of producers.

Trusts make for good in so far as combination saves the duplication of controls, abolishes wasteful competition, or saves labour. Trusts make for ill in so far as combination enables the combined producers to league themselves against the public, and to "hold up" their goods for monopoly prices.

In a Free Trade country, in trades where the consumer can protect himself by having recourse, if necessary, to foreign supplies, a combination of producers is unable to hold up prices against the consumer, and can only benefit in so far as combination makes for economy of production.

In a Protectionist country, a trust has the consumer at its mercy, up to the limit of the tariff. For the consumer can only import by paying the duty, and therefore the trust can exact the amount of the duty on all that it sells, acting as a private tax-gatherer. Thus the American Tinplate Trust is enabled to make a heavy tariff profit on the tinplates which it sells, this profit being in addition to its legitimate trade profit.

As soon as the Dingley Tariff passed into law in 1897, American tinplates were raised to nearly £20 per ton, the British price for tinplates being a little over £12 a ton, and the American duty being nearly £7 per ton.

**UNEMPLOYMENT**—Until recent years the great problem of unemployment has received little attention. It cannot be said that there has been yet produced a literature worthy of the subject. This is exceedingly unfortunate, and not a little remarkable. We can only attribute the neglect to lack of faith in the power of man to overcome social evils by wise laws, and a consequent resignation both of study and of effort. I cannot pretend myself to have completed my own studies of this particular phase of poverty, but I think I may usefully put before the reader a survey, if an incomplete one, of the chief causes of unemployment, which are many. I do not purpose to deal with what have been called the "unemployables"—those unfortunates who, not by any means through their own fault always, are not fit to be economically employed. I confine my observations to causes which affect the able-bodied workman willing to work who cannot find work to do—the man who engages the sympathies of us all, whatever our politics.

So many of us live in the towns through the industrial revolution that it is to be feared that few realise how much variations of rainfall at home and abroad have to do with unemployment. The greatest industry in the world, and in every country of the world, is still agriculture. The size and value of the product of this industry varies in different countries very greatly from year to year, chiefly through climatic influences which man has not yet learned to control. Agricultural products exchanged for other products are a great factor in trade, and trade must necessarily vary, therefore, with variations of rainfall. Drought in several regions of the world may raise the price of food and consequently reduce spending power upon goods in Britain. Drought in Australia may at any time raise the price of wool and cause unemployment in Yorkshire. The condition of the weather in our own islands is a considerable factor every year, depressing one trade or increasing another.

We have only to remind ourselves of these very important facts to see that neither Free Trade nor Protection has relevance to this great cause of unemployment, and that at present Governments are largely powerless, save in conserving forests, carrying out irrigation, &c., to cope with it. All they can do, and what they must do, is to provide against the distress following the cause.

In part allied to the first cause we examined is the problem of supplies of material. Here climate, of course, plays its part, as in the well-known case of Australian wool a few years ago. Apart from climate there is the wanton wastage of material for which man himself is responsible. Take the case of rubber as an illustration. The world's rubber-trees have been ravaged with such ruthless hands in so short a space of time that rubber has become very dear, and that dearness becomes a cause of unemployment. Timber, again, has been thoughtlessly exploited to such an extent that there has been a considerable appreciation in the price of this important material in recent years, a fact which has depressed employment in the building trades in all countries. These causes man may remedy, although not quickly, by careful planting and cultivation on a gigantic scale.

But it is not climate and waste which we have here alone to consider. There may be combination amongst material suppliers, long threatened by the American cotton planters, in order to secure monopoly prices. And fiscal policy plays a great part. In connection with access to materials, Protection cannot be acquitted as a cause of unemployment. Under Protection it is difficult to restrain the home producers of raw, crude, partly manufactured, and wholly manufactured materials from securing import duties to promote their own trades, and therefore necessarily to cause unemployment in other trades. The owner of the granite quarry, the master of the tanyard, the proprietor of the paper mill, the producer of feeding-stuffs, must be forgiven if, when the nation decides that import duties are necessary, they claim that while granite is the raw material of building and construction, leather the raw material of boots, paper the raw material of newspapers and books, and feeding-stuffs the raw material of meat and milk, these materials are the manufactured articles—the finished products—of those who have invested capital in producing them. That is why every Protectionist nation finds itself compelled to tax raw materials when once it starts putting Protection into practice. Thus, Protectionist nations possess a cause of unemployment which we, happily, are free from.

We have next to consider season as a considerable cause of unemployment, and here Free Trade and Protection are again entirely irrelevant, having power neither to help nor to hinder. There are summer trades and winter trades employing masses of labour which sometimes, but not often, are able to find alternative employments in their off-seasons. The building trade is the outstanding example, with its tens or hundreds of thousands unemployed for many weeks or even months in the winter in great countries like Britain, America, and Germany.

Here a system of labour bureaux may help a little to dovetail together summer and winter trades, but only a little, and insurance is necessary to preserve those who suffer from seasonal fluctuations. We cannot abolish the seasons, but we can abolish the distress which now results from the seasons.

Not less fruitful as a cause of unemployment is the progress of invention and science exercised to produce labour-saving appliances. It cannot be too clearly borne in mind that this is an increasingly important cause. In the old days the march of progress was very slow, and units of capital were small. To-day new inventions come into use very suddenly, for units of capital are large and those who exercise them are more awake to the advantages of economising labour. Outstanding instances of rapid displacement are furnished by the building industry and the cab industry. In the last ten years the use of re-inforced concrete in building has displaced tens of thousands of craftsmen in the building trade so rapidly that the displaced men have been quite unable to find other work. This cause, which at present affects large buildings only, may come to affect all sorts of building and construction, as the value of ferro-concrete is more widely recognised.

The London cab industry is a smaller matter in bulk, but just as important in principle and to the men concerned. In the course of a few years the hansom cab has been swept from the streets in thousands by the motor-cab, and, as a consequence, thousands of expert drivers find themselves thrown out of their old trade and too aged for the new one. It is a terrible and cruel process.

We have to try to perfect arrangements to protect and tide over men so dispossessed. Admittedly, the task is a difficult one, but that fact should not bar continuous and generous experiments. To leave such men to the tender mercies of our existing Poor Laws is unworthy of our civilisation.

The incidental ruin caused by progress takes another shape when it breaks up not employees alone but employers also. The amalgamation of businesses, the crushing of little firms by big ones, the displacement of all lines of trade by new inventions, the entry into retail business of a well-equipped joint-stock company, spreading its stores all over the land—these and allied movements, matters of daily occurrence, break up master and man alike. The community at large gains by the amalgamation of two firms, the consequent cessation of useless competition, and the consequent cheapening of production. But that is small consolation to the managers, clerks, and travellers sent adrift. So commonplace are these things that there is probably no commercial reader of these lines who could not name, from his own personal experience, many cases of dire hardship, the direct result of industrial and commercial change. There can be no question that at any given moment a large percentage of the working community is suffering bitterly from progress in an unorganised society.

I come next to causes set up chiefly by the caprices of feminine fashions. The dominion of fashion has rapidly extended its borders in recent years, and the effect upon the employment of hundreds of thousands of people is exceedingly unfortunate. Has the reader ever thought how rapidly trades have to adapt themselves to the ever-changing forms in which women delight to appear? Suddenly every dress must be braided; result, plenty of employment in the braid trade. As suddenly it becomes hopelessly out of date to appear with an inch of braid; result, sudden unemployment in the braid trade. This is but one instance of thousands which might be adduced. The cause here lies in what we call human nature, and surely nothing is more obvious than that tariffs are beside the point. I do not know how regularity of employment is to be secured in many of the trades which clothe us as long as we so rapidly change our ideas as to what particular furs or feathers or braids or buttons or embroideries or laces should be worn. As things are, a very large number of highly skilled workers are played with by the vagaries of taste and fashion.

Another cause of importance which is little realised is change of fashion in respect of locality and residential neighbourhoods. When a locality is first "taken up" as a desirable place in which to live, there is for a time a great and growing demand for workmen in it. Houses and shops are built in serried rows, and many workers and their families attracted during a period, it may be, of many years. Sooner or later comes a check, and it may even be that speculators carry the development beyond the limits of prudence, when there comes a slump in employment in the district. This sort of thing has occurred again and again round London, with the result that considerable bodies of under-employed men are found. The same result occurs sometimes through the migration of industries within the country, as when a London manufacturing firm goes out to seek better quarters twenty or forty miles from the metropolis, leaving stranded workers who are not always able to follow it, or who, again, in so far as they follow it, are a cause of unemployment in the deserted neighbourhood through the withdrawal of wages from it. In the rough and tumble of these far-reaching changes, thousands of citizens are thrown idle.

As every thinking man knows, war has far fewer victims than are caused by the casualties of industrial operations, and it is also true that while war is a cause of unemployment, it is not one of the greatest causes. War in its economic aspect means a sudden diversion of employment into certain trades, such as the making of arms and ammunition, of clothing, of provisioning, &c. While the war is proceeding, certain trades flourish exceedingly at the expense of other trades. When the war is over, the trades which have received stimulation are as suddenly depressed, and great misery is consequent. There is also the important fact that able-bodied men have been called out of their employments for the field, and that, when they return to their homes, they often find it exceedingly difficult to replace themselves in situations. The effects of war upon employment may be felt, and are usually felt, long after the war has ceased, and I should not forget to remind the reader that employment is also seriously affected by the diversion of capital during a war from peaceful enterprises.

We have examined a number of specific causes of the disorganisation of labour which we call unemployment. I now pass to a general cause which affects the greater part of industry. I refer to the fact that industry, as we know it to-day, is for the most part carried on in haphazard fashion. Let me contrast organised with unorganised industry. Take first the Post Office or a railway as a specimen of organisation. Each is a monopoly which, as the sole employer of its kind in the country or in a certain district, completely controls the necessary employment in the industry. As a consequence, it is enabled to work with a definite body of workers who enjoy regular employment. Save at special seasons, such as Christmas, the Post Office works with a definite army of men who have no fear of unemployment, and so within certain limits it is with a railway company. Now let the reader contrast the building industry. This is carried on by a great host of large and small masters who are continually scrambling for contracts. As each contractor wins a contract, he takes a dip into a great body of workmen and engages the amount of labour which he needs for his work. The system, if system it can be called, is one of customary in-and-out employment. It is not too much to say that unemployment is tacitly counted upon as part of the general conception. If a house is needed, tenders for erecting it may be invited from a large number of builders, each of whom is prepared to carry out the conditions of his tender if he secures the contract. This means, of course, that each contractor knows of the existence of an army of builders' workmen upon which he may safely rely for labour if he wins the contract. Thus in the building trade in all countries we find a large number of under-employed workmen who get a job one day and are unemployed again in a few weeks or months when the job is finished. If the reader builds a house and inquires amongst the men who build it, he will assuredly find that a proportion of the men, sometimes a large proportion, have been unemployed for some time before they started to make him a home. The considerable size of the manufactures produced make this unorganisation easily observed in building, but, of course, similar conditions, only varying in degree, exist in a great variety of trades.

The great mass of casual labourers in our towns, the result of unorganisation, is a public shame which brings its punishment upon us all. Chronic unemployment is the lot of thousands. On any given day in the winter, in Britain or Germany or America, there are tens of thousands of unemployed. A week after that day there will again be tens of thousands of unemployed, but not wholly composed of the same units as were unemployed on the first day. It is in and out, in and out, all the year round, and sometimes months may pass without a casual job being found by many workmen. It is a matter of faulty organisation, which ought not to be tolerated by a self-respecting people. We do not treat our horses thus, as Thomas Carlyle long ago pointed out. We do not work a horse to-day and turn him out to starve to-morrow. But that is what we do with a large part of our working population. Take the actual earnings of a typical London dock labourer as given in "West Ham" (published by J. M. Dent & Co.) :

EARNINGS OF A CASUAL WEST HAM DOCKER IN THREE MONTHS OF 1904

| | s. d. |
|---|---|
| Week ended May 7 ... ... ... ... | 33 9 |
| " " 14 ... ... ... ... | 30 4 |
| " " 21 ... ... ... ... | nil |
| " " 28 ... ... ... ... | nil |
| Average for May ... ... ... ... | 15 0 |

| | s. d. |
|---|---|
| Week ended June 4 ... ... .. ... | nil |
| " " 11 ... ... ... ... | 5 9 |
| " " 18 ... ... ... ... | 28 0 |
| " " 25 ... ... ... ... | nil |
| Average for June ... ... ... ... | 7 6 |

| | s. d. |
|---|---|
| Week ended July 2 ... ... ... ... | 32 2 |
| " " 9 ... ... ... ... | 15 9 |
| " " 16 ... ... ... ... | 30 3 |
| " " 23 ... ... ... ... | 11 8 |
| " " 30 ... ... ... ... | 5 3 |
| Average for July ... ... ... ... | 17 6 |

When a man earns 25s. or 30s. one week, not knowing whether he will earn anything at all the next week, can we wonder if he becomes careless of consequence? "Let us eat and drink, for to-morrow we die." I wish that some of those who preach at the poor, and are so wanting in humour as to believe themselves "courageous" because they "tell the working man of his faults to his face," would reflect on what their own characters would probably, almost certainly, have become, if they had "graduated at the docks behind a bale of wool," as a docker once put it to me, at an early age, and earned such casual sums as I have indicated for some ten or fifteen years.

Casual labour is necessary, but casual employment is quite unnecessary. It needs but a better—in the true sense of the word a business-like—organisation to eliminate the factor. Even at the London Docks, one of the old companies, by sensible management, long ago found it possible to make regular the employment of a large number of their men. The casual labour question demands our best energies. From the casuals come the hopeless unemployables. Human nature is not strong enough to withstand hopeless uncertainty. Every day the victims of chance deteriorate—every day a proportion of them sink into the abyss. And we stand by and wring our hands and ask each other what we shall do to rid ourselves of the trouble, overlooking the root cause of it all—disorganisation. We let the machine go creaking on, grinding out its inevitable thousands of human wrecks, and then apply ourselves vainly to the rehabilitation of those we have allowed to become degraded. Surely it were more profitable to attend to the machine.

I next come to what is known as the cycles of trade—to those at first sight mysterious alternations of good years and bad years which are a feature of commerce in all industrial nations. These are again a symptom of unorganisation. Supply and demand are as yet uncorrelated, and it is impossible to hope for any substantial correlation for many years to come. An enormous number of producers are making goods for the consumption of an enormous number of consumers all over the world, the units involved numbering some 1,500,000,000 people. It is impossible for the producers accurately to gauge the quantities required by the consumers, and periodic overproduction becomes inevitable under the circumstances, especially as the producers are competitive with each other to meet the calls of the consumer. Hence we get alternations of booms and slumps in trade, good and bad years succeeding each other in a constant succession. The existence of the bad years, indeed, chiefly forces unemployment as a problem upon the public mind, and, as in the case of all incurable diseases, the quack is always to the fore. That Protection cannot help us here is shown, not only by the above plain statement of the cause, but by the existence of good and bad years in Protectionist countries. Our own slumps in trade are mild as compared with those of America, as is illustrated by the American panic of 1907–8.

Finally, a new form of foreign competition may have an effect similar to the introduction of a new machine, and in this case an import duty might, by reducing the competition, prevent a labour fluctuation, but it can only do so with the same economic effect which would obtain if, by legislative action, the use of a new invention were prohibited because it caused a labour fluctuation—*i.e.*, the general effect on trade and employment would not be for good but for ill.

Thus it needs but to consider these various causes of unemployment to understand (1) that Protection has nothing to offer as a solution of unemployment, and (2) why unemployment is only too well known in all industrial nations, whatever their fiscal policies, good, bad, or indifferent.

Some evidence as to the worldwide character of the unemployment problem may usefully be added. In 1908 the Washington Department of Commerce and Labour employed an official investigator, Mr. W. D. P. Bliss, to prepare a report upon unemployment in Europe, and in their official "Bulletin" for May they published a long and valuable document from the pen of Mr. Bliss, entitled, "What is Done for the Unemployed in European Countries." It runs to some 200 pages. It is not irrelevant to ask ourselves in the first place why Washington needs this report. Is it that the American Department has a purely academic interest in a great European social question? Not at all. As Mr. Bliss points out, unemployment is a commonplace in America itself. He says:

> "There are hundreds of thousands of people in the United States who never come before the charitable, and who dislike and even denounce charity, who are nevertheless, at least for periods of time, bitterly in need of work. Very few working men pass through life without being, for a time at least, in need of work."

That, it is to be feared, is the truth about unemployment in the richest industrial country in the world—the country which, above all others, has been gifted by Nature with the means of doing work. Mr. Bliss's report is intended to help America to deal with the problem which we also have to deal with; that should give Protectionists something to think about. Tariff after tariff has been employed in the United States, until the full effect of Protection as a cure for unemployment should surely by this time have been realised. Yet we find Mr. Bliss, an American official, not even mentioning Protection as among the reputed remedies available. His 200 pages ignore Protection altogether.

In this, I may remind the reader, the American writer agrees with both the Majority and Minority Reports of our own Poor Law Commission, which differed in many things, but which agreed in ignoring Protection.

Another consideration will suggest itself. If Protection is a remedy for unemployment, our American investigator would have found in Europe one country in particular, the United Kingdom, cursed with unemployment, and Germany, France, Austria, Italy, Spain, Russia, Switzerland, with considerable or high tariffs, and no unemployment at all. His report would have been a simple one. We can imagine him, impressed by the exceptional unemployment in Britain, returning to America and saying: "The matter is perfectly clear: England has Free Trade and unemployment, Germany has 'Tariff Reform and work for all.'" That, of course, is what our Protectionists assure the British people is the fact of the case. Mr. Bliss, viewing Europe with impartial eyes as the citizen of a country where tariffs and unemployment are a commonplace, sees a Europe in which unemployment is rife in every country, and describes a multitude of different methods of combating a general and prevalent evil.

Not only so, but Mr. Bliss has much less to say about Britain than about some other countries in Europe. He does not seem to have been specially impressed with the quantity of unemployment here, and, of course, so far as Government efforts are concerned, he has much more to say about Continental than about British efforts.

I quote from the American synopsis:

"The most important agencies for providing work for the unemployed who are employable are the public employment bureaus. These are largely developed in a number of European countries, but especially in Germany . . . other efforts made consist in attempts either to colonise them across the seas [here is obviously a reference to this country] or in some way to get them back to the land.

"In connection with the temporarily out-of-work, consideration is given to trade union out-of-work benefits; under this are included the attempts, mainly in Switzerland, at insurance against unemployment, and the 'Ghent' system, now largely developed throughout Belgium and spreading into other countries, notably France, whereby the Government may supplement the trade union out-of-work benefit by adding to it an equal sum.

"The subject of temporary relief works is considered, and the experience of Great Britain, Germany, and France is given. *In Germany, and to a less extent in France, the provision of municipal relief works has come to be the rule almost every winter in all the large and not a few of the smaller cities.*"

Mr. Bliss gives an account of the German relief stations, which assist German workmen travelling in search of work, which is worth reproducing, not only because it shows the existence of out-of-work Germans, but for its own sake:

"These relief stations are already organised in many portions of the German Empire in such numbers as to be within walking distance of each other, and all are connected by telephone. A workman travelling in search of work can go from shelter to shelter, and at every point learn in which direction he can look for work with the most hope of success. A man who patronises these stations is compelled to have and to show at every shelter at which he applies a little book showing his occupation, last place of employment, reason of discharge, &c. His being at each place of shelter is carefully noted, and it is indicated to which shelter he will next apply. All is under complete Governmental or police control; and if the worker, securing work, departs from his appointed route or has recourse to begging, or in any way violates the rules, he can be, and is, arrested. If unable to pay for his shelter he is required to work in the morning and travel in the afternoon."

Switzerland also has this system in some cantons, and in both countries it is claimed that by its means tramps and vagrants have been almost entirely abolished. It should be added that the national railways carry travelling workmen searching for work at half or one-third the ordinary fares. I have myself suggested in the House of Commons, and repeat here, that our railway companies should be compelled to give similar facilities to unemployed workmen.

Mr. Bliss also describes the efforts made by the German Government so to distribute their orders for work as in part to regularise employment as between good and bad years. He also describes the German, Swiss, Belgian, Dutch, British labour colonies, and so forth. He does not pretend to know the numbers of the unemployed in the different countries, but very sensibly points out that no man knows those numbers. He shows that in 1906 3,187,660 nights' lodgings were furnished to transient guests at the German relief shelters, but no man knows how many individuals were concerned. He shows that in Germany about 1,250,000 and in Austria about 400,000 situations are filled for unemployed workmen in a year by the various employment bureaus, but, again, no one can pretend to know how many individual men are represented by these figures. They indicate an enormous amount of unemployment, but we cannot give a precise or even approximate figure. We cannot, with truth, pretend to decide which country carries off the unenviable palm of unemployment; we are only able to say with certainty that the problem of unemployment is grave and great in all the industrial countries.

On this head I may add the following quotation from the book "Poverty," which Robert Hunter, the well-known sociologist, wrote a few years ago:

"There are probably in fairly prosperous years no less than 10,000,000 persons in poverty—that is to say, underfed, underclothed, and poorly housed. Of these about 4,000,000 persons are public paupers. Over 2,000,000 working men are unemployed from four to six months in the year. About 500,000 male emigrants arrive yearly and seek work in the very districts where unemployment is greatest. Nearly half of the families in the country are propertyless. Over 1,700,000 little children are forced to become wage-earners when they should still be in school. About 5,000,000 women find it necessary to work, and about 2,000,000 are employed in factories, mills, &c. Probably no less than 1,000,000 workers are injured or killed each year while doing their work, and about 10,000,000 of the persons now living will, if the present ratio is kept up, die of the preventable disease, tuberculosis."

Mr. Robert Hunter recently informed me (1908) that these statements had all been the subject of fierce controversy in America, and that they remained unshaken by criticism.

It is the peculiar vice of the tariff controversy that it concentrates attention upon one particular form of Government interference, and drags every conceivable subject into a false relation with itself. The fiscal question is, in point of fact, largely irrelevant to the question of unemployment, as I have shown in these pages, and it is necessary for both Free Traders and Protectionists to grasp that fact before we shall attain to a sufficient devotion to the many forms of effort which are necessary if we are gradually to decrease the evil.

Above all, it is necessary to keep clear heads, and to remember that (1) the cure of unemployment and (2) the cure of the distress which arises from unemployment are two entirely different things. To illustrate my meaning in the concrete, I may refer to State insurance against unemployment, which we are about to put our hands to. Insurance against unemployment helps the man in distress and remedies that distress, but do not let us forget that the unemployed workmen on the funds is still *out of work*, and that insurance, therefore, leaves *unemployment* precisely where it was.

**UNEMPLOYMENT, COMPARATIVE** — The available statistics relating to unemployment in different countries are not precisely comparative, and it is advisable to preface any remarks on the subject by repeating what the Board of Trade say every month in their official *Labour Gazette*, that the figures from abroad "*cannot be properly used to compare the actual level of employment in the United Kingdom with that of foreign countries.*" The reason for this will be obvious on a moment's reflection. The chief statistics available are those relating to Trade Unionists out of work. As some trades are more fluctuating than others it follows that if a country like the United Kingdom has included in its unemployment statistics a large number of men employed in shipbuilding, a violently fluctuating industry, its statistics will look worse than those of a country which, like France or Germany, has few Trade Unionists who are shipbuilders. Moreover, the different returns vary from other causes, such as the conditions of membership. With this said, I give the latest (I write early in December, 1909) Trade Union unemployment statistics available:

UNEMPLOYMENT AMONGST TRADE UNIONISTS

(In each case the figures relate to persons all out of work simultaneously)

| Country | No. of Trade Unionists Reported upon | Date of Report | Proportion Reported Unemployed Per Cent. |
|---|---|---|---|
| United Kingdom ... ... | 694,930 | Oct., 1909 | 7·1 |
| France ... ... ... | 259,832 | Sept., 1909 | 6·8 |
| Germany ... ... ... | 1,355,964 | Sept., 1909 | 2·1 |
| Belgium ... ... ... | 48,512 | Sept., 1909 | 2·1 |
| Russia ... ... ... | 13,896 | Feb., 1909 | 20·8 |
| Norway ... ... ... | 9,795 | Sept., 1909 | 3·8 |
| Massachusetts, U.S.A. ... | 113,464 | Sept., 1909 | 3·4* |
| New York State, U.S.A. ... | 89,227 | June, 1909 | 13·1* |

* All unemployment from sickness, accident, and strikes excluded.

It will be seen that the proportions of unemployed vary very greatly, the highest figures being those of New York State and Russia, and the lowest those of Belgium. In the United States, employment in the State of Massachusetts, although bad, is

## BRITISH TRADE UNION UNEMPLOYMENT, BASED BY THE BOARD OF TRADE ON RETURNS BY TRADE UNIONS

(Contrasted with our Imports of Manufactures for Home Consumption)

| Year | Trade Union Unemployment | | | (4) Imports of Manufactures only for Home Consumption |
|---|---|---|---|---|
| | (1) Engineering, Shipbuilding, and Metal Trades only | (2) All other Trade Unions making Returns | (3) Mean of Columns 1 and 2 | |
| | Per Cent. | Per Cent. | Per Cent. | Million £ |
| 1860 ... ... ... ... | 1·9 | 1·8 | 1·85 | 22·2 |
| 1861 ... ... ... ... | 5·5 | 1·9 | 3·7 | 24·0 |
| 1862 ... ... ... ... | 9·0 | 3·1 | 6·05 | 26·7 |
| 1863 ... ... ... ... | 6·7 | 2·7 | 4·7 | 27·7 |
| 1864 ... ... ... ... | 3·0 | 0·9 | 1·95 | 31·2 |
| 1865 ... ... ... ... | 2·4 | 1·2 | 1·8 | 32·2 |
| 1866 ... ... ... ... | 3·9 | 1·4 | 2·65 | 36·6 |
| 1867 ... ... ... ... | 9·1 | 3·5 | 6·3 | 36·9 |
| 1868 ... ... ... ... | 10·0 | 3·5 | 6·75 | 40·9 |
| 1869 ... ... ... ... | 8·9 | 3·0 | 5·95 | 41·5 |
| 1870 ... ... ... ... | 4·4 | 3·1 | 3·75 | 47·2 |
| 1871 ... ... ... ... | 1·3 | 2·0 | 1·65 | 41·3 |
| 1872 ... ... ... ... | 0·9 | 1·0 | 0·95 | 47·3 |
| 1873 ... ... ... ... | 1·4 | 0·9 | 1·15 | 48·7 |
| 1874 ... ... ... ... | 2·3 | 0·9 | 1·6 | 53·3 |
| 1875 ... ... ... ... | 3·5 | 0·9 | 2·2 | 57·9 |
| 1876 ... ... ... ... | 5·2 | 1·6 | 3·4 | 58·4 |
| 1877 ... ... ... ... | 6·3 | 2·5 | 4·4 | 61·8 |
| 1878 ... ... ... ... | 9·0 | 3·5 | 6·25 | 61·3 |
| 1879 ... ... ... ... | 15·3 | 6·1 | 10·7 | 57·2 |
| 1880 ... ... ... ... | 6·7 | 3·8 | 5·25 | 65·0 |
| 1881 ... ... ... ... | 3·8 | 3·3 | 3·55 | 62·7 |
| 1882 ... ... ... ... | 2·3 | 2·4 | 2·35 | 65·4 |
| 1883 ... ... ... ... | 2·7 | 2·5 | 2·6 | 67·4 |
| 1884 ... ... ... ... | 10·8 | 3·5 | 7·15 | 63·1 |
| 1885 ... ... ... ... | 12·9 | 4·2 | 8·55 | 63·8 |
| 1886 ... ... ... ... | 13·5 | 5·6 | 9·55 | 63·3 |
| 1887 ... ... ... ... | 10·4 | 3·9 | 7·15 | 63·0 |
| 1888 ... ... ... ... | 6·0 | 2·3 | 4·15 | 69·6 |
| 1889 ... ... ... ... | 2·3 | 1·8 | 2·05 | 74·4 |
| 1890 ... ... ... ... | 2·2 | 2·0 | 2·1 | 73·5 |
| 1891 ... ... ... ... | 4·1 | 2·7 | 3·4 | 76·0 |
| 1892 ... ... ... ... | 7·7 | 4·7 | 6·2 | 75·6 |
| 1893 ... ... ... ... | 11·4 | 4·0 | 7·7 | 75·4 |
| 1894 ... ... ... ... | 11·2 | 3·2 | 7·2 | 77·8 |
| 1895 ... ... ... ... | 8·2 | 3·8 | 6·0 | 84·7 |
| 1896 ... ... ... ... | 4·2 | 2·5 | 3·35 | 92·1 |
| 1897 ... ... ... ... | 4·8 | 2·1 | 3·45 | 94·7 |
| 1898 ... ... ... ... | 4·0 | 1·9 | 2·95 | 96·1 |
| 1899 ... ... ... ... | 2·4 | 1·7 | 2·05 | 104·1 |
| 1900 ... ... ... ... | 2·6 | 2·3 | 2·45 | 110·1 |
| 1901 ... ... ... ... | 3·8 | 2·9 | 3·35 | 109·4 |
| 1902 ... ... ... ... | 5·5 | 2·9 | 4·2 | 115·6 |
| 1903 ... ... ... ... | 6·6 | 3·4 | 5·0 | 116·3 |
| 1904 ... ... ... ... | 8·4 | 4·4 | 0 4 | 115·8 |
| 1905 ... ... ... ... | 6·6 | 3·9 | 5·25 | 121·4 |
| 1906 ... ... ... ... | 4·1 | 3·3 | 3·7 | 130·2 |
| 1907 ... ... ... ... | 4·9 | 3·0 | 3·95 | 127·9 |
| 1908 ... ... ... ... | 12·5 | 4·8 | 8·65 | 119·8 |

much better than in New York State; that is partly because of the fact already referred to, that the proportion of fluctuating trades included in the figures varies as between the two States. Unfortunately, only these two States make such returns, but the figures serve a useful purpose in warning us how absurd it is to compare offhand the statistics of, say, Britain and Germany. The German and Belgian figures must be considered in relation not only to the warning already given, but to the fact that the employers of both these countries very largely practise the system of working short time all round instead of discharging workmen. As to Germany, we know that the public labour exchanges find situations for about 1,250,000 unemployed per annum, but again there are no figures for other countries with which this may be fairly compared.

My only reason for printing the above statistics at all is that they are so frequently misused that it is necessary to point out their true nature. We are not entitled to compare them, or to draw conclusions from them as to comparative unemployment rates in the various countries. All we are entitled to do is to assert that they prove most conclusively that Protection does not, as Mr. Chamberlain alleged on May 17, 1905, in addressing Trade Unionists, offer "two jobs for one man."

Our own Board of Trade Trade Unionist unemployment figures are widely misunderstood. They relate in a considerable proportion to fluctuating trades. This fact is brought out very clearly in the figures, on p. 283, published by the Board of Trade in Blue Book Cd. 4954.

Here the reader has before him all the facts necessary to decide whether or not imports of manufactures cause unemployment.

*The first column shows unemployment in the fluctuating trades* which bulk up our Trade Union unemployment rate. The second column shows unemployment in the other trades reported upon. The third column shows the mean of the other two columns. The fourth column shows our imports of manufactured articles year by year.

If imports cause unemployment, then the first three columns

would show a continuous rise corresponding to the rise in imports. As a matter of fact, what is actually shown is that unemployment goes up and down, up and down, and that at times when imports fall, unemployment grows worse and not better. It will also be seen that when employment improves, our imports almost invariably rise. Look, for example, at the very good year 1899, when the fluctuating trades had only 2·4 per cent. unemployed, and other trades only 1·7 per cent. In that year imports of manufactures rose by £8,000,000. Take, again, 1908, when employment declined. In that year, imports of manufactures fell by £8,000,000.

I have noticed that the Tariff Reform League circulate as representative American unemployment statistics, and as comparable with ours (indeed, actually compared with ours) the figures of the American Federation of Labour. It should be understood that these figures relate to only about 90,000 men in a population of nearly 90,000,000 and that they are worthless for purposes of comparison.

**UNEMPLOYMENT AND THE "TARIFF REFORM" AGITATION**—I think it necessary to illustrate in this work the methods by which the neo-Protectionists are endeavouring to convert the working classes to what they call "Tariff Reform." A London newspaper, the *Daily Express*, which for many months printed prominently on its front page the words

TARIFF REFORM

MEANS

WORK FOR ALL,

published, between May 18 and June 21, 1909, thirty-five articles, of considerable length, professing to be a detailed "Inquiry" into the effects of a tariff on the employment of labour. The articles were freely decorated with such headings as these:

"More Work for Over 74,000 Hands."

"Work and Wages for 40,000 More."

"ASTONISHING RETURN FROM THE SILK TRADE."

"FREE TRADE RUIN."

In gross, the articles promised that, given an average duty of 10 per cent. on imports of manufactures, certain British industries could employ 534,675 "extra hands," and increase their wages bills by £765,372, or £39,799,344 PER ANNUM.

Let us see how this cheerful result was arrived at. The *Daily Express* issued a circular to a proportion of the firms in certain trades, asking them to answer the following questions:

> "A.—If the Government by an Order in Council imposed an *ad valorem* duty of 10 per cent. on imported manufactured goods and parts in your line of manufacture, do you think your trade would be increased thereby?
>
> "B.—How many extra hands do you estimate you would be enabled to employ?
>
> "C.—What would you estimate your weekly wage bill would be increased by?"

These naïve inquiries were addressed indiscriminately to all sorts of producers, without qualifications or warnings as to the range of the trades circularised. Thus the *Express* addressed bootmakers without telling them that it was also asking the leather-makers how many extra hands leather-makers could employ if given a duty of 10 per cent. to enable them to tax the bootmakers.

In the industries which it "examined," the *Daily Express* tells us, in the course of its articles, that it "believes" there are firms numbering 26,400. By diligently adding the numbers which it tells us it has circularised, we find that 4,800 of these firms were addressed. Of the 4,800 addressed, only 636 were foolish enough to give definite answers to the *Express* questions. This fact is a tribute to the common sense of the overwhelming majority of the firms circularised.

To exhibit the method in more detail, let me give the figures of the *Daily Express* for electrical engineering. The *Express* tells us:

There are some 2,000 firms in the industry.

188 of these were circularised.

Only 78 of these replied.

Of the 78, 30 were " evasive " or " unfavourable."

Of the balance of 48, only 18 gave definite estimates of what they thought they might gain by a 10 per cent. duty.

Thus, on its own confession, the *Express* obtained definite information from only 18 firms out of 2,000 which it says it knows of. Yet, while making this confession, it coolly argues from the 18 firms to the entire trade.

The 18 firms, it appears, told the *Daily Express* that, given a 10 per cent. duty, they could employ:

Extra hands, 74,060.

Extra weekly wages, £119,600.

The problem before the *Daily Express* was how to magnify these figures to make them, in the terminology of its headline, " striking." This is how it went about the business. I quote its own words:

" The 18 firms who give figures form 23 per cent. of the total number who replied. Approximately, there are 2,000 firms engaged in the manufacture of electrical apparatus, fittings, and machinery. If only 23 per cent. of these could provide increased employment and wages in the same proportion as the firms who give figures, the totals would be, estimated for whole trade:

" Extra hands, 74,060.

" Extra weekly wages, £119,600."

This childish application of rule of three promises the payment of:

£6,219,200 *per annum in extra wages in the electrical industry.*

Let us think what that means. The very lowest value of the electrical goods which would have to be made for the wages bill to rise £6,219,200 is twice that sum, or £12,438,400. That is to say, imports of these goods would have to be reduced by £12,438,400. What, then, were our imports of electrical goods and machinery last year?

They amounted to only £1,678,000. That is to say, if a 10 per cent. duty shut out *all* electrical imports, and the goods shut out were made here, the wages bill would not rise by more than £880,000. As a matter of fact, even this figure is an exaggeration, for 50 per cent. of the value of production is too high as an estimate of wages.

As a matter of fact, a duty of 10 per cent. would reduce our electrical imports very little.

By the wholesale application of the "method" just exposed in detail, the *Daily Express* considers a number of important trades, and arrives at results which I now summarise in the table on p. 289. In the first column I show the absurdly small number of definite answers upon which the *Express* "calculates." The second and third columns show the *Express* "calculations." *The fourth column shows the extra product which would be needed to yield the extra wages, taking wages as half product.* The fifth column shows our imports in the industry, in 1908, where it is possible to state them.

It will be seen that upwards of £79,598,680 additional product would have to be made in order to yield the extra wages in these industries promised by the *Daily Express*. But our total imports of manufactures for home consumption in 1908 only came to £120,000,000. Is it pretended that a trumpery import duty of 10 per cent. would reduce this figure by £79,598,688? The imports of manufactures by Germany and the United States amount in each case to about £100,000,000 per annum, and if high duties do not keep manufactures out of those countries, how can it be contended that small duties here would have such a tremendous effect?

If the table is carefully examined it will be seen that there is no logical relation between the import column and the "extra wages" column. If the *Express* inquiry had been genuine there would have been a fairly constant ratio between the imports and the extra trade promised.

In some cases the amount of extra wages promised is greater than the total import. For example, quarrymen are promised £1,990,040 of extra wages, whereas the imports are valued at only £1,219,000. In quite a number of cases the amount of extra product needed to yield the extra wages is greater than the amount of the actual imports. See in par-

ANALYSIS OF *DAILY EXPRESS* INQUIRY

| Industry | Number of Definite Replies | *Express* Calculation | | Extra Output needed to yield Extra Wages | Imports for Home Consumption in 1908 |
|---|---|---|---|---|---|
| | | Extra Hands | Extra Wages per Annum | | |
| | | | £ | £ | £ |
| Motors and cycles | 29 | 40,320 | 3,197,376 | 6,394,752 | 3,948,000 |
| Silk ... ... | 13 | 11,780 | 573,248 | 1,146,496 | 9,897,000 |
| Electrical ... | 18 | 74,060 | 6,219,200 | 12,438,400 | 1,677,000 |
| Leather, boots ... | 39 | 28,875 | 1,938,300 | 3,876,600 | 10,503,000 |
| Hardware ... | 38 | 27,840 | 2,081,040 | 4,162,080 | ? |
| Glass ... ... | 21 | 7,245 | 546,030 | 1,092,000 | 2,705,000 |
| Optical ... ... | 13 | 3,430 | 280,280 | 560,560 | 925,000 |
| Jewellery ... | 20 | 6,916 | 484,120 | 968,240 | 1,102,000 |
| Fancy leather ... | 13 | 5,580 | 330,460 | 660,920 | ? |
| Lace ... ... | 15 | 6,630 | 663,000 | 1,326,000 | 1,930,000 |
| Woollen ... ... | 39 | 51,000 | 3,198,000 | 6,396,000 | 8,393,000 |
| Quarrying ... | 18 | 26,875 | 1,990,040 | 3,980,080 | 1,219,000 |
| Guns ... ... | 8 | 7,560 | 751,296 | 1,502,592 | 97,000 |
| Musical instruments ... ... | 8 | 6,528 | 726,648 | 1,453,296 | 961,000 |
| Cutlery ... ... | 21 | 2,369 | 230,308 | 460,616 | 157,000 |
| Pottery ... ... | 16 | 3,224 | 210,912 | 421,824 | 791,000 |
| Cement ... ... | 13 | 1,891 | 133,224 | 266,448 | 115,000 |
| Tobacco pipes ... | 4 | 442 | 32,448 | 64,896 | ? |
| Engineering ... | 113 | 69,720 | 5,722,080 | 11,444,160 | 3,472,000 |
| Cotton, linen, hosiery, and dress goods generally (!) ... | 26 | 49,680 | 2,511,600 | 5,023,200 | ? |
| Wood-working ... | 27 | 8,208 | 673,920 | 1,347,840 | 1,750,000 |
| Brush ... ... | 6 | 3,744 | 232,128 | 464,256 | 338,000 |
| Fancy box ... | 15 | 1,150 | 54,600 | 109,200 | ? |
| Paper and stationery ... | 58 | 14,070 | 775,320 | 550,640 | 5,650,000 |
| Chemical ... | 15 | 4,032 | 329,472 | 658,944 | 8,414,000 |
| Iron and steel ... | 30 | 66,528 | 5,559,840 | 11,119,680 | 7,390,000 |
| Miscellaneous ... | ? | 2,478 | 159,484 | 318,968 | ? |
| Milling ... ... | ? | 2,500 | 195,000 | 390,000 | 7,020,000 |
| Total ... | 636 | 534,675 | £39,799,344 | £79,598,688 | ? |

ticular the lines electrical, quarrying, musical instruments, cutlery, cement, engineering, brushes, iron and steel, and guns. In the last case imports are only £97,000; yet the *Express* promises gun-makers £751,296 more wages! This fact alone reduces the inquiry to nonsense.

It will be seen that in the fifth column a note of interrogation appears opposite some items. This is because the imports are either so small as not to be noted at the Customs House (*e.g.*, fancy boxes and tobacco pipes), or the *Express* classification is obscure or ridiculous. For example, under "hardware" the *Express* actually includes wood flooring, and it does not tell us what it means by "fancy leather."

The implied promise to tax raw materials to protect their producers should not go unnoticed. The *Express*, throwing overboard Mr. Chamberlain's programme, promises quarrymen to put a 10 per cent. tax on stone, slates, and granite. If these are not "raw materials," what substances can be described as such? And if the man who owns a stone-quarry is to have a duty, how can we refuse one to the owner of an iron-mine or a tin-mine or a copper-mine? If granite coming in is a real cause of unemployment, imports of iron ore, pyrites, tin, &c., must also rob the British workman of wages. But if we tax all these articles, what is to become of the work and wages of the tens of thousands of British workmen who work on imported raw material, and who would have no work to do if they were made dearer by taxes?

As I remarked at the beginning, the *Daily Express*, in its circularising, made no reference to taxes on materials. Let me supply the all-important questions which the *Express* forgot to ask when it addressed itself to bootmakers, bag-makers, purse-makers, saddlery-makers, machine-belt makers, and other users of leather:

(*a*) If the Government by an Order in Council imposed an *ad valorem* duty of 10 per cent. *on the imported leather which you use as a material*, do you think your trade would be decreased thereby?

(*b*) How many hands do you estimate you would be *enabled to discharge?*

(*c*) What would you estimate your weekly wage bill *to be decreased by?*

The *Express* shows itself completely incapable of appreciating the importance of untaxed materials. On June 1, 1909, it said:

"While the exports of boots and shoes exceeded the imports by £1,370,166, the imports of leather exceeded the exports by no less than £7,261,605. These figures indicate in a striking manner how the injury inflicted by dumped foreign leather has been out of all proportion to the advantages derived by the boot manufacturers."

Thus the *Express* showed that it imagines export trade alone to benefit by untaxed leather imports. It altogether forgets that by far the greater part of our boot and other leather-using trades is concerned with the home market, and that Free Leather is absolutely indispensable if these trades are to flourish.

It would be bad enough if the *Express* inquiry was simply an exhibition of sheer ignorance, for in such a serious matter the public have a right to demand from newspapers a sober attempt to understand trade and industry. On June 10th the *Express* clearly exhibited something worse than ignorance. It had to deal with the cotton trade, that industrial miracle which is a just cause of national pride and foreign admiration (*see* COTTON). The *Express* knew this much at least—that it would not do to treat cotton by itself. There was no excuse for not giving cotton separate treatment, for it is one of our greatest industries, and has a total product valued at over £176,000,000 per annum. What did the *Express* do? Knowing that no possible "calculations" could conceal our astonishing supremacy in this trade, the *Express* mixed it up with other trades with which it has nothing whatever to do. The *Express* heading runs: "Cotton, linen, hosiery, and dress goods generally." By mixing cotton manufactures with scarves, collars, cravats, mantles, costumes, and so forth, the *Express* audaciously applied to a great trade which would be ruined by Tariff "Reform" its absurd Rule of Three calculations, based on a few vague assertions made by persons who have no more to do with cotton than the Editor of the *Daily Express*.

The *Daily Express* applied the same method of obscuration to the proud British shipbuilding industry. We may wonder to how many British shipbuilders the *Express* addressed its question about a 10 per cent. duty. No ships are imported into this country, and a 10 per cent. tax on iron and steel, and other shipbuilding materials, would ruin our great shipbuilders. What does the *Express* do in this case? It carefully mixes shipbuilding with engineering generally, and then, on the strength of a small proportion of Protectionist engineers, applies its calculations to the whole. If the *Express* desired to give its readers a fair view of British industry, surely it would have given shipbuilding, like cotton, a line to itself. The *Express*, however, found it impossible to suppress the statement it received from Harland and Wolff, the great Belfast shipbuilders, who declared that a 10 per cent. duty would be "*disastrous to shipbuilding and engineering and other trades.*"

If the reader will turn again to the table of trades which were the subject of this *Express* "inquiry," he will be struck by a number of significant omissions. The *Daily Express* turned a blind eye to the industries which employ the largest number of people, viz., railways, mining, cotton, building, agriculture, printing, iron and steel, engineering, and shipbuilding. It is thus the most important of our industries which the *Express* has either ignored altogether, or obscured by connection with less important trades. To these let us not forget to add shipping, which, directly and indirectly, gives profit and honour and commercial prestige to this country, and which, in common with other industries we have named, is totally ignored by this farcical exposition of a policy which would bring it disaster.

It may be thought by some that it is scarcely worth while to pay such arguments as these of the *Daily Express* the compliment of serious criticism. Let it not be forgotten, however, that it is precisely such arguments which form the stock-in-trade of the Protectionist agitation as it makes its appeal to the popular ear.

Few people have at hand the means to check such "statistics" as those of the *Daily Express*, and it is idle to ignore the fact that converts to Protection are readily made by such means. The *Daily Express* has a circulation of about 200,000 a day, I believe; I put this article on record, therefore, as a description of a form of Protectionist argument, which no man would dare to utter in the House of Commons, but which many men make it their business to disseminate throughout the country. If the nation is to be converted to Protection, let us have on record the means of conversion used.

**UNITED KINGDOM**—The United Kingdom in two most important points is favoured by Nature in respect of the primary conditions of trade and industry. The first is that she is one of the three great coal producers (*see* COAL), and the second that she has an excellent seaboard, no part of her interior being over 100 miles from tide-water. She has also an excellent geographical position at the gates of Europe. On the other hand, Britain has poor mineral resources other than coal. Free Trade has made the most of coal and seaboard by permitting her coal to draw all the world's materials to her shores (*see* COAL), and by making her a universal free port, to the great gain of her commerce and shipping. British wealth, it cannot too clearly be borne in mind, has been created not by working upon British resources, but by developing within her borders products brought from the three corners of the world. The Open Port policy has triumphed. Without it the 121,000 square miles of British area would not, in 1909, sustain as many as 44,000,000 people. (*See* FREE TRADE and PROTECTION.)

The progress of British commerce before and after Free Trade is exhibited in the following figures:

COMMERCE OF THE UNITED KINGDOM IN A CENTURY

(In Millions of £)

| Year | Total Imports | Imports Re-exported | Exports of British Goods | Total Visible Commerce |
|---|---|---|---|---|
| 1805 ... ... ... | Not known | Not known | 38 | ? |
| 1810 ... ... ... | ,, | ,, | 48 | ,, |
| 1815 ... ... ... | ,, | ,, | 52 | ,, |
| 1820 ... ... ... | ,, | ,, | 36 | ,, |
| 1825 ... ... ... | ,, | ,, | 39 | ,, |
| 1830 ... ... ... | ,, | ,, | 38 | ,, |
| 1835 ... ... ... | ,, | ,, | 47 | ,, |
| 1840 ... ... ... | ,, | ,, | 51 | ,, |
| 1845 ... ... ... | ,, | ,, | 60 | ,, |
| 1850 ... ... ... | ,, | ,, | 71 | ,, |
| 1855 ... ... ... | 143 | 21 | 96 | 260 |
| 1860 ... ... ... | 210 | 29 | 136 | 375 |
| 1865 ... ... ... | 271 | 53 | 166 | 490 |
| 1870 ... ... ... | 303 | 44 | 199 | 546 |
| 1875 ... ... ... | 374 | 58 | 223 | 655 |
| 1880 ... ... ... | 411 | 63 | 223 | 697 |
| 1885 ... ... ... | 371 | 58 | 213 | 642 |
| 1890 ... ... ... | 421 | 65 | 263 | 749 |
| 1895 ... ... ... | 417 | 60 | 226 | 703 |
| 1900 ... ... ... | 523 | 63 | 291* | 877 |
| 1905 ... ... ... | 565 | 78 | 330* | 973 |
| 1907 ... ... ... | 646 | 92 | 426* | 1,166 |
| 1908 ... ... ... | 593 | 80 | 377* | 1,050 |

* From 1900 onwards these figures include exports of ships, which were not recorded before 1899.

Unfortunately, the values of British imports were not recorded until the year 1854, but the exports of the first half of the nineteenth century are known and given above.

Here the reader has before him the stationary character of British commerce during fifty years of Protection, and the magnificent growth of British commerce during fifty years of Free Trade.

It should not be forgotten that our shipping earnings and other "invisible exports" are not shown in the export column, but what they earn in imports is, of course, shown in the import column. Indeed, the import column most truly exhibits the progress of British commerce, *because a nation only exports in order to gain imports.*

The nature of British commerce is analysed in the following table:

COMMERCE OF THE UNITED KINGDOM ANALYSED

(In Millions of £)

| | Imports for Home Consumption | | Exports of British Make | |
|---|---|---|---|---|
| | 1900 | 1907 | 1900 | 1907 |
| Food, tobacco ... | 207·9 | 235·1 | 14·2 | 22·7 |
| Raw materials ... | 138·8 | 188·7 | 44·5 | 55·0 |
| Manufactures ... | 110·6 | 127·9 | 228·8 | 342·0 |
| Miscellaneous ... | 2·6 | 2·2 | 3·7 | 6·3 |
| Total ... | 459·9 | 553·9 | 291·2 | 426·0 |

The table may be summed up by saying that Britain chiefly imports food and raw materials, and chiefly exports manufactured articles. The years compared in the above table were both boom years, so that the comparison is a fair and valuable one.

The foregoing tables give a broad idea of the nature and development of British commerce. I give on page 298 a more detailed view of our oversea trade, based on the Board of Trade Blue Book (Cd. 4954). It will be seen that our oversea trade has *far more than kept pace with our increase of population.* How, in view of these facts, it is possible for the Protectionists to continue to spread their fancy pictures of a declining British commerce it is difficult to say. The responsibility incurred in proclaiming the ruin of British trade to the world at large is very great, and it should not be lightly incurred. I regret to say that Tariff "Reform" jeremiads have even found their way into foreign Consular Reports. In the United States Daily Consular Report of April 18, 1904, I found a striking instance of this. In the index appeared "Great Britain losing her Colonial Trade," and on turning to the page named I found an official report beginning as follows:

"GREAT BRITAIN LOSING HER COLONIAL TRADE

"A report has been received here [Washington] of a lecture delivered in London by Mr. W. A. S. Dewins, Secretary of the Tariff Commission, in which he claimed that, taking the whole of the British possessions in a group, the same movement had been observed in each instance—the percentage of British trade diminished in comparison with the foreign trade of the Colonies."

And so forth. These American Consular Reports are sent gratis to the American newspapers, who quote from them freely, and so the words of Mr. "Dewins" (a misprint, of course, for Hewins) were circulated all over America, and something more was neatly and effectively done to destroy British commercial prestige. I myself took the trouble to write to the Washington officials and give them the facts of the case, but I fear my effort never caught up the misrepresentation. The report, I should add, reached Washington from the United States Consulate-General at Halifax, Nova Scotia, which shows that Mr. Hewins's unfortunate utterance reached Canada before it reached America, and proves how these things go round the world. How was the American Consul-General at Nova Scotia to know what was the real meaning of the "percentages" referred to? How could he imagine that the facts relating to British exports to British possessions are as follows?

BRITISH EXPORTS TO BRITISH POSSESSIONS ONLY, 1855–1907

| | £ |
|---|---|
| Average of 1855–59 ... ... ... ... | 37,000,000 |
| ,, 1865–69 ... ... ... ... | 50,000,000 |
| ,, 1875–79 ... ... ... ... | 67,000,000 |
| ,, 1885–89 ... ... ... ... | 79,000,000 |
| ,, 1895–99 ... ... ... ... | 81,000,000 |
| In the year 1907 ... ... ... ... | 137,000,000 |

If the American Consul had known the facts he would never have gathered from Mr. Hewins, or stated in his report, that "Great Britain is losing her Colonial trade." Another point should be noticed. The Consul refers gravely to the Tariff

"Commission." How was he to know that a private body of British Protectionists had adopted the title of "Commission," a word which all over the world implies in such a connection the status of State appointment?

In view of the table on page 298 and its wonderful record of progress we may well recall the opening speech of Mr. Chamberlain's fiscal campaign (Glasgow, October 6, 1903), in which he said (speaking to a brief made by a sensational journalist—Mr. J. L. Garvin):

> "What are the facts? The year 1900 was the record year of British trade. . . . The year 1902—last year—was nearly as good, and yet, if you will compare your trade in 1872, thirty years ago, with the trade of 1902—the export trade —you will find that there has been a moderate increase of 22 millions. That, I think, is something like 7½ per cent. Meanwhile, the population has increased 30 per cent. Can you go on supporting your population at that rate of increase, when even in the best of years you can only show so much smaller an increase in your foreign trade?"

The facts, as we have seen, are entirely at variance with this statement. The British population has rapidly increased, but our oversea trade per head has increased even faster. What Mr. Chamberlain did was to compare the exceptional year 1872, when our trade rose abnormally through the effect of the Franco-German War, to the year 1902, when our trade suffered by our own war in South Africa.

The distribution of British commerce between foreign countries and British Possessions is worth careful examination. In the table printed on page 299 the facts on this head since 1854 are presented in a form which enables the respective proportions of our foreign and imperial trade to be seen at a glance. The really remarkable fact about these figures is the persistency of the proportion of foreign to colonial trade. It is not true that "trade follows the flag." While our Colonial trade is happily great and increasing, our foreign trade is not less expansive and prosperous. Yet at the beginning of the fiscal controversy in 1903 nothing was

UNITED KINGDOM OVERSEA TRADE

(Showing: Total Imports; Exports of Imported Goods; Imports for Home Consumption; Exports of British Produce and Manufactures, 1854–1908)

| Years | Imports | | Re-exports (Exports of Imported Goods) | | Imports for Home Consumption (Imports less Re-exports) | | Exports of British Goods Only | |
|---|---|---|---|---|---|---|---|---|
| | Total | Per Head of Population | Total | Per Head of Population | Total | Per Head of Population | Total | Per Head o Population |
| | Million £ | £ s. d. | Million £ | £ s. d. | Million £ | £ s. d. | Million £ | £ s. d. |
| 1854 ... ... | 152 | 5 10 2 | 19 | 0 13 6 | 133 | 4 16 8 | 97 | 3 10 3 |
| Average 1855–9 ... | 169 | 6 0 3 | 23 | 0 16 7 | 146 | 5 3 8 | 116 | 4 2 4 |
| „ 1860–4 ... | 235 | 8 1 2 | 42 | 1 8 5 | 193 | 6 12 9 | 138 | 4 14 8 |
| „ 1865–9 ... | 286 | 9 8 2 | 49 | 1 11 11 | 237 | 7 16 3 | 181 | 5 19 0 |
| „ 1870–4 ... | 346 | 10 17 2 | 55 | 1 14 10 | 291 | 9 2 4 | 235 | 7 7 4 |
| „ 1875–9 ... | 375 | 11 3 5 | 55 | 1 13 1 | 320 | 9 10 4 | 202 | 6 0 0 |
| „ 1880–4 ... | 408 | 11 11 8 | 64 | 1 16 5 | 344 | 9 15 3 | 234 | 6 13 2 |
| „ 1885–9 ... | 380 | 10 7 6 | 61 | 1 13 4 | 319 | 8 14 2 | 226 | 6 3 8 |
| „ 1890–4 ... | 419 | 10 19 4 | 62 | 1 12 3 | 357 | 9 7 1 | 234 | 6 2 10 |
| „ 1895–9 ... | 453 | 11 6 7 | 60 | 1 10 2 | 393 | 9 16 5 | 238* | 5 18 11 |
| „ 1900–4 ... | 533 | 12 14 3 | 67 | 1 12 1 | 466 | 11 2 2 | 283* | 6 14 9 |
| 1905 ... ... | 565 | — | 78 | — | 487 | — | 325* | — |
| 1906 ... ... | 608 | — | 85 | — | 523 | — | 367* | — |
| 1907 ... ... | 646 | — | 92 | — | 554 | — | 416* | — |
| 1908 ... ... | 593 | — | 80 | — | 513 | — | 366* | — |
| Average 1905–8 ... | 603 | 13 14 9 | 84 | 1 18 1 | 519 | 11 16 8 | 368* | 8 7 11 |

* The figures given exclude Exports of Ships.

UNITED KINGDOM: OVERSEA TRADE WITH FOREIGN COUNTRIES AND BRITISH POSSESSIONS

| Years | Imports | | | | | Exports (British Goods only) * | | | | |
|---|---|---|---|---|---|---|---|---|---|---|
| | Total | From Foreign Countries | | From British Possessions | | Total | To Foreign Countries | | To British Possessions | |
| | | Amount | Per Cent. of Total | Amount | Per Cent. of Total | | Amount | Per Cent. of Total | Amount | Per Cent. of Total |
| | Mill. £ | Mill. £ | | Mill. £ | | Mill. £ | Mill. £ | | Mill. £ | |
| 1854 ... ... | 152 | 118 | 77·6 | 34 | 22·4 | 97 | 63 | 64·9 | 34 | 35·1 |
| Average 1855–9 ... | 169 | 129 | 76·5 | 40 | 23·5 | 116 | 79 | 68·5 | 37 | 31·5 |
| ,, 1860–4 ... | 235 | 167 | 71·2 | 68 | 28·8 | 138 | 92 | 66·6 | 46 | 33·4 |
| ,, 1865–9 ... | 286 | 218 | 76·0 | 68 | 24·0 | 181 | 131 | 72·4 | 50 | 27·6 |
| ,, 1870–4 ... | 346 | 270 | 78·0 | 76 | 22·0 | 235 | 175 | 74·4 | 60 | 25·6 |
| ,, 1875–9 ... | 375 | 292 | 77·9 | 83 | 22·1 | 202 | 135 | 66·9 | 67 | 33·1 |
| ,, 1880–4 ... | 408 | 312 | 76·5 | 96 | 23·5 | 234 | 153 | 65·5 | 81 | 34·5 |
| ,, 1885–9 ... | 380 | 293 | 77·1 | 87 | 22·9 | 226 | 147 | 65·0 | 79 | 35·0 |
| ,, 1890–4 ... | 419 | 323 | 77·1 | 96 | 22·9 | 234 | 156 | 66·5 | 78 | 33·5 |
| ,, 1895–9 ... | 453 | 355 | 78·4 | 98 | 21·6 | 238 | 157 | 65·9 | 81 | 34·1 |
| ,, 1900–4 ... | 533 | 422 | 79·2 | 111 | 20·8 | 283 | 177 | 62·7 | 106 | 37·3 |
| 1905 ... ... | 565 | 437 | — | 128 | — | 325 | 212 | — | 113 | — |
| 1906 ... ... | 608 | 466 | — | 142 | — | 367 | 246 | — | 121 | — |
| 1907 ... ... | 646 | 489 | — | 157 | — | 416 | 281 | — | 135 | — |
| 1908 ... ... | 593 | 463 | — | 130 | — | 366 | 242 | — | 124 | — |
| Average 1905–8 ... | 603 | 464 | 76·9 | 139 | 23·1 | 368 | 245 | 66·6 | 123 | 33·4 |

* Ships Excluded.

commoner than the assertion that our Colonial trade alone saved our commerce from decline. In the articles which "briefed" Mr. Chamberlain, published in the *Daily Telegraph* by Mr. J. L. Garvin in 1903, we read :

"The result of thirty years' trading, we say, is that our commercial supremacy, except in the case of our commerce under the flag, *has been destroyed.*"

Apparently believing this, Mr. Chamberlain, speaking at Liverpool on October 27, 1903, said :

"In almost exactly the same proportion in which the trade with these foreign protected countries has continuously fallen off, trade with our Colonies and possessions has continuously risen ; and if we have good trade to-day, if the last year, 1902, was one of the best years that British trade has known, it is not thanks to the foreign trade, which has decreased, but it is thanks to the Colonial trade, which has increased."

It is pleasant to turn from the misguided misrepresentations of British trade in which Protectionists have permitted themselves to indulge to matters which demand our serious attention as a nation. In dealing with German progress (*see* GERMANY), I have pointed out what I believe to be the real causes of her success since 1870. She has since that date redoubled her exertions to educate her people, so that at the present time she is far ahead of us in scientific training. She has given her citizens a magnificent State insurance system which saves them from the worst vicissitudes of industrial life. She has labour bureaux to grease the creaking wheels of unorganised industry. She has a State canal and railway system which gives her more *internal* Free Trade (and in a larger population and area) than we possess. In all these points it is necessary for the United Kingdom to "wake up." If we have done so much without these things, how much more we could hope to do if in the United Kingdom scientific captains of industry led a better trained people.

**UNITED STATES OF AMERICA**—The United States of America is by far the richest country in point of natural resources in the world. In mere area she has 3,600,000 square miles against our 121,000, but that is the least part of it. The great American area is rich in natural fertility and range of climate, in coal and water power, in petroleum and natural gas, in iron and copper and silver. Above all, the United States is the greatest coal country in the world (*see* COAL). Here is a comparison of the United Kingdom and the United States in respect of natural resources in the year 1906:

NATURAL RESOURCES OF BRITAIN AND AMERICA

| Production of— | UNITED KINGDOM | UNITED STATES |
|---|---|---|
| Coal (tons) ... ... | 251,000,000 ... ... | 370,000,000 |
| Iron ore (tons) ... | 15,500,000 ... ... | 43,000,000 |
| Copper (lb.) ... ... | 130,000,000 ... ... | 298,000,000 |
| Silver (oz.) ... ... | 3,000 ... ... | 56,500,000 |
| Petroleum (barrels) ... | nil ... ... | 126,500,000 |
| Natural Gas (dollars)... | nil ... ... | 46,900,000 |
| Wheat (bushels) ... | 60,800,000 ... ... | 735,000,000 |
| Cotton (bales).... ... | nil ... ... | 13,300,000 |
| Wool (lb.) ... ... | 130,000,000 ... ... | 298,000,000 |

The reader will see from these figures how thoughtless it is to compare the two countries in point of prosperity or industry, without reference to what Nature has given them. The fact is that America is a world in herself, and that Protection cannot therefore work the harm in her economy that it would work in ours. Either the Dingley Tariff or the new American tariff of August 5, 1909, would ruin either Britain or Germany if they were foolish enough to adopt it.

I give on page 302 the American official analysis of United States commerce in the same form as that in which I stated British commerce.

Unlike Britain, the United States chiefly imports manufactured articles, and chiefly exports food and raw materials. The average Protectionist is quite unaware of these facts, and will probably rub his eyes when he sees the figures on page 302. He can obtain confirmation of them by consulting the official American trade returns at the Commercial Intelligence Office of the Board of Trade.

COMMERCE OF THE UNITED STATES

(In Millions of £)

| | Imports (almost entirely for Home Consumption) | | Exports of American Produce | |
|---|---|---|---|---|
| | 1900 | 1907 | 1900 | 1907 |
| Food ... ... | 48·1 | 64·2 | 113·7 | 106·9 |
| Raw materials ... | 57·6 | 99·4 | 67·8 | 123·6 |
| Manufactures ... | 70·3 | 133·0 | 101·0 | 154·2 |
| Miscellaneous ... | 1·1 | 2·2 | 3·1 | 1·5 |
| Total ... ... | 177·1 | 298·8 | 285·6 | 386·2 |

A ridiculous degree of Protection has prevented the United States from becoming a great competitor of Britain and Germany in the world's markets, and it has ruined her oversea shipping, which has fallen from 2,546,000 tons in 1860 to 871,000 tons in 1907. (*See* also Exports, Comparative, and Imports, Comparative.)

**WAGES**—Wages, the remuneration of labour, can only be paid out of the product of labour, *or out of what can be exchanged for the product of labour.* The last point is of profound importance, because of the distinction between real and nominal wages. Nominal wages are the money wages, or mere coins which a man receives from his employer. Real wages are the commodities—food, fuel, housing, clothes, and other necessaries and comforts—which a man can purchase with his nominal wages. Under Free Trade a workman is enabled to exchange his labour, by means of his nominal wages, for real wages in the shape of the cheapest and best commodities which the whole world has to offer.

The Board of Trade showed in the Fiscal Blue Book of 1903 that, comparing the prices of articles in 1871 with their prices in 1902, there was an all-round fall which may be expressed by saying that you could buy as much in 1902 for £78 16s. as

# BRITISH WAGES

## STATEMENT SHOWING BY THE METHOD OF INDEX NUMBERS THE GROWTH OF MONEY WAGES IN THE UNITED KINGDOM

(Wages at the end of 1900 are represented as 100)

| Years | Agriculture | Coal Mining | Textile | Building Trades | Engineering | Unweighted Mean of Preceding Groups of Trades | |
|---|---|---|---|---|---|---|---|
| | Ordinary Labourers (Mean of 115 Rates) | Hewers (Weighted Percentage changes in Principal Districts) | Cotton Spinners and Weavers, and Linen and Jute Operatives | Bricklayers, Carpenters and Joiners, and Masons (Mean of 74 Rates) | Fitters, Turners, Ironfounders and Patternmakers (Mean of 36 Rates) | Including Agriculture | Excluding Agriculture |
| 1874 | 93·22 | 88·90 | 106·67 | 81·11 | 88·77 | 91·73 | 91·36 |
| 1875 | 93·79 | 79·38 | 104·89 | 84·45 | 88·99 | 90·30 | 89·43 |
| 1876 | 94·92 | 70·66 | 104·89 | 87·78 | 88·86 | 89·42 | 88·05 |
| 1877 | 94·92 | 65·65 | 102·22 | 90·00 | 88·86 | 88·33 | 86·68 |
| 1878 | 94·35 | 61·98 | 92·45 | 88·89 | 88·05 | 85·14 | 82·84 |
| 1879 | 92·09 | 62·11 | 88·01 | 86·67 | 87·86 | 83·35 | 81·16 |
| 1880 | 91·53 | 61·45 | 89·78 | 85·55 | 88·05 | 83·27 | 81·21 |
| 1881 | 91·53 | 63·23 | 94·23 | 85·55 | 89·36 | 84·78 | 83·09 |
| 1882 | 91·53 | 67·91 | 94·23 | 85·55 | 89·94 | 85·83 | 84·41 |
| 1883 | 92·09 | 69·24 | 93·33 | 84·45 | 90·09 | 85·84 | 84·28 |
| 1884 | 91·53 | 65·67 | 93·56 | 84·45 | 89·99 | 85·04 | 83·42 |
| 1885 | 90·40 | 63·10 | 90·22 | 84·45 | 89·96 | 83·63 | 81·93 |
| 1886 | 89·83 | 61·09 | 89·34 | 84·45 | 89·60 | 82·86 | 81·12 |
| 1887 | 89·27 | 60·85 | 90·22 | 84·45 | 90·29 | 83·02 | 81·45 |
| 1888 | 89·27 | 64·80 | 93·78 | 84·45 | 91·29 | 84·72 | 83·58 |
| 1889 | 89·83 | 75·79 | 94·67 | 85·55 | 91·72 | 87·51 | 86·93 |
| 1890 | 90·96 | 85·85 | 95·12 | 86·67 | 92·68 | 90·26 | 90·08 |
| 1891 | 93·22 | 86·52 | 96·89 | 87·78 | 93·31 | 91·54 | 91·13 |
| 1892 | 93·22 | 78·88 | 96·00 | 88·89 | 93·31 | 90·06 | 89·27 |
| 1893 | 92·66 | 80·44 | 94·97 | 90·00 | 92·60 | 90·13 | 89·50 |
| 1894 | 92·66 | 76·13 | 94·97 | 91·11 | 92·56 | 89·49 | 88·69 |
| 1895 | 92·66 | 72·54 | 94·97 | 92·22 | 93·18 | 89·11 | 88·23 |
| 1896 | 92·66 | 71·90 | 94·97 | 93·33 | 96·75 | 89·92 | 89·24 |
| 1897 | 93·79 | 72·60 | 94·97 | 94·45 | 98·18 | 90·80 | 90·05 |
| 1898 | 95·48 | 78·60 | 94·97 | 97·78 | 99·19 | 93·20 | 92·64 |
| 1899 | 96·61 | 83·53 | 98·22 | 98·89 | 99·61 | 95·37 | 95·06 |
| **1900** | **100·00** | **100·00** | **100·00** | **100·00** | **100·00** | **100·00** | **100·00** |
| 1901 | 101·13 | 93·95 | 100·00 | 100·00 | 100·29 | 99·07 | 98·56 |
| 1902 | 101·13 | 87·53 | 100·00 | 100·00 | 100·29 | 97·78 | 96·96 |
| 1903 | 101·13 | 84·92 | 100·00 | 100·00 | 99·93 | 97·20 | 96·21 |
| 1904 | 101·33 | 82·31 | 100·00 | 100·00 | 99·93 | 96·71 | 95·56 |
| 1905 | 101·22 | 81·02 | 102·67 | 100·00 | 100·05 | 96·99 | 95·94 |
| 1906 | 101·25 | 83·36 | 106·22 | 100·00 | 100·83 | 98·33 | 97·60 |
| 1907 | 101·25 | 96·25 | 108·89 | 100·00 | 102·00 | 101·68 | 101·79 |
| 1908 | 101·25 | 93·30 | 108·89 | 100·00 | 101·68 | 101·02 | 100·97 |

you could buy for £100 in 1871. That means, of course, a great rise in real wages. In the same period nominal wages rose considerably in the United Kingdom. Thus, representing the average wages of building, mining, engineering, and the textile industries in 1900 by 100, the Board of Trade show that the wages of 1878 are represented by 82·8. Combining the increase in nominal or money wages with the great fall in prices referred to, the rise in real wages is seen to be very great indeed.

In two most interesting reports issued in 1908–9 the Board of Trade compare British, French, and German money wages for the year 1905. The official figures are as follows:

WEEKLY MONEY WAGES IN ENGLAND, FRANCE, AND GERMANY

| Trade | England | France | Germany |
| --- | --- | --- | --- |
| | s. d. s. d. | s. d. s. d. | s. d. s. d. |
| Bricklayers ... ... | 37 6 to 46 6 | 21 7 to 28 10 | 26 11 to 31 3 |
| Carpenters ... ... | 36 2 ,, 39 4 | 24 0 ,, 30 3 | 26 11 ,, 31 3 |
| Plumbers ... ... | 35 4 ,, 39 9 | 24 0 ,, 28 10 | 24 0 ,, 28 6 |
| Painters ... ... | 31 6 ,, 37 6 | 21 5 ,, 26 5 | 24 0 ,, 29 8 |
| Builders' labourers... | 23 6 ,, 27 0 | 15 10 ,, 19 10 | 19 6 ,, 24 0 |
| Engineers' fitters ... | 32 0 ,, 36 0 | 24 0 ,, 28 10 | 26 0 ,, 32 0 |
| Engineers' labourers | 18 0 ,, 22 0 | 15 7 ,, 19 2 | 18 0 ,, 22 0 |
| Compositors ... ... | 28 0 ,, 33 0 | 22 10 ,, 28 10 | 24 0 ,, 25 11 |

Taking the group of trades compared, including both skilled and unskilled workmen, the Board of Trade's general conclusion is that money wages in England, France, and Germany respectively are as 100 to 75 to 83.

But, taking into consideration the fact that hours of labour are longer in France and Germany than in England, the average earnings per hour in England, France, and Germany respectively are as 100 to 64 to 75.

Further, the Board of Trade show that the cost of living in Germany is one-fifth greater than in England, and in France one-seventh greater than in England. (*See* COST OF LIVING.)

In the table on page 303 a careful examination of the growth of British wages by the Board of Trade will be found. The rates of 1900 are taken as 100, and the other years therefore represent percentages of the rates of 1900. (*See also* under the various trades.)

**WATCHES**—In the manufacture of watches and chronometers of the highest class British makers are unsurpassed, but our manufacturers were for long content to resign the great market for popular watches to Continental and American makers. In recent years, however, the British manufacture of watches for the multitude has considerably extended, with the result that the imports have fallen greatly.

BRITISH COMMERCE IN WATCHES

| | Imports for Home Consumption (c.i.f.) £ | Exports of British Make (f.o.b.) £ |
|---|---|---|
| 1900 (good year) ... | ... 1,313,000 ... | ... Not known |
| 1907 (good year) ... | ... 728,000 ... | ... Not known |
| 1908 (bad year) ... | ... 707,000 ... | ... 12,000 |

The export trade is very small, and was not even recorded before 1908. The imports for home consumption have fallen by one-half in eight years. As the consumption of watches must be increasing, it is clear that British makers are rapidly atoning for their past neglect of the popular watch market.

**WHEAT**—In order to show quite clearly the position and recent variation of our wheat supplies, I have constructed the table on page 306, which distinguishes the home and chief foreign and Colonial supplies. The figures are expressed to the nearest million, so that when the supply from any country is merely a few hundred thousand cwts. it is not shown at all in the table.

This table will repay examination. We get the wheat we want year by year, but the sources of supply vary greatly, and none of them is to be depended upon individually. Free Trade cannot guarantee harvests, either at home or abroad, but what it does do is to place at our disposal freely the best harvests of the world available in any year. Wheat is tending to become dearer because the number of wheat-eaters in the world is increasing more rapidly than the wheat supply. This makes Free Trade not less important but more important, for it is easier to bear a bread tax when wheat is naturally cheap than when it is naturally dear.

The lack of necessity for a Colonial preference on wheat is also shown by the table; it will be seen that the Colonies are

UNITED KINGDOM WHEAT SUPPLIES

(In millions of cwts., and in round figures to the nearest million)

| | 1898 | 1899 | 1900 | 1901 | 1902 | 1903 | 1904 | 1905 | 1906 | 1907 |
|---|---|---|---|---|---|---|---|---|---|---|
| 1. Homegrown ... | 37 | 34 | 27 | 27 | 29 | 24 | 19 | 30 | 30 | 28 |
| 2. Foreign Imports: | | | | | | | | | | |
| Argentina ... ... | 4 | 12 | 19 | 8 | 5 | 14 | 22 | 24 | 19 | 22 |
| Austria ... ... | 1 | 1 | 2 | 1 | 1 | 1 | 1 | 1 | 1 | 1 |
| France ... ... | 1 | 1 | 1 | 1 | 1 | 1 | 2 | 1 | 1 | 1 |
| Germany ... ... | 1 | 1 | 2 | 1 | — | — | 1 | 1 | — | — |
| Roumania ... ... | — | — | 1 | 1 | 2 | 3 | 1 | 2 | 4 | 3 |
| Russia... ... ... | 6 | 3 | 4 | 3 | 7 | 17 | 24 | 24 | 15 | 11 |
| U.S.A. ... ... | 62 | 60 | 58 | 67 | 65 | 47 | 18 | 14 | 36 | 33 |
| Total Foreign ... | 77 | 78 | 87 | 82 | 83 | 85 | 72 | 71 | 78 | 74 |
| 3. Colonial Imports: | | | | | | | | | | |
| Australia ... ... | — | 3 | 3 | 6 | 4 | — | 11 | 11 | 9 | 8 |
| New Zealand ... | — | 1 | 1 | 1 | — | — | — | — | — | — |
| Canada ... ... | 8 | 9 | 8 | 9 | 12 | 14 | 9 | 8 | 14 | 15 |
| India... ... ... | 9 | 8 | — | 3 | 9 | 17 | 25 | 23 | 13 | 18 |
| Total Colonial ... | 17 | 21 | 12 | 19 | 25 | 32 | 46 | 43 | 35 | 42 |
| Total Imported ... | 94 | 99 | 99 | 101 | 108 | 117 | 118 | 114 | 113 | 116 |
| Total Supply ... | 131 | 133 | 126 | 128 | 137 | 141 | 137 | 144 | 143 | 144 |

quite naturally increasing their wheat supplies and it is quite unnecessary to tax bread on their behalf. (*See* Canadian Farmers and Preference.)

In 1909, owing to the natural rise in the price of wheat, British farmers are enjoying a "natural protection" at the expense of their fellow-countrymen. In 1909 wheat has been over 40s. a quarter, or about twice the price it fetched in the lowest year on record, 1894, and more than 10s. per quarter more than the average of the past ten years. To add a duty, even a small one, to this natural rise in price, which has made bread dearer, would be an act of folly.

On page 308 I reproduce the Board of Trade's comparison of wheat prices, in Britain, France, Germany, and the United States, from Blue Book Cd. 4954. This table shows how wheat prices have been affected by import duties in France and Germany.

The American wheat duty may be neglected, for it is, of course, a sham. It was inserted in the American tariff to reconcile American farmers to taxes on imports of the manufactures they need to buy; to put it quite plainly, it was enacted to gull them. An American tax on imported wheat is like a British tax on imported coal.

In comparing the effects of a wheat duty in Britain, France, and Germany, it should be remembered that France is in some years almost or quite independent of imports, because of her stationary population and larger area per head of population. The population per square mile in Britain, France, and Germany compares as follows:

POPULATION PER SQUARE MILE

(Last Census in each case)

| | |
|---|---|
| Britain ... ... ... ... ... ... | 342 |
| France... ... ... ... ... ... ... | 190 |
| Germany ... ... ... ... ... ... | 290 |

In spite of her comparative paucity of population, the French wheat duty affects price considerably in most years, it will be seen.

In Germany we have a nearer approximation to British conditions, and in nearly every year, it will be seen, wheat is higher in price in Germany than in Britain by approximately the amount of the German wheat duty.

Britain is more dependent than Germany upon imported wheat, and it is clear that not merely the imported supply, but the entire British supply of wheat, home, foreign, and Colonial, would be raised in price by the amount of any import

# WHEAT PRICES AND IMPORT DUTIES

| Year | United Kingdom | | | France (Official Average) | | Germany (Official Average for Prussia) | | United States (Average Price of Winter Wheat, New York Market) | |
|---|---|---|---|---|---|---|---|---|---|
| | Average Price of British Wheat | Imported Wheat (Average) | Import Duty | Average Price | Import Duty | Average Price | Import Duty | Average Price | Import Duty |
| | s. d. | s. d. | s. d. | s. d. | s. d. | s. d. | s. d. | s. d. | s. d. |
| 1854 | 72 5 | 68 2 | 1 0 | 67 1 | Free | 55 3 | 2 11 | 68 8 | 20 % *ad val.* |
| 1855 | 74 8 | 72 7 | " | 68 3 | Free | 60 10 | " | 79 2 | " |
| 1856 | 69 2 | 62 5 | " | 71 7 | Free | 57 10 | " | 60 5 | " |
| 1857 | 56 4 | 55 8 | " | 56 8 | Free | 43 8 | 1 2 | 54 5 | 15 % *ad val.* |
| 1858 | 44 2 | 42 8 | " | 39 0 | Free | 39 0 | " | 40 2 | " |
| 1859 | 43 9 | 43 7 | " | 39 0 | Free | 38 4 | " | 50 1 | " |
| 1860 | 53 3 | 56 4 | " | 47 1 | 0 7 | 45 0 | " | 47 7 | " |
| 1861 | 55 4 | 55 1 | " | 57 2 | 0 10½ | 47 4 | " | 44 1 | 6 10½ |
| 1862 | 55 5 | 48 6 | " | 54 1 | 1 0½ | 45 10 | " | 44 1 | " |
| 1863 | 44 9 | 42 3 | " | 46 0 | " | 39 5 | " | 35 11 | " |
| 1864 | 40 2 | 39 5 | 1 0¾ | 40 11 | " | 34 1 | " | 43 11 | " |
| 1865 | 41 10 | 40 0 | " | 38 2 | " | 34 11 | Free | 32 6 | " |
| 1866 | 49 11 | 48 1 | " | 45 8 | " | 41 11 | " | 56 5 | " |
| 1867 | 64 5 | 61 10 | " | 60 11 | " | 55 3 | " | 72 7 | " |
| 1868 | 63 9 | 57 11 | " | 62 0 | " | 53 6 | " | 61 2 | " |
| 1869 | 48 2 | 44 5 | " | 47 4 | " | 41 7 | " | 39 10 | " |
| 1870 | 46 11 | 45 1 | Free | — | " | 43 8 | " | 37 1 | " |
| 1871 | 56 8 | 50 9 | " | 59 8 | " | 50 2 | " | 49 6 | " |
| 1872 | 57 0 | 53 3 | " | 53 11 | " | 51 9 | " | 51 1 | " |
| 1873 | 58 8 | 55 9 | " | 59 7 | " | 56 6 | " | 53 8 | " |
| 1874 | 55 9 | 52 1 | " | 58 5 | 1 1 | 51 5 | " | 45 2 | " |
| 1875 | 45 2 | 45 5 | " | 45 0 | " | 41 11 | " | 40 6 | " |
| 1876 | 46 2 | 44 8 | " | 47 11 | " | 45 0 | " | 41 1 | " |
| 1877 | 56 9 | 53 6 | " | 54 7 | " | 49 3 | " | 52 11 | " |
| 1878 | 46 5 | 47 1 | " | 49 5 | " | 43 3 | " | 42 4 | " |
| 1879 | 43 10 | 45 3 | " | 51 6 | " | 41 11 | 2 2 | 40 3 | " |
| 1880 | 44 4 | 47 6 | " | 51 8 | " | 46 10 | " | 43 8 | " |
| 1881 | 45 4 | 47 4 | " | 51 8 | 1 0½ | 47 1 | " | 45 4 | " |
| 1882 | 45 1 | 45 9 | " | 44 11 | " | 44 7 | " | 43 11 | " |
| 1883 | 41 7 | 42 0 | " | 44 3 | " | 39 7 | " | 40 5 | " |
| 1884 | 35 8 | 36 1 | " | 41 4 | " | 37 0 | " | 33 6 | " |
| 1885 | 32 10 | 33 7 | " | 38 3 | 5 2 | 34 8 | 6 6½ | 33 2 | " |
| 1886 | 31 0 | 32 4 | " | 38 6 | " | 33 7 | " | 30 5 | " |
| 1887 | 32 6 | 32 9 | " | 41 2 | 8 8 | 35 2 | " | 30 7 | " |
| 1888 | 31 10 | 32 11 | " | 43 9 | " | 37 3 | 10 10½ | 33 5 | " |
| 1889 | 29 9 | 32 11 | " | 42 1 | " | 39 2 | " | 30 4 | " |
| 1890 | 31 11 | 33 5 | " | 44 1 | " | 41 2 | " | 33 9 | " |
| 1891 | 37 0 | 38 1 | " | 47 10 | 5 2 | 47 6 | " | 37 7 | 8 7 |
| 1892 | 30 3 | 32 10 | " | 41 6 | 8 8 | 40 6 | 7 7½ | 31 3 | " |
| 1893 | 26 4 | 27 7 | " | 37 9 | " | 32 6 | " | 25 5 | " |
| 1894 | 22 10 | 22 11 | " | 34 6 | 12 2 | 28 11 | " | 21 0 | 20 % *ad val.* |
| 1895 | 23 1 | 23 7 | " | 32 9 | " | 30 0 | " | 23 0 | " |
| 1896 | 26 2 | 26 6 | " | 33 4 | " | 32 9 | " | 26 10 | " |
| 1897 | 30 2 | 31 11 | " | 43 9 | " | 35 5 | " | 32 10 | 8 7 |
| 1898 | 34 0 | 34 4 | " | 45 8 | " | 39 10 | " | 32 9 | " |
| 1899 | 25 8 | 28 8 | " | 34 11 | " | 33 2 | " | 27 4 | " |
| 1900 | 26 11 | 29 2 | " | 33 8 | " | 32 1 | " | 27 8 | " |
| 1901 | 26 9 | 28 5 | " | 35 3 | " | 34 8 | " | 27 7 | " |
| 1902 | 28 1 | 28 8 | 1 0 6/7 from 15.4.02 to 30.6.03, then free | 37 9 | " | 35 2 | " | 28 9 | " |
| 1903 | 26 9 | 29 1 | | 39 8 | " | 33 2 | " | 29 4 | " |
| 1904 | 28 4 | 30 0 | Free | 37 11 | " | 36 2 | " | 38 1 | " |
| 1905 | 29 8 | 31 0 | " | 40 10 | " | 36 7 | " | 35 4 | " |
| 1906 | 28 3 | 30 2 | " | 41 0 | " | 37 3 | 11 10 from 1.3.06 | 29 9 | " |
| 1907 | 30 7 | 32 11 | " | 40 7 | " | 43 1 | " | 33 1 | " |
| 1908 | 32 0 | 36 0 | " | 38 5 | " | 43 8 | " | 36 1 | " |

duty levied. I add particulars of the growth of the wheat duties in France and Germany:

FRANCE: GROWTH OF WHEAT DUTIES

| | Customs Duty Per 100 kilogs | English Equivalent Per cwt. |
|---|---|---|
| | fr. cts. | s. d. |
| Law of June, 1861, modified in 1862 | 0 60 | 0 3 |
| ,, December, 1873 ... ... | 4% on above | 4% on above |
| ,, May, 1881 ... ... ... | 0 60 | 0 3 |
| ,, March, 1885 ... ... | 3 00 | 1 2¾ |
| ,, March, 1887 ... ... | 5 00 | 2 0½ |
| ,, July, 1891 ... ... ... | 3 00 | 1 2¾ |
| ,, January, 1892 ... ... | 5 00 | 2 0½ |
| ,, February, 1894 ... ... | 7 00 | 2 10¼ |

GERMANY: GROWTH OF WHEAT DUTIES

| | Customs Duty Per 100 kilogs | English Equivalent Per cwt. |
|---|---|---|
| | mks. pf. | s. d. |
| Law of 1879 ... ... ... ... | 1 00 | 0 6 |
| ,, 1885 ... ... ... ... | 3 00 | 1 6 |
| ,, 1888 ... ... ... ... | 5 00 | 2 6 |
| ,, 1892 (reduced by treaty) ... | 3 50 | 1 9 |
| ,, 1906 ... ... ... ... | 5 50 | 2 9 |

Contemplation of these tables should be useful to a nation which is being urged by Protectionists to adopt food duties on the ground that they cannot do much harm because they are "so small." As a matter of fact our industrial Protectionists hate food duties as heartily as any Free Trader; they are compelled to stomach them to secure the votes of the landed interest in the Tory Party. By the same interest they would most unwillingly be compelled to increase the duties, just as the German Agrarians have worked their ends in the making of German tariffs. (*See* GERMANY.)

**WOOL**—Our imports of wool are very great, and three or four times as great as our home clip. Between home-grown and imported wool and hair, we consumed in the last three years about 800,000,000 lb. a year on the average. The wonderful growth of wool consumption in this country will be gathered from the fact that whereas in the last days of Protection the wool consumption was under 7 lb. per head, it rose to nearly 17 lb. per head in 1908, reaching nearly 21 lb. per head in 1907. Under Protection, between 1775 and 1846, British wool consumption was stationary.

There is, of course, danger of the taxation of wool under a preferential system. If we are to give a preference on Australasian mutton, as suggested by Mr. Chamberlain, it will be difficult to resist the logical demand for a preference on the wool which grows outside the mutton. At the recent Imperial Press Conference a New Zealand delegate told me that we certainly ought to tax wool, and that it would not do us any harm!

**WOOLLENS AND WORSTEDS**—The highly satisfactory present position and progress of this ancient British industry is shown in the following table:

BRITISH WOOLLEN AND WORSTED PRODUCTION AND COMMERCE

| | Wool, Hair, &c., consumed by the Industry | Imports for Home Consumption (c.i.f.) | Exports of British Make (f.o.b.) |
|---|---|---|---|
| | lbs | £ | £ |
| 1860 | 300,000,000 | 2,145,000 | 16,148,000 |
| 1870 | 410,200,000 | 4,731,000 | 26,964,000 |
| 1880 | 529,700,000 | 8,921,000 | 22,034,000 |
| 1890 | 576,600,000 | 9,874,000 | 27,476,000 |
| 1900 | 654,600,000 | 10,659,000 | 23,796,000 |
| 1907 | 833,400,000 | 9,667,000 | 34,159,000 |
| 1908 | 741,300,000 | 8,393,000 | 28,392,000 |

The most important column of the above table is the first, since it measures the growth of the entire production, and not merely the production for export.

As to external trade, it is noteworthy that imports in 1907 were of less value than in 1890, and that imports in 1908 were of less value than in 1880. Our exports, checked in 1890–1900

# BRITISH WOOLLEN AND WORSTED EXPORTS IN ANALYSIS

| Year | Flocks and Shoddy | Tops, Noils, and Waste | Yarns | | | | Manufactures | | | | | | Apparel (Estimates down to 1900) | Grand Total |
|---|---|---|---|---|---|---|---|---|---|---|---|---|---|---|
| | | | Woollen | Worsted | Alpaca and Mohair | Total Yarns | Woollen Stuffs | Worsted Stuffs | Flannels and Blankets | Carpets | All other Sorts | Total Manufactures | | |
| | £ | £ | £ | £ | £ | £ | £ | £ | £ | £ | £ | £ | £ | £ |
| 1860 | 145,796 | — | Included in "Worsted" | 3,578,088 | 265,362 | 3,843,450 | 2,996,000 | 7,013,000 | 848,000 | 667,000 | 634,000 | 12,158,710 | 700,000 | 16,847,956 |
| 1870 | 116,162 | — | 97,708 | 4,896,541 | 188,687 | 5,182,926 | 4,749,000 | 13,788,000 | 1,078,000 | 1,393,000 | 654,000 | 21,664,953 | 700,000 | 27,664,051 |
| 1880 | 546,671 | — | 106,922 | 3,237,818 | 877,953 | 4,222,693 | 6,736,000 | 7,241,000 | 897,000 | 1,133,000 | 1,256,000 | 17,265,177 | 1,900,000 | 23,934,541 |
| 1890 | 406,517 | 1,390,065 | 197,733 | 3,888,725 | 1,174,477 | 5,260,925 | 6,016,000 | 10,326,000 | 1,097,000 | 1,115,000 | 1,864,000 | 20,418,482 | 1,700,000 | 29,175,989 |
| 1900 | 328,324 | 2,125,939 | 95,500 | 4,397,773 | 1,506,643 | 6,123,349 | 5,906,000 | 6,468,000 | 718,000 | 919,000 | 1,669,000 | 15,682,154 | 1,700,000 | 25,946,037 |
| 1907 | 474,796 | 4,380,411 | 256,083 | 5,758,024 | 2,303,463 | 8,569,994 | 10,311,000 | 7,393,000 | 690,000 | 1,232,000 | 2,525,000 | 22,151,174 | 2,544,895 | 38,121,270 |
| 1908 | 284,326 | 3,523,000 | 192,410 | 4,416,820 | 1,764,804 | 6,616,952 | 9,641,000 | 5,932,000 | 524,000 | 776,000 | 2,278,000 | 19,150,769 | 2,229,398 | 31,804,445 |

recovered admirably, and in 1907 reached £34,159,000. Even in 1908—a year of worldwide depression—they were far better than in 1890 or 1900, both good years of trade.

It is sometimes asserted—as, for example, in the so-called Tariff "Commission's" Report on the subject—that our imports of woollen fabrics compete unfairly with the home product, and that duties are needed to keep them out. Our woollen imports come chiefly from France:

IMPORTS OF WOOLLEN STUFFS, 1907

| | Yards |
|---|---|
| From France ... ... ... ... ... | 60,019,000 |
| From all other places... ... ... ... | 14,371,000 |
| Total ... ... ... | 74,390,000 |

The explanation of these striking facts is simple. Our woollen imports consist almost entirely of stuffs which do not directly compete with our own, *being of a sort in which we do not specialise.*

This was explained by the special Committee appointed by the Bradford Chamber of Commerce in 1903 to consider this particular subject. They reported that neither in the yarn-making nor in the dyeing of delicate shades were we able to equal the French woollen-makers, and their opinion is confirmed by my own inquiries. The remedy, it was recognised, was to be found in study of the methods by which French dress goods were produced. Yorkshire is setting herself to do this with every hope of success.

I give in the table on page 311 an analysis of our woollen and worsted exports since 1860, taken from the records of the Bradford Chamber of Commerce. Here the development of our exports is pictured in some detail, and it is, on the whole, a satisfactory record. The grand totals of this table are larger because more complete than those of the table on page 310. During the fifty years reviewed, foreign and Colonial tariffs have again and again made their impression on the various branches of the export trade, and many a "retaliator" has been made by those tariffs. It should be remarked on this head that under Free Trade the British woollen and worsted industries have very successfully "fought tariffs with free imports," to use the phrase of Sir Robert Peel. This will be realised by contrasting British and French exports of this character, which is done in the following table:

BRITISH AND FRENCH EXPORTS OF MANUFACTURES OF WOOL

| | United Kingdom Million £ | France Million £ |
|---|---|---|
| 1882 ... ... | 23·6 ... ... | 17·7 |
| 1884 ... ... | 26·0 ... ... | 14·7 |
| 1886 ... ... | 26·6 ... ... | 16·8 |
| 1888 ... ... | 26·4 ... ... | 14·4 |
| 1890 ... ... | 27·4 ... ... | 15·8 |
| 1892 ... ... | 24·9 ... ... | 13·9 |
| 1894 ... ... | 21·6 ... ... | 10·4 |
| 1896 ... ... | 27·7 ... ... | 12·9 |
| 1898 ... ... | 22·5 ... ... | 10·1 |
| 1900 ... ... | 23·8 ... ... | 10·5 |
| 1902 ... ... | 23·3 ... ... | 10·2 |
| 1904 ... ... | 26·9 ... ... | 9·7 |
| 1905 ... ... | 29·1 ... ... | 9·4 |
| 1906 ... ... | 31·8 ... ... | 11·1 |
| 1907 ... ... | 34·2 ... ... | 12·1 |

Both Britain and France are experts in the manufacture of wool, while each excels in different branches. It will be seen how much more successful we have been than France in fighting tariff obstacles. In 1897 the American Dingley Tariff reduced both British and French woollen exports—see the figures for 1898. By 1904 British woollen exports recovered, but those of France did not. Even in the boom year 1907 French woollen exports were only at parity with those of 1906. Yet France has what has been termed the "big revolver" of a general tariff to use as a weapon of "Retaliation." Such is the true value of a tariff as a fighting weapon.

The Census of Protection (1907) Preliminary Tables show that the output of British woollen and worsted factories in 1907 was as follows:

BRITISH WOOLLEN AND WORSTED OUTPUT

| | Quantity | Value £ |
|---|---|---|
| Wool, sorted, blended, &c., lb. ... ... | 37,954,000 | 648,000 |
| Woollen Rags, lb. ... ... ... | 51,192,000 | 418,000 |
| Tops, lb. ... ... ... ... ... | 188,769,000 | 2,695,000 |
| Noils, lb. ... ... ... ... ... | 31,589,000 | 608,000 |
| Flocks, lb. ... ... ... ... ... | 26,947,000 | 142,000 |
| Waste, lb. ... ... ... ... ... | 33,988,000 | 659,000 |
| Shoddy, &c., lb. ... ... ... ... | 137,056,000 | 1,798,000 |
| Yarns: Woollen, lb. ... ... ... | 62,225,000 | 2,414,000 |
| ,, Worsted, lb. ... ... ... | 159,940,000 | 16,058,000 |
| ,, Alpaca, Mohair, &c., lb. ... | 20,316,000 | 2,362,000 |
| ,, Other, lb.... ... ... ... | 10,942,000 | 406,000 |
| Woollen Tissues, yds. ... ... ... | 183,596,000 | 16,508,000 |
| Worsted ,, yds. ... ... ... | 201,391,000 | 15,718,000 |
| Damask, Tapestry, &c., yds. ... ... | 2,608,000 | 247,000 |
| Wool and Mohair Plushes, yds. ... | 3,077,000 | 330,000 |
| Flannels and Delaines, yds. ... ... | 49,749,000 | 1,753,000 |
| Carpets, yds. ... ... ... ... | 26,159,000 | 3,337,000 |
| Rugs ... ... ... ... ... | — | 647,000 |
| Blankets, pairs ... ... ... ... | 3,115,000 | 1,450,000 |
| Shawls, No. ... ... ... ... | 1,290,000 | 227,000 |
| Coverlets, &c., No. ... ... ... | 828,000 | 236,000 |
| Braids, &c. ... ... ... ... | — | 107,000 |
| Miscellaneous ... ... ... ... | — | 1,563,000 |
| Total Gross Product ... ... ... ... ... ... | | £70,331,000 |

The cost of material and of work given out in producing this £70,331,000 of gross product is returned at £50,879,000, giving a net profit and wages fund of £19,500,000. Thus an extra cost of 10 per cent. for material and work would reduce the profit and wage fund to £14,500,000.

Comparing output with net imports and exports in 1907, we get:

BRITISH WOOLLEN AND WORSTED TRADE, 1907

| | £ |
|---|---|
| Value of British production ... ... | 70,300,000 |
| ,, ,, imports for home consumption... | 9,667,000 |
| ,, ,, exports of British make ... ... | 34,159,000 |

The value of our imports of woollen and worsted manufactures thus amounts to about one-seventh of the value of our home production.

**ZINC**—We import about £2,500,000 of zinc every year, chiefly in a crude state. It is of interest to note that this large import of raw material, being strictly speaking a "manufacture," is classified under imports of manufactures in the Board of Trade Returns, and consequently included in the total of £120,000,000 worth of imported manufactures which the Protectionists assert in millions of leaflets and thousands of speeches to be the cause of unemployment!

**ZOLLVEREIN**—This German word means Customs Union. All the German States, together with Luxemburg, have Free Trade with each other, and a general Customs tariff against all countries outside them. (*See* CUSTOMS UNION.) The case against the pseudo-Zollverein of Mr. Chamberlain is discussed under PREFERENCE.

The Gresham Press,
UNWIN BROTHERS, LIMITED,
WOKING AND LONDON.